KANT'S CRITIQUE OF
PURE REASON

The posthumous works

Beethoven: The Philosophy of Music
Introduction to Sociology
Problems of Moral Philosophy
Metaphysics: Concept and Problems
Kant's Critique of Pure Reason

KANT'S *CRITIQUE OF PURE REASON*

(1959)

Theodor W. Adorno

Edited by Rolf Tiedemann

Translated by Rodney Livingstone

Stanford University Press
Stanford, California

Stanford University Press
Stanford, California
© 1995 Suhrkamp Verlag
This translation © 2001 Polity Press
First published in Germany as *Kants 'Kritik der reinen Vernunft'* by
    Suhrkamp Verlag
Originating publisher of English edition: Polity Press in association with
    Blackwell Publishers Ltd.
First published in the U.S.A. by Stanford University Press, 2001
Published with the assistance of Inter Nationes

Cloth ISBN 0-8047-4292-8
Paper ISBN 0-8047-4426-2
A catalog record for this book has been applied for from the Library of
    Congress.
This book is printed on acid-free paper.

Last figure below indicates year of this printing:
09   08   07   06   05   04   03   02

CONTENTS

Identity and non-identity (II); knowledge as tautology (I) Hegel's solution to the problem of knowledge • Attitude towards reason: identification with the Enlightenment and the accusation of blasphemy • 'Protestantism'; knowledge of the Absolute and erotic metaphor • Attitude towards utopia: the making real of reason and 'This shall not be'; the concept of the infinite; the concept of depth (I) • Knowledge and faith • Theology and philosophy; spirit and organic nature • The construction of Kantian philosophy: theoretical and practical reason • The signature of the history of philosophy in Kant (I): class thinking and 'spokesperson of mankind' • Interpretation as objective expression • On method (II): interpretation as extrapolation; interest in contradictions

On method (III): revised view of non-contradiction; fissures and chinks • Against a prejudgement in favour of identity • Negativity as the self-movement of the thing; Nietzsche's critique of logic • Contradiction and expression; salvaging of ontology (II) • Ontology as the forecourt to metaphysics • The mediation of pure existence and existent beings; dialectics or the dualism of form and content • Attitude towards Hume • The concept of the self • The unity of personal consciousness • The category of causality (I) • The concept of the thing

Reinstatement of the objectivity of 'naturalistic' concepts; the unity of consciousness as the correlative of the unity of the thing • On the theory of the thing: Kant's 'law' and Hume's 'rule' • Transcendental idealism/empirical realism • 'How we are to understand the idea that the mind prescribes laws to nature' • On the distinction between form and content; subjectivity as creator of form; the undetermined nature of material; 'creative spirit' • The concept of law and of the given; categories as the ground of the laws of nature • Synthesis and the unity of consciousness; the apprehension in intuition and *Gestalt* theory • Synthesis within a temporal horizon: memory and expectation • A functional theory of the thing • The ambiguity of '*Erscheinung*' (I)

Difficulties and equivocations in the subject matter; the ambiguity of '*Erscheinung*' (II) • The unity of consciousness as the correlative of the unity of the thing • The category of causality (II); the dualism of object and thing-in-itself • The double nature of the concept of the thing and the doubling of the world; Kant as '*Hinterweltler*' • Metaphysical experience: to live without fear and alienation in the Absolute • 'As if', allegory, the Absurd • The moral law as an 'inner light' • Idealism and reification • Reification as function of subjectivity: thought and labour; the antinomy of bourgeois society: rationality and impotence

Concerning salvage operations • 'Upwards to idealism' • The dialectic of reason • Critique and apologia for reason; Kant's history of philosophy (II): between dogmatism and heteronomy • Subjectivity and receptivity • The qualitative as trans-subjective minimum • Nothing without mediation • Nominalism and realism • The Deduction of the Pure Concepts of Understanding (I): objectivity as the secret of subjectivity

The known: a problematic concept; knowledge as tautology (II) • Knowledge as the organization of materials and as self-adjustment to the material • The function of the Schematism chapter • Intuition and category as essentially different • Time as schema • Resignation and triumph of the natural sciences • Subjectivism and practical philosophy; the truth and untruth of idealism • Tautology as imprisonment within ourselves

Subject and object: *constituens* and *constitutum* • Necessity and causality • Causality as synthesis • Universality as *a priori* • Critique of concept-formation • Objective and subjective reason; universality and consensus • The social and the transcendental subject • Society and epistemology; the *constituens* not detachable from the *constitutum* • Obligation to move towards dialectics; against the absolute first principle

The 'we' cannot be eliminated • The 'we' and the universality • Plurality as the synthesis of singularities • The form of personality;

form and factual consciousness • The Amphiboly chapter • Mediating the transcendental • Formal and transcendental logic; the 'question of origins'; spontaneity • The critique of idealism and of naive realism; against the idea of the absolute first principle; the impossibility of ontology

Reciprocity of *constituens* and *constitutum*; *prima philosophia* always an idealism • 'God is in the detail' • Residual theory of truth as dogmatism; subject and object: the separation is historically determined • Hegel's *Phenomenology of Spirit*; lack of interest in mediation today • Differentiation and need for unity • Social substance; genesis and validity; the idea that truth is immutable • Transition from the Kantian problem of constitution to history • Against sociologism; Durkheim's position

'I and we' as starting-point of epistemology • Epistemology as reflection of the labour process • Truth and untruth of the transcendental subject; the concept of mankind in the *Critique of Practical Reason*; Kant's formalism and the reversal into materialism • The Kantian 'block' and the universal exchange relation • Relation to the natural sciences; knowledge and the domination of nature • Positivism and metaphysical mourning • The 'block' as the expression of indecision • The distinction between appearance and essence unimportant; the world view of a blunted bourgeois sensibility

Critique and affirmation • Utopia as undertaker • The problem of a binding authority; practical philosophy; the neutralization of culture • The concept of depth (II) • Against the alleged depth of the irrational • Protestantism; inwardness; the tragic • Depth and depth psychology; attitude towards psychology • Continuation and conclusion of the lecture course

Relation to psychology; Kant and Hume • Kant's demotion of psychology; philosophy versus psychology in Germany; state-of-mind

[*Befindlichkeit*] in Heidegger; denial of the element of drives; Kant's 'authorization' of psychology as a science • The psychological paralogisms; the doubling of the concept of the self; unity of consciousness and the existing soul; inner experience is like outer • Kant's concept of synthesis and thought that dominates nature; the one and the many • Unity of consciousness and the privileging of the subject • Against the substantiality of the soul; the singularity of the self of apperception; the non-identical identity of the subject in advanced art [Proust]

• Critique of the second thesis: space and time are necessary ideas • The third thesis: space and time are not concepts • Critique of the fourth thesis: space and time are 'infinite givens' • The reciprocity of intuitions and the forms of intuitions • En route to dialectics: universal mediation and immediacy; identity and non-identity (III)

LECTURE ONE

12 May 1959

Methods and Intentions

Let me begin with the fiction that you do not yet know anything about the *Critique of Pure Reason*. This fiction is simultaneously legitimate and illegitimate. It is illegitimate since it is obvious that even today a work like Kant's epistemological *magnum opus* radiates such authority that everyone has heard something or other about it. However, in a deeper sense it is less of a fiction than it seems. We might begin by saying that whenever one aspect of a philosophy becomes public knowledge it tends generally to obscure its true meaning rather than to elucidate it. The formulae to which philosophies are commonly reduced tend to reify the actual writings, to sum them up in a rigid fashion and thus to make a genuine interaction with them all the harder. To make the point more specifically in relation to Kant, you have undoubtedly all heard that Kant's so-called Copernican revolution consisted in the idea that the elements of cognition that had previously been sought in the objects, in things-in-themselves, were now to be transferred to the subject, in other words to reason, the faculty of cognition.[1] In such a crude formulation this view of Kant is also false because, on the one hand, the subjective turn in philosophy is much older than Kant – in the modern history of philosophy it goes back to Descartes, and there is a sense in which David Hume, Kant's important English precursor, was more of a subjectivist than Kant. And on the other hand, this widely held belief is mistaken because the true interest of the *Critique of Pure Reason* is concerned less with the subject, the turn to the subject, than with the objective nature of cognition.

If I may make a start with a programmatic statement, a sort of motto, encapsulating what you are about to hear, I would say that the Kantian project can actually be characterized not as one that adopts subjectivism in order to do away with the objectivity of cognition, but as one that grounds objectivity in the subject as an objective reality. It stands in contrast to the previously dominant view which downgraded objectivity by emphasizing the subject, and restricted it in a spirit of scepticism. This, we might say, is Kant's project in the *Critique of Pure Reason,* and he himself has said so in a not very well-known passage in the Preface to the *Critique of Pure Reason.* I shall read it out to you at once because it may help to dispel a significant misunderstanding from the very outset. His enquiry, he says, has two sides, one of which is concerned with objects, while the other seeks 'to investigate the pure understanding itself, its possibility and the cognitive faculties upon which it rests; and so deals with it in its subjective aspect'.[2] He goes on to say that, important though this exposition is, it is not essential to his 'chief purpose', 'for the chief question is always this – what and how much can the understanding and reason know apart from all experience? Not: – how is the faculty of thought itself possible?'[3] I believe, therefore, that if you accept right from the start that the interest of the *Critique of Pure Reason* lies in its intention to establish the *objective nature* of cognition, or to *salvage* it, if I may anticipate my future argument, this will afford you a better access to the work than if you simply surrender to the widespread idea of Kant's so-called subjectivism.[4] This remains true even though these two aspects of Kant's philosophy are in constant friction with one another. *How* this process of friction, how these two aspects, relate to one another in a series of configurations and how this gives rise to a whole set of problems – to explore this will be the task I have set myself in this lecture course.

But let me return to the fiction I started with. It is reasonable for me to assume that you have no preconceived notions about the *Critique of Pure Reason* because the traditional beliefs surrounding this work no longer survive. Once, some forty years ago, a very important philosopher of the day remarked wittily that a philosopher was someone who knew what was said in the books he had not read. And this remark could probably be said to have applied to the *Critique of Pure Reason.* In other words, the aura surrounding this book was so extraordinary at the time that even people unfamiliar with the text seem to have had a 'feeling' for what it contained – if you will pardon my use of this word; no other word will really do. The intellectual situation of our age is one in which no work belonging to the past really enjoys such authority any more, and certainly not Kant's *magnum opus*, for the simple reason that the school that dominated the German universities until around forty years ago has faded somewhat and has become something of a dead dog.[5] This was the Neo-Kantian school in its various guises – mathematical in Marburg and arts-orientated in south-west Germany. In consequence the *Critique of Pure Reason* is no longer able to derive any sort of traditional nourishment from that source either. I imagine, therefore, that you may well approach the *Critique of Pure Reason* with something of the feeling that it is like an old statue of the Great Elector,[6] an idol standing on its plinth gathering dust, something that the professors keep on discussing because, regrettably, they have been in the habit of doing so for the past 150 years, but not anything that need concern us overmuch today. What indeed are we supposed to do with it? You will probably have an idea that the *Critique of Pure Reason* is concerned on the one hand with particular questions of scientific theory and that it is filled with discourses pertaining to the individual sciences, discourses that for the most part have now been superseded. For example, you will all have heard something to the effect that the Kantian theory of the *a priori* nature of time and space has been undermined by relativity theory, or that the Kantian theory of causality as an *a priori* category has been refuted by quantum mechanics. On the other hand, however, the narrower, more specifically philosophical questions of the *Critique of Pure Reason* – that is to say, those not connected with the grounding of the sciences – may well have lost something of their exalted status in your eyes. For when you hear the concept of 'metaphysics' – to mention the other term that forms the subject of the Kantian critique – you will not generally be thinking of the same concepts as formed the essence of metaphysics in Kant's eyes – that is to say, the concepts of God, freedom and immortality, or of the independence or the existence or non-existence of the soul. You have instead been brought up to find the true essence of metaphysics in such concepts as *Being* [*Sein*]. Let me say right away that the so-called question of 'Being' does not represent an innovation when compared to the *Critique of Pure Reason*, or a happy rediscovery. We could rather say that Kant has some very definite and unambiguous comments to make about the question of 'Being' in a very central chapter of the *Critique of Pure Reason*, namely the chapter on the Amphiboly of Concepts of Reflection. And I may perhaps add that if you do not wish to capitulate to the current talk about 'Being' and to succumb helplessly to the suggestive power of this so-called philosophy of 'Being', it would be a very good thing for you to familiarize yourselves with these matters. It is not my wish to eliminate the problems involved here by proclaiming in a professorial

manner that the *Critique of Pure Reason* is a God-given work with
the kind of authority enjoyed by, say, Plato for the last two thousand
years, or to assert that we feel paralysed when confronted with these
eternal values and unable to muster the necessary respect and the
necessary interest. I would say that, on the contrary, such admonitions
themselves smack of the impotence and hollowness implicit in any
such concept of unchanging, eternal values.

I should like instead to do something else. I cannot deny that I still
believe that this work is one that deserves the very greatest respect.
It does so for quite objective reasons, albeit for reasons that are
very different from those to which it owed its position when it first
appeared. What I should like is to make this book speak to us. I should
like to show you what interest the matters that are discussed in it can
still hold for us today. And I should like to rehearse the experiences
that underlie this work as objective realities, as experiences forming
an essential part of the history of philosophy. I attempted something
of the sort in my memorial lecture on Hegel that some of you may
have heard.[7] So what I would like to do is to retranslate this philosophy from a codified, ossified system back into the kind of picture
that results from a sustained X-ray examination. That is to say, I
should like to urge you to conceive of this philosophy as a force field,
as something in which the abstract concepts that come into conflict
with one another and constantly modify one another really stand in
for actual living forces. At the same time and as a matter of course –
if I have any success at all in achieving my aims – an essential task will
be to enable you to read the – very extensive – text of the *Critique of
Pure Reason* for yourselves. I hope you will learn how to distinguish
between its essential and less essential aspects, a crucial matter when
reading Kant. And I hope also to make things come alive by presenting
them in terms of a number of models. It is not my intention to give
you lengthy paraphrases of the *Critique of Pure Reason,* or to supply
you with commentaries on particular passages. All that has been done
countless times and those of you who would like such an approach
can find more than enough examples of it in the secondary literature.
Instead I shall try to introduce you to the core philosophical problems through the discussion of particular questions that I regard as
being of central importance. But I shall do this, as I have said, not
through the exposition of Kant's ideas as a complete philosophy, but
as a kind of transcript of the intellectual experiences that lie behind
them. And the concept of experience (or what I wish to show you of
it) is not one that can be explained abstractly in advance. I would ask
you not to expect me to start with a definition of what I mean by it;
its meaning will become clear in the course of these lectures.

You will be curious to learn about the actual source of the intimidating reputation of this work as *the* philosophical work *par excellence*. A point in time when a tradition has come to an end and when the authority of books is no longer taken for granted has the advantage that it is possible to put such questions. I should like to tell you that if I have spoken of the loss of authority of the *Critique of Pure Reason*, this is not just an invention of mine. There are in fact philosophical trends today that really do regard the whole of Kant's philosophy as nothing more than a cult object that has now been superseded thanks to advances in scientific knowledge, and that far from calling for philosophical labour it can at best hope for a certain antiquarian interest. An example is Hans Reichenbach, the logical positivist, who has defended this point of view, with great courage, if not always with the requisite sensitivity, in his book *The Rise of Scientific Philosophy* and in a number of other writings.[8]

You may well wonder from where a book like this one of Kant's actually derives its great authority – particularly when you see that it says nothing about the major topics which might be thought to be of interest. To make this brutally clear to you: if you expect to find in the *Critique of Pure Reason* proofs for or against the existence of God or the immortality of the soul or of freedom, you will be sorely disappointed. It is true that there is no lack of such proofs, above all in the great second part of the Transcendental Logic, namely the Transcendental Dialectic. However, these proofs suffer from the grave defect that Kant has always arranged them ambiguously because he has always advanced them in the form of antinomies. What this means is that he has demonstrated that both the truth of these concepts and that of their opposites can be proved. What we have here is a theory of cognition, but a theory of cognition in a double sense. The first meaning is that it attempts to lay the foundations of the sciences that in Kant's eyes are established and free from doubt, that is to say, of mathematics and the natural sciences. The second meaning lies in his attempt to restrict the possibility of knowledge of those absolute concepts that you may be disposed to regard as the most important. You have to be clear about this. The *Critique of Pure Reason* does not polemicize against these concepts; for example, he does not deny the existence of God. And when Heine remarked, in the *History of Religion and Philosophy in Germany*, that the upshot of the *Critique of Pure Reason* is that even the Lord of Lords is dying, 'wallowing – unproven – in his own blood', then the emphasis must be placed on the word *unproven*.[9] That is to say, what is limited is the possibility of proof; judgements about these categories as such are not made in the book. What constitutes the enormous significance of the book and what really changed the whole intellectual climate in a way that reverberates down to the everyday life of our minds today is probably the fact that it denied that certain questions were rational and hence banished them from our horizons. Bernhard Groethuysen, the historian of ideas, has attempted to show in his writings how God and the devil disappeared from the world in the course of the later seventeenth and early eighteenth centuries – not as part of a trend towards atheism, but because the questions about them ceased to be asked.[10] Now we might say that the achievement of the *Critique of Pure Reason* is that a whole series of these great metaphysical, fundamental concepts vanished from the horizon of what could be rationally decided. And in the same way, modern theology, as it has been developed by Karl Barth, following Søren Kierkegaard, has insisted with great feeling on placing the categories of theology in extreme opposition to knowledge and has argued that what applies to them is the paradoxical concept of faith. If this has been possible it is because it is implicit in the Kantian situation, in the sense that the sharp distinction that Kant made between knowledge and those metaphysical categories is a fundamental premise for us today.

Thus if we are to speak of the *critique* of pure reason, this critique must be regarded as neither a negative reply, nor indeed as a reply of any sort, to the fundamental questions of philosophy. It is rather a critique *of* those questions. It is a critique of the ability of reason to pose such questions, to do them justice. We may say perhaps that the enormous impact of the *Critique of Pure Reason* has its source in the circumstance that it was in effect the first work to give expression to the element of bourgeois resignation, to that refusal to make any significant statement on the crucial questions, and instead to set up house in the finite world and explore it in every direction, as Goethe phrased it.[11] This is a very different kind of outlook from the radical atheism of the *philosophes* of the Enlightenment such as Helvétius or La Mettrie or Holbach, who really did give negative answers and in whose thought reason was sufficiently confident to make statements about the Absolute. It is precisely this that is restricted in Kant. The crucial feature of the Kantian work (and this will perhaps give you an insight into its inner nature) is that it is guided by the conviction that reason is denied the right to stray into the realm of the Absolute, to 'stray into intelligible worlds', as he terms it.[12] This explains why we can stand with both feet firmly planted on the ground and it is thanks to this that we really know what it is that we can positively and definitely know.

We might almost say, then, that what has been codified in the *Critique of Pure Reason* is a theodicy of bourgeois life which is conscious of its own practical activity while despairing of the fulfilment of its own utopia. The power of the *Critique of Pure Reason* resides not so much in its responses to the so-called metaphysical questions as in its highly heroic and stoical refusal to respond to these questions in the first place. What makes this possible for Kant is the self-reflexive nature of reason. By this I mean that, as a rational being, I am capable of reflecting on my own reason, and through this reflection I am able to give myself an account of what it can and cannot achieve. This dual aspect of self-reflexivity is what enables Kant to claim that he has established the foundation of experience – in other words the original leading concepts of our knowledge of nature; and on the other hand, it is what prevents us from going beyond this knowledge and entering into speculations about the Absolute.

Nevertheless, I should say at this point that the idea of the self-reflexivity of reason contains a difficulty and also a challenge that only emerged fully in post-Kantian philosophy and the philosophy of German idealism in the narrower sense. The difficulty is that we can enquire, how can reason criticize itself? Does not the fact that it criticizes itself mean that it is always caught up in a prejudice? That is to say, when reason judges the possibility of making absolute statements, does this not necessarily imply that it has already made statements about the Absolute? And in fact post-Kantian idealism did take up this quite simple idea and turn it *against* Kant. Perhaps the crucial distinction between Kant and his successors is that in Kant the reflexivity of reason is conceived in a quite straightforward way, much as with the English empiricists who similarly dissect the mechanisms of reason. It is true that at one point Kant does make fun of the concept of the physiology of reason that he found in Locke and which ventured something of the sort.[13] But when we look more closely at what he has himself done in the *Critique of Pure Reason*, we discover that it is not all that far removed from such a physiology of reason, that is, from a dissection of reason, albeit in the case of Kant 'on the basis of principles'. In contrast his successors then faced up to the question of what it *means* for reason to criticize itself – and they were led by that question both to criticize Kant and to infer a series of answers that Kant himself was initially unwilling to provide with his critique.

But I believe that it would be good for you to grasp the idea that, for all Kant's notorious reputation for difficulty, he was a relatively straightforward writer inasmuch as he believed – without wasting too much time thinking about it – that reason is able to treat of the realm of reason, the realm of knowledge, just as effectively as any other field of knowledge. Connected with this – and this is a further prerequisite for understanding Kant that is absolutely indispensable if you wish to see what is involved in his philosophy – connected with this is the fact that underlying Kant's philosophy lies a huge confidence in the mathematical natural sciences; and that his philosophy is absolutely full of the spirit of these sciences. If we wish to grasp the chief inspiration of the whole *Critique of Pure Reason*, we might locate it in the idea that the attempts of metaphysics to arrive at absolute certainties by spinning them out of mere thought have all failed – and Hume was right to criticize them. But this does not mean that we should despair because, thanks to the persuasive force of the mathematical sciences – particularly mathematics itself and what today we would call theoretical physics – we possess an entire body of knowledge that actually does satisfy the criterion of absolute truth. Kant's achievement only becomes comprehensible on the assumption that science provides the absolute knowledge which merely abstract speculation had failed to deliver.

I believe that to say this is enough to eliminate one of the difficulties that tend to crop up in the mind of the so-called naive reader who embarks upon the *Critique of Pure Reason* for the first time. For Kant begins with the question '*How are synthetic a priori judgements possible?*' (This comes in the Introduction and it is explored at length in the course of the book.[14]) This is one of the chief questions of the *Critique of Pure Reason*. Without bothering with any long drawn-out preambles I should like to say something about the significance of this question. But first I want to comment on the shock contained in the expression '*How* are they possible?' For when the speculative philosopher approaches this book he expects a completely different question, namely, *Are* synthetic *a priori* judgements, in other words, absolutely valid statements, possible? This question is not put in the *Critique of Pure Reason*.[15] You can see here plainly how difficult it is to understand a work simply by reading the text, without any prior assumptions. And if a lecture course like this one (and every lecture course on comparable topics) has any justification beyond the mere fact that it is advertised in the university lecture programme, this justification must surely be sought in the realization that such works cannot simply be understood on their own. This is not meant in the ominous schoolmasterly sense that you need to know the historical context so as to be able to place them correctly – I am quite indifferent to such matters – but in order to grasp the fact that the problems under discussion are only comprehensible if you are familiar with certain force fields within which philosophies may be said to move.

Kant's work is called *The Critique of Pure Reason*, and the emphasis here doubtless falls on the word 'critique'. In essence there is nothing new in this since we might say that the entire history of philosophy is nothing but one vast nexus of criticism which has led consciousness to its ideas, its concepts and ultimately to itself. In this sense the *Critique of Pure Reason* is an encounter of philosophy with itself. Thus what I wish to say is that this strange formula '*How* are synthetic *a priori* judgements possible?' does become meaningful and at the same time it reveals something of the entire complexion, the inner workings of Kant's thought. It does so because what is truly substantial, the element that seems to constitute its unquestionable truth, manifests itself in the shape of the synthetic *a priori* judgements and because it does not spin the truth abstractly from within itself, but proceeds from the truth, as Kant calls it, as if from a 'given', and sticks to knowledge that it holds to be true and absolute.

Let me tell you right away what synthetic *a priori* judgements are. Forgive me if I speak at a rather basic level, but if I am to take seriously my own fiction that you know nothing of Kant, there is no other way forward. I must start by telling you what a *judgement* is. You all have a more or less vague idea of what is meant, but I am sure it is vague. In the old tradition of logic, judgements were defined as the union of subject, predicate and copula – that is to say, an object which corresponds in grammatical terms to a subject has something *different* predicated of it. This is expressed in the form of 'is', as in 'A is B'. This is a somewhat superficial characterization of a judgement because it presupposes that these components are discrete entities, which is not in fact the case. Moreover, the implied identity of A = B is problematic because in general the concept beneath which a specific thing is subsumed is always broader than that thing, so that the judgement is both identical and non-identical. You encounter difficulties of all kinds here with the consequence that a judgement is defined as a state of affairs of which it is meaningful to ask whether it is true or false. If such a state of affairs is expressed in words it is customary to call it a *proposition* [*Satz*], but this distinction plays no significant role in Kant. In Kant we hear generally of 'judgements', even though it is propositions that are generally meant and not the interconnections between primitive, pre-linguistic concepts.

Judgements may be synthetic or analytic. This means that the concept in the predicate adds something to the concept in the subject, or, more precisely, the concept in the predicate is not contained in that of the subject. Where that is *not* the case, that is to say, if we have a judgement that adds something new and is what we may call an 'ampliative judgement', then we speak of synthetic judgements. And where *that* is not the case, where the predicate is simply a repetition of the subject, where it is implied in the definition of the subject, then we speak of analytic judgements. In that case the judgement is a mere analysis, a mere analysis of its own subject; it merely makes explicit what is already contained in the subject. In other words, analytic judgements are really all tautologies.

Kant combines these concepts with the additional concepts of *a priori* and *a posteriori*. It is self-evident that the analytic judgements are all *a priori*, that is to say, they are valid absolutely and unconditionally – precisely because they are tautologous. Because they are actually not judgements at all, they cannot be refuted. They are simply repetitions of definitions that are presupposed. Synthetic judgements, on the other hand, can be either *a priori* or *a posteriori*. This means that if you make a statement about something, form a judgement about it, then this judgement may either arise from experience (Kant would say) or it can be necessary even though it is not already contained in the concept. Thus if you say, 'All men are mortal', that is a judgement of experience, since mortality is not implicit as such in the concept of 'men'. However, when you say 'All bodies are extended', that is a synthetic *a priori* judgement.[16] It means that extension is not contained in the concept of the body, but notwithstanding that all bodies necessarily possess the quality of extension.

You will now ask me – and this brings me back to the Great Elector and to the question of whether he has a wig or a pigtail – you may well object: for goodness' sake, this is supposed to be the most important work in the history of philosophy and now we have to endure an account of how synthetic *a priori* judgements are possible. We have to put up with listening to the assertion that judgements are possible which say something new, but which are valid for all time . . . On this point we have to say that the concept of truth in Kant – and this is profoundly bound up with bourgeois thought – is itself that of a timeless truth. 'To be absolute' for Kant means as much as to be irrefutable by the passage of time; an absolutely secure possession; something that cannot be taken away from you, that you can keep safe in your own hands for ever. The concept of a timeless truth, the concept that only that which is timeless can be genuinely true, whereas whatever can be refuted cannot really aspire to the concept of truth – that is one of the innermost driving forces of Kantian philosophy. And if, finally, the idea of immortality appears as one of the supreme ideas, that provides you with the key to the enormous emotional weight that this concept of an *a priori* status has in Kant. What he is concerned with in his work is a kind of tendering of accounts in which he seeks to crystallize those truths that I end up possessing with absolute certainty, without incurring any debts and without their being exposed to any claims through the passage of time. Incidentally, what may seem to you to be rather philistine ana-logies from the bourgeois world of commerce play a major role in Kant and in the *Critique of Pure Reason*. And I may tell you that they are profoundly related to what is magnificent about Kant, to his particular kind of sobriety, of self-possession, even when confronted by the most sublime and impressive objects. It is all quite inseparable from his bourgeois and philistine cast of mind. In all probability you will do better to seek the core of Kantian metaphysics in this sobriety than at the point where he seems more directly metaphysical.

Thus this interest in synthetic *a priori* judgements is connected with the fact that Kant really does require truth to be timeless. I should like to point out to you already at this stage that this is the site of one of the profoundest difficulties in Kant. On the one hand, he perceives, like no one before him, that time is a necessary condi-tion of knowledge, and hence of every instance of allegedly timeless knowledge, and that it exists as a form of intuition. On the other hand, he perceives the passage of time as a kind of flaw, and some-thing that truly authoritative knowledge ought to avoid. This explains why the question of whether and how synthetic *a priori* judgements are possible occupies such a key position in the *Critique of Pure Reason*.

LECTURE TWO

14 May 1959

The Concept of the Transcendental (I)

I should like to begin by correcting a misunderstanding or rather a crude blunder that I made in the heat of battle, so to speak, towards the end of the last lecture. I gave you a completely idiotic example of a synthetic *a priori* judgement – it is the kind of thing that sometimes happens when you try to compress too much into the final moments of a class. Needless to say, the statement 'all bodies are extended' is an analytic judgement, not, as I stupidly said, synthetic – at least, inasmuch as we are speaking of the definition of bodies in geometry, or more precisely, stereometry. An instance of a synthetic judgement – and this is the classical example that is always cited – 'all bodies are heavy'. This is because the concept of weight is not already contained in three-dimensionality.[1]

But the need to clarify this misunderstanding gives me the opportunity to point to a problem that really does exist here – a very serious problem, as it happens. This is that it is very difficult to make a clear distinction between analytic and synthetic judgements on the basis of single examples. There is, for example, the question of whether propositions in mathematics are synthetic, as Kant claimed, or analytic, as Leibniz believed and as has since been reiterated by modern mathematicians. I may refer you to Henri Poincaré's well-known assertion that the whole of mathematics is nothing but a single tautology. The answer to this question depends largely on the context within which such claims are made. For example – I am improvising somewhat here, without being able to guarantee the scientific accuracy of my statements, but I am concerned more with the general argument than with what happens to be the case in the different sciences – if you take the definition of a body in chemistry, where weight is one of the basic elements, then the proposition that all bodies are heavy can be analytic, while it was synthetic in the realm of mathematics. These are highly complex questions, as is in general the question whether logical forms such as judgement, inference and concept can be defined in isolation or whether they can only be grasped in the context of the intellectual systems or structures in which they appear. These are questions that have emerged only in the course of modern developments in logic.[2] Hence in order to understand Kant, or indeed in order to understand any thinker, you need to make certain assumptions; this holds good for all intellectual activities that are to be found between heaven and earth. If you refuse to make any assumptions, if you attempt to understand a thing purely on its own terms, then you will understand nothing. I shall return to this point in a moment. In the case of Kant you have to assume – and this is essential for an understanding of the *Critique of Pure Reason* in general – that the whole of traditional logic is in place. There is a passage in the *Critique of Pure Reason* where he asserts in all innocence that, apart from a few improvements, logic has made no progress since Aristotle, and nor could it have done.[3] In consequence, in his conception of logic he simply cleaves to the traditional Aristotelian logic which makes a clear distinction between the different categories in ways familiar to us – namely in accordance with the practice of a linguistic analysis, and without taking any notice whatever of the interconnections between the categories of logic and the systems to which they refer.

I shall also take this opportunity to draw a further point to your attention, one that has a bearing on the importance of the concept of reason for an understanding of the *Critique of Pure Reason*. You will come to hear of all sorts of concepts of reason in Kantian philosophy. There is the concept of reason in the mathematical natural sciences which I spoke about last time and which I told you was appropriate for synthetic *a priori* judgements since it refers to highly generalized propositions that provide a foundation for judgements of experience. Then comes the concept of empirical reason that refers to material, factual judgements falling within our experience. After that we have the metaphysical judgements about which I shall have something to say today and which provide the critical, or if you prefer, the negative object of the *Critique of Pure Reason*. And lastly, there are the judgements of practical philosophy that in a certain sense establish links between them all. Now, I believe – and this is something that is very easily overlooked in discussions of Kant – that you can only understand the interconnections between all these realms, which Kant himself sometimes brings together and sometimes sharply contrasts, if you realize that the distinctions between them presuppose an element of sameness, of identity, that enables them to be measured against one another. This unifying factor is reason itself. In other words, then, reason is the canon of propositions as they have been codified in the traditional, bivalent logic, that is to say, in a system of logic that is based pre-eminently on the principle of identity – in other words, the postulate that a concept should retain the same meaning – and the principle of contradiction, namely that where there are two contradictory judgements only one can be true. In Kant's view every procedure that adheres to these principles is rational. And the unifying factor, the factor that joins these different aspects of philosophy together and is tested out in its various fields, is the mode of reason as defined once and for all by the principles of formal logic, accepted uncritically though these may be. For their part, the distinctions arise from the application of this same reason to different objects. By distinctions I am referring here both to the distinctions operating within the *Critique of Pure Reason* and, on a larger scale, the distinctions obtaining between the various elements of the Kantian system of which theoretical reason forms only a part. That is to say, the distinctions in this entire system of thought, in the critique of reason and beyond, always arise from a reason that is thought of as identical in its application to different objects. It remains identical however it is applied. It may be applied to sensible matter, to the so-called pure intuitions. Or it may be applied to the employment of reason beyond the realm of any conceivable experience and as a guide to action – where it is assumed that inasmuch as these actions are freely performed, they are not subject to any fixed obligation. Or finally, it may be applied to its use in formal logic, that is to say, in the quintessential realm of reason, the realm of formal rules without regard to any content whatever. Kant's concern is always that reason should not be criticized from the point of view of pure logic, that is to say, the task facing reason is not to discover whether it is internally coherent – for the validity of logic is everywhere taken for granted and reason itself is held to be identical with logical thinking. Instead the meaning of Kantian reason is always that reason should reflect on its own possible relationship with objects of different kinds. And as I pointed out last time, it is always assumed – and this is a very bold assumption – that reason is capable of making an authoritative statement, a really compelling statement about its own relation to these objects. I wanted to make these points as footnotes to what was said previously.

I should like now to return once more to the question of the enormous burden represented in Kantian philosophy by these so-called
synthetic *a priori* judgements which I attempted to explain to you in
some detail last time. Perhaps you will allow me to return at this
point to my fiction that you have come here without any knowledge
of Kant. In addition, many of you will have come to a course of
lectures on philosophy bringing with you some idea of thought without any preconceptions. That is reasonable enough since in your
specialist subjects you will often find yourselves confronted by material or formal disciplines that are themselves based on a variety of
assumptions. You will then be told that we are not competent to test
these assumptions, we are not competent to say anything definitive
about the nature of time or space, or to decide what history is or
the essence of humanity, or whatever it happens to be. But to test
assumptions *in general* – that is said to be the task of philosophy . . .
The consequence of this, of course, is that you will expect philosophy
to be free of assumptions because it is philosophy that makes possible the assumptions underlying every conceivable individual discipline of whatever sort.

There are two points to be made here. First, to insist on this is
to make excessive demands on philosophy – or rather, you are in
effect coming to philosophy with a highly specific preconception, one
that is indeed sanctioned in great measure by the history of Western
metaphysics, but which turns out on closer inspection to be not quite
as self-evident as might be imagined. A mode of thought that is absolutely free of assumptions would in reality be a kind of thought that
is tied to nothing but pure thought itself. In other words, the philosophical problem *par excellence*, namely the problem of the relation
of consciousness to its objects, of the subject to the object, would be
prejudiced in a quite specific sense, namely in the idealist sense that
everything that exists is the subject, that is, consciousness or spirit.
Only if that were the case, only if spirit could itself generate all the
preconditions of all knowledge without reference to anything alien
to itself, would the postulate of a knowledge free of assumptions
be satisfied. Even then it would be problematic, since the supreme
presupposition, the assumption that might be thought of as the basis
of every conceivable judgement, could not itself be inferred from
anything prior. At this point even Fichte may be said to have come to
terms with the fact that there are givens; although Fichte's is the only
philosophy to have made a serious attempt to implement this project
of a philosophy without assumptions. In reality what we see here in
this entire clamour for a philosophy without preconceptions is something I have described, somewhat disrespectfully, as the mania for

foundations [*Fundierungswahn*].[4] This is the belief that everything which exists must be derived from something else, something older or more primordial. It is a delusion built on the idealist assumption that every conceivable existent thing can be reduced to mind or, I almost said, to Being – and 'Being' is itself a mediated, mental concept. And I would say that one of the overdue revisions that philosophy today should demand from your pre-philosophical expectations of it is that you should liberate yourselves from this 'mania for foundations', and that you should not always feel the need to begin at the very beginning. For such a presumption implies the belief that there is nothing new under the sun and that everything can be reduced to what has always existed – and the consequence of that would be to make the problems of history and of change in general absolutely insoluble.[5] So you should relinquish any expectation that Kantian philosophy should dispense with every assumption, and in general you should desist from making any such demands on philosophy at all. Instead you should seek to understand the role of so-called assumptions *within* the movement of a system of thought. I believe that if you do this you will make more progress than simply by posing mechanical questions such as, Yes, but does this not assume that such-and-such is the case . . . ? and does this not presuppose something or other . . . ?, a type of question that I would call infantile. For that is precisely what children do when they reply, Yes, but . . . , to every explanation you give, and when they find that they cannot stop asking questions because they do not understand the matter in hand, but instead just keep on asking questions mechanically. That is to say, they just keep on asking for the sake of asking without ever responding to the resistance in the matter in hand, the resistance created by what it actually refers to.

The second point to be made is that Kant's philosophy is no more devoid of assumptions than any other. And it is certain (and this is what actually motivates me in my entire approach to inducting you into the critique of reason) that if you were to attempt to understand his philosophy without any presuppositions, entirely on its own terms, without any knowledge of the status of the categories in his thought, you would fail utterly. Take, for example, the central concept that his critique of reason is based on, the concept of the transcendental, of which he maintains in one of the decisive passages of the book that it (namely the synthetic unity of apperception) is the highest point to which he has 'attached' his entire philosophy.[6] Even this concept is not derived by Kant from something else but is in a certain sense assumed in the course of his account. I shall read you an instance of this, one that is interesting because it concerns the spiritual

core of Kant's philosophy, the inner essence of reason, which, how-
ever, manifests itself, curiously enough, as something simply given.
He states in a note to the Transcendental Deduction of the Pure
Concepts of Understanding – which we shall have to examine in
detail since Kant regarded it as the central section of the *Critique of
Pure Reason*,[7] and that is no doubt exactly what it is – he states:

> But in the above proof there is one feature from which I could not
> abstract, the feature, namely, that the manifold to be intuited must be
> *given* prior to the synthesis of understanding, and independently of it.
> How this takes place, remains here undetermined.[8]

This is illuminating. It asserts that what comes to me from outside,
the material of experience, in other words, the sense impressions –
that these must be given to me and that I have no power over them.
This is a relatively straightforward assertion that the given is for-
tuitous by nature and that no further explanation of sense data is
possible – and it is also familiar ground to the whole of empiricist
thought. However, Kant goes beyond this in a very remarkable para-
graph at the end [of §21] where he writes as follows – and I would
ask you to pay particular attention since it shows how far Kantian
thought is from claiming to be free from assumptions.

> This peculiarity of our understanding, that it can produce *a priori*
> unity of apperception solely by means of the categories, and only by so
> much and so many, is as little capable of further explanation as why
> we have just these and no other functions of judgement, or why space
> and time are the only forms of our possible intuition.[9]

Thus you can see here that what stands opposed to the concept of the
given, namely the organization of mind to which something *is* given –
is something that Kant himself regards as a kind of given – and you
could even read this very profound passage as one that Kant intended
to be understood as pointing to what Hermann Cohen – who had
a very sensitive ear for such matters – described as 'intelligible contingency'.[10] That is to say, measured by any absolute standard, if we
could or wished to transport ourselves outside the prison of our own
mind, the organization of our mind, we might almost say the entire
logic and the very mode of our relations, our inescapable relations to
objects of whatever sort would itself be contingent ones, in other
words, an ultimate given beyond which we cannot go.[11]

I would just like to indicate here that it would be an extraordinarily fascinating task to track down all the so-called assumptions that

Kant makes in the *Critique of Pure Reason*. The reason for its importance – and this is why I place such great stress on it – is that it would
enable you to see something of fundamental significance for an
understanding of Kant. This is the distinction between Kant and
what is usually called idealism. This distinction is normally signalled
in the usual trivial histories of philosophy by their habit, a by no means
unhealthy one, of setting German idealism in the narrower sense
– that is, Fichte, Schelling, Hegel and, if you like, Schopenhauer –
in opposition to Kant. The reason for this – and I would ask you to
take a firm grip on this idea – is that while Kant does situate the unity
of existing reality and also the concept of Being in the realm of
consciousness, he simultaneously refuses to generate everything that
exists from that realm of consciousness. The consciousness of what
the modern expression calls 'ontological difference', that is to say, of
the fact that a thing is not fully reducible to its concept, that object
and subject are not to be collapsed into each other – this consciousness is powerfully developed in Kant. So much so that he would
rather accept inconsistency, that he would rather allow all sorts of
unexplained phenomena to enter his philosophy whenever he encounters something given, than, as sometimes appears to be the case,
to reduce everything to the unity of reason, 'on its weightless merry
journey', as Kafka phrases it.[12] This gives rise to not inconsiderable
difficulties, for at the same time Kant's aim is to create a system. As
early as the Preface he remarks that pure reason cannot be conceived
other than as a system, that is to say, as a coherent deductive unity.[13]
The idea of such a system actually precludes the non-identical, that
is, whatever does not fit into it.

On the other hand, he always has the consciousness – and I should
like to use the term that Horkheimer and I have been using increasingly in our discussions of these matters recently – the consciousness
of a 'block'. By this I mean the awareness that even though there
is no unity other than the one I have already told you about, namely
the unity that lies in the concept of reason itself – this is not the
whole story and we always come up against some outer limit.[14] We
might even say that in a sense the vital nerve of Kant's philosophy as
a whole lies in the conflict between these two aspects, the impulse
towards system, unity and reason, and, on the other hand, consciousness of the heterogeneous, the block, the limit. These two elements
are in a state of constant friction and he is always being brought up
short by this block. The vehicle of this process is this concept of the
given nature of transcendental conditions.

I have already mentioned the difficulties of the transcendental and
last time I told you about the concept of synthetic *a priori* judgements.

Up to now, however, I have said nothing about the concept of the transcendental itself, even though it is the crucial concept of Kantian philosophy, which has been rightly called a transcendental philosophy. I am also fully aware (following my original fictional assumption) of the formidable reputation of this term. You doubtless imagine that the transcendental is so sublime and remote as to rule out any discussion of it – much as at school the difficulties of integral calculus were thought to be frightfully off-putting and comprehensible only to the select few. That is an illusion and I believe I can quickly dispel this fear of the concept of the transcendental. This fear partly arises from the proximity of the word 'transcendent'; both concepts have their roots in medieval philosophy. I do not wish at present to enter into the complex question of the relations between them. We shall have ample opportunity for that later on. What I intend to do instead is simply to tell you what meaning the term 'transcendental' has in the *Critique of Pure Reason*, and you will soon find, no doubt to your own surprise, that after what I have said already, even though it does not amount to all that much, the meaning of this so-called difficult concept will more or less just fall into your lap. I shall now read out to you Kant's definition of the concept of the transcendental:

> I entitle *transcendental* all knowledge which is occupied not so much with objects as with the mode of our knowledge of objects in so far as this mode of knowledge is to be possible *a priori*.[15]

In other words, then, to put it quite simply: transcendental means all those enquiries that relate to the possibility of synthetic *a priori* judgements. But not just to the possibility of synthetic judgements; over and above that, transcendental in Kant means every investigation of basic concepts or, let me put it more precisely, basic forms of a conceptual or intuitive kind, that enables our reason, according to the Kantian theory, to make such synthetic *a priori* judgements. Thus a transcendental enquiry is an enquiry of mind or consciousness from the standpoint of how far it is possible for this mind to posit valid synthetic *a priori* judgements, that is, judgements that are independent of experience. This transcendental enquiry is articulated in the positive part of the *Critique of Pure Reason*. It breaks down, on the one hand, into the Transcendental Aesthetic, that is, the doctrine of the forms of intuition that are necessary and constitutive givens which are not reducible to anything else and through which all our intuitions are filtered if they are to be 'our' intuitions at all. In addition, there are the categories, that is, the basic *concepts* – for instance, the concept of causality or the concept of substance or the concept of reciprocity – beneath which our understanding must necessarily subsume the given objects of intuition. The whole of the so-called positive part of the *Critique of Pure Reason*, namely the Transcendental Aesthetic and the analytical section of the Transcendental Logic, is concerned to crystallize these elements.

One further point should be made here, if you are to understand Kant's intentions properly. Unlike Aristotle, he is not content simply to liberate these basic concepts from their linguistic forms. Incidentally, as you may be aware, in Aristotle there is often no clear distinction between the intuitive forms and the conceptual ones: they are all mixed up together in his table of categories like apples and oranges. Moreover, Kant criticizes Aristotle for having assembled these basic forms of the mind 'rhapsodically', as Kant says, that is, haphazardly, without any canon or guiding principle, namely as necessary aspects of language.[16] For his part, while Kant must indeed accept the forms of intuition as something ultimately given because they are not conceptual in nature, he believes that the forms of thought have to be derived from the unity of thought, that is, from the unity of logical reason itself. This attempt to derive the forms from the original unity of our thought as an activity is what he has undertaken to do in the principal section of the *Critique of Pure Reason*, namely the so-called Transcendental Deduction of the Pure Concepts of Understanding.

Let me just make a brief comment on the relationship between 'transcendental' and 'transcendent'. Where words are related like this, where they are so obviously connected, there is generally more involved than pure historical chance: the connections are a matter of essentials. Transcendent means 'going beyond' and the concept of 'going beyond' is capable of a variety of meanings; in fact, there are three meanings of significance here. You may speak of logical transcendence; that is found when you measure a proposition not on its own terms, but as it were from outside. For example, a transcendent critique would be one where a cultural conservative criticizes Samuel Beckett from his culturally conservative point of view. That would be a case of logical transcendence. Secondly, there is a narrower, epistemological concept of transcendence that refers to a concept of being that is different from consciousness, beyond consciousness: thus, for example, the difference between the thing-in-itself and the consciousness through which it becomes known. Lastly, there is the consciousness of metaphysical transcendence. That would be the kind of transcendence that is found if we go beyond the limits of the possibility of experience, as Kant would put it, and make judgements about absolute matters, such as God, freedom, immortality, the essence of being, or whatever else occurs to us.

In the Kantian use of the term 'transcendental' you may well have to recollect this third meaning of transcendent in order to grasp the specific distinction between 'transcendent' and 'transcendental'. For both 'transcendental' and this third meaning of 'transcendent' belong together in their common opposition to the concept of experience; they are both concerned with whatever is independent of experience. But the concept of the transcendental conceives of whatever precedes experience, what makes experience possible, as an attribute of reason, an attribute of mind. This stands in contrast to metaphysical dogmatism, which, according to Kant, understands the transcendence of experience as something otherworldly in the sense of an absolute substance – something that even goes beyond the mind itself – a divine substance, in short. Thus the transcendental in Kant represents the transcendent nature of our minds in the sense that it supplies the conditions that make something like experience possible, and in that sense may be said to go beyond experience, but on the other hand – and this is one of the most remarkable difficulties of the *Critique of Pure Reason* – these conditions can only be held to be valid if they do ✳ in fact relate to experience. They do indeed transcend experience, but they possess no absolute, transcendent truth; they possess truth only in so far as they relate to experience, to possible experience, and in general are saturated with the objects of experience. Thus we might say that the concept of the transcendent is significantly restricted by its translation into the transcendental; and it is at the same time *interiorized* to a significant degree. This means that it ceases to be a dogmatically postulated principle standing beyond and opposed to human beings, and becomes instead a principle of mind itself and an attribute of human consciousness as such.

So much for the concept of the transcendental. But whenever you find yourself in difficulties with the concept, your best recourse is to reflect that transcendental means simply the quintessence of all enquiries that relate to the possibility of synthetic *a priori* judgements. If you do not wish to take this Kantian definition too literally, you can regard the transcendental as the realm through which experience becomes possible although it does not itself arise from experience – as you can see from the first sentence of the main text of the *Critique of Pure Reason*:

> There can be no doubt that all our knowledge begins with experience. For how should our faculty of knowledge otherwise be awakened into action . . . ? But though all our knowledge begins *with* experience, it does not follow that it arises *out of* experience.[17]

Thus in Kant all enquiries that are concerned with these propositions that are independent of experience, these synthetic *a priori* judgements, may be said to be transcendental. At the same time, the concept
refers to all enquiries that extend to the possible relation of mind to
experience and hence to objects in general. This, then, is the concept
of the transcendental. Thus the sphere of the transcendental is neither
one of formal logic – because it is concerned with the possible knowledge of objects – nor is it a sphere concerned with the contents of
knowledge – because it does not presuppose such contents, but only
the possibility of possessing such contents. It is, then, a curious *no
man's land* of knowledge positioned somewhere between psychology
and logic (if I can put it in this somewhat provisional way).[18] This
curious intermediary realm is the realm in which the *Critique of Pure
Reason* unfolds, and it is this that has earned it the title of a transcendental enquiry.

It goes without saying that the existence of such a realm poses
great difficulties. It remains to be seen whether such a realm exists in
fact; whether there is a realm that is neither purely logical (because
it has a material content), nor somehow empirical or psychological
(because in that event it could not exist *a priori*) – I just wish to point
out to you that this is just one of the most difficult metacritical
questions raised by the *Critique of Pure Reason*. But here, too, I
would counsel you not to be too hasty with your criticisms, but
simply to allow for the fact that, by establishing this highly curious
sphere of the transcendental, Kant has made it possible to open up
something that seemed to him to harmonize with the ideal of knowledge, namely the sphere of *a priori* knowledge.

The actual source of this interest in the *a priori* and what it involves
is a subject we shall turn to in the next lecture.

LECTURE THREE

26 May 1959

The Concept of the Transcendental (II)

You will remember that last time we looked a little more closely at the concept of synthetic *a priori* judgements the possibility of which forms the central theme of the *Critique of Pure Reason*. What I now owe you is an explanation of the enormous importance ascribed to these synthetic *a priori* judgements, however they are to be understood in detail. We are talking here of judgements which are valid independently of experience or which hold good for all future experience. Your initial response to this will probably be to say that if we judge in this way, if we can secure knowledge in this manner, the fact that this knowledge is absolutely and necessarily valid is not so terribly important to us. We are generally interested – at a fairly basic level – to know whether these judgements suffice for us to orientate ourselves and, after that, whether they possess enough plausibility, power and penetration, or however you want to phrase it. Whether they are absolutely valid is not so terribly important to us. I believe that a certain lack of interest in philosophy is to be attributed to the fact that traditional philosophy makes truth claims that seem so excessive that we are not able to make them fit our own spiritual needs. I should like to say that the distrust of philosophy that we find here is not without its justification; in general, philosophy really does act as if the idea of a timeless truth, valid for all future experience, were the only one worthy of mankind – whereas it is not entirely appropriate for us, at least in the form stated, and I may add that its unquestioned acceptance by the entire philosophical tradition is something that can no longer be tolerated by a critical philosophy.

I then pointed out to you that at this crucial point Kant does not represent anything absolutely new, but he can be situated within a particular philosophical tradition. I may even say, without being unkind, that he is actually positioned within the philosophical mainstream, and that the general interest in the *Critique of Pure Reason* can really only be explained if this connection between Kant and the tradition has been properly understood. According to this tradition there is a world of truth that stands opposed in principle to the fleeting nature of the world of phenomena. This world of phenomena represents something of a delusion, and is therefore inferior when compared to that truth. This motif is regarded as being self-evidently true in the current of philosophy I have termed the mainstream. It begins with the Eleatics and passes via Plato and Aristotle through the great Aristotelian tradition of the Middle Ages, through Descartes and the rationalists, right down to Kant.

The fact that the truth of such ideas of truth is by no means self-evident in reality can be seen when you encounter them for the first assest and at the same time most shameless form, 's dialogue *Meno*. In the *Meno* Plato provides the eory of ideas and with it the doctrine of the eternally immutable realm of truth which is still the concern of Kant's critique of reason. What you find there is the statement, which is obviously felt to be self-evident, that human concerns – the basic moral principles, for example, according to which we must act, the idea of what is good or what is just – that all these things must be known with the same degree of certitude as the propositions of geometry. Plato evidently remained quite unshocked by everything that had to be omitted and by the violence of the process of abstraction that is necessary before a concept of truth borrowed from mathematics can be applied to the concrete activities of human beings.[1] I have already pointed to certain features that surface again in Kant's philosophy. And it has rightly been pointed out many times that the relationship between Kant and Plato is very profound, although in one crucial respect there is a decisive distinction to be drawn. This is in the approach to the absolute realm of ideas which plays a role in both philosophers. The distinction is, to put it in Kantian terms, that in Plato the ideas have a constitutive meaning, that is to say, they are the only essential and real things, while Kant allows them validity only as regulative principles, roughly, as 'unending tasks' to which reality itself cannot simply be reduced.

Thus in Kant, as I attempted to show you last time, you have a mathematical model very similar to Plato's, and you also have a method very similar to Plato's, one that modern epistemology would term a *reductive method.* This means that everything that can be regarded as ephemeral, transitory, deceptive, and illusory is left to one side, so that what remains is supposed to be indispensable, absolutely secure, something I can hold permanently in my hands. I have called this idea of truth the residual theory of truth.[2] As I have said, it is common to almost the entire philosophical tradition and includes Descartes and Leibniz among Kant's immediate predecessors. This theory asserts that truth is whatever remains once everything sensory, everything ephemeral and hence deceptive has been subtracted. To put it in economic terms, it is the profit that remains after deducting all the costs of production. For sensory experience cannot entirely be dispensed with – all these philosophers concede this after their own fashion, even old Plato. It is merely that in this tradition the epistemological value of experience is highly problematic: it must be regarded as the point of departure, but it may not be regarded as the actual source of knowledge – as we can see from the very first sentence of the *Critique of Pure Reason*, which is in complete agreement with the view of experience I have just outlined:

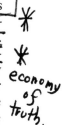

economy of truth.

> There can be no doubt that all our knowledge begins with experience. For how should our faculty of knowledge otherwise be awakened into action . . . ? But though all our knowledge begins *with* experience, it does not follow that it arises *out of* experience.[3]

Now, so as to extract from knowledge everything that does not spring from experience and that therefore does not change and perish with experience – this is what we may broadly, less technically, describe as the motivation that leads us to a preoccupation with synthetic *a priori* judgements and that then becomes inextricably linked with the attempt to provide a grounding for the exact natural sciences by reflecting on their epistemological foundations. It would be important to reflect on how this ideal actually arose. It is a remarkable business. In your normal lives as knowing subjects, you probably do not give a damn about this idea of what Thucydides calls 'enduring gain'.[4] However, when it comes to philosophy, you will probably all automatically accept this concept of truth. The fact is that we are saturated with all sorts of philosophical ideas of which we are unaware; and not the least task of philosophy is to make us conscious of ideas that we have automatically adopted without really thinking them through, and to examine them critically. So I would say that we need to consider in all seriousness – the greatest thinkers of the post-Kantian period, Hegel and Nietzsche, have both raised this question insistently – whether this equation of the truth with what is permanent, eternal and timeless, is actually a sufficient definition, or whether it does not predetermine the truth in line with a particular model, a model characterized by the handiness of its methods, reliable scientific methods for all eventualities. We might indeed argue that this handiness, this ease of application to all future eventualities, wherever possible, says nothing about the nature of truth in reality, even though the truth is the goal of the method.

We should really ask ourselves how this equation of binding truth with timeless or eternal knowledge comes about.[5] You then realize that you are dealing with something primordially bourgeois. I have no wish to indulge in sociological discussions here and to say that such ideas as timeless truths can be socially inferred, because such inferences always imply a particular concept of truth and we would then land in a vicious circle we would be best advised to avoid. But since it is my task, or rather since I regard it as my task to make Kant speak to you, I should like to make you aware that this strange idea of the truth as something lasting and enduring somehow always appears where urban exchange societies have developed. That is to say, underlying this is an idea that nothing new should come into being, that the new is actually a source of insecurity, a threat, something worrying. There may even be something quite archaic underlying it, namely the fear of difference, the fear of anything that is not cocooned in the web of our concepts and which therefore frightens us when we encounter it. There is, then, a kind of taboo on the new and on change that declares itself in the way in which the right to truth, the emphatic claim to be true, is given only to what is permanent, while whatever changes and is new is degraded in the first instance to the illusory, the transient, and condemned to inferior status. But over and above that, what is at stake here is the way in which this archaic need for security can be extended into ideas of property.

What is so magnificent about Kant is that he still possesses something of the uninhibited frankness of a man who is not ashamed of his bourgeois attitudes, but who gives them expression and who thereby expresses something of their truth. In Kant you constantly encounter these homely comparisons – like the famous one of the 300 imagined thalers and the 300 real ones.[6] You will constantly hear about 'firm' or 'lasting' ownership and similar figures of speech in reference to propositions we possess. A fundamental analysis of the metaphoric language of Kant's philosophy would undoubtedly be a fruitful undertaking, for the similes and metaphors in a text are not neutral, but reveal something of its deepest intentions, intentions that are mostly imposed on the author. However that may be, behind this whole enterprise stands the model of fixed possessions that is transferred to knowledge and is supposed not to be transitory. But a further element lies behind it, one I regard as decisive. What is lurking somewhere in this idea that there should be nothing new is the exchange relationship. I believe that this is the profoundest thing that can be said about the bourgeois nature of this kind of philosophy. I am not using 'bourgeois' here in a derogatory, aestheticizing sense, but simply phenomenologically, in order to define the specific character of this kind of philosophy in the history of mankind . . . Thus in this philosophy we find lurking the idea that the act of cognition is a kind of exchange in which equivalents, namely efforts and products, are exchanged so that debts are settled and the sums work out. There *economy of philosophy* is a relationship of equivalence such that in principle nothing can emerge without entering into it, that is, nothing that does not have to be paid for by whatever has first been *posited*. And in the process only this exchange relation of knowledge, that is, the effort, the exchange between the labour of thinking and the object which thought then appropriates, and the products of this process, namely the fact that the ideas *work out* – only this becomes the thing that endures, the lasting product.[7]

I have already pointed to the ambiguity that lies in the concept of synthetic *a priori* judgements. The ambiguity is whether synthetic *a priori* judgements are valid *independently* of experience, which is how Kant generally formulates it, or whether it means that they are valid *for* every experience. This apparently trivial distinction conceals a crucial point, one you can learn from. One of the demands that philosophy makes on common sense, and which you cannot evade if you intend to take philosophy seriously, is that the crucial philosophical problems almost always lie concealed in such nuances. That (if I may be allowed to say so) also explains why linguistic problems, so-called questions of formulation – in other words, the effort to state matters as precisely as possible and to hit the nail on the head as cleanly as you can – have such an enormous importance throughout the whole field of philosophy. This is because the only way to do justice to nuances of meaning is to make the very greatest efforts to achieve precise linguistic expression. So if there is a gulf between 'independently of experience' and 'for every future experience', this must conceal a problem, a very serious problem, and, as I believe, a key problem for Kantian philosophy and for epistemology in general.

I would like to explain this problem to you in a few words so as to provide you with a model for the theoretical method that underpins this lecture course as a whole. It is that a system like Kant's, that to all intents and appearances seems to be a coherent totality, held together in a deductive unity, is in reality a force field, one that can

only be properly understood if you understand the forces that come
together in a kind of productive friction and if you are able to bring
such a text to life. The assumption of the inferiority of experience
about which I have been speaking is one that permeates the whole of
philosophy, and is ultimately connected with the separation of manual
and mental labour and the making absolute of mind in fixed logical
forms. This assumption demands that synthetic *a priori* judgements
should be free of experience of every kind. What this conflicts with,
however, is the fact that these synthetic *a priori* judgements are simply full of elements of every conceivable kind that are drawn from
experience and about which I could know nothing in the absence of
experience. I have already read out to you for a second time the key
sentence from the celebrated Introduction to the *Critique of Pure
Reason*, and this idea is expressed there in the statement that while
it is true that all our knowledge *begins* with experience, it does
not *arise from* experience. But I should like to say that this crass
dichotomy has something dogmatic about it. If something begins at a
certain point, it cannot be wholly unconnected with its origins. It is
quite true – and this really does lead us into a discussion of Kant's
core concerns – that time and space or the forms of our thought
cannot simply be inferred from experience and that logical propositions are not simply facts of experience comparable to the observations we make of the physical world. But on the other hand, if there
were no such thing as experience, if we did not receive from experience the elements that are formulated in these propositions, even
these allegedly experience-free propositions would not be possible –
and this is the source of the variant reading: '*for* all future experience'.
I can easily produce any number of propositions – my old teacher
Cornelius always enjoyed doing this[8] – that could be classified as
synthetic *a priori* judgements in the sense understood in the *Critique
of Pure Reason*, but which notwithstanding this cannot be said to be
independent of experience. For example, 'Orange comes between red
and yellow on the colour scale.'[9] As long as you are familiar with red
and yellow, this statement has an absolutely compelling truth; it remains valid for all future experience. This means that it is a synthetic
a priori judgement according to *this* definition of the term. However,
it unquestionably arises from experience and not from pure thought.
For pure thought alone can tell you nothing whatever about colours.
Colours are sense data, and if you have not *seen* red and yellow then
you do not know what a colour scale is, and hence do not know
what orange is either. I should say here for purposes of clarification
that you must always distinguish the source of the so-called deictic
from other definitions: that is to say, a reference to some sensory

phenomena or other that cannot be defined. You cannot define red. At most you can say what is playing upon your retina, and even then you still will not know what red is. A further source of knowledge is definition by means of concepts as this has been understood in traditional logic. Now there is a whole series of deictic definitions that are *a priori* in nature, but which necessarily refer to experience. I should like to say, however, that this all sounds splendid and it helps you to circumvent one of the difficulties with the *Critique of Pure Reason*, namely, that you underestimate experience and therefore exclude from the realm of synthetic *a priori* judgements an infinite number of propositions that undoubtedly possess an *a priori* character as Kant understood it. However, in so doing – and here you come to something which is highly characteristic of Kant's philosophy – you introduce as a source of knowledge the very thing that has been excluded from it in the course of the critique of reason: namely, experience itself.

It might nevertheless be asked: well, if such a synthetic *a priori* judgement arises from experience, why should experience be deemed inferior when compared to absolute truth, as has been repeatedly claimed by rationalist and idealist philosophers ever since Plato? If I include Kant in this tradition I can only do so with a significant reservation – and this brings me to what is specifically new about Kant. This specifically new aspect lies not so much in the thesis he advances as in the general direction of his gaze. What is new in Kant is not the doctrine of the synthetic *a priori* judgement as the truly authoritative shape of truth. Something similar can be found, for instance in Descartes's 'innate ideas', which can be regarded as the ancestors of all these Kantian ideas. Or you can find it in Leibniz's '*vérités de raison*', which we might then describe as the grandfather of the Kantian concept. What is particular to Kant – and I believe that this will convey a much more specific understanding of Kant's point of departure – is that these truths of reason are not simply inferred by him, they are not simply taught. Nor are they 'asserted' [*gesetzt*], as Fichte would have called it, but instead they are '*reflected upon*'. This means that if they are to be proved, if they are to be valid, they must be subjected to a kind of process of inspection. You can say, therefore – and I believe this is important for an understanding of the *Critique of Pure Reason* as a whole – that the theme of the *Critique of Pure Reason* is not just the speculative production or generation of these synthetic *a priori* judgements, but rather the scrutiny of their validity.

In the *Critique of Pure Reason* Kant's concern is to test the validity of judgements whose validity is assumed. This is closely linked to something else I have mentioned: Kant takes the existence of the

mathematical natural sciences for granted. The emotional force of
the *Critique of Pure Reason* lies in the fact that he is convinced of
the overwhelming power and dignity of these theories. What he
then does is to conduct a huge audit in order to establish why these
sciences whose existence is taken for granted can be said to be truly
valid – without making any attempt to generate them from pure
thought or speculative philosophy. This is what distinguishes Kant's
philosophy both from the philosophy that preceded his own and
from that of his immediate successors who appealed to his authority.
What is at issue here is not so much that these absolute truths should
emerge from the philosophy as that a kind of process of reflection, of
testing, should take place. The effect of this process is to consolidate
the validity of this entire structure whose truth is already assumed on
the basis of the positive validity of the sciences. And this is actually
what Kant means by 'critique'. The path then taken by his successors
is one in which they said: by practising critique in this fashion, I must
always also say that by virtue of a critical reasoning I actually produce and generate and create what the criticized reason is able to
express as its particular finite and limited truth. This element of
reflecting on knowledge in order to test its validity is the feature that
Kant shares with empiricism, above all with Hume. You will all have
heard or read at some point that Kant claimed that Hume had aroused
him from his 'dogmatic slumber'.[10]
    You will all be familiar with the general statement that is to be
found in textbooks and lectures to the effect that Kant's philosophy
represents a union of the Leibniz–Wolff school from which he came
and Hume's empiricism. And if you wished to provide a rough-and-
ready summary of the force field I have been speaking about, this
rather unsophisticated formula would do well enough. But I believe
that for a more sophisticated, less elementary view it is necessary to
achieve greater clarity about the relative importance of these elements in Kant's philosophy. On this point my view would be that the
vérités de raison, the synthetic *a priori* judgements, in short, the in-
controvertibly true and valid modes of knowledge that far surpass
mere logic, may be described as the roast, the Leibnizian or Cartesian
roast, while Hume and English scepticism provide the dialectical salt.
That is to say, this scepticism is the method through which the critical scrutiny is undertaken, but the empirical strand does not play so
very great a role in the plan of the entire system. The fact is that
scepticism already finds expression in the demonstrable existence of
the sciences since it is only their validity which is to be reviewed.
Kant's philosophy makes use of doubt, of critical examination, so
as to ensure that what it perceives as incontrovertible truth should

shine forth in all its glory because it has withstood even that sceptical inspection.

What you never find in Kant is what might be termed metaphysical scepticism, that is, a scepticism that is directed, for instance, at the absolute character of these truths. Thanks to this we may say that Kant's distance from Hume, which occasionally seems to be minimal, a matter of fine distinctions, is in reality a matter of his philosophy as a whole. This is something frequently encountered in philosophy, where the same, the identical theses may have completely different meanings within the general parameters, the general emotional thrust of a given philosophy. The solution Kant provides – to sum it up rather crudely – is that the truths he is concerned with and whose validity he demonstrates with the aid of the sceptical analysis of consciousness that he has borrowed, are indeed supposed to be valid for all time, but they are not timeless as such. They are not free-floating entities, but are timeless only with regard to experience; they are the supreme principles that actually make experience possible, rather than truths detached from experience. His method, then, is that of analysis of the faculty of cognition as a whole in so far as it makes experience possible. Or, as Kant puts it in his own language: he is interested in the elements or features of the faculty of cognition that constitute experience or knowledge in general.

It will not have escaped you that there is a very serious problem here, one that I am not able to resolve today, but which I should like to bring to your attention, so that you should not think that we are just skating over the difficulties. The fact is that I had said to you, on the one hand, that Kant is concerned with the constitution of timeless, absolutely valid modes of knowledge. Now you suddenly hear from me that these modes of knowledge should only exist if they constitute something like experience. With this we arrive at the point where the scepticism to which he has subjected his truths of reason has left its scars. So, on the one hand, he wishes to salvage the timeless, absolutely valid experience of independent truth;[11] and we shall have to talk at length about Kant's desire to salvage what is threatened.[12] The *Critique of Pure Reason* is in general a supreme attempt to salvage ontology on a subjectivist basis, if I may speak so grandiloquently. But on the other hand, despite this rescue attempt his analysis does extend ultimately into the realm of concrete consciousness and therefore also assumes an element of experience. And he cannot uphold these [absolute?] propositions as something substantive independently of experience because they can never be free of some substantive elements or other. And this is how he arrives at the highly curious theory that they constitute experience.

I should like to tell you now what we shall be looking at later on. This is one of the genuine difficulties of the *Critique of Pure Reason* and it is my view that you will best deal with these difficulties if you refrain from saying, 'Look, he has made a mistake! He has got it wrong! Old Kant has really made a fool of himself here.' Instead, you would do better to try and understand that the difficulties you discern in the *Critique of Pure Reason* have their roots in this constant friction created by opposing strands of thought that then inflict all kinds of damage on each other. The entire *Critique of Pure Reason* is acted out in a peculiar no man's land. On the one hand, it cannot be a purely formal logic, since in that case the propositions that are crucial to it could not be synthetic propositions. On the other hand, however, they may not have any content since in that event they would be empirical propositions and would once again not be synthetic *a priori* propositions. Through this peculiar difficulty you enter into the true realm in which Kantian ideas have their being. This is the realm that could properly be called the *transcendental* realm – in a less pedantic sense than when I expounded it to you last time. It could be thought of here as a speculative realm where the need somehow or other to reconcile two otherwise irreconcilable concepts leads to intellectual constructs that cannot refer to any immediately given, positive realities, but which are motivated by the forward march of the analysis. Only if you make allowances for the peculiar structure of the philosophy of Kant and even more of his successors will you be in a position to understand the entire thrust of this philosophical idealism.

What is generally referred to as Kant's Copernican revolution is essentially concerned with the fact that those absolute truths are independent of experience but form the object of criticism so that criticism drives a trench through the middle of their realm, accepting some propositions and rejecting others. Kant's Copernican revolution is nothing other than the fact that this entire realm is no longer simply visited so that these things can be discussed and judged directly, but instead they are involved in the process of reflection. When I said to you earlier that the novel aspect of the *Critique of Pure Reason* was the reflection of reason on itself, that reflexivity is what lies at the heart of the Copernican revolution. The truths that are the object of concern in the *Critique of Pure Reason* are not supposed to be externally demonstrated and presented or asserted any more – as free-standing things as in Plato's theory. Instead, they are to prove their worth by the fact that reason examines itself and then discovers in itself the constitutive elements thanks to which something like a universally valid and objective knowledge can be made

knowledge that transcends the bounds of what can be supplied by experience. If I remind you here of the themes of Kant's theory of ideas, of questions about God, immortality, the soul, the nature of Being, you will be able to form a more concrete idea of what is meant by metaphysics in this book. The concept of metaphysics has also been used in a *positive* sense as a focal point from which to gain an understanding of the *Critique of Pure Reason*. An example is Martin Heidegger,[1] who believes that the problem of time provides a key to the work. However, he reads a specific interpretation of metaphysics into the *Critique of Pure Reason*, namely the relationship of Being and time,[2] which I would say is not directly a central theme in the work. I have no desire to castigate Heidegger on this account, since the ideas I intend to examine with you also involve considering a number of questions which are not raised as such in the *Critique*, but may be said to be extrapolations from it. But since my intention in talking about the problem of metaphysics is the more modest one of introducing you to the *Critique of Pure Reason*, I believe that the appropriate method is an immanent procedure, that is to say, I wish to examine the way the concept or concepts of metaphysics are actually used in the book.

As to the question of the relationship between the problem of metaphysics and the problem of synthetic *a priori* judgements (and my seeming neglect of the former), I would like to make two points – the second of which will lead us into the substance of the problem. The first point is: do you recollect my saying that the main section of the *Critique of Pure Reason* was divided into two main parts – that do not wholly coincide with the slightly artificial division described in the table of contents? There is, to oversimplify, a positive part and a negative part. Both of these are included in the so-called Transcendental Doctrine of Elements. Compared to this the Transcendental Doctrine of Method is more of a corollary: it is readily comprehensible and does not throw up any particular difficulties. But on the other hand it is not an integral part of the work in the sense of being absolutely essential for an understanding of it.

The so-called *positive* sections of the *Critique of Pure Reason* consist of the First Part of the Doctrine of Elements, that is, the Transcendental Aesthetic [pp. 65–91], and from the Second Part (i.e. the Transcendental Logic), we must include the First Division, that is, the Transcendental Analytic [pp. 102–296]. And at the end of Book II of the First Division, in the Analytic of Principles [pp. 170ff], you do in fact discover what I might very loosely call the 'positive' conclusion of the *Critique of Pure Reason*. The System of all Principles [pp. 188–256] with which this part concludes is in fact nothing

other than the systematic arrangement of the synthetic *a priori* judgements as these emerge fully armed, as it were, from the interaction of
the elements of intuition, or more accurately, the forms of intuition,
with the forms of the understanding that were deduced in the critique
of reason, in short, the categories. What I am saying here is not to be
taken quite literally.[3] Particularly since Kant would claim that these
principles yield only the most general statements from which the
actual synthetic *a priori* judgements still have to be deduced, which
then in their turn constitute the supreme propositions of the pure
natural sciences. But the essential labour of this process of deduction
can be regarded as having already been accomplished in them; and
Kant himself did not carry out the work of what he would have
called an *elaborated* metaphysics of nature, that is, a doctrine of the
supreme synthetic propositions of the natural sciences.

In contrast to all this the Second Division, that is, the Transcendental Dialectic [pp. 297–570], is the negative side. It is the part of
the *Critique of Pure Reason* that concerns itself with the contradictions in which reason necessarily becomes entangled. At the same
time, it is the part that is devoted to metaphysics in a significant
meaning of the term, since Kant equates metaphysical problems (we
shall have more to say about this in the course of this lecture) with
the contradictions in which reason must necessarily be caught up,
but which reason is also said to be able to resolve – one of the most
remarkable features of the *Critique of Pure Reason*.

If I began by placing such great emphasis on the synthetic *a priori*
judgements, I may say in my own defence that this at least had the
merit of enabling me to include some reflections on what may be
thought of as the positive side of the *Critique of Pure Reason*. I
should like to add that Book II, chapter III of the First Division, The
Ground of the Distinction of all Objects in general into Phenomena
and Noumena [pp. 257–75], already represents the transition to dialectics; and that, strictly speaking, the extremely important Appendix
on the Amphiboly of Concepts of Reflection [pp. 276–96] that has
been placed here really forms part of the Transcendental Dialectic
and does not properly belong in the Transcendental Logic. I should
like to recommend very strongly that you direct your attention to this
slightly neglected chapter, in contrast to the Transcendental Doctrine
of Method, because it really provides the solution contained in Kant's
philosophy to what nowadays has become the fashionable problem
of *Being*. But all this is a somewhat superficial response to the question of the nature of our interest in synthetic *a priori* judgements.
Much more to the point is the fact that the question of metaphysics
cannot really be separated from the question of synthetic *a priori*

judgements. That is to say, the different parts of the architectu.. ..
the *Critique of Pure Reason* are so inextricably interwoven, so closely
bound together, that to divide them into a positive section and a
negative one as I have just done is really a childish undertaking,
as childish as Hegel would claim every division is into a so-called
positive and a so-called negative part. I have only attempted this to
give a very rough-and-ready outline to those of you who have not yet
familiarized yourselves with the structure of the work.

But let me begin first with the question of metaphysics in Kant
himself, and the way it is posed in the *Critique of Pure Reason*. I
shall then attempt to show you how it is connected to the problem of
synthetic *a priori* judgements. We are looking here at the Introduction, the end of the Introduction, to be precise, where this question
is explicitly raised – as indeed I have shown you indirectly in my
earlier lectures and, I hope, without your having noticed it too much,
with reference to the problems raised in the two Prefaces and the
Introduction to the *Critique of Pure Reason*. You will now discover
there that the question of metaphysics is divided into two further
questions, namely, 'How is metaphysics as a natural disposition
possible?' and 'How is metaphysics possible as science?'[4] Let me try
to help you understand this better by interpreting the first question
in the light of what we have already said. For after what you have
already heard about the plan of the *Critique of Pure Reason*, and
in particular the fact that it is concerned not with a psychological
approach, but with a transcendental one, that is, one investigating
the necessary conditions of thought, you may well be moved to say:
Why the devil should we be interested in metaphysics as a natural
disposition? That is exactly the same as wishing to discuss the question of the dorsal vertebrae or other anthropological topics in the
Critique of Pure Reason; and it is completely unnecessary to raise
such questions of what might be called intellectual anthropology in a
work devoted to epistemology and metaphysics.

If you approach this question guided by such thoughts, as is your
right, you will encounter great difficulties. It is necessary for thinking about Kant – and to a far greater degree about Hegel – that the
process of thought should carry out a double movement. On the one
hand, it should immerse itself in the text, and keep as closely to it as
possible; on the other hand, it should retain a degree of self-control,
remove itself from immediate contact and look at the ideas from a
certain distance. This is because very many of the difficulties in Kant
and Hegel, but also in Fichte and Schelling, arise when you scrutinize
the texts too closely and so fail to recognize their intentions, whereas
these can be perceived much more clearly at a distance.

So let us return to the first question of what is meant by metaphysics as *natural disposition*. After what I have said to you in general
terms, you will readily understand what is meant without confusing
it with psychology. Whereas if you just looked at the text, you might
easily fail to grasp that point. You have to think of it in conjunction
with the passage I have now mentioned several times and that we
shall have occasion to return to again. This is that by virtue of its
own disposition reason is necessarily compelled to keep asking
certain questions, but by the same token it is unable to answer them.[5]
And it is this, the logic that leads to metaphysical questions being
asked, that concerns us here. What is at issue here is not a sort of
physiology of mind – as Kant ironically called it, with reference
to Locke,[6] for example – of the kind frequently encountered in the
Enlightenment. Such a 'physiology' would set out to discover which
human drives would lead people to ask certain metaphysical questions: fear, for example, or wish fulfilment. We are not concerned
with such matters here. Instead we have a genuine intellectual question: by what means, with the aid of which immanent mechanisms,
is reason driven towards those problems that we call metaphysical
problems? And the answer – to cut a long story short – is simply that
metaphysics is nothing but reason asserting itself absolutely; that is
to say, reason which regards its own use as the warranty of truth,
quite independently of the materials it has to work on.

Perhaps I may be allowed at this point to shed some light on an
aspect of the history of idealist philosophy to which Kant belongs.
Reason appears there as something *negative*, in the sense that it may
be said to be doomed to follow its own impulse and obey its own
laws, without regard to whatever may land it in contradictions. Kant's
successors, however, transformed this negative element – just because
it is a necessity, because it is inevitable, a compulsion inherent in
logic – into something *positive*, into the organ of truth. This transformation of what Kant calls dialectics with purely negative connotations into dialectics as a method for the discovery of the truth and
simultaneously as truth revealing itself – that, in a nutshell, is the
crucial factor distinguishing Kant from the philosophers of German
idealism who came after him. In other words, when we speak here of
a natural disposition what is meant is simply that reason, by following its own destiny, marches on and on, transcending its own finite
conditions. And finally, so as not to end up in an infinite progression,
it finds that it must somehow postulate the existence of a frontier in
the shape of an ultimate cause, an ultimate form of existence, an
ultimate absolute being in which everything can be anchored. And,
Kant asserts, this is an entirely legitimate and unavoidable need that·

is simply rooted in the impulse to ground knowledge in other foundations, and hence in its logical structure. It is rooted in the circumstance that we have no right to judge unless we can provide a reason
for it. But by acceding to this entirely legitimate and unavoidable
coercion, we end up in these difficulties. So the question that appears
in this first category as the question about metaphysics as a natural
disposition is nothing other than the question of how we are driven
to ask the kinds of question that Kant calls metaphysical.

The second question is, 'How is metaphysics possible as *science*?' I
would like to ask you to consider this question, too, in the light of
what I have already said. If you do that, it will not sound as strange
as it may seem at present. The question can be found at the end of
the Introduction,[7] and thereby points – this must surely be conceded
– to the most important theme to which the *Critique of Pure Reason*
aspires. In contrast to the question about the *necessity* with which
reason is driven towards metaphysics – the question here relates to
the *validity* of metaphysical propositions; in other words, the really
critical question: to what extent questions about God, freedom,
immortality, the soul, Being, infinity and the like are actually valid,
how far they may be thought legitimate. Now, I think that in this
context, now that the concept of science has cropped up, we ought to
pause briefly and note that there is a problem in the relationship of
philosophy to science, a problem that dominates the entire history
of philosophy and that is given its supreme and most logical expression, at least in the history of philosophy up to Kant, in the *Critique
of Pure Reason*. Looking somewhat further, and considering the
question more broadly, we can say that the question of how metaphysics is possible as science in fact describes the impulse underlying the whole of modern philosophy. We may say that the terrain
of philosophy and science is one that has been fought over from the
very outset, since the earliest times, until it finally crystallized in this
Kantian question.

On the one hand, philosophy would like to utter the unconditional;
it would like to make a statement about the crucial questions that lie
beyond the everyday activities of the understanding, activities that
are determined by the division of labour and are linked to the business of human self-preservation. It would like to make a statement
about how matters really lie and what the *Being* is that lies behind all
things. On the other hand, the positive sciences have removed from
philosophy more and more of the kinds of question that target this
unconditioned absolute. If you look at the ancient Ionian philosophers of nature, you will find that their thought contains countless elements that belong to natural science or the theory of nature in

modern terminology, and that have been wrested from philosophy by the advances of science. And if you read a book of such high metaphysical ambition as Plato's *Phaedo*, a work that stands at the pinnacle of Greek philosophy, you will find it addressing a problem that is also encountered in the *Critique of Pure Reason*, namely the problem of immortality, or what we might also call the problem of the substantiality and indivisibility of the soul. At the same time, however, this highly metaphysical book also contains a series of statements that from a modern perspective would simply belong in the field of geography: statements about the rivers that form the frontiers of the ocean, that lead down into the underworld, and other mythological claims of the same sort. Scientific and speculative metaphysics had not yet parted company. You need only read some of the truly fantastic stories Plato tells about these rivers to realize the extent to which science has liberated itself from philosophy – or I might as well say, metaphysics. Furthermore, if you wish, and if you will allow me to make this point, even though it has no direct connection with Kant, you may regard the entire project of Aristotle's philosophy as a magnificent, and actually the first, attempt on a grand scale to combine the ideal of science with the ideal of metaphysics.

In the *Critique of Pure Reason* the way this is done is to apply to philosophy the criteria that have established themselves as the criteria of valid science. These criteria are those of testability and the absence of logical contradiction. This means that philosophy has taken over the spirit of science but still retains its claim to be philosophy. In this sense it can be asserted that Kant's philosophy stands on the dividing line between philosophy and science: it is *still* metaphysics and at the same time it is *already* a theory of science. To put it another way, in Kant this process of wresting from philosophy the specific pieces of scientific knowledge that had once belonged to philosophy, to speculative metaphysics, has reached the point where only a limited number of ideas remains.

In Kant metaphysics is actually no more than a residue: it is what is left over once every conceivable scientific discipline has made itself independent of the κόσμος νοητικός of the old metaphysics, which was itself the product of an earlier process of emancipation from the magical and mythological idea of the oneness of nature. What Kant actually does in the *Critique of Pure Reason* is to examine this residue of knowledge, assertions, theses and propositions that cannot be dissolved into scientific knowledge. He then judges this residue according to criteria that have been derived from the sciences whose validity is uncontested. Of these sciences he says at one point that pure mathematics and pure science exist and are proved by the fact that they exist.

To discover *how* they can exist is the task of rational critique. This can be found in the same Section VI of the Introduction to the *Critique of Pure Reason* to which I have just referred.[8] You can see exemplified here what I have said to you about the residual character of truth in all philosophies of this kind – that is, the truth is always what remains when you eliminate the apparently ephemeral, transitory and historical. But it is even more striking that this idea of truth has its own deeply historical meaning. It is not a residue simply in a logical sense, but also in the sense that it is literally what remains to poor old philosophy after the individual sciences have plundered it and stripped it of everything they can in order to enrich their own disciplines. It is this terribly impoverished and deprived thing that is then supposed to be the entire substance of philosophy. Kant undoubtedly belongs in this residual conception of philosophy. There have been no more than a handful of philosophers who have seriously waged war on this residual concept of truth and have systematically laid bare its poverty. Hegel and his dialectical successors are among them, on the one hand, as is Nietzsche, on the other. For his part, Kant was evidently not even conscious of this poverty, even though it is the consideration of his philosophy that leads us to draw attention to it.

The question here, however – and this brings me back to my opening remarks in this lecture – is inextricably bound up with the question of synthetic *a priori* judgements. For if metaphysics is thought of as a science, then, according to Kant, it requires the same rationale as the pure sciences. This means in his view that the supreme propositions of metaphysics must be synthetic *a priori* judgements – or else they cannot exist at all. For the conviction that the propositions of metaphysics are not analytical judgements is one of the key assumptions of the *Critique of Pure Reason*. Of course, it is easy to say this and you may not think it so very important when you hear it, and you will think to yourselves: Well, I guess we can swallow the idea that the propositions of metaphysics have to be synthetic *a priori* judgements. But I should like to point out to you that the proof of this is one of the chief arguments of the *Critique of Pure Reason*, one that lies at its very heart.

This is the argument that no matter of substance can be inferred from pure concepts alone, but that substantive statements about such things as God, freedom and immortality assume more than their mere concepts. They assume the confrontation of the concept with its material. After all, the traditional ontological proof of the existence of God unquestionably forms part of what Kant means by metaphysics, and this asserts that the idea of an absolutely perfect being is not complete unless we include among its attributes the attribute of *existence*. Kant has shown, in one of the most penetrating analyses in the entire *Critique of Pure Reason*,[9] that the idea of such an absolutely perfect being implies nothing about its existence, and that even the absolutely adequate and perfect idea of 300 thalers – that is the example that Kant gives – says absolutely nothing about whether I am just imagining these 300 thalers or whether, as he would presumably have said, I have locked them up in my desk.[10]

This is a passage of such outstanding importance for the *Critique of Pure Reason* that I would ask you to make very special note of it. What he is saying is that the propositions of metaphysics have a content, that they are synthetic propositions and of course synthetic *a priori* propositions, since they are supposed to possess absolute validity. This is a premise or a conclusion of the *Critique of Pure Reason* – it is very hard to decide which; it seems to form a sort of logical circle at this point. What he means is that the pure concept alone cannot entail the validity of these propositions because every proposition that asserts existence, for example, 'There is a God' or 'The soul is immortal' contains something that is not present in the pure concept of the soul or of God – so that we must really be dealing with synthetic propositions. The idealist philosophers that came after Kant revised this. Their reason was that they made an absolute of reason, an absolute metaphysical entity, whereas for Kant reason acted as a critical authority; it had a cognitive, scrutinizing function. This cannot be discussed further here. But I believe that the entire Kantian critique of metaphysics can only be understood if you realize that all the metaphysical propositions that are criticized in Kant within the framework of the *Critique of Pure Reason* must be held to be synthetic *a priori* judgements.

Over and above that, however, there is a much more profound, internal connection between the synthetic *a priori* judgements and the propositions of metaphysics. The connection is this: I have already told you – and this is really the way in which to characterize the *Critique of Pure Reason* in general – that the answer to all the questions that arise in the *Critique of Pure Reason* is to be found by interrogating the knowing subject. It is this process that I have attempted to explain and to present to you as what Kant meant by the Copernican revolution that he had accomplished. So if a pure natural science and if synthetic *a priori* judgements about nature are to be at all possible, the guarantee of their validity must lie not in something, of whatever kind, that comes to consciousness from outside; it must lie not in some kind of material, but simply in the subjective conditions of my knowing, without which knowledge as such would not be possible. However, these subjective conditions that make the natural

sciences possible are identical with those that ma
sible. There is thus no real difference between
hand and μετὰ τὰ φυσικά, whatever comes 'af
other. In other words, what we discover in Kant
in line with the eighteenth century and the Enl
extraordinarily strict and, if you like, undiffere
the unity of reason throughout the various sph   ___ ....owicuge.
It follows from this, however, that the question of metaphysics can
really only be the question of these conditions of reason, these indispensable conditions implicit in reason – that is, of thought and the
necessary forms of intuition – and their relation to different kinds of
material.

Or, to put it more radically, metaphysics asks questions about
whether there is material of any kind available to me; whether these
conditions of reason can be applied to any sensory experience of
whatever kind; whether they can be said to run amok and freewheel;
whether they spontaneously perpetuate themselves and imagine that
they can make all the crucial decisions on their own. Thus the unity
that exists between the question of a priori synthetic judgements and
the question of metaphysics in Kant is the unity of reason itself, or
more precisely, of the propositions about experience that I am justified in making. The distinction between the two is only to be found
in the question of whether these conditions of reason can be filled
with something else, with something that is not them, with something non-identical – or whether they retain their absolute identity
and may be said to produce the Absolute from within themselves.

With this I have brought you to a problem, to a pair of concepts
that are fundamental to the understanding of the *Critique of Pure
Reason*, and that we have now arrived at without too much effort,
or so I hope. These are the twin concepts of the *form* of knowledge
and the *content* of knowledge. In line with what I have already said,
and with the primacy of reason in his philosophy, the content of
knowledge in Kant is always what comes to me from outside: it is
the contingent, or, as he sometimes says, the chaotic, the sensory
manifold over which I have no control, but to which my knowledge
refers. Moreover, it does not refer to it in the sense that we know the
sensory. The fact is that we do not know the sensory; it is something that we *possess*, it is *given* to us. But it is opaque, blind and
impenetrable.

However, what is known as knowledge in an emphatic sense in
Kant is something we might really describe as a question of organization. It is a question of whether and how far we succeed in unifying,
in organizing the sensory elements that are given to us with the aid of

he forms both of our intuition and also the forms of our thought. By 'organize' we mean both to differentiate and distinguish between them and also to bring them together with the aid of unified points of view. Now since this content is something accidental and contingent, something changeable, which therefore does not belong in philosophy as Kant understands it, it follows that the whole of philosophy cannot really be anything other than the *analysis of form*. This element of form is really decisive for the whole of Kantian philosophy. You should note, incidentally, that this is the point at which Kant's philosophy has always been the target of the ugliest criticism. When Kant is accused of formalism – as he was by Max Scheler[11] – what this represents is the price Kant had to pay for his preoccupation with the transcendental, that is, with the possibility of synthetic *a priori* judgements: in other words, with the fact that he had to confine himself to formal constituents because he had no control over the constantly changing contents.

At this point, however, we encounter a very subtle problem that I have to tell you about and that will perhaps enable you to understand the specific nature of the *Critique of Pure Reason* more precisely. It is this: it is true enough that according to Kant reason has no control over its material; rational critique does not have it in its power to bring order into the chaos of the sense data that we receive from time to time. Notwithstanding this, it claims to have the power – and this implies a claim that you may well think to be a purely wilful assertion on the part of the *Critique of Pure Reason* – to decide whether modes of knowledge can be applied to sense data or not. Please do not misunderstand me here; it is true that no single sensory element can become the object of rational critique; not a single sensory element can enter the theory, the critique of knowledge as such. But whether *in general* such a thing as absolutely valid knowledge is possible depends according to Kant on whether our knowledge relates in general to sense data or not. I would just like to indicate that this 'whether' obviously contains an implied 'the fact that'. That is to say, Kant has already conceded entry to sensory material against his will, even though he had earlier excluded it, rather artificially, in favour of *a priori* knowledge. So what we have here is a place where two alien ideas join together, a suture that constantly threatens to come apart and that should not be relied on too heavily. But (if I can say this much by way of conclusion) the point you must grasp is this: on the one hand, the *Critique of Pure Reason* is a formal doctrine of consciousness inasmuch as consciousness possesses valid knowledge. On the other hand, however, it is also a doctrine about the relation of these forms, not to a specific content, but to the fact that such a thing as content actually exists; it is about their relation to some possible contents or other. In this respect the question of metaphysics is identical with that of synthetic *a priori* judgements. This is because Kant believes that the distinction between valid judgements and mere metaphysical speculations consists in whether this connection with the realm of the senses, with sensory fulfilment, is present or not.[12]

LECTURE FIVE

4 June 1959

Metaphysics (II)

Last time we mainly talked about the fact that the *Critique of Pure Reason* is divided into parts that point in different directions, not so much in its external structure as in its meaning, and we considered what it is that unites them. In the course of this discussion I fixed upon the synthetic *a priori* judgement as the canonic concept, the concept that comes foremost in the themes of the *Critique of Pure Reason*. I should now like to add a final comment on this and to say that the propositions that Kant regards as metaphysical are what the mathematicians call invariants. In other words, they do not refer to changing contents, but instead make the claim that they are absolutely valid for all time. This characteristic is one that the propositions of metaphysics – at least, in the traditional sense with which Kant is concerned – share with synthetic *a priori* judgements. Thus the idea that there could be metaphysical or speculative propositions of the sort that assert that Being contains movement within itself or that contradiction is a constituent of Being, propositions that then occur in Hegel's *Logic* as immutable truths or rather as changing variants – such an idea is quite foreign to Kant. This implies a final and in my view decisive congruence between the question of metaphysics and that of the possibility of synthetic *a priori* judgements.

Historically – and this is something that has more far-reaching implications than I can pursue at this moment – we may add that the propositions that Kant attempted to establish as synthetic *a priori* judgements represent secularizations, that is to say, experiential versions, transformations into experience or propositions constitutive of experience, of the very things that metaphysics claimed in all naivety, or perhaps innocence, independently of any such reflection. I do not need to tell you, but I should at least remind you, since it is not unimportant for our own purposes, that the *Critique of Pure Reason* does not contain a direct critique of metaphysics. If we were to take it as providing such a critique we would go badly astray. The so-called Copernican revolution means, among other things, that what is criticized is not metaphysical propositions as such, but rather the possibility that our reason can rationally articulate them, or utter valid judgements about them without violating the rules of discursive logic.

This limiting comment on the scope of the Kantian critique of metaphysics has far-reaching implications because it reveals the flaw in the Copernican revolution. For whereas the turn to the subject appears initially as the sign of strength, of a radical disposition, it overlooks the fact that the *Critique of Pure Reason* has nothing further to say about such matters as God, freedom and immortality. To put it simply, the intellectually innocent person who takes the *Critique of Pure Reason* in his hand because he knows that it deals with the so-called problem of metaphysics, and who imagines that it will tell him whether such things as God, immortality or freedom actually exist, is doomed to disappointment. Direct propositions of this kind are prohibited here because the *Critique of Pure Reason* is concerned not with objects as such, not even the objects of metaphysics, but simply, as Kant puts it, with our faculty to obtain knowledge of such objects. This means, however, that positive or negative judgements cannot be made about the existence of such objects; instead what the so-called negative conclusion of the *Critique of Pure Reason* amounts to is an embargo on further enquiry. Reason does not suffice, Kant asserts, to enable us to say anything absolutely authoritative about these matters of supreme importance; they remain up in the air.

The remarkable neutrality to be found in the conclusion of the *Critique of Pure Reason*, thanks to this turn to the subject, inevitably has its consequences – and it is vital that you should understand this, if you wish to understand the larger context in which the work must be viewed. The chief consequence is that this neutrality points to a critique of metaphysics as a science, on the one hand, while at another level, in a different dimension, it leaves open the possibility of reinstating or salvaging metaphysics. The point I wish to make is that the turn to the subject is a radical shift in the sense that instead of enquiring into the validity of our knowledge, we now look to the root of the matter and reflect on our ability to know. But on the other hand, because of this process of reflection decisions about the essential questions of metaphysics are suspended, at least as far as questions

of cognition are concerned. If you wish – and if you will permit me
to put this point in a broader historical context – you can see here
something of the bourgeois neutralization of metaphysical and theological ideas. On the one hand, they are stripped of their authority,
while on the other hand, they are allowed a shadowy existence on
the grounds that we do not really know much about them. Within
the bourgeois household they are all postponed until Sunday and
they are permitted a kind of Sunday-existence. You may feel that this
is very unfair to Kant, but if you compare him with the main current
of the Enlightenment you will see a very real difference on this point
– even though I would also claim that the Enlightenment critique of
metaphysics is by no means as unambiguous as is generally assumed.
There is always a sceptical element that leaves scope for traditional
metaphysics to creep back in. This is particularly true of Voltaire,
who, as is well known, started out from theism and whose faith in
that was shaken somewhat, but who nonetheless never offered any
explicit criticism of certain traditional metaphysical ideas.

I believe that following these remarks we are now more or less in
a position to understand what Kant means by metaphysics. In this
connection I should like to read to you a passage from the Preface to
the Second Edition of the *Critique of Pure Reason*. It goes as follows:

> *Metaphysics* is a completely isolated speculative science of reason, which
> soars far above the teachings of experience, and in which reason is
> indeed meant to be its own pupil. Metaphysics rests on concepts alone
> – not, like mathematics, on their application to intuition. But . . . it
> has not yet had the good fortune to enter upon the secure path of a
> science.[1]

It is this state of affairs that moved Kant to make his critique.

Let me just say a few words about the concept of the *speculative*
as we find it in Kant, and how it differs crucially from its meaning in
Kant's successors – although the change in meaning is one that throws
light on the subject itself and is no simply arbitrary verbal alteration.
In Kant speculative knowledge, we can say, is synonymous with metaphysics. Looked at subjectively, metaphysics is all knowledge that owes
its existence to pure speculation. I would ask you to think of the
word 'speculative' in a completely straightforward sense, in the sense
which will presumably occur to you if you have not been affected by
Hegelian philosophy: namely, as a form of knowledge that is acquired
purely by the application of reason, without its deriving any sustenance
or limits or anything non-identical from experience, or any element, in
short, that would create resistance or friction with it. Thus speculative

thought is the same as pure thought; speculative knowledge is knowledge that is spun out of thought itself without measuring itself in any way against material emanating from experience.

I have already indicated that Kant's successors no longer regard the concept of experience as one of mere material, as something that comes to the subject from outside. For very weighty reasons these philosophers believed that the contents of experience itself were to be inferred from the mind. It follows fairly compellingly that this must give a new twist to the concept of the speculative. According to this way of thinking, it means that reason is *everything* and that it therefore contains the element of the material in itself. It follows from this that when reason reflects on itself it thereby becomes capable of recognizing the truth and even the Absolute. Thus the concept of the speculative, which is negative in Kant, a critical concept, becomes positive in his successors. This follows directly from the criticism which the post-Kantian thinkers levelled at Kantian philosophy. I draw your attention to this so that you can see Kant in the context of what follows him and not just what precedes him. However, I must add that you should not run away with the idea that Kant's critical achievement was simply forgotten by the post-Kantian philosophers, starting with Salomon Maimon.

Kant's successors, Hegel in particular, did not take issue with the negative part of the *Critique of Pure Reason* in which Kant demonstrates that transcendent propositions – that is, propositions that go beyond the possibility of experience – lead to contradictions. They merely placed a different value on this Kantian insight from that which Kant himself had done. What they said was that these contradictions, or rather the conflict that constantly arises between finite knowledge and infinite knowledge, between experience and the Absolute, that such contradictions are actually the organ, the medium, in which what we think of as knowledge is constituted. Consistently with this, the concept of the speculative that we find in Hegel is that speculative thought does not tackle contradictions from outside; it does not find itself in a state of conflict with them which ends up in its own defeat. It is a kind of thinking that absorbs the contradictions into itself and discovers its own natural movement in the contradictions that are contained in the situation itself.[2]

This is all very different from Kant; basically, for him the concept of metaphysics is problematical from the outset, thanks to its definition as something speculative. Moreover, that definition rigidly severs all links between the concept and any possible experience, any possible content. The separation of form and content of which I spoke to you last time leads – with a dualism that recalls that of Descartes – to

[margin handwritten note: speculative – if reflection of reason upon itself]

a rigorous distinction between the sphere of consciousness, on the one hand, the sphere of thought as a sphere of forms; and, on the other hand, to a sphere of contents confronting it. Furthermore, the contents do not determine the forms, nor do the forms have any influence over the contents. There is a precise sense – and I do not say this to belittle it, but simply to describe it – in which the relation between form and content in Kant is external. That is to say, you really must imagine the forms as a sort of container through which the materials coming from outside are filtered. Once these materials have passed through the forms, what emerges at the other end are the valid modes of knowledge, the synthetic *a priori* judgements. The relation between the two elements, however, the way in which these two elements each presuppose and produce the other, is not even examined in the *Critique of Pure Reason*.

In this respect Kant quite simply regards the matter much like the English psychologists: on the one hand you have reason, the faculty of intuition, man as a kind of *tabula rasa*, who finds himself bombarded with sense impressions, without really knowing where they come from. On the other hand, we do not really know what these sense impressions are. This is because they acquire all their properties through this filtering process, and unless it takes place they are quite indeterminate. But he really does conceive of this in the naive terms that we use in ordinary life: thus we are mental creatures, endowed with powers of intuition and thought, and then various stimuli come along (to use the language of the physiology of the senses, albeit one somewhat alien to Kant), and the collision of these two elements or the friction between them is what constitutes knowledge. This basic idea of the relation between subject and object – before any analysis of the way it is constituted – is something that you must take for granted in Kant if you wish to understand him at all. And, as I have told you, the crucial idea in metaphysics is that metaphysics is actually nothing but form which misapprehends itself as content. Or, to put it in other terms, the propositions of metaphysics arise when some determinants which are really no more than determinants of thought, but without any content, are extrapolated and extended to an infinite degree, beyond any possibility of fulfilment, just as if they constituted valid forms of knowledge of something or other.

I believe that after all this you will now be in a better position to understand the starting-point of the *Critique of Pure Reason*, since the concept of metaphysics in Kant contains an incipient dialectical element. When I told you that the concept of the speculative was a negative concept in Kant, we should add – as I am sure you will almost have guessed by now – that the concept of dialectics is no less

negative in his eyes.[3] That is to say, freedom from contradiction is
assumed by him to be the sole criterion, whereas only a type of
thought that takes the reciprocal relation between form and content
as its starting-point has been able to reach the point at which contradiction can be regarded in a much more positive light.

With this in mind I should now like to say something about the
first few sentences of the Preface to the First Edition – in the hope
that this will bring about for the first time what I have been promis-
ing you from this course of lectures: namely, that all these things will
start to speak to you, that they will become eloquent.

> Human reason has this peculiar fate that in one species of its know-
> ledge it is burdened by questions which, as prescribed by the very
> nature of reason itself, it is not able to ignore, but which, as transcend-
> ing all its powers, it is also not able to answer.
> The perplexity into which it thus falls is not due to any fault of its
> own. It begins with principles which it has no option save to employ in
> the course of experience, and which this experience at the same time
> justifies it in using. Rising with their aid (since it is determined to this
> also by its own nature) to ever higher, ever more remote, conditions,
> it soon becomes aware that in this way – the questions never ceasing –
> its work must always remain incomplete; and it therefore finds itself
> compelled to resort to principles which overstep all possible empirical
> employment, and which yet seem so unobjectionable that even ordin-
> ary human consciousness readily accepts them. But by this procedure
> human reason precipitates itself into darkness and contradictions; and
> while it may indeed conjecture that these must be in some way due
> to concealed errors, it is not in a position to be able to detect them.
> For since the principles of which it is making use transcend the limits
> of experience, they are no longer subject to any empirical test. The
> battle-field of these endless controversies is called *metaphysics*.[4]

I should like to draw your attention to the stroke of genius in that
last definition of metaphysics as a 'battle-field'. This sentence shows
you how much greater a great philosophy is than it knows. Take this
definition, according to which the realm that he calls metaphysics is
not static, is not simply a collection of ready-made propositions, but
a force field in which motifs of different kinds come together in
conflict. It amounts to the positive definition of dialectics that Kant
has effectively rejected in these introductory sentences to the *Critique
of Pure Reason*. We might say that his metaphor, his metaphor of the
battle-field, has driven his thinking well beyond what it actually
claimed to do.

I believe that we have a contradiction here, one that arises because
although reason is driven by its own impetus to arrive at ultimate

principles, it is not able to gain control of its own further development. He goes on to say that this conflict, this battle, is so destructive and irrepressible because it lacks a final authority that might provide arbitration. This absence of a final court of appeal arises because the only authority that might be applied to – namely, experience – has been ruled out by definition, since what is at stake is a knowledge that oversteps the bounds of experience. Now, I cannot explore whether the contradiction we find here is a 'judgement' on metaphysics or its first proposition, its first basic principle. This question is one that has been taken up by post-Kantian philosophy and has no place here. However, I should like at least to give you a pointer to a problem that is lurking here. At the same time, I would like to encourage you through this example to approach the Kant text in what appears to me to be the only appropriate way, namely, to read it with X-ray eyes. This means reading it in such a way as to make its hidden content and its hidden puzzles as transparent as the Cabbalists of old tried to make the Torah. Incidentally, any other approach to the great philosophical texts seems to me to be impossible; and what I regard as the 'cognitive theory' of such a procedure is something I hope to be able to explain to you very clearly.

When Kant says that we are driven by our nature to go further and further in order to arrive at some sort of primary and absolute knowledge, it is legitimate for us to cast doubt on this supposed natural disposition. Or, to put it less anthropologically, since that is not how Kant meant it to be understood, he believes that the compulsion lies in the matter itself. I should like at least to invite you to consider whether it is not an illusion that if our knowledge is to be secure everything that is known has to be traced back to some ultimate truth or to some primary certitude. That raises the question whether what Kant regards here as something absolutely self-evident and given is in truth the primordial pseudo-reality, the authentic, original delusion that characterizes metaphysical thinking in general; whether we are not faced here with what I have elsewhere called the 'mania for foundations' [*Fundierungswahn*].[5] This is the idea that no piece of knowledge can be understood simply within the framework in which it just happens to be located. I can only be satisfied with it once I have pursued it back to infinity, to the point where nothing further can happen, and nothing can deprive me of this piece of knowledge. You should be quite clear in your minds that this principle – which is indeed a principle accepted in the entire tradition of Western philosophy – actually implies that there is a match between the knowing mind and the objects of possible knowledge that allows us to reduce every object of cognition to such an absolute. Only if I start from this metaphysical premise of an ultimate, conclusive identity between the object of cognition and the cognitive faculty can I legitimately require everything I know to be able to demonstrate its credentials in terms of its own founding principles.

In this respect philosophers have all been of one mind, and it makes no difference whether we are talking about Plato with his Ideas or Kant with his synthetic *a priori* judgements, or rather with his notion of original apperception, or whether we are thinking of Heidegger, who has made an absolute of the concept of origin and turned it into a metaphysical entity. I only want to make sure that you understand that an extremely intractable problem emerges at this point which we may regard as the natural starting-point of Kant's critique of reason. The difficulty is that we can never be certain whether this reductive urge to discover an ultimate cause that cannot itself be reduced to anything further, whether this urge is not itself a delusion in which the mind's absolute desire for mastery is lodged – by which is meant, in the last analysis, the simple power we wish to exert over nature. This suggests that a seemingly self-evident assumption such as the one I have been speaking about contains a very far-reaching problem. I wish here only to put this idea in your heads and apart from that to refer you to the Introduction to my book *Against Epistemology*.[6] I have tried there to provide an analysis of the principles involved in this problem which I see as the starting point of all epistemology, and I believe that what I say there about modern philosophy holds good for the Kantian approach of which we are speaking.

I should also like to draw your attention to the fact that in the passage of Kant we have been considering the separation of metaphysics and experience is taken to be self-evident and even the insolubility of the problem of metaphysics is taken to be justified by the avoidance of every appeal to experience or indeed to any superior authority. By way of objection to this we should remind ourselves that the contents of every concretely available or even conceivable metaphysics are always a matter of experience. If I were to rely on existing metaphysics in the way in which Kant thinks he can rely on the natural sciences in the *Critique of Pure Reason*, we would quickly discover that this rigid dichotomy of experience and reason does not exist in the form he imagines. At all events, from the passage I have just read out to you we discover what is really at stake in the *Critique of Pure Reason*: his intention is to resolve this very dispute *after all*, even though he says that it cannot be resolved. There is evidently a certain contradiction here. If, on the one hand, someone *objects to* metaphysics that here reason wishes to be its own pupil, it follows

that in a discourse in which reason sets itself up as the *critic* of
reason, reason will quite assuredly be its own pupil to no less a
degree. At all events, the description of the *Critique of Pure Reason*
as a problem is the consequence of this.

The indifference which according to Kant will be the fate of metaphysics in more modern, enlightened times, is, he says, 'the effect not
of levity, but of the matured *judgement* of the age' – here we have the
enthusiasm of the youthful bourgeoisie which has not yet started its
never-ending complaints that reason cannot solve anything, but which
still feels confident of its ability to achieve things by virtue of the
power of its own reason –

> which refuses to be any longer put off with illusory knowledge. It is a
> call to reason to undertake anew the most difficult of all its tasks,
> namely, that of self-knowledge, and to institute a tribunal which will
> secure for reason its lawful claims, and dismiss all groundless preten-
> sions, not by despotic decrees, but in accordance with its own eternal
> and unalterable laws. This tribunal is no other than the *critique of
> pure reason.*[7]

If you think your way through the implications of the metaphors of
this passage, it will not escape you that the tribunal he is speaking of
is a curious affair: it is a tribunal in which the judge, the prosecutor
and the accused are actually one and the same person. However, I
believe it would be a little facile to ridicule Kant for this because
what we might call this paradoxical idea is actually the heart of the
Kantian conception and points to a feature that is a motivating impulse rather than a mere presupposition or even a logical error that
can be lightly dismissed.

What lies behind it – and in this respect we cannot really separate
Kant's theoretical philosophy, that is, the critique of reason, from his
practical philosophy, the *Critique of Practical Reason* – is Kant's
remarkable conception which actually supplies the unifying factor
that must not be made the subject of mockery, but which must rather
be properly understood. It is the idea that the freedom and sovereignty of spirit amounts to what he calls *autonomy*. This element is
represented here by the judge who can freely resolve all these matters; it is the ability to give oneself laws, to restrict oneself and to
determine one's own limits. Autonomy literally means that you give
yourself laws – and autonomy is the supreme concept in Kant's moral
philosophy, and by implication also of Kant's theory of knowledge.
The concept of autonomy actually contains that paradox, that contradiction, which I have drawn your attention to: namely, that the

judge and the accused are one and the same; that the authority that is free and independent simultaneously represents the law. This is the founding conception of his entire universe. It contains the idea – I believe you can only picture this if you attempt to translate it into a kind of experience – it contains the experience of bourgeois society in its conviction that only by virtue of this autonomy can society become free, mature and able to escape the bonds of tutelage – only with the aid of this conviction can it organize everything and arrange matters for itself so that it will be able to manage its own life in a proper and meaningful way. In short, acting in accordance with laws appears as a function of freedom – or, conversely, freedom manifests itself as a function of law. This idea, that freedom and obedience to the law are one and the same thing, means that there is indeed an end to tutelage, but that freedom ends up merely as something that is determined by law. This is the kernel of Kant's philosophy. It does in fact articulate a very dark secret of bourgeois society. This secret is the reality that the formal freedom of juridical subjects is actually the foundation of the dependency of all upon all, that is to say, it is the foundation of the coercive character of society, its conformity with law. This is what lies behind this very strange theory that in Kant reason is a tribunal which has to sit in judgement over reason as the accused.

This is followed by the definition of a critique of pure reason:

> I do not mean by this a critique of books and systems, but of the faculty of reason in general, in respect of all knowledge after which it may strive *independently of all experience*. It will therefore decide as to the possibility or impossibility of metaphysics in general, and determine its sources, its extent, and its limits – all in accordance with principles.[8]

This, then, is what Kant is concerned with in the *Critique of Pure Reason*; and I hope that what we have said up to now will have been enough to make you fully aware of his position. I should merely like to remind you quite explicitly that it is difficult for someone unfamiliar with philosophy to know how to approach the *Critique of Pure Reason*, since what we generally understand by criticism (and Kant also alludes to this) is criticism of specific books, arguments and matters of that sort, and we do not really know how to react when confronted by a criticism which actually has no object. Now, we may say that in Kant the criticism of literary texts, a criticism that is in fact implicit in his work, is radicalized to such a degree that it becomes a criticism of the faculty of cognition itself. But this very criticism leads to the paradox that I have already referred to, namely, that the critic and the object of criticism are actually the same thing.

I should like to add the further point that the dialectical path of the history of philosophy expresses itself in the fact that the entire history of philosophy is in reality a history of criticisms, and by that I mean criticisms in a very tangible sense. We might just as easily argue that Aristotle's *Metaphysics* is a major criticism of Plato's theory of Ideas, much as we can say that the *Critique of Pure Reason* represents a criticism of Wolffian philosophy, on the one hand, – that is to say, the systematization of Leibniz's thought – and of Hume's philosophy, on the other. In other words, then, the movement of philosophy, even when it looks as if it is putting so-called radical questions and starting once again from the very beginning, is always criticism of texts already in existence with which it is in a constant state of friction. The more philosophers insist on their own radicality, the truer this is. If you compare the chaotic, centrifugal character of philosophy with the much more cohesive shape of the positive sciences, we may perhaps say that the most philosophy may lay claim to by way of a unifying factor is precisely the unity represented by this element of criticism, or as I would prefer to express it with greater feeling, the unity of the problem. The unity of the problem does not lie in its solutions, for example, in the idea that the solutions of philosophy would yield a coherent set of interconnections, but in the fact that in their historical shape the different philosophies are mediated through one another; that they are linked by the problems raised in them in a way that above all in retrospect appears coherent and even consensual.

Let me finish by outlining for you a programme for the coming lectures. I can do so by saying that the programme that Kant proposes is in fact one of *Enlightenment*. If you think of the critique of metaphysics as in one sense a critique of the faculty of cognition, this points to the enlightened habit of anthropomorphism taken to a radical extreme. That is to say – and this reflects the negative side of the *Critique of Pure Reason* – metaphysics can be thought of as a gigantic projection, a hypostatization of mind, and where mind imagines that it apprehends objective beings, what it encounters in reality is *nothing more than* mind; that is, nothing more than the human being himself. It is in this sense that the critical design of the *Critique of Pure Reason* falls into the general rubric of the problem of Enlightenment and the themes of Enlightenment. But next time I shall try to explain to you the view of the Enlightenment espoused by Kantian philosophy.

LECTURE SIX

9 June 1959

Enlightenment

Last time I told you something about Kant's approach in the *Critique of Pure Reason,* focusing particularly on the problem of metaphysics, and I had reached the point of reading you the relevant passages in the text dealing with this problem and offering a brief interpretation of them. In the course of these passages in which Kant tells us about his intentions and about the meaning of the critique of reason there is a form of words that is extremely revealing about the problem I should like to discuss with you today. This concerns the relation of the *Critique of Pure Reason* to the Enlightenment. He says there that in his book the answer to these metaphysical questions 'has not been such as a dogmatic and visionary insistence upon knowledge might lead us to expect – that can be catered for only through magical devices, in which I am no adept.'[1] This is an allusion to his celebrated pamphlet against Swedenborg, the *Dreams of a Spirit-Seer,* a pamphlet directed against the occult and one that attacks all dabbling in the occult with an incisiveness that has never been surpassed.[2]

> Such ways of answering them are, indeed, not within the intention of the natural constitution of our reason; and inasmuch as they have their source in misunderstanding, it is the duty of philosophy to counteract their deceptive influence, no matter what prized and cherished dreams may have to be disowned.[3]

There are two reasons why this is an openly and explicitly enlightened statement: firstly, because it assumes that reason is part of our

natural constitution, because, if I may put it like this, the metaphysical inspiration is shifted onto the concept of reason itself. It is
assumed that reason contains a particular kind of intention, namely,
the secret design to achieve freedom or the fulfilment of the destiny of
mankind. This was part of the common stock of ideas throughout
the eighteenth century, and was especially important in the philosophy of Rousseau, who had an enormous influence on Kant, as is
well known from a whole host of detailed studies, as well as his
own admission. Secondly, this form of words is characteristic of the
Enlightenment because the task of reason, whose existence as part
of our natural constitution is viewed essentially as positive, is to do
away with all dogma, delusion and knowledge that has been merely
handed down. This had been the general attitude of the emerging
bourgeoisie towards the entrenched religious authorities it had re-
belled against in the late seventeenth and eighteenth centuries, using
the weapons of the Enlightenment. So Kant joins forces with the
Enlightenment here, but I think it would be simplistic just to acquiesce in his own view of himself as a man of the Enlightenment.

The relationship is actually highly complex. I believe that if you wish
to understand the broader implications of an apparently technical
work of epistemology such as Kant's *Critique of Pure Reason*, you
have to be aware of the complex nature of his relation to the Enlightenment. This complexity has not escaped the attention of the traditional historians of philosophy. But they have generally used what I
would call a Sunday phrase to describe it, to demolish which is one
of the tasks I have set myself here. This cliché is the phrase that Kant
was indeed the completer of the Enlightenment, but at the same time
the Enlightenment was overcome in his philosophy. We shall shortly
have more to say about what this 'overcoming' amounts to. First,
however, we would do well to remind ourselves that the tradition of
German thought and the German philosophy of which Kant was
a part never achieved a full, authentic Enlightenment. It was once
remarked – accurately, I believe – that there never was an Enlightenment in Germany, but only an enlightened theology. When you look
at the most illustrious names of the representative figures of German
intellectual history who are in any way connected with the concept of
the Enlightenment, you will find this saying confirmed. This holds
good whether you think of Leibniz, in whom this feature emerged
very clearly for the first time in Germany, as I believe; or whether you
think of Lessing, in whose writings this element of an enlightened
theology is immediately obvious; or indeed of Kant himself. But it is
not my intention to expound the historical situation to you, because
I regard it as my task to give you not a *historical* introduction to the

Critique of Pure Reason, but an introduction to the *substance* of the book, that is, to the philosophical problems it raises. In line with this I shall now attempt to explain how the problem of the Enlightenment appears in Kant.

I have already told you that Kant is enlightened in the sense that he is a critic of dogmatism. It must be pointed out, however, that the concept of dogmatism undergoes a curious enlargement at his hands. Whereas the older Enlightenment and the Western Enlightenment mainly used the term to refer to theology proper, Kant uses the term, as I have already suggested, to apply also to metaphysics. This, too, is a feature that Kant shares with the mature Enlightenment. Those of you who have studied French will be aware that one of Voltaire's chief works, certainly the book that is best known in Germany, is his *Candide*. *Candide* is an attempt to expose the dogmatic character not so much of theology as of German metaphysics, namely, Leibniz's theodicy. To a degree, then, this critique of the dogmatic side of reason is to be found among the themes of the *Critique of Pure Reason*. I shall attempt later on to look a little more closely at the peculiar difficulty contained in the notion of the dogmatic nature of reason.[4] However, nothing should be accepted without questioning it, neither theology nor metaphysics and the allegedly eternal truths of reason, nor even, as Kant would doubtless have said, the empirical objections that have been advanced against a rationalist metaphysics. It is this refusal to accept statements unquestioningly that marks the rather more incisive version of Enlightenment thought in Kant in which reason broadens its critical, anti-dogmatic activities to embrace everything that is not completely transparent and self-evident. I should like to say that the programme of Enlightenment shares this feature with the entire movement of modern Western thought. If, for example, you read the demands made by Descartes in the *Discours de la Méthode*, you will discover that one of his most essential requirements is that we should not accept any assertions that are not clear and distinct.[5] But we can probably say that Kant's critique of reason was the first to take this old programmatic demand really seriously and to import it into the so-called question of the constitution of reason – the 'basic' question, if you like.

Kant has gone into greater detail about the concept of Enlightenment in an essay entitled '*Answer to the Question: What is Enlightenment?*' This essay is not very widely known, but it is very instructive. If you just take an uninformed look at Kant's own statements, you make some very striking and surprising discoveries. I should like to acquaint you with some of these statements, both for their own sake, and because of their value from the standpoint of method. The fact is

that if you occupy yourselves with philosophy and with Kantian philosophy in particular, you have opportunities to learn the value of the
micrological gaze in exemplary fashion and you can then attempt to
apply it elsewhere. What this means is that you should learn to look
closely and critically at statements which we often tend to read cur-
sorily without paying much attention. You should study them until
they begin to speak. When I told you that I regard it as my task to
present philosophy in general, and Kant's philosophy in particular,
as a kind of force field,[6] what I had in mind was precisely this micrological method. On the surface – although I do not really want to say
'on the surface' – but in terms of its own explicit doctrines every
philosophy with well-developed ambitions aspires to present a more
or less coherent deductive (or indeed inductive) system. You have
to ponder its details if you wish to gain access to the interplay of
conflicting forces within this coherence, this logical harmony, this
balanced system, if you wish to gain access to that internal life of
philosophy with its mutually conflicting forces that consists to a not
inconsiderable degree in its latent contradictions. The ability to dissolve the congealed, fixed, systematic edifice of a philosophy and to
make it speak involves a particular talent for dwelling insistently on
individual arguments as they make their appearance. You should
look at the *Kant-Lexikon* of Rudolf Eisler – a book that is still extremely valuable even today – if you wish to gain a picture of all sorts
of problems that arise in Kant with the aid of references to sources
that are frequently widely separated. In the *Lexikon* you will find a
collection of Kant's most important statements on the Enlightenment. You will find, for example, this passage from the *Critique of
Pure Reason*, which is to be found in chapter 1 of the Transcendental
Doctrine of Method:

> Freedom in the critique of reason can only be beneficial to the interests
> of reason, both theoretical and practical. Therefore, reason must be
> left to resolve its own disputes for itself, and not be subjected to coer-
> cion. 'For it is indeed absurd to look to reason for enlightenment, and
> yet to prescribe beforehand which side she must necessarily favour.'[7]

In this critique of what might be called the pre-established answer
in philosophy Kant describes very incisively and elegantly a danger
that philosophy frequently succumbs to when it attempts to function
as an apologia, and I am not even completely certain whether Kant
himself always contrives to escape it. This is the danger of the *thema
probandum*, that is to say, the danger that the argument may in
reality have been determined in advance, in the sense that you know

in advance how it will end, what will emerge and indeed what ought to emerge. In general, this takes the form of justifying something already known and existing. Whether it is ever entirely possible to think without this element, whether we can think in the absence of any intention or any desire to prove something or other, is a question I should like to leave open for the time being. But there is evidently a genuine problem here. Moreover, it is undoubtedly the case that the interminable boredom aroused by much philosophy – and perhaps something of the resistance that many of you may feel if you have come to philosophy from outside, under some compulsion, rather than from an inner need – may stem from the fact that you often know in advance how an argument will end, and that the whole thing is reminiscent of that conversation with Coolidge, a former president of the United States. Coolidge had been to church and his wife asked him what was in the sermon. He replied in his usual laconic manner that the clergyman had talked about sin. 'And what did he say?', his wife asked. To which he answered: 'He said he was against it.' The danger of statements like this one is ever present in philosophy. I would say that one of the tasks that should be attended to with more than the usual lip service is that we should try to avoid this kind of thing and work consciously to eliminate it. It should actually be an obligation for philosophers to follow the logic of the matter in hand rather than to allow the course of the argument to be dictated in advance by some goal or other. It may even be the case that certain modern philosophical trends, phenomenology, for example, have come into being in response to this demand to follow the logic of the matter in hand and to abstain from any *thema probandum*. As I have said, however, the difficulties of doing so are considerable and we may question whether it is in fact possible. I would only suggest that genuine thinkers must reflect on this problem – that is, it is vital for a thinker to become conscious of the relation between the intention implicit in a problem, what the problem itself implies, and the organization of a line of thought in terms of a specious argument in the interests of an already fixed *thema probandum*.

Reason is tamed by reason itself; and it stands in need of the disagreements that criticism provokes since it is thanks to these that quarrels fade away naturally. Enlightenment is 'a great benefit which the human race must reap even from its rulers' self-seeking schemes of expansion, if only they realize what is to their own advantage. But this enlightenment, and with it a certain sympathetic interest which the enlightened man inevitably feels for anything good which he comprehends fully, must gradually spread upward towards the thrones and even influence their principles of government.'[8]

This, then, is a very powerful statement of his faith in enlightenment. It is to be found in Kant's philosophy of history, more specifically, in the *Idea for a History with a Universal Intention.*
Lastly, he asserts that

Enlightenment is *man's emergence from his self-incurred immaturity.* *Immaturity* is the inability to use one's own understanding without the guidance of another. This immaturity is *self-incurred* if its cause is not lack of understanding, but lack of resolution and courage to use it without the guidance of another. The motto of enlightenment is therefore: *Sapere aude!* Have the courage to use your *own* understanding!'[9]

Elsewhere he states: '*To think for oneself* means to look within oneself (i.e. within one's own reason) for the supreme touchstone of truth; and the maxim of thinking for oneself at all times is *enlightenment.*'[10] You can see, then, that on the positive side the concept of enlightenment, as Kant developed it, corresponds precisely to what I have shown you as being the kernel of the Kantian method in the *Critique of Pure Reason.* That is to say, it consists essentially in the demand for the unfettered use of reason and the installation of reason as the supreme authority. The disputes in which reason becomes involved, including those disputes with itself, are to be seen as reason's own life-blood. On the negative side, however, a couple of points will no doubt have occurred to you. The first is that in Kant enlightenment always refers to thought that does not allow itself to be dictated to; you have to have the courage to think for yourself as far as possible according to the principle of autonomy, that is, the laws of thought. But enlightenment does not really mean to be critical of the structures of objective spirit, that is, to be critical of whatever is not thought. We may say, then, that the concept of enlightenment in Kant is subjectively restricted from the outset: it is restricted to the way the individual behaves within the world of his own thoughts. The question of the objectification of spirit and therewith the institutions and arrangements of the world is not really included in this definition of enlightenment. Closely related to this is a second factor. This is that there is no real connection between enlightenment and the concept of practice, of action – even though this does indeed play a major role in Kant. Enlightenment as a pure mode of behaviour of reason is exclusively theoretical in nature.

This brings us to a statement that in my view leads into the heart of the problem of enlightenment in Kant in a way that amounts almost to parody or caricature. It leads us into the peculiar ambivalence that marks the concept of enlightenment in his thought. 'For, enlightenment nothing is required but the freedom "to make *public use* of one's reason in all matters", both as writer and scholar, not however as servant of the state, who as such may not reason.'[11] Here, then, you find the definition of enlightenment restricted in all innocence by that disastrous word 'as' that plays such a dubious role in our age too. You find it when people say in the course of a discussion, '*As a German*, I cannot accept that...' or '*As a Christian*, I must react in such-and-such a way in this matter...'. This predicative use of 'as' signals a restricting of reason in line with the division of labour in which human beings find themselves involved; the restriction imposed on enlightenment here is in fact a matter of the division of labour. The purely theoretical human being – and that means quite concretely, the independent writer; in other words, the writer who is not paid for specific services and for propagating opinions that serve specific causes to a greater or lesser degree – the purely theoretical human being is free to be enlightened in a radical sense. The moment he has a particular function, the post of civil servant, for example, all reasoning is at an end. At that moment the unfettered use of reason becomes precisely what is concealed in the double meaning of 'reasoning', namely, a kind of unseemly grumbling, and hence to a kind of practical criticism of given institutions. Such a person shakes his finger at you and says, 'Wait on, that is not really what is meant by enlightenment at all; as long as you remain pure and free within the realm of a self-sufficient reason, all will be well. But as soon as you leave it and start to act the enlightened man directly and in walks of life that are laid down, that is a very different matter...' I think that this is to let the cat out of the bag, and to expose the peculiar ambiguity to be found in Kant's relation to enlightenment. It may well be a sort of Freudian slip that underlies the curious ambivalence of the *Critique of Pure Reason* and which then tells us something about the passages where reason is exalted to the skies. I cannot resist reminding you that Hegel is evidently following in Kant's linguistic footsteps when we find critics rebuking him for his apologetic, affirmative stance. What I am referring to is the way in which Hegel's immeasurable efforts of speculation are alleged to end up by legitimizing existing institutions. Critics have noted that when he sets limits to the use of reason as a weapon with which to criticize existing circumstances, he, like Kant, always has recourse to the [derogatory] term 'reasoning' [*Räsonieren*]. However, this tendency both to exalt reason to the skies and, at the same time, to reduce it to a mere reasoning, is rooted in Kant, the allegedly radical exponent of enlightenment. Moreover, this is part of the tradition of bourgeois rationalism as a whole. On the one hand, reason is deemed to be the supreme and indeed the only authority by which to regulate human relations; on the other hand, this is always accompanied by warnings to the effect that reason must not be 'taken to extremes'.

What this expresses, of course, is a genuine social situation. On the one hand, the world with all the resources at its disposal is caught up in a constant process of rationalization: in the production process, in its shaping of individual human relations, in bourgeois society generally. It is permeated with science to a constantly increasing degree. At the same time, the irrationality of the whole, that is to say, the blindness of the forces at work, and with that the inability of the individual to determine his own life in accordance with reason, remains intact. This peculiar oscillation between rationality and irrationality characteristic of bourgeois society at its very core is reflected in the ambivalent attitude of philosophy, especially the greatest philosophy, towards reason. I feel it is important to point out that this does not apply just to Hegel, in whose writings it is shouted from the rooftops, but it is no less true of Kant. This holds good even though in Kant the emotional appeal of reason as the eighteenth century understood it is even more fully intact than in Hegel, in whose writings existing reality is given a very different status, thanks to his insistence on the objective nature of the concept of reason.

You can probably see from all this that the claims that enlightenment has been overcome, completed and then simultaneously superseded, are not entirely unproblematic. This Sunday phrase, as I have called it, assumes from the outset this very desire to stop enlightenment in its tracks, to call a halt to the advance of reason, and I have drawn your attention to the reasons for this. I should now like to go into greater detail about these reasons as they appear in the philosophy of Kant. The essence of it is that they all belong in the realm of apologia. In general, I believe that few concepts have been such a catastrophe for the history of German thought as the cliché that labels enlightenment 'superficial' or 'facile'. It was perhaps the greatest curse of this development that the effect of the Romantic, and ultimately theological, belittling of enlightenment was to ensure that much of the enlightened thought that flourished in Germany actually assumed the shape imagined by the obscurantists.

However, in order to bring the discussion back to the specific problems of the *Critique of Pure Reason*, I should like to say that the *Critique* belongs in the overall context of the European Enlightenment in a much broader and more important sense than I have suggested hitherto – though I must point out that I am taking the liberty of using the term 'enlightenment' in the comprehensive meaning given to it in our *Dialectic of Enlightenment*.[12] We use it there to describe the general trend of Western demythologization that may be said to have begun in Greek philosophy with the fragments of Xenophanes that have come down to us. The broad thrust of this process of demythologization is, as has frequently been shown, to demonstrate the presence of anthropomorphism. This refers to a practice in which objectivity, existence and absolute dignity have been ascribed to a whole series of assertions, doctrines, concepts and ideas of whatever kind, which in reality can be reduced to the products of human beings. In other words, they can be seen to be what the language of psychology would call mere projections, and since it is merely man that has produced these concepts from within himself they are not entitled to any absolute dignity. Now it is the supreme goal of the *Critique of Pure Reason* to conceive of its criticism of traditional metaphysical ideas as a piece of enlightenment, in the strict sense – and you may regard it, if you wish, as the final proof of this subtle process of sublimation – that these supreme metaphysical concepts are actually no more than a game played by reason with itself.

In its second, negative section the *Critique of Pure Reason* undertakes to show that the contradictions reason necessarily becomes entangled in have their origins in the fact that, as I have already remarked,[13] reason freewheels, or we might also say, runs amok. That is to say, it simply produces propositions about the world from synthetic *a priori* judgements, spinning them out of pure forms, without measuring them against anything that is not reason, anything that is not a human being, but something else, something objective, in other words, something external to them. In attempting to demonstrate this, the *Critique of Pure Reason* can be said to be secretly pursuing the Enlightenment programme of the critique of anthropomorphism. We could say, then, putting it rather freely and at a distance from Kant's own words, that the metaphysical ideas whose absolute validity he is challenging are nothing more than hypostatizations of human beings as rational creatures; they are nothing other than attempts to translate the forms inherent in reason into absolutes without reference to anything that is not identical with or inherent in them. In this sense we may say that Kant's supreme critical intention is in tune with that of the Enlightenment.

What I have just said contains, I believe, an intention that tells us something quite crucial about the general design of the *Critique of Pure Reason*, and I should like to invite you to concentrate on it for

the few remaining minutes of this lecture, since I hope it will enable
me to lead you deeply into the mechanics of this work. You will
remember that I have explained to you that the *Critique of Pure
Reason* is essentially an analysis of form. Moreover, I have shown
that its tendency is subjective, that is, instead of making naive judgements about this or that thing or entity, it aims to employ the tools
of reason to judge the adequacy of reason itself. On the other hand,
you must bear in mind what I have just said about this element of
enlightenment, namely, that critical thinking wishes to eliminate the
illusion that reason can produce the Absolute from within itself, or,
in other words, the illusion that man as a cognitive creature is himself
the Absolute. This leads to the general problem that seems to me to
be crucial for the *Critique of Pure Reason*.

We may describe this general problem as follows. On the one
hand, we think of the *Critique of Pure Reason* as a kind of identity-
thinking. This means that it wishes to reduce the synthetic *a priori*
judgements and ultimately all organized experience, all objectively
valid experience, to an analysis of the consciousness of the subject.
It wishes to do this because – to use the language of the later idealists
– there is nothing in the world that is not mediated. This means that
we have no knowledge apart from what we know through the medium
of our reason, apart from what we know as knowing beings. On the
other hand, however, this way of thinking desires to rid itself of
mythology, of the illusion that man can make certain ideas absolute
and hold them to be the whole truth simply because he happens to
have them within himself. In this sense Kantian philosophy is one
that enshrines the validity of the *non-identical* in the most emphatic
way possible. It is a mode of thought that is not satisfied by reducing
everything that exists to itself. Instead, it regards the idea that all
knowledge is contained in mankind as a superstition and, in the spirit
of the Enlightenment, it wishes to criticize it as it would criticize any
superstition. It wishes to say that to make an absolute of everything
human is not significantly different from endorsing the customs of
shamans who regard their own rites as objectively valid, even though
in reality they are no more than subjective abracadabra.

Now the greatness of the *Critique of Pure Reason* is that these two
motifs clash. To give a stark description we might say that the book
contains an identity philosophy – that is, a philosophy that attempts
to ground being in the subject – and also a non-identity philosophy –
one that attempts to restrict that claim to identity by insisting on the
obstacles, the *block*, encountered by the subject in its search for knowledge. And you can see the double nature of Kant's philosophy in the
dual organization of the *Critique of Pure Reason*.

But we can go even further than this. The *Critique* has always been criticized (and we shall discuss thi particular kind of contradiction. The best-known of the one hand, Kant insists that his starting-point is immediately present to me, what is 'given', and he w all transcendent premises. At the same time, however, he speaks of the 'affections', that is, of the fact that what is immediately given to me, my sense data, originates in an external world that affects me. This inconsistency is so straightforward that it would be crystal-clear to a child. You will probably realize – and this is much more interesting – that this particular contradiction exists for a very good reason. So we may say that what Kant has been doing is a formal analysis, but he has also realized that if all knowledge were nothing but form, and if all knowledge were totally submerged in the subject – then it would be nothing but a gigantic tautology. For in that event the knowing subject would really know nothing but it, and this act of merely knowing it would be nothing more than a regression to the identical mythological thinking that Kant, as a champion of the Enlightenment, had striven to overcome.

In order to avoid this regression Kant prefers to accept the contradiction contained in asserting, on the one hand, that we know absolutely nothing about things-in-themselves; things are something that we constitute, that we bring into existence with the aid of the categories. On the other, it is claimed that our affections arise from things-in-themselves, for only in that way can his theory of knowledge introduce the notion of the non-identical – that is, the element that is more than just mind or reason. For it is only in this way that this element of non-identity makes its appearance in his thought.

We may say, then, that this contradiction, this apparent lapse of thought in the *Critique of Pure Reason*, objectively contains the entire question of the *dialectic*, and that the relation of identity and non-identity is mapped onto the two sides of the Enlightenment. One side is the elimination of an epistemological dogmatism that assumes something which cannot withstand the scrutiny of reason. The other side imposes limits on what is made by human beings, that is, this human product must not be allowed to mistake itself for objective reality, but must become conscious of itself as something internal to human beings and hence limited. This second element, this criticism that enlightenment directs at identity, that is, at the assertion that everything which exists is absorbed into reason, contains the possibility of an intellectual somersault that turns against the Enlightenment and against reason. Thus when I said that Kant's philosophy is ambivalent in its attitude towards the Enlightenment, I would ask you not to think of this in any superficial way. It is not just a matter of attitude, but of the difficulty of substance I have tried to explain. The moment reason restricts itself from the motives I have mentioned, and the moment it makes this restriction the subject of its own concern – and with good reason – it necessarily acquires the potential to turn against itself and to start considering reason in a negative light. The way this happens is linked in the most remarkable way with the anti-intellectualism that the *Critique of Pure Reason* shares with the *Protestant* tradition. I shall say something about this next time.

LECTURE SEVEN

11 June 1959

Knowledge as Tautology

Last time I told you something about the curious and, as it seems to me, deeply rooted, dual attitude of the *Critique of Pure Reason* towards its own object, that is, to reason. I argued that, on the one hand, the *Critique of Pure Reason* contains the elements of an identity philosophy since it attempts to derive authoritative, universally valid knowledge from the analysis of reason. On the other hand, however, it strives with equal vigour to bring the element of nonidentity to the fore. This means that Kant is conscious of a problem that was not perceived so clearly by his successors precisely because of their greater consistency. This is the problem of knowledge as a tautology, that is to say, the problem that if everything that is known is basically nothing but a knowing reason, what we have is no real knowledge but only a kind of reflection of reason. That we are confronted here with Kant's own clear philosophical decision – and not, as is frequently imputed to him, the mere vestiges of a position not properly thought through – is evident. It was demonstrated as a matter of historical fact by his impassioned resistance to the interpretations placed on his critique of reason by his first great successor, Fichte, who regarded himself, not without cause, as a consistent Kantian. This is why he argued that Kant's critique of reason still appeared to contain dogmatic elements, particularly in its insistence on the thing-in-itself which is said to exist outside the sphere of consciousness, but to impinge on us nevertheless.[1] The fact that this leads to inconsistencies in the *Critique of Pure Reason* and that in consequence the book really does find itself forced into contradictions

it is unable to resolve is a story so often told in the history of the
literature on Kant that I have no need to dwell on it here. I should
like only to say about these contradictions or inconsistencies that if
they have been defined as *necessary* contradictions, this testifies to
the influence of the most consistent method to have succeeded Kant,
namely Hegel's. For what Hegel did was to analyse the contradictions necessarily contained in the method of the critique of reason in
an attempt to arrive at a solution to the problem of knowledge in
general and ultimately to the problem of philosophy as such. I may
also add that in the process Hegel explicitly embraced that element of
tautology that I have described as the essence of identity philosophy.
This means that in his philosophy the culmination of thought in
'absolute spirit' is actually identical with the Absolute with which it
began – except that everything is placed inside the process which
leads to this tautology. Here, too, the elements that made their appearance in Kant against the will of philosophy and took the form of
its aporetic limits have been made conscious of themselves and transformed into the instruments of knowledge. But I do not wish to spend
more time on these matters now, even though I think it perfectly
legitimate to use my rather broadly conceived introduction to the
Critique of Pure Reason to give you some idea of the way in which
philosophy developed after Kant. For there is a sense in which this
further development is already implicit in Kant himself and it is important to see this instead of treating each philosophy in a separate
compartment.

   More important than this perspective on future developments, however, is the peculiar duality with which the *Critique of Pure Reason*
regards its own object, namely reason itself, and the genuine ambivalence towards enlightenment of which I have already spoken. I told
you last time about the positive elements of enlightenment – 'positive' in the sense of a simple identification of the critique of reason
with enlightenment – and I argued then that the true element of
enlightenment in Kant is the assertion that nothing may be held to
be true that cannot withstand the scrutiny of thought, above all, subjective thought. This view of reason is not the only one to be found
in the *Critique of Pure Reason*, however. You will discover a different view in one of the most famous passages of the *Critique of Pure
Reason*, a passage I should like to read out to you now so as to give
you a precise idea of what is at stake. Kant is talking about the
positive introduction of the supreme categories of metaphysics – God,
freedom and immortality – categories which are regarded only negat-
ively in the book on the grounds that they are theoretically unknowable. He says of these ideas in the Preface to the Second Edition:

[From what has already been said], it is evident that even the *assump-tion* – as made on behalf of the necessary practical employment of my reason – of *God, freedom*, and *immortality* is not permissible unless at the same time speculative reason be deprived of its pretensions to transcendent insight. For in order to arrive at such insight –

in other words, to arrive at the thesis that the existence of God, freedom and immortality can be proved on the basis of pure thought alone –

it must make use of principles which, in fact, extend only to objects of possible experience, and which, if also applied to what cannot be an object of experience, always really change this into an appearance, thus rendering all *practical extension* of pure reason impossible.[2]

In this 'always really change this into an appearance', if we reflect on what lies behind it, reason is reproached for something like blasphemy if it believes it can prove the existence of the highest goods – to use the expression current in the older language of philosophy – purely from within itself. It is a kind of hubris on the part of 'the mere light of nature'[3] to attempt to transcend what is given to it, namely, the world of the finite and the phenomenal, and to appropriate the Abso-lute even while leaving the latter's absolute status intact. This is made quite explicit in the following, famous statement:

I have therefore found it necessary to deny *knowledge* in order to make room for *faith*. The dogmatism of metaphysics, that is, the pre-conception that it is possible to make headway in metaphysics without a previous criticism of pure reason, is the source of all that unbelief, always very dogmatic, which wars against morality.[4]

You perceive here a very different side of Kant. This is the side that wishes to impose restrictions on reason on the grounds that because reason is natural it can be concerned only with the natural, and must therefore detract from the dignity of everything supernatural.[5]

This places Kant in a tradition that is of extreme importance for his practical philosophy. I am speaking here of the tradition of German Protestantism, in which, as you know, the concept of reason is narrowly circumscribed in favour of faith. The emphasis placed on faith, which puts it in sharp contrast to Catholicism, was gained by downgrading knowledge and natural reason – quite in opposition to the views of High Scholasticism and to Thomas Aquinas. You will all have heard mention of Martin Luther's reference to 'that whore, reason',[6] and its echo can still be heard here. Incidentally, this Lutheran description of reason as a whore reminds us how frequently the language of philosophy has recourse to erotic metaphors when it wishes to set limits to reason or to rebuke reason for its arrogance. In the *Critique of Pure Reason*, when Kant desires to impose limits on reason and restrict it to the world of appearances, while declining to extend it to the Absolute, he uses the expression about 'straying into intelligible worlds'.[7] It is as if the speculative inclination of mind to go in the direction of the Absolute, to refuse to allow oneself to be cut off from the Absolute by a wall, went hand in hand with a kind of sexual curiosity from the very outset. Later psychologists homed in on this particular point by showing that there is a profound link between the impulse to know and a curiosity that is ultimately sexual in nature. That is to say, if this curiosity is knocked on the head by the hand of authority as soon as it stirs, the faculty of knowledge will be damaged. We are talking here of the phenomenon of neurotic stupidity and it is on the side of this stupidity that Kant places himself here, doubtless without intending to do so. Moreover, the same kind of metaphoric language is to be found in Hegel when he is discussing Kant's view of this problem. He says there that if philosophy does as Hegel wishes and *thinks* the Absolute, it will be moving into a region where, as he puts it, there are 'houses of ill-repute'.[8] This phenomenon recurs over and over again. I shall leave you to make up your own minds about it.

I have already said that the denigration of reason (I believe that I told you about this last time) accompanies self-sustaining reason like a shadow.[9] That is to say, reason is held to be legitimate; it is to be tolerated where it serves to control nature and to introduce a kind of order into the world. But as soon as it goes beyond that, as soon as it touches the true ground of existence, it finds itself accused of sacrilege and unwarranted curiosity. This affords a parallel to the way in which the gnostics were always being criticized for their excesses, their antinomianism, in short, their illegality, their violations of the law. We might say that the more Kant attributes to reason as a *criticizing* activity – the more he regards it as the authority that presides over the possibility of judgements in general – then the more he seems to subtract from the individual act of subjective reason, that is, reason as something *criticized*. You will discover in him the tendency to give emotional emphasis to a completely abstract concept of reason, entirely divorced from actual, individual, rational human beings. In consequence the individual human being who makes unfettered use of his reason without making the concessions that Kant insisted on in servants of the state and that I told you about last time,[10] finds himself accused of 'pseudo-rationality' and the like.[11]

Thus Kant can be seen to add his voice to the ancient complaint about a consistently critical reason, decrying it as mere sophistry. His reasoning contains an anti-utopian element: the insistence that this shall not be. You can observe the peculiar ambivalence of Kant's attitude towards the utopian very clearly in the highest concept to which his metaphysics aspires, namely the concept of the infinite. On the one hand, Kant is enough of a champion of the Enlightenment to demand again and again that the requirements of reason be satisfied. Although reason for him is an essentially formal principle, he does necessarily (I would say) provide quite concrete and comprehensible definitions of what it is supposed to achieve – humanity, for example, in the *Critique of Practical Reason*, or again, the absolute reconciliation of mankind, absolute peace between nations and individuals in such writings on the philosophy of history as the tract *On Eternal Peace*. At the same time, the idea has the character of a task that is postponed to infinity – quite apart from the fact that it demands that human beings should strive constantly and tirelessly, much as Max Weber does in the case of the Protestant ethic. In short, human beings must slave away in the service of this idea to the point of infinity, without ever being allowed to rest. This motif is then intensified to the utmost degree in Fichte. On the other hand, this concept of infinity also contains a negative meaning. It is that the fulfilment of the utopia which is demanded of us should never take place, that it is no more than a dream, and we might almost say that it *ought to* remain a dream. The great difficulty of Kant's practical writings in particular is that these two elements are in permanent conflict with each other. I mean by this the utopian, enlightened element that strives for the making real of reason despite everything, and the critical – and hence no less enlightened – element, but one that is intertwined with the strand of thought taken from Protestant theology. This [critical] strand of thought would like to thwart all that and in the spirit of Protestantism it calls for submission to existing circumstances, regimes or governments, of whatever kind.

To come to a conclusion about what we were discussing last time, we might say that in this sense Kantian philosophy does not really transcend the Enlightenment and bring about a consummation of philosophy, as we are constantly told. The case is rather that in Kant an ambiguity of Enlightenment thought itself reaches a culmination and finds itself in an antinomic situation. On the one hand, enlightened and enlightening thought really does aspire to a utopia, to the making real of reason; while, on the other hand, it turns its critical gaze on the concept of reason and thus restricts its own validity, recoiling from the complete establishment of utopia, the Absolute.

To wish to perceive a particular merit in this peculiar ambiguity, in this curious backwardness of philosophy, in the light of the challenges confronting it, is the mark of a specific and highly dogmatic concept of *depth*. (I thought I would take the opportunity to say something to you about the fundamental underlying principles of this notion of depth in connection with Kant's philosophy, which is renowned as the 'deep' philosophy *par excellence*. But we have not yet reached the point where this would be appropriate.[12])

It is commonly claimed – and the claim has something of the Enlightenment about it – that even reason, like everything else, can become a dogma. You will constantly hear objections of this kind made if you occupy yourselves with theological studies of the *Critique of Pure Reason*. You will hear people say that indeed, there is faith in reason just as there is religious faith – and by reducing this faith in reason to a 'mere faith', the door is opened wide to the true faith. I hold this argument to be false, and I believe that there is a kind of equivocation in the concept of faith here, a sort of ambiguity that you would be well advised to think about. When we speak of faith in the strict sense what we mean is that something is said to be true because – or although – it lies beyond the scope of our reason; because it conflicts with reason; or because in a weaker version, more commonly encountered, reason has not yet been able to make it its own because no decision has yet been reached about its truth or untruth. Thus the concept of faith lies in its opposition to knowledge. If we then take the concept of faith as defined in this way and use it to refer to the acceptance of everything that exists, this blurs the distinction according to which faith can refer only to things that are accepted as being true *without* being grounded in reason. In contrast to this the acceptance of propositions validated by reason has a very different character, a transparency, that is necessarily absent from the concept of faith. It follows (to return to our previous theme) that when Kant says that he is placing restrictions on knowledge in order to leave scope for faith, this is not really reconcilable with the intention of the *Critique of Pure Reason* as a whole. This is because of his principle that only those propositions are permissible that are evident to our reason; it derives from his idea of absolute maturity as this was represented in the essay on Enlightenment from which I read you some crucial statements last time.[13] And these restrictions on knowledge are of course quite incompatible with a view that suddenly introduces a different, no less legitimate cognitive source – even if it is only in the realm of *practical* cognition – which is the very antithesis of knowledge [grounded in reason]. Philosophy in the emphatic sense can no more tolerate the placing of restrictions on reason through reason than it can condone a concept of faith that aspires to be independent of thought and superior to it. This is because the moment it did so it would introduce an element that would be beyond the reach of philosophy itself.

In this respect the theologians who have simply abandoned philosophy or who, like Søren Kierkegaard, became its enemies, are infinitely more consistent, and, if I may say so, more profound than the representatives of the tradition of semi-theological philosophy – among whom Schopenhauer included Kant[14] – with their belief that space could be found for the category of faith in a philosophy conceived of as the speculative employment of reason. The vehicle of this ambiguity I have been telling you about is the limitation placed on the critical findings of the critique of reason, the fact that these findings are not themselves unambiguous and so do not come down clearly on one side or other of a question like the existence of God. This in turn is connected with the fact that these findings are methodological in nature and hence refer simply to the *ability* to *gain knowledge* of such matters, and not to knowledge of these things *themselves*. The block placed on the method, in Kant's view, the assumption of an irreducible residue, of something non-identical, the *negative* side of Enlightenment, which has the profundity and the greatness that comes from asserting absolute limits to the arrogance of a reason that asserts itself absolutely – this block also has the curious weakness that when confronted by superstition it ceases to function as an authority. It is no accident that the adherents of a consistent positivism – and positivism is basically the rationalism of an absolute self-limitation – that positivists are never immune to superstition. When they find themselves faced by occult phenomena of one sort or another, they exhibit a casualness that would be unthinkable in a speculative philosopher of the calibre of Hegel, who would never let such things pass without comment. On the other hand, it should be said – and since these matters are extremely complex I have to present them to you in their full complexity as it would never do to convey to you a crude or primitive idea of such difficulties – on the other hand, then, because of the Kantian block and even more because of this theological idea that reason *cannot* be asserted absolutely, we see that there is an ultimate barrier which prevents reason, spirit, the very thing that in the final analysis has separated itself off from manual labour, from being asserted in an absolute way. This barrier prevents something which is deeply embedded in nature from behaving as if it were a transcendent category, utterly superior to nature. We may well say that the spirit that forgets that it is rooted in nature, and that consequently truly asserts its own absolute status, is committing an act of hubris that condemns it all the more to fall victim to its own roots in nature. We may say, in other words, that it will be doomed to perpetuate blind natural conditions.

I should like at this point to say something of relevance to the structure of Kantian philosophy as a whole. You would be making a mistake if you were to imagine that this strange ambivalence towards Enlightenment and reason simply coincided with the twofold division of the Kantian system in general, an assumption that is easily made. In other words it would be all too easy to claim that the Kant who championed the Enlightenment is the Kant of the *Critique of Pure Reason*; this Kant was an agnostic who said that we are only able to have knowledge of, and to organize, the world of appearances, while we have no true knowledge of God, freedom and immortality; when it comes to such matters we do not rightly know where we are and cannot allow ourselves to make judgements. In contrast we might assert that the Kant of the practical philosophy who introduced such ideas as *regulative* ideas, this Kant really just smuggled them in. In that sense the Kant of practical reason was opposed to the Enlightenment. But matters are not so simple. I believe you would do well, now that we are meditating on the place of the *Critique of Pure Reason* within the whole Kantian system, to take cognizance of the fact that the fissure I have been telling you about is one that runs right through the entire Kantian system. It is not simply one of a divide in Kant between theoretical, scientific knowledge and practical, that is, moral knowledge. The situation, then, is one in which, on the one hand, theoretical reason is anti-dogmatic and denies itself the right to go beyond the limits of possible experience. In so doing, it embraces the Enlightenment.

On the other hand, however, it is this selfsame theoretical reason that actually installs this block which prevents reason from going beyond that point. It is theoretical reason in Kant that commands reason to stop and prevents it from carrying out its original task, namely, to think the Absolute. Instead, it ponders the question of whether thinking the Absolute can be possible as a science, and only resolves it in the context of science itself. That is to say, it refuses to recognize any truth apart from scientific truth. This is the sense in which the anti-Enlightenment side of Kant, that is, the side that paralyses reason and binds it in fetters, limiting it simply to organized science, is deeply embedded in the *Critique of Pure Reason*. On the other hand, it is perfectly true that the theological categories that are criticized in the *Critique of Pure Reason* and are excoriated throughout the Enlightenment, then make their reappearance in the *Critique* of *Practical Reason*. However, precisely because they do reappear there, we can say that this *Critique* really does make space for elements that can be called authentically utopian – that is to say, the creation of humanity and of human solidarity – all the elements mentioned in the concluding sections of the *Critique of Practical Reason* and for which there was no room in the *Critique of Pure Reason*. You see, then, how the structure I have shown you is really a fundamental feature of Kantian philosophy as a whole, and, I should like to add, of bourgeois thought. It is a structure, or so I would claim, that is only obliquely reflected in the division of Kant's critique of reason into two great sections.

If you place Kant's philosophy at the very beginning of the liberal era, you could perhaps add the speculative idea – which is in fact rather more than mere speculation – that bourgeois thought in its cradle – that is to say, at the turn of the eighteenth to nineteenth centuries – was both bourgeois and also something that pointed beyond it. The outlook of any given class at the point at which it becomes the subject of history represents of course the history of that class, but it also points beyond it. That is to say, the moment a class bursts through the barriers of antiquated social relations of production, it feels itself – and with justice – to be the executive arm of *mankind* as a whole. This double role is evident in the *Critique of Pure Reason* with particular force. On the one hand, you feel at every turn a certain homely bourgeois rationality, as well as countless bourgeois virtues, such as prudence, righteousness, judicious appraisal, and a specific type of humanity that is highly characteristic of Kant, in contrast to his successors. But you also gain the strong impression that the moment this class begins to determine its own ideals, and to define them in a self-critical manner, it transcends the horizons of its own particular interests, and in a sense starts to act as spokesperson on behalf of humanity as a whole. This is a peculiarity of Kant, one he shares with the greatest thinkers of his age in the realm of social theory – an example is the great French social theorist Saint-Simon. It is my belief that this remarkable ambiguity, this flirtation with the anti-utopian and repressive, with duty and the insistence on definite set tasks, in short, the commitment to all such ideas, on the one hand, and, the idea on the other hand, that the world as a whole must become rational – the tension between these two strands of Kant's philosophy has its roots ultimately in this point in the history of philosophy. The hour had struck when this philosophy ceased for an instant simply to represent its own particular interests and really became the voice of the World Spirit, to use Hegel's expression, an ability which it went on to lose soon enough.

These observations and the remarks I let fall last time have of course taken me well beyond the limits of what is usually understood by the interpretation of Kant. I have not simply given you a faithful and straightforward account of what there is in the text, and translated Kant's more difficult expressions into easier ones – something I cannot at all regard as my task. Nor have I attempted to explain to you what thoughts were in Kant's mind when he was writing, a task of supreme indifference for the understanding of philosophy. Instead, I have kept within a framework which I would like to think of as being the appropriate framework within which to discuss Kant *objectively*, that is, in terms of the philosophy of history. I would of course ask you to take the term 'philosophy of history' in a very definite sense. I am not concerned with Kant's precise position in the history of mind or actual history (such an approach would strike me as relatively primitive and indeed pre-philosophical). What I wish to explore is what Kant reveals to us of the movement of mind itself, of what we might term the internal history of truth, as this has been expressed on the sundial of truth itself. I refer explicitly to whatever Kant's philosophy contains that is *over and above* the immediate meaning of the text – in the spirit in which Hegel observes in one of the great passages of the *Logic* that certain propositions (Hegel means the principles of identity or contradiction) contain more than what is actually meant by them.[15] This is what I have set out to do – and not to show you what philosophers had in mind when they wrote their philosophies, something we are not able to reconstruct anyway, and certainly not to indulge in such trivial activities as to discuss Kant's place in the history of philosophy between Leibniz and the German idealists, something you can easily read up in any textbook. What I am concerned with is what a philosophy objectively expresses, over and above its own opinion: that is what is at stake. In other words, I am concerned with the constellation of truth – and this constellation is identical with the force field I have talked about so often – that has crystallized into such a philosophy, that is the decisive point. I am fully aware that I am making considerable demands on you, that is to say, I am doing something that deviates from everything you will have learnt about interpretation in either the disciplines of philology or jurisprudence, for example, in the interpretation of a particular law, where to my layman's eye the thoroughly mysterious 'intentions of the legislator' feature in such a striking way.

I believe, then, that it is incumbent upon me to give you an account of my own methodology here, for two main reasons. Firstly, so that you should know where you are, so that you are not just drifting and do not have the feeling of being swept along over an abyss. And secondly, because there are genuine difficulties here that cannot simply be passed over by anyone unwilling to offend against the virtue of intellectual integrity which Kant demands. I can define this problem of methodology for you quite sharply and succinctly. On the one hand, you will be aware how unprofitable it is to reflect on what someone thinks about his own thoughts; that what matters is what is objectively expressed in those thoughts, what their truth content is, what significance they have over and above their immediate meaning. My belief is that *this* is the crucial aspect of a philosophy, and *not* the task of eliciting the philosopher's opinions. For this mere eliciting of opinions basically presupposes their objective meaning; it would only be sensible to do this if we already know that what he means is something of objective importance. And all this is just repeated parrot-fashion in the histories of philosophy which have contrived to include so-called great philosophers like the Great Elector or Dante in their pantheon. But the very proof of importance is exactly what would have to emerge from an objective scrutiny. On the other hand, you may rightly say, 'That's all very well, but isn't what you are saying completely arbitrary? Are you not just reading things into a philosophy in an entirely speculative way? Or perhaps it is just a kind of sociology of knowledge, that is, a process of relating a particular body of thought to some social trend or other, even though such links are quite unproven and it is very debatable whether they have anything to do with the philosophy in question.

I should like to say in reply that there are definite limits to arbitrary interpretation, and these limits that are set by a text of whatever kind – and I know I am in agreement here with the philologists – these limits really are set by the *text*. This means that no analysis of this type can be released from the necessity of making a quite explicit appeal to statements on the page. If I may distinguish my approach from another, likewise speculative, method, namely that of the school of Martin Heidegger (and I think it my duty to do so), the distinguishing feature can be found at this point. For *I* think it wholly impermissible simply to twist what is *said* in a text like the *Critique of Pure Reason*, and to turn it upside down. But even more important is the question of how to justify the claim that *more* is said in such an interpretation than can be found on the page. I can speak only briefly about that here. Basically, the justification is nothing but the demonstration of an immanent tension within such a text; the method of interpretation is actually one of extrapolation. In other words, it consists in focusing on the way in which such contradictions as the one about identity or non-identity are anchored in the text, and the way in which they define its specific character. If you then refuse to accept these contradictions simply as intellectual flaws, and attempt instead to show how they are motivated within the structure of the text overall, you really do arrive at the point of understanding the ideas as containing more than appears on the surface: they are the precipitate of a force field. Once you have defined such a force field, and have identified the forces at work in it, forces that are in a state of constant friction with each other, you then acquire the right to call such forces by their names, and in so doing, you go beyond the immediate meaning on the page. My task here is not to present the Kantian system to you as a coherent totality, free from contradictions. In this respect I find myself in disagreement with the most recent approach to Kant, that of what might be called the neo-Marburg School of Ebbinghaus[16] and, above all, Klaus Reich. You can find an example of their work in Klaus Reich's extremely rigorous book on the completeness of the table of judgements.[17] I, on the contrary, am much more interested in the inconsistencies, the contradictions in Kant. I regard these inconsistencies and contradictions as providing far more compelling evidence of Kant's greatness than any harmonious system. This is because they express the life of truth, whereas smoothing over the contradictions and creating a superficial synthesis is an easy task.

LECTURE EIGHT

16 June 1959

The Concept of the Self

I should like to carry straight on with the methodological remarks we had begun with last time. You may have had the experience of finding yourself in a discussion in which, instead of focusing on the subject in question, people have tried to pin you down by arguing that you have contradicted yourself. They mean by this that you have failed to use a concept consistently, or that before using a particular concept – usually a highly emotive one – it is important to arrive at a clear definition of it. For example, when discussing guilt, you regularly hear people say that such a thing cannot be discussed without its being defined, otherwise you just land up in contradictions.[1] Similarly, it will not have escaped your attention that there is a certain kind of inferior philosophical criticism that makes a virtue of attacking writers like Nietzsche, or more recently, Spengler, on the grounds that they have been guilty of some so-called logical contradiction or other. This makes such critics feel good even though the reader does not have the sense that writers like Nietzsche are at all diminished in consequence. I do not wish to discuss the psychology of this approach. It is in reality a kind of compartmentalized thinking, that is to say, the thinking of the ordinary man, the petty bourgeois who likes everything to be neat and tidy, and who feels secure if his machinery does not break down and his ideas all function smoothly and without disruption. But such criticism makes us forget what philosophy is all about and what justification we can give for it – if, indeed, one is possible. Such a justification must go in the direction of saying that our aim is *not* to juggle concepts, arranging and rearranging them as neatly as possible like a stamp collection, but to deploy concepts in order to bring the subject, whatever it may be, to life. The unending problem arises because what that subject and that life are is not something we have in our pockets. Nevertheless, philosophy directs its efforts precisely towards the recuperation of what has been lost through this conceptual cleansing operation, this so-called contradiction-free, bland presentation of philosophical problems. This appears to me to provide the profoundest reason, the deepest justification of the claim that the philosophical interpretation of a text should focus less on the absence of contradictions, less on systematic consistency, than on its opposite, on the contradictions themselves. The aim should be not to nag away at these contradictions, but to discover the fissures, the chinks, that – if I may use an image from mountain-climbing – enable us to get a foothold and eventually to reach the peak from where we can obtain a freer view of whatever intellectual panorama we are examining.

Please, do not misunderstand me here. It is not the case that I despise conceptual clarity and order – by no means! It goes without saying that the so-called positive sciences cannot survive without precisely defined concepts and a discourse free of contradiction. But philosophy is really a matter of 'thinking on thinking',[2] as Aristotle defined it, and so the thought processes of logic and the positive sciences have to be subjected to a second critical scrutiny. This means that you cannot put too much reliance on a discourse free of contradictions. I should almost like to assert that the profundity of a philosophy – a concept I hope I shall be able to enlarge on in a more fundamental way in a later lecture – is not a matter of its capacity for resolving contradictions, but rather of its ability to bring to the surface contradictions that are deeply embedded in the subject under investigation, to raise such contradictions to the level of consciousness, and at the same time, to understand the necessity for them; that is, to understand their meaning. The discussion that I presented you with as a kind of model, a discussion of Kant's dualistic view of reason, will, I hope, give you some idea of my thoughts on this subject.

To justify this in a more principled way I would like you to consider a quite simple matter. The reason why I am placing so much emphasis on this is that all of you – I should really say, all of *us* – are 'conditioned' to accept that our discourse should be free of contradictions. Consequently, the demand that we should liberate ourselves from this principle comes very hard indeed, and so you are right to expect me to explain *why* I proceed as I do – and not in some other way. The deepest reason I can offer is that we have no guarantee that the problem we are investigating is itself free of contradiction. If we were to assume that it is free of contradiction, that would be a prejudgement with immense implications. These implications would not be rendered more anodyne by the fact that in general we are not conscious of them when we privilege such contradiction-free knowledge. By insisting on this assumption we are inserting a sort of clause in a will: we are *assuming* that the reality that is the object of our knowledge is identical with our knowledge, and that, in the final analysis, it is fully coextensive with it. This means that we would have begged the question, presupposing in advance a solution to the problem of knowledge, by assuming that reality is identical with *us*. For only when the *knowing subject* is identical with the *object known* can we conceive of knowledge as being free of contradiction; only then may we assume that all contradictions will be resolved in the unity of our reason, in the unity of logical thought, because what we perceive forms part of this unity in our thinking from the outset and obeys its laws. But this assumption is one that we simply *cannot* take for granted, or so it seems to me. On the contrary, our entire experience, our entire living, pre-scientific experience – even more than our scientific knowledge which in a certain sense has already been shaped in advance – compels us to doubt the validity of this premise.

It is this train of thought that leads me to focus on the interpretation of the contradictions in a philosopher's arguments, rather than to attempt to reconcile disparate ideas. It is not hard to smooth everything out so that everything in a philosophy fits together. That is, to use Hegel's phrase, 'a step that is soon learnt'. It is not so easy, firstly, to realize how, just beneath the surface of a coherent body of thought, the various strands that make it up come into conflict with one another; and although the philosopher has sought to reconcile them, they retain their distinct identity. Nor is it a simple matter, secondly, to grasp just what a specific configuration of ideas means.

This is a crucial methodological point and I would like to cite two sentences from Hegel's *Logic* – from the 'Logic of Essence' – to show you that the self-reflexivity of thought, that is, thought that enters into itself in order to discover its own essence, was already preoccupied with these questions. I do not say this in order to appeal to any external authority, or to strut around in borrowed plumes. I say it simply to enable you to see that what I am doing here is to apply an insight of advanced dialectics retroactively to philosophy itself. In Section I of Book II of the *Science of Logic*, Hegel says:

Only when the manifold terms have been driven to the point of contradiction do they become active and lively towards one another, receiving in contradiction the negativity which is the indwelling pulsation of self-movement and spontaneous activity.[4]

And a little further on, he adds:

In general, our consideration of the nature of contradiction has shown that it is not, so to speak, a blemish, an imperfection or a defect in something if a contradiction can be pointed out in it.[5]

It is in this sense that I would ask you to understand what I have to say to you about contradictions in Kant. I said earlier that Nietzsche is often subjected to quibbles about contradictions in his writings – the best-known is that Nietzsche rightly thought of his ideas as the extreme culmination of Enlightenment, but at the same time, as the philosopher who had in a sense repudiated rationality and who opposed it on the grounds that it was 'inimical to life'. A further contradiction is that he described himself as a *décadent*, and simultaneously declared war on decadence and nihilism. When I said earlier that this kind of criticism of Nietzsche was the mark of an inferior mind, I can now add that Nietzsche himself did not simply overlook these and other contradictions from carelessness or inattention. On the contrary, Nietzsche's philosophy is remarkably coherent in a higher sense; it is constructed in a pre-eminently consistent manner. There can be no doubt that he was as acutely aware of the so-called contradictions as the worthy professors of philosophy, such as Rickert,[6] who have given him bad marks because of them. They undoubtedly originate in one of his very well-founded theses that nothing that we know actually obeys the laws of logic, but that we employ logic to organize the world in a particular manner. In the light of this Nietzsche represents the conscious attempt to heal knowledge, to rescue it from this process of organization, from the illusion of its own logicality, but he uses the methods of logic to achieve this. Incidentally, there is a profound agreement between Hegel and Nietzsche on this point – even though Nietzsche knew very little about Hegel. Despite this, the affinity between them leads me to conclude that this healing of thought from the wounds that it inflicts on its own objects is in actual fact the true task of philosophical reflection.

All this by way of introduction. I should now like to move on to tell you at least something about what it is that Kant's philosophy *expresses*. That is to say, what it expresses over and above what it just *states* (to pick up the idea I mentioned last time). This involves telling you about ideas that exhibit this contradictory character for the most part, and indeed, about ideas whose expressive value and expressive force can only be read off from that contradictory core.[7] At the head of the list I should like to place something that is perhaps less shocking today than it undoubtedly was in Kant's own lifetime, and continued to be long after. After what I have already said in this course of lectures what I have to say now will not be exactly new to you, but I wish to elevate it into something of *thematic* importance. I am drawing your attention to this particular feature because I believe that by making it clear, it will provide you with the key to the *Critique of Pure Reason* as a whole. Within the German tradition of philosophy – which as you know retained its dogmatic character far longer than elsewhere in Western Europe – Kant's critique of reason has been perceived essentially as a *negative* achievement; later on it would have been described as a subversive, destructive achievement. You need only recall Kleist's famous utterance on the subject,[8] or the epithet of the 'all-destroyer' that was applied to Kant.[9] More recently, however, I believe that with the passage of time the precise opposite has come to be seen to be the truth about Kant.

The thrust of Kant's philosophy as a whole – and that includes the really critical work, namely the *Critique of Pure Reason* – is aimed at *salvaging*, and the salvaging of *ontology* in a quite specific sense. He wishes to salvage specific fundamental spiritual realities that can be said to be valid for all time and that are secure from the vicissitudes of history as well as from what Kant would have called a 'reasoning' reason. This definition of the thrust of Kant's critique of reason may appear astonishing to you at first sight, but I believe that it can be supported by certain passages in the *Critique of Pure Reason*, even though these may conflict with yet other passages. I have in mind here the statement from the Preface to the Second Edition that 'criticism is the necessary preparation for a thoroughly grounded metaphysics . . . as science.'[10] The only meaning we can give to such a statement, assuming that we take the words at face value and make no attempt to twist them, is that the 'preparation' for metaphysics as a science must have been intended by Kant in a positive sense – despite the contrary statement that metaphysics is not possible as a science, but only as the repository of the regulative ideas, and thereby as a purely practical discipline.

It is my belief that the form of words I used before about the 'salvaging' of ontology, even though it goes beyond this, can nevertheless be made to agree with the Kantian formula without doing violence to it; to do this we need only look at Kant's use of the term 'ontology'. I believe, further, that the specific nature of Kant's project lies in this contradictory element, that is to say, that, on the one hand, the *Critique of Pure Reason* is concerned with rescue, with salvaging ontology, while, on the other hand, some doubt is cast on this positive aspect. In other words, Kantian metaphysics is to be found in the constellation between these two poles, which cannot easily be reconciled.[11]

Listen now to the definition of ontology in the *Progress of Metaphysics*:

> Ontology is the science (as part of metaphysics) which constitutes a system of all the concepts and principles of the understanding, but only in so far as they apply to objects that are given to the senses and can therefore be confirmed by experience. It is not concerned with the supra-sensual which is after all the ultimate aim of metaphysics, and hence forms part of the latter only as a propaedeutic, as the vestibule or forecourt of metaphysics proper,

– and metaphysics is evidently viewed here in a positive light –

> and is known as Transcendental Philosophy because it contains the conditions and primary elements of all our *a priori knowledge*.[12]

You can see here very clearly that, as the precondition of the possibility of knowledge in general, the Kantian concept of the *a priori* is not just to be understood in functional terms, that is, not just with reference to the constitution of knowledge, the grounding of experience. Over and above that Kant ascribes a kind of ontological meaning, that is, a kind of ideal existence, to these root concepts, to the categories and forms of intuition, and it is this ideal existence that he is attempting to salvage. Moreover, he is attempting to salvage it in the sense that it is to be independent of all experience, that is, it should not be thought of as dependent on the vagaries of experience. At the same time, ontology is not something that exists purely in itself, but its existence in itself exists only for others, that is, it does not exist in a realm beyond experience, but only as constituted by an other, and as fulfilled through experience. This is the crux, the *Pointe*, as Nietzsche would have called it or the *Witz*, as Kant would have said. Here you have a very precise picture of the curious – we might even say, paradoxical – constellation of ontology in Kant. This salvaging of ontology really is a rescue at the moment of greatest need; at this stage of the Enlightenment we are looking at a rescue in the nick of time: the thing that has to be saved has almost drowned, and Kant only just manages to hold its head above water. What I mean by this image is that, on the one hand, concepts that are beyond experience, removed from the realm of relativization and retaining their absolute validity, may indeed *exist*; but, on the other hand, this intrinsic existence is *not* a hypostatization, that is to say, the ontological status of these pure ideas is defined by Kant as tied to existing reality.

If I may express this by employing the all-too common notion of 'ontological difference' here – that is, the difference between pure existence and existent beings – then Kant would have said (even though this way of speaking would have been quite foreign to him) that there is such a thing as existence, but that this existence is only there to the extent that it refers to existing things. The moment it is severed from them, he would say, the moment it loses its relation to things in time and space, to individuated realities, to actually existent beings – it sinks to the level of a mere preconception. This means, then, that the ontological difference has the meaning that τὰ ὄντα are indeed constituted through the ὄν, through pure existence, but that conversely, pure existence only acquires truth in so far as it relates to τὰ ὄντα. If dialectical philosophy was subsequently able to develop from Kant, you can see here very clearly how these two elements could interact with one another. In other words, the supreme concepts to which philosophy can aspire, the concept of form and the concept of actual existence [*Dasein*], are each mediated through the other at the core of their innermost being. The only problem is that Kant did not make this the object of reflection. However, this mediation is implied. For, on the one hand, there can be no existing things, no factual reality, that is not constituted by the forms available to us; factual reality is mediated by these forms. Released from these forms, factual reality would be entirely vague and undefined – in Hegel's parlance, it would be a nothing. Conversely, however, the forms are in their turn mediated by existing reality. This means that the forms, too, have no validity in themselves – there are no logical or categorical absolutes[13] – they have no absolute status, they cannot for their part be turned into things or reified. They exist only in so far as they relate to the things that are thought of through them, to the extent that they connect with experience.

In this respect we may say that dialectical thought is already contained objectively, already implied, *in* the Kantian theory even though Kant himself left it in the shape of a crass dualism of form and content. But the crucial idea is that the properties he ascribes to the forms can only hold good, can only have existence, if they refer to contents; while the contents, for their part, remain quite indeterminate and cannot be the objects of thought until they have passed through these forms. This complex in fact expresses the idea that these two supreme concepts, form and content, are each mediated by the other. You can see here, then, that the dialectic does not involve

sorcery, but that the transition to dialectics is a necessary consequence
of the objective shape of Kantian philosophy. You can see likewise
that the contradiction involved in the concept of 'salvaging' is not a
simple intellectual contradiction, but a dialectical one. That is to say,
it is only possible to rescue ontology in the shape of this dialectical
contradiction, in this pattern in which existence and existent things
are mutually interrelated and interdependent – as opposed to an
abstract conception of ontology as pure existence standing in absolute
opposition to existing beings.[14]

However, everything I have said up to now is not enough to justify
my contention that the *Critique of Pure Reason* objectively contains
an attempt to rescue ontology. It goes without saying – and I am the
last to want to deny it – that you could find as many or more negative passages about metaphysics and ontology as the positive ones I
have told you about, and as long as you are content to trawl through
a great philosopher in search of simple proofs of what are said to be
his intentions, the arguments and counter-arguments will never come
to an end. As I have already told you, when you are attempting to
assess a philosopher's thought, the least important evidence is that
philosopher's own opinion about it. It is the same with a literary
work, where it is just as idle to enquire into the convictions which
inspire a work and which enable a writer to express himself directly.
Thus when I claim that the *Critique of Pure Reason* was written to
rescue ontology, I need rather stronger evidence and, above all, more
objective evidence grounded in the subject matter than can be obtained
simply from Kant's own 'opinion'. I believe that I can provide this
evidence quite simply by reminding you of the position of the *Critique of Pure Reason* in contrast to the philosophy of David Hume.
As you will know, or as you ought to know if you wish to gain
anything from a course of lectures on Kant, David Hume applied an
empiricist critique, that is, an analysis of the forms of our experience,
which resulted in the *dissolution* of three fundamental concepts, three
categories. He showed that they were really no more than conventional notions to which no substantial reality or – we might say in this
context – to which no ontological reality corresponded. These three
concepts are those of the *thing, causality* and the *self*. You must
now bear in mind that one of the positive intentions of the *Critique
of Pure Reason,* and at the same time, one of the points at which we
can obtain a glimpse of its ontological ambitions, is to adopt and
continue this Humean critique. At the same time, however, Kant is
concerned to turn Hume's arguments against him – with the consequence that these three concepts of the self, causality and the thing-
in-itself are *salvaged*.[15]

On the first point, we should say that he mobilizes a strict and powerful argument against Hume's analysis of the concept of the self. I believe it is important that you should make yourselves familiar with this line of argument, which only makes its appearance at a later stage in the *Critique*.[16] This takes the view that the laws of association or custom, and in general all the elements through which the changing contents of consciousness enter into relations with one another, cannot be imagined save in the unity of a conscious mind. This brings us to the truly central concept of the *Critique of Pure Reason*, one which we have not yet discussed and yet which holds the key to Kant's entire solution to this problem – and that is the unity of consciousness. You cannot – and this is the burden of Kant's criticism of Hume – even conceive of all the psychological facts that Hume uncovers and which he uses to undermine the assumption of a self, unless you accept that they are included within the 'synthetic unity of apperception' or the ' "*I think*" that accompanies all my representations'.[17]

The concepts of the synthetic unity of apperception and the 'I think' that accompanies all my representations are not concepts we can fully analyse at this juncture. Instead, I should like to give you at least a very simple pointer to their meaning in order to show you the general direction of Kant's line of argument. Before rushing to put a metaphysical or speculative gloss on that 'I think', you should merely think first of all of what the simplest experience will tell you about the unity of your own personal consciousness. For example, consider the laws of association, that is to say, laws that enable you to bring different ideas together because they resemble one another or because they are contiguous in time or place – to take two of the laws of association mentioned by Hume.[18] You would not be able to say anything about experiencing such associations if you did not conceive of them as your *own* experiences. Thus if you have toothache today and someone else had toothache yesterday, but did not tell you about it, you would not be able to associate your toothache with his. Only if you yourself had the toothache yesterday would you be in a position to ascertain the similarity or difference in intensity between these two toothaches. This is a terribly primitive and basic example, but this very basic fact that there can only be knowledge of this kind where the individual has some continuity – this really is the key to an understanding of Kant. Moreover, when he says that the 'I think' accompanies all my representations, this contains something else, namely the idea of spontaneity or activity, about which we shall hear more in the coming lectures. For the moment, however, we should be aware that this statement about what 'accompanies all my representations' contains nothing other than the fact that all my representations – irrespective of what kind – do have something in common because *I* have them, that is, they are *my* representations and no one else's. This simple unity, which has its roots in psychology, has a kind of ontological significance for Kant. If this unity of personal consciousness did not exist, if there were nothing to unite all these different perceptions, then there would be no knowledge as such, but only a chaos. But this unity does exist and in consequence the self is a kind of basic ontological foundation of knowledge.

I would add only that the problem of which subject is under discussion is in no way resolved, since the critique of reason has made it its task to ground empirical facts and not to presuppose them. This means that the empirical self, the individual person that everyone in this room is, cannot be taken for granted. On the other hand, the assumption of a specific individual consciousness which is able to unify disparate perceptions is absolutely indispensable to the Kantian critique. We thus find ourselves confronted by a contradiction (and I do not imagine, after what I have already said, that you will perceive this as an impudent criticism of Kant, rather the contrary, in fact) – namely, the contradiction that, on the one hand, the concept of subjectivity cannot be conceived of without the personal subject from which it has been derived; but that, on the other hand, the personal subject has first to be constituted and so cannot be presupposed in advance. Kant, however, could not bring himself to stop worrying away at this contradiction. In the attempt to resolve it he kept coming up with new restatements in his various writings, notably in the *Prolegomena*, where his terminology differs from that of the *Critique of Pure Reason*.

So much for what we might term the ontological significance of the concept of the subject in Kant. The actual inference that can be drawn from this that is of relevance for the overall plan of the work is that everything else, that is, all the specific forms which enable me to have any knowledge of whatever kind, has to be inferred from this unity of consciousness, this 'I think' that accompanies all my representations. This unity ranks highest in the hierarchy of forms and everything that can be thought is subordinated to it; it is the ultimate source from which the wealth of individual forms – of intuition and the categories – all arise. And as for the famous central section of the *Critique of Pure Reason*, the Deduction of the Pure Concepts of Understanding – you can now easily understand what is at stake here. Kant's task is to deduce the categories, the important, individual, basic concepts that enable me to organize my experience, from this very unity of personal consciousness, and from nothing else. That, in broad outline, is the strategy on which the edifice of the *Critique of Pure Reason* is founded.

I do not wish to spend much time on causality. In Kant causality is a category that follows from this unity of personal consciousness. It is nothing but the general form of a conformity to law which compels me to synthesize the different phenomenal aspects of the same thing that succeed each other in time. He agrees here with Hume in not ascribing causality to things-in-themselves, that is, he does not conceive of causes naturalistically. In contrast to Hume, however, he believes that an ordered knowledge, a lawful succession of events, is only possible in the context of this form. Thus, whereas Hume would say that causality is merely *subjective*, Kant would reply, indeed, it is merely subjective, but this supposedly subjective element is the necessary precondition without which *objectivity* cannot come into being. In this sense the category of causality, too, acquires an ontological meaning, in contrast to Hume.[19]

Finally, we come to the concept of the thing, where the position is at its most opaque. At this point I should like to offer you a little assistance for your own work on Kant. The concept of the thing or object is ambiguous in Kant, like very many of his concepts. And even if we have established that equivocal or ambiguous concepts do not come about by chance, but are in some way connected with the life of the thing to which they refer, this does not absolve us from the necessity of giving ourselves an account of the different meanings of a given concept. So please make a note of this: in the *Critique of Pure Reason* a 'thing-in-itself' means roughly: the entirely unknown and indefinite cause of phenomena, the cause of the 'affections', the cause of sense data – which, as I have already said to you, are conceived as something indeterminate, but which in Kant are seen also to be caused by such an unknown thing. I do not wish at this point to  explain how Kant arrives at such an unknown thing, and even to postulate a causal connection between it and our experiences. He posits this causal connection even though causality is defined as an immanent category in his writings, that is, a category concerned with the ordering of phenomena and not, say, with transcendent matters, inaccessible to experience. I believe that I have said enough by showing you that the seemingly dogmatic assumption of the thing has no explanation beyond the fact that he wished to avoid the duplication of knowledge by itself and to retain a concept of reality which is nonidentical, that is to say, it does not simply coincide with consciousness. But in contrast to this concept of the *transcendent* thing-in-itself – which the neo-Kantians then attempted to appropriate and interpret as a marginal concept, as in mathematics – Kant also has a second concept of the object or thing, which we may call an *immanent* concept. According to this, a thing is nothing other than the laws that underlie the individual phenomena, the individual data of my consciousness. We should remind ourselves here that Kant maintained that phenomena could only be brought together with the aid of such a law – that phenomena could only be made to relate to one another through force, necessity. In this way he rejected the concept of the thing or else turned it into something quite vague and banished it from the gates of transcendental philosophy. But then he imported a second definition of the thing into transcendental philosophy as a positive fact – in contrast to Hume, who dismissed out of hand the idea of such a concept of things.

LECTURE NINE

18 June 1959

The Concept of the Thing (I)

I should like to remind you briefly of Kant's main line of thought so that you will be in a position to appreciate the importance of the more detailed analyses I shall give you today. I have told you – and this is one of the metaphysical experiences articulated by Kant's book – that in the midst of all Kant's criticism, in spite of it and even through it, there is a sense in which you must discern an attempt to rescue ontology in the *Critique of Pure Reason*. In the process I tried also to elucidate the term 'ontology'. I explained further that this rescue attempt can be most clearly explained by showing how some of the central concepts of ontology, what I have termed the naturalistic concepts,[1] succumbed to Hume's criticism; that is to say, thanks to Hume's criticism they lost every claim to objectivity and stood revealed as merely conventional terms. These concepts had their objective status restored by Kant, but their road to objectivity *passed through the subject*. I exemplified this with the concept of the self, the concept of the subject, about which we shall have a lot more to say later on. I also tried to illustrate it briefly with reference to the concepts of causality and the thing. We are dealing, then, with three so-called naturalistic concepts which are viewed in Kant as objectivities constituted by categories – so that we might think of them as *subjectively* constituted, if you wish.

Of the three, the third concept, that of the thing, plays an outstanding part. You can best picture to yourselves its central role if you remind yourselves that the overall design of the *Critique of Pure Reason* is objective in the sense that it is not concerned primarily to

analyse the objective mechanisms of cognition for their own sake;
that is to say, it has no wish to provide a physiology of thought or
knowledge. It wishes, rather, to analyse these mechanisms with a
view to discovering what kind of objectively valid knowledge is available to us. In the nature of the case this means the knowledge of
nature, since, as you will recollect, the *Critique of Pure Reason* proceeded from the assumption that the mathematically based natural
sciences are valid, and then set itself the task of consolidating their
validity through reflection on the knowing subject. But it is quite
obvious that the epitome of nature or of the world is a concept of the
thing, that is, the supreme synthesis, the all-inclusive ensemble of all
existing things in general. We may say, therefore, without too many
ifs and buts that the success of Kant's search for the truth, the objective proof of truth, depends in actuality upon the success of his analysis
of the objectivity of things, of individual things, as constituted by the
subject. He can then advance from there to the connections between
things, and finally, to the objectively valid concept of a world.

You may then add a second observation, one that will become
fully clear to you in due course, but which I would like at least to
mention right now. This is that the concepts of a constitutive subjectivity, that is, the concepts by means of which the unity of consciousness actually comes into being and which I described to you in some
detail last time – in short, the real kernel of Kant's conception – this
unity of consciousness is conceived as the correlative of the unity of
the thing, the unity of the object. That is to say, the mechanisms that
Kant represents as the truly transcendental mechanisms, those which
provide the foundations for subjective unity, are indistinguishable in
reality from those which enable us to perceive things, objective existent beings, as identical objects. This has the effect that throughout
the entire *Critique of Pure Reason* you must always conceive of the
two concepts, the object of knowledge and the subject of knowledge,
in tandem. The possibility of the objective knowledge of things really
leads to an insight into constitutive subjectivity, and conversely, you
arrive at the objective existence of things only through these subjective factors. I shall return to this later on.

I believe, however, that now that I have undertaken to show you
in what sense Kant salvages the concept of ontology, or, in other
words, the possibility of absolutely valid knowledge, I owe it to you
to clarify Kant's theory of the thing and to make it seem a little more
plausible to you. I told you last time[2] that Kant's answer to the
problem of the thing can be summarized in the proposition that a
thing is the law of its possible appearances. As always in the decisive questions of philosophy the distinction between this position and

opposing views is minimal. Here, you really need to take Kant's concept of 'law' in a very strong sense if you wish to distinguish it clearly from that of Hume. It is the form in which things are necessarily connected with one another. As I have said, on this question of naturalistic concepts and their salvaging with the aid of the transcendental, what this amounts to is the polemical engagement of the *Critique of Pure Reason* with Hume's *Treatise*.[3] You may well take the view that although these two thinkers are so opposed to each other, on this matter their ideas are so similar that we could say loosely of Hume – and also of John Locke, though far less loosely – that he too speaks of conformity to law as the determining factor in constituting the objectivity of things. Furthermore, when Hume explains our practice of speaking of permanent existent beings in terms of association or contiguity or the like, as I reported to you last time, he is obviously concerned with certain regularities that must be observable by us in our analysis of human consciousness. Thus the distinction between his views and those of Kant are reduced in actual fact to the difference between the two terms 'regularity' and 'law'. The point is that in Hume these regularities are purely empirical: they may exist, or they may not exist. Hence the objectivity to which these psychological laws lead is in a sense contingent; or we might equally say that it is merely subjective and that it depends upon the more or less accidental nature of the organization of the psyche. In Kant, on the other hand, these laws are such that without them we would be unable to conceive of a unified consciousness, and thus a unified experience of reality.

All of this may appear to you as involving an extraordinary subtlety, an almost Talmudic dispute among epistemologists, about a minimal distinction between an empirical rule and what amounts to a law of logic. In its consequences, however, we see that an entire conception is at stake. It is because Kant understands these laws as the necessary condition of a unified consciousness, and thereby of a unified world of objects, that there can be such a thing as the objectively valid knowledge of nature, the objective valid knowledge of things and of reality or – as Kant terms it in a celebrated expression – 'empirical realism'. For the Kantian formula for this complex of ideas is one that I should certainly mention to you, and it is undoubtedly one of which you will have already heard. It is the idea of 'transcendental idealism/empirical realism'.[4] This means that in transcendentalist terms, that is, in terms of synthetic *a priori* judgements, we are talking about an idealism – that is, something arising exclusively from the mind; this objectivity is rooted in mind. On the other hand, it is empirical realism in the sense that the interaction of these transcendental conditions with the data of reality in fact leads to the constitution of the world which surrounds us as the world of our experience. It would be a gross misunderstanding of Kantian idealism if we were to conceive of it as an acosmic philosophy, as a denial of empirical reality; or if we were even to go so far as to impute to Kant the desire to suggest that the world is no more than a dream – a suggestion made by Descartes in his *Meditations,* as many of you will know.[5] It is this very hypothesis that Kant ridiculed so scathingly under the title of 'dreamy idealism' in his now famous polemic against the empirical idealism or spiritualism of Berkeley.[6]

In order to understand the objectivity claims of subjectivity in Kant it is vital to treat this concept of law with extreme rigour. It must be seen as an indispensable precondition without which something like an organized consciousness, a consciousness that is logically consistent and coherent, and hence an organized, logically consistent world of objects, is not conceivable. The most general proposition in the *Critique of Pure Reason* that is of relevance here is one that states that the law governing phenomena is the law that actually regulates the connections between my ideas. I should like at this point to read you the critical passage from the second version of the Transcendental Deduction which refers to this problem and which you will be able to comprehend even though you will not be wholly conversant with the conception of that deduction – that is to say, the way in which the categories are linked to the unity of consciousness – in all its details.

> Categories are concepts which prescribe laws *a priori* to appearances, and therefore to nature, the sum of all appearances (*natura materialiter spectata*).

– that is to say, nature as perceived in a specific material.
The question therefore arises – and this is actually the central question of the *Critique of Pure Reason –*

> how it can be conceivable that nature should have to proceed in accordance with categories which yet are not derived from it, and do not model themselves upon its pattern (because otherwise they would be empirical);

– this is the central paradox of the *Critique of Pure Reason*: that the mind prescribes laws to nature; that the intellect should constitute thinghood as a rule-bound complex of appearances that conform to laws –

that is, how they can determine *a priori* the combination of the manifold of nature, while yet they are not derived from it.

– that is, from the content, the material of knowledge –

The solution of this seeming enigma is as follows. That the *laws* of appearances in nature must agree with the understanding and its *a priori* form, that is, with its faculty of *combining* the manifold in general, is no more surprising than that the appearances themselves must agree with the form of *a priori* sensible intuition.[7]

He asserts, then, that there is nothing surprising about our subsuming the data that we possess under the concepts of the understanding and combining them with these concepts; it is just as unsurprising as the fact that our individual sense data are given to us in sensory forms as such, to wit, the forms of time and space.

Of course, we might cogently object at this point[8] that all this is exceedingly odd. How does it come about that these givens over which we have no control can behave in such a way that they coincide with the forms of our subjectivity without any contradiction – and that thanks to this coincidence something like objectively valid knowledge comes into being? Let me say straight away that Kant himself was very conscious of this problem and did not dismiss it out of hand, as the sentence I have just read to you may suggest. We are talking here about the very profound and intractable problem of 'schematism', about which I shall have more to say in a future lecture.[9] For the moment I would prefer not to lead you into these abysses and would like instead simply to explain in a straightforward fashion what Kant is asserting here, to wit, that it is the forms of the understanding which enable us to make connections between sense data, and that it is in this way that objectivity comes into being.

Furthermore, there is nothing surprising in all of this. The answer that this calls for is, if you like, no proper answer in the sense of a synthetic judgement, that is, of a new piece of knowledge, but it refers ultimately to the entire set of underlying premises of the *Critique of Pure Reason* as I have explained them to you – and you will now realize why I have explained them at such length. It comes down to a distinction between form and content. I have told you that this distinction is extremely radical in Kant, in the sense that all the determining factors – everything that makes a thing what it is – lie on the side of form, of the subject. If we then subtract all these determining factors, what remains is the given that is to be subsumed under the forms of consciousness and then synthesized by these forms; and this

given something is in fact completely indeterminate, as indeterminate (we might almost say) as the thing-in-itself from which all these
givens are supposed to arise. These givens are completely chaotic, in
complete disorder. They cannot even be said to exist. Their existence,
the assertion that they exist, already implies their relation to a subject
to which they belong. Kant calls this their 'apprehension in intuition'.[10] This means that their very existence is already mediated – so
that it is really no more than a small step beyond Kant when Hegel
states that the pure existence that is said to characterize the ultimate data of knowledge is nothing at all; that it might just as well
be a something.[11] However, even if we set aside for the moment
this question of something and nothing, we can at least say that the
completely undetermined nature of this material of knowledge has a
negative aspect that fits perfectly into the Kantian system – just as we
may say in general, even though this is frequently overlooked in
philosophical discussion, that the claim to objectivity, the claim to
the validity of some knowledge or other, consists not just in a positive side, in something given in the materials or forms of what is
known, but in a στέρησις, a negative element, a factor that is missing.

This absolute absence of determinations is based ultimately on the
Cartesian division into form and content; it is something that suits
Kant's book all too conveniently. For it means that there is no real
resistance to this act of subsumption – that is, this synthesizing of my
ideas with the aid of the understanding, of the forms of my consciousness – on the part of whatever is synthesized. This is because
whatever is being synthesized is so lacking in qualities that it is infinitely malleable by the forms of consciousness. The absence of qualities, the indeterminate nature of the material of knowledge, confers
on it a kind of plasticity – this is not stated explicitly in the *Critique
of Pure Reason*, but we have to try and picture these things to ourselves – that allows us to synthesize these givens without their placing
any obstacles in our path. This means that our minds can manipulate
them at will. They do not need to have any particular taste; it is
enough if there is something to bite on. Thus this wholly abstract
something is what gives me the right to claim that I am processing
my experience. As long as I have something between my teeth, my
sovereign will can do with it whatever I please. This, then, is the
ultimate source of the vast claims of the sovereign, creative spirit that
were proclaimed later on by Fichte and Schelling.

I shall now read you the relevant passage in Kant:

> For just as appearances do not exist in themselves but only relatively
> to the subject in which, so far as it has senses, they inhere, so the laws

do not exist in the appearances but only relatively to this same being, so far as it has understanding.[12]

In other words, he says that, looked at ontologically – that is, in terms of their absolute nature – there is no vast difference between the concept of laws and the concept of givens even though they lie at the opposite poles of knowledge. For just as I may not speak of a given without postulating a subject – in the absence of a subject all talk of givens is meaningless – so too, at the other pole of the understanding, I may not speak of laws without presupposing an act of thinking that could be said to think those laws. For conformity with law is nothing other than thinking as such, that is, it is a logic (you might say) that necessarily refers back to thinking, and thus to a subject. According to Kant, then, it is in this sense that it is no paradox to ascribe the objectivity of things to the subject, because the guarantee of that objectivity is nothing but the fact of laws, and we can speak of laws only as the laws of our thought. This is the central answer to the question: how can our minds prescribe laws to nature?

Thus 'things-in-themselves' – that means, then, transcendent things, not the things of our experience with which we actually have dealings, but the famous unknown cause of appearances which make their entrance, like the person or persons unknown in the reports of court proceedings, to whom all sorts of things are ascribed, but whom no one has ever seen.

> Things-in-themselves would necessarily, apart from any understanding that knows them, conform to laws of their own. But appearances are only representations of things which are unknown as regards what they may be in themselves. As mere representations they are subject to no law of connection save that which the connecting faculty prescribes. Now it is imagination

– in other words, the ability to conceive of absent things as present –

> that connects the manifold of sensible intuition; and imagination is dependent for the unity of its intellectual synthesis upon the understanding, and for the manifoldness of its apprehension upon sensibility. All possible perception is thus dependent upon synthesis of apprehension, and this empirical synthesis in turn upon transcendental synthesis, and therefore upon the categories. Consequently, all possible perceptions, and therefore everything that can come to empirical consciousness, that is, all appearances of nature, must, so far as their connection is concerned, be subject to the categories. Nature . . . is dependent upon these categories as the original ground of its necessary conformity to law.[13]

ır the relevant passage from Kant.

ɔynthesis in this sense means simply that the chaos of givens is conditional upon a unity that – as I explained to you last time – is none other than the unity of our consciousness. This unity is to be understood in a double sense, to wit, a successive and a simultaneous unity. You must think about consciousness in a quite concrete way, namely, as your own consciousness, indeed as a stream of consciousness – I almost used the modern term: a *monologue intérieur*; at any rate, as the continuous flow of your ideas, desires and experiences, and whatever else goes on in each of us. Now Kant says that the synthesis of this manifold is either successive or simultaneous. *Simultaneous* is what I meant when I referred before to the 'apprehension in intuition'; that is to say, I perceive the scattered, chaotic elements that appear to me as a unified phenomenon and am able to achieve something like a unified perception.

I have no wish to intervene in the controversy among psychologists, which, incidentally, cannot be separated at this point from the debates on the theory of knowledge – about whether this doctrine of apprehension can be reconciled with modern *Gestalt* theory. Modern *Gestalt* theory would repudiate the idea of the fragmentation, of the chaotic nature of individual sensory data, and would claim that I perceive these fragmentary elements as a unity from the outset. In this respect it stands in apparent contradiction to the *Critique of Pure Reason*. I believe, however – if I may make these comments for those of you who are interested in the psychology of knowledge – that the distinction here is illusory, as I have already indicated. The reason is that according to Kant this simultaneous synthesis – that is, the fact that you apprehend these sensory data, as a conscious unity, as something unified – is not something we perceive in retrospect. Indeed, while we are of sound mind we can apprehend a manifold only as long as we do perceive it as a unity and organize it with the aid of this unity. This unity is not something tacked on as an afterthought; it is – Kant would claim – the *a priori* condition for every act of perception. In practice, then, he would agree with *Gestalt* theory, or so it appears to me.

The point at which he would part company with *Gestalt* theory – and I would tend to agree with him – is that he would say that the immediately given figures, shapes [*Gestalten*] and structures that are the subject of *Gestalt* theory stand in need of mediation. They need the mediation of a subject. They exist only if there is a comprehending subject. This condition is suppressed by *Gestalt* theory, and this goes hand in hand with the scientific division of labour, namely, with the fact that psychology is necessarily concerned with subjectivity, since that is its field. Hence it does not explicitly focus on subjectivity as such because everything it treats is enacted within subjectivity from the outset. Philosophy, however, differs here (as I do not tire of reminding you) because the relation between subjectivity and objectivity is precisely the object of its reflections; that explains why this relation of *Gestalt* to a possible subject that can create meaning is of central importance to philosophy.[14] Philosophy just adds a further element to modern psychology at this point, namely, the element of subjective mediation, or, as Kant himself would have phrased it, subjective preconditions. This remains true even though at the same time it would be a mistake to accuse Kant of having succumbed to an atomistic psychology (of which the English have rightly been accused), since in his philosophy even the most elementary level of knowledge – to wit, immediate perception as the apprehension of the fragmentary in intuition – is a synthesis, a unity. Moreover, it is an unconscious synthesis, that is, a synthesis that we do not arrive at by thinking, by reflecting, by working on the state of chaos. Rather, we frame it within this unity by making it *our own*, by appropriating it, by thinking of it *as something*; we can no more set this unity aside than, according to the *Gestalt* theorists, we can set aside the structural unity of phenomena. So much for the simultaneous unity as we find it in experience.[15] As far as the *successive* unity is concerned, it consists simply in the fact that we unify phenomena by regarding them as existing not merely in the here and now, but we also relate them to what we have seen or heard, and what we shall see and hear. In other words, the given also operates within a temporal horizon.

Setting aside that primary simultaneous unity of apprehension, it is upon this temporal horizon that the entire theory of the thing can be said to depend in a radical manner. The line of argument that leads Kant to assert that we live in an empirical reality, that things truly exist as the objects of our experience, but that this experience is grounded in our subjectivity – that argument runs as follows, and I shall try to present it to you with very broad, perhaps crude, brush-strokes, so that you will all be able to grasp the very essence of the *Critique of Pure Reason*.

Simply picture to yourselves this lecture hall for a second. It might perhaps be the case that the room had no rear wall, because it had been bombed out, or that it seemed to have no ceiling if you had not been looking upwards. Now you turn round and perceive it from a second angle, and make the welcome discovery, for the time being, at least, that it does have both a rear wall and a ceiling and that it may be said in a sense to 'hang together'. You may finally establish to your own satisfaction that the lecture hall is situated in this university by

leaving this room at the end of the lecture and orientating yourselves
by noting the relationship between this lecture hall and the corridor
or other parts of this splendid building. As you do so, you will find
that at each moment you have only one, partial point of view, or (as
we may express it in the idiom of the modern theory of knowledge)
we perceive the object, the thing, this lecture hall, only in a particular
adumbration [*Abschattung*].[16] However, the law that signals to you
that when you turn round you may expect to see a wall, etc., and
that when you undertake these different operations the phenomena
will arrange themselves in a unified way – that is to say, the law that
is the sum of these relations between isolated momentary perceptions
which you bring together by means of your memories of the past and
your expectations for the future – all that together constitutes a thing.
In other words, a thing is nothing but the law which tells you that
by linking a present perception, connecting it in accordance with
laws, with past and future perceptions, and with whatever expectations you may have – the law, in short, that tells you what will happen
and what has transpired – this law is in fact the thing you are concerned with at that particular moment. This, then, is Kant's concept
of the thing, and we may add that it is the idealist notion of the thing
and perhaps even the concept that operates in the theory of knowledge in the narrower sense. Much can be said in criticism of this
concept of the thing, but I do not think it my duty to rush in with
criticism at every juncture. Instead, I would urge you to picture this
concept to yourselves before you start to reflect on its validity. Let me
add that by polishing and refining this concept of the thing – both in
regard to Hume and to Kant, and by conceiving of it as the functional
unity of the phenomena covered by it – you finally end up conceiving
of it mathematically, as a functional concept, to wit, as the functional
equation of the phenomena concerned. This functional theory of
the concept of the thing was really anticipated by Kant himself. I
shall show you that Kant himself already perceived this functional
character of the concept of the thing for what it is, namely, as the
concept of what he termed a mere relation. In other words, he already
perceived the crucial difficulty that we perceive things as relations,
not as existent beings.
But let me at this point read and interpret a very characteristic
passage about the theory of things from somewhat further on in the
text, namely, in the chapter on the Amphiboly of Concepts of Reflection. This forms the transition to the Transcendental Dialectic; we
might say that it is in this chapter that Kant deals with the confusion
of the pure object of the understanding with its [empirical] appearance. At this point you will discover the definition of things as a set

of functions as well as a discussion of the difficulty I have drawn your attention to already. The passage can be found in a context to which it does not really belong and which I cannot go into at the moment, but picks up the discussion on the nature of things and is in fact extremely important on this question.

> All that we know in matter is merely relations (what we call the inner determinations of it are inward only in a comparative sense).

That is to say, mere relations are external, Kant maintains, in the sense that we place our individual appearances, our individual experiences as subjects in relation to one another, and only through these relations do we arrive at a consciousness of things, whereas the question of whether they are things, that is, things-in-themselves, independently of us, whether they are defined as things, is something we have no knowledge of in the first instance because, as Kant says, they are not things-in-themselves, but merely appearances:

> But among these relations some are self-subsistent and permanent, and through these we are given a determinate object.[17]

These relations, these functional concepts that refer to something relatively self-subsistent and permanent – these are in fact what we mean by things. In this sense no distinction can be made between things and the concepts of things; instead, the things *qua* laws to connect the appearances are themselves just concepts.

> The fact that, if I abstract from these relations, there is nothing more left for me to think does not rule out the concept of a thing as appearance, nor indeed the concept of an object *in abstracto*. What it does remove is all possibility of an object determinable through mere concepts, that is, of a noumenon.[18]

This means, then, that the moment I abstract from these relations, the moment I attempt to make a statement about the pure existence of this lecture hall here, without referring to the relations between its various phenomenal aspects, that is, between the aspects of the hall given to me through experience – nothing remains to me at all. This proves that the thing of which I am speaking empirically belongs in fact on the side of appearance; it is a complex of appearances, and not a thing-in-itself.

It is certainly startling to hear – and there you have the difficulty that I have drawn your attention to, as formulated by Kant himself –

that such a thing is to be taken as consisting wholly of relations. Such a thing is, however, mere appearance, and cannot be thought through pure categories; what it itself consists in is the mere relation of something in general to the senses.[19]

I should like to conclude this lecture with a remark about terminology. The word *Erscheinung* [appearance] in Kant has a number of different meanings, and I believe that you will find it easier to read the *Critique of Pure Reason* if you bear in mind the following two, a narrower meaning and a wider one. The narrower meaning is that of 'appearance' in the sense of a 'perception': the image, if I may put it crudely and naturalistically, that you have of this lecture hall, the field of vision you have before you. That is 'appearance' in a literal, immediate sense. It is what appears to you without the addition of any mental act on your part. Over and above that, Kant also uses 'appearance' to mean the object, the thing concerned, as long as you do not imagine this to mean any transcendent 'thing-in-itself', but simply this relation conceived by my mind between these single perceptions, between the single immediate givens: in short, it is a thing, inasmuch as it can be verified or falsified in my experience and *by* my experience. In this sense the entire empirical world, the whole world in which we live, is appearance, according to Kant, almost in the same sense as Schopenhauer had in mind when he said that the world is 'my idea' [*meine Vorstellung*]. We may say that Schopenhauer's use of the term 'idea' corresponds pretty exactly to this wider meaning of *Erscheinung*. According to this broader meaning, things, to wit, empirical things or empirical objects, are in fact appearances, in Kant's view. If Kant speaks of a thing as an appearance, this is, generally speaking, a fairly loose expression, and what is meant by it  is the thing conceived as a relation between the immediately given data of experience as prescribed, regulated and constituted by the understanding. In other words, a thing is nothing other than the synthesis of its individual appearances.

LECTURE TEN

23 June 1959

The Concept of the Thing (II)

When we look at the difficulties presented by the *Critique of Pure Reason*, we see that we can divide them into two groups. The first type consists of superficial difficulties that can be overcome by giving useful pointers. Then there are the difficulties that lie in the subject matter and in the ideas themselves. As to the latter, I can only see it as my task in these lectures to intensify them rather than to play them down. That is to say, I have to show you *problems* where there seem to be *solutions*. As for the avoidable problems of the first type, I would say that the duty of an introductory course of lectures is to minimize them as far as possible. This is best done by resolving ambiguities. Wherever one word is used in a number of different senses, we should try to read with some understanding so that we can assign the correct meaning to specific passages. However, I must remind you of what I have frequently had to stress in this course of lectures and elsewhere. This is that the method used by the positivists, the semanticists, will not do. They attempt to resolve such difficulties by eliminating ambiguities and then saying 'That is that',[1] as if that were all one had to do to rid oneself of problems. In general, where you find ambiguities, that is to say, where the same term is used to refer to different things, there is a genuine connection between the things referred to. Last time, I told you about the plurality of meanings given to the word 'appearance' [*Erscheinung*] in Kant, or rather, I had begun to tell you, and I should now like to take this a little further, by way of offering you this assistance. I should preface my comments by pointing out that the two meanings of 'appearance' nave one thing in common and that is their *immanence*; that is, they both refer to the sphere formed by the unity of consciousness – and not some form of being or other that is conceived as something completely independent of consciousness. The first of these meanings is the stricter and narrower. It is the momentary perception, or, more broadly, the immediate given, regardless of whether you think of it as Kant seems to suggest in a number of passages, as completely devoid of qualities, chaotic or, if you like, abstract; or whether you think of it as something already structured, as is implied in the doctrine of apprehension. In the second meaning of 'appearance', on the other hand – and this is the difficulty I should like to eliminate – appearance really is the object, the immanently constructed thing about which I talked in detail last time, in the sense that this thing is no thing-in-itself, no unknown cause of my appearances, but, as we saw, nothing but a law governing the connections between specific givens.

This is what he means by appearance in the following passage, for example, which I should now like to read to you in order to make you aware of this usage. I would almost go so far as to say that as the text of the *Critique of Pure Reason* progresses, and the further it distances itself from the passive reception of sense impressions, the more this second meaning of appearance gains in importance. Here, in §17 of the Transcendental Deduction, Kant writes of the 'principle of the synthetic unity of apperception' as the 'supreme principle of the employment of the understanding':

> *Understanding* is, to use general terms, *the faculty of knowledge*. This knowledge consists in the determinate relation of given representations to an object.

Object here means simply the unifying element to which the different representations refer and which gathers them together. It does not mean a thing-in-itself in the transcendent sense which we have described as one meaning of the concept of the thing in Kant:

> And an *object* is that in the concept of which the manifold of a given intuition is *united*. Now all unification of representations demands unity of consciousness in the synthesis of them.

This means that, after all, we think of things that are different as one, as an identity.

> Consequently it is the unity of consciousness that alone constitutes the relation of representations to an object, and therefore their objective

validity and the fact that they are modes of knowledge; and upon it therefore rests the very possibility of understanding.[2]

Here, then, you have a very clear example of the second meaning of 'thing' as an object. I should like here to draw something to your attention even though it is a little out of place. It is something that emerges very clearly here in a passage of central importance in the *Critique of Pure Reason*. What I have in mind is the peculiar inter-action between the concept of a unified consciousness and that of the unity of the object. It is self-evident that because this unity is supposed to be created through our act of thinking, and ultimately through its *logical* unity, in *genetic* terms, that is, in terms of the way it is actually created, the subject has priority in bringing the object into being.

But if you examine the passage closely you will see that the unity of consciousness is conceived on the model of the unity of the thing. Thus in a certain sense the two aspects – the coherent, unified con-sciousness and the coherent thing identical with itself – mutually condition each other. It is true that a thing is constituted by the unity of consciousness, but by the same token, the idea that the unity of a thing should exist itself calls for the unity of consciousness, a syn-thesizing unity. We might say, therefore, that Kant proceeds – as in the natural sciences – from experience, that is, from the given fact of identical things as opposed to the manifold nature of appearances, as physics always had to, at least in its traditional form. Further-more, starting from there, he is forced into the assumption of a uni-fied consciousness, just as, conversely, the mechanism of the unity of consciousness brings forth something like the unity of the thing. This is why it is so typical of him when he says: 'Now all unification of representations demands unity of consciousness in the synthesis of them.' This means that if the representations are as unified as we experience them as being in our consciousness of things, then, so Kant concludes, there must be some such thing as a unity of con-sciousness in the sense that I explained earlier on.[3] This means that there must be a unified personal consciousness which perceives given realities that cannot be replaced by the given realities of any other consciousness because in that event the synthesis could not come into being. This implies, for example, that it is impossible to create a synthesis, a unity, by taking the facts of consciousness that yesterday were in the mind of the gentleman who is sitting in front of me now, and putting them together with the facts of my consciousness today, facts of which he is ignorant. This is the simple idea that I am trying to convey.

Thus the object that Kant imports into the world of appearances, that is to say, the object that is conceived by Kant to be nothing other than the law governing appearances, distinguishes itself in a crucial sense as a *phenomenon*. By this I mean that it is no more than an abbreviation for appearances; it possesses the quality that is generally ascribed to the fleeting nature of appearances. In other words, it is not characterized by apodeictic certainty, but rather by the fact that it is exposed to deception and disillusionment, and also to change. Moreover, it is this link between something constituted as law, on the one hand, and the possibility of disappointed expectations – that is, the possibility of changes to which it is subject – on the other, that compels Kant to introduce the concept of *causality*. For causality enables him to require that in order for something that conforms to laws to be subject to change, it must itself be subjected to a *law of change*. And in Kant's philosophy causality means simply this most universal law of all which governs every change in the world of objects that cannot be thought of as accidental. Accordingly, you have objects that can be known, that differ from the fleeting nature of their appearances, but that also belong in the world of appearances; objects that can be apprehended by experience and that are capable of change. These, then, are what Kant generally thinks of as objects.

I believe that I have already read you a number of passages that confirm this. There are more. For example, here is a further instance from the Solution of the Cosmological Dialectic:

> The faculty of sensible intuition is strictly only a receptivity, a capacity of being affected in a certain manner with representations, the relation of which to one another is a pure intuition of space and of time (mere forms of our sensibility), and which, in so far as they are connected in this manner in space and time, and are determinable according to laws of the unity of experience, are entitled *objects*. The non-sensible cause of these representations

– that is, the actual thing-in-itself – 'is completely unknown to us'.[4] Thus you have to reckon in Kant with this dualism of things as objects, or as the rule-bound complexes of the phenomena as they appear to us, of the data of our consciousness, *together with* the absolute things that have allegedly produced them.

It is quite obvious, therefore, that this duality in the concept of things inevitably leads to certain difficulties, huge difficulties, in fact, for the theory of cognition. The effect is that the world can be said to be doubled, in the paradoxical sense that true existence at the same time becomes something wholly undefined, abstract and ethereal, while conversely what we definitely know, positive existence, is turned into the mere delusion of appearances, the mere interconnection of the phenomena at our disposition. And at the same time we are denied the right to reach compelling conclusions about the true nature of existence.

This is the source of that remarkable dual structure of Kantian philosophy that the philosophers have always attacked and that Nietzsche summed up in the pun on the American expression 'backwoodsman' [*Hinterwäldler*] when he described Kant as an 'otherworldsman' [*Hinterweltler*].[5] By this he means someone who supposes that behind the world of our experience there lies a second world even though we know nothing whatever of this second, other world. It is fairly evident that this duplication of the thing – and therefore the duplication of the world, since the world is in reality nothing more than the supreme unity of all the things that exist – that this duplication of the world leads to the very gravest epistemological difficulties. It leads either to a kind of agnosticism, that is, to the conclusion that whatever we know, we do not know it with any certainty. Alternatively, it leads to the conclusion that what we know is merely a mirror of the real world, or a mere copy of the real world, without our being able to say anything definite about the relation between the two. Moreover, this idea of two worlds, this idea that we perceive copies and not the world itself, leads to paradoxes and muddles at every turn. I have no need to list them here, but if you look up the theory of images and signs in the theory of cognition contained in Husserl's *Ideas*, and also in his *Logical Investigations*, you will find everything that needs to be said about them.[6] Now, this difficulty of a duplication of the world is all too evident in the *Critique of Pure Reason* and I must also add that Kant talks explicitly about the duplication of objective existence in a number of passages.

It is noteworthy that this talk of duplication occurs not only when he is talking about the dual nature of things, but that it recurs in the *Critique of Practical Reason*. I regard this fact of duplication as being of such central importance for the entire structure of Kantian philosophy that, exceptionally, I should like to refer to a particular passage in the *Critique of Practical Reason*. I have in mind a passage in the theory of conscience (which comes late on in the *Critique of Practical Reason*), where he writes that conscience is a kind of court in which the subject sits in judgement on himself, in which the subject, that is to say, the human being, has to be imagined as judge and accused simultaneously: on the one side stands the intelligible character, who corresponds to the thing-in-itself, the Absolute, and on the other stands the empirical character corresponding to the actual, empirical thing.[7] I bring this to your attention because I believe that this figure of speech – as well as Kant's frequent practice of underlining the concept of the duplication of the thing – really does point to the question I wish to expound to you and for the sake of which I have given you this very detailed account of Kant's theory of the thing. It is for the sake of the metaphysical experience that can be said to lie behind it, for this metaphysical experience is actually identical with that duplication.

Thus underlying that duplication stands the idea that our world, the world of experience, really has become a world familiar to us; the world in which we live has ceased to be ruled by mysterious, unexplained powers. Instead, it is something we experience as *our* world in the sense that we encounter nothing that is incompatible with our own rationality. The experience that in this world we stand on our own two feet, and that we inhabit a known world without dreading the intervention of demons, without magical and mythical anxieties – all that is implicit in Kant's immanent concept of the thing. The world has ceased to be permeated by the ruins, by the surviving vestiges of a metaphysical meaning that even in its present fragmentary and elusive shape assumes the frightening and demonic visage that it possessed in the art and philosophy of the baroque age with which we are essentially concerned here. This process of disenchantment strips the world of its uncanny aspect. It is a bourgeois element that finds expression in Schiller when he makes the wealthy Stauffacher say in *Wilhelm Tell*, 'I stand here on my own property.'[8] It is an idea that is expressed in the assertion that the world of experience, of things, is my own product: it is my own world. But here is the crucial motif, I mean the objective motif, the motif of metaphysical experience, that of the position of the sundial of world history that led Kant to venture into this concept of duplication, even though he was by no means deceived as to its inherent difficulties.

By making the experienced world, the immanent world, the world in its this-ness, commensurate with us, by turning it into *our* world, so to speak, something like a radical metaphysical alienation is achieved simultaneously. It may be that the expression 'achieved' is a shade too idealistic; perhaps it describes an objective state of affairs too much as if it were merely the product of philosophical reflection. The more the world is stripped of an objective meaning and the more it becomes coextensive with our own categories and thereby becomes *our* world, then the more we find meaning eliminated from the world; and the more we find ourselves immersed in something like a cosmic night – to express it in a modern way. The demystification or disenchantment of the world – to employ an expression taken from Max Weber – is identical with a consciousness of being locked out, of a darkness in which we are enclosed. In one of the coming lectures I shall give you a theory of the Kantian 'block' and its significance. But I can say already that the meaning of this block is that the more the world in which we live, the world of experience, is commensurate with us, the less commensurate, the more obscure and the more threatening the Absolute, of which we know that this world of experience is only a detail, becomes. The situation is really one in which knowledge becomes a kind of idyll for *Homo sapiens*, an idyll that is acted out within the tragedy of existence, a cosmic tragedy in the face of which we are completely helpless. It is comparable (and I believe that the comparison is not far-fetched) to [Goethe's] *Hermann und Dorothea*, a work contemporary with Kant's, in which an idyllic happiness is purchased at the price of leaving in utter darkness the great drama of world history from which it may be said to have been excerpted. In other words, this darkness, that is, this consciousness, means that the more secure we are in our own world, the more securely we have organized our own lives, then the greater the uncertainty in which we find ourselves in our relations with the Absolute. The familiarity with our own world is purchased at the price of metaphysical despair. It is this paradox that is expressed in Kant's duplication of the world. It means that we accept an entirely undefined, obscure and, if you like, demonic world as a world 'behind' our own world, even though we have no way of knowing how it relates to the world of experience that we inhabit.

Now it is important, I believe, that you should be clear in your own minds that even the world of experience in which we find ourselves is not neutral. Because we downgrade it into *mere* appearance, *mere* phenomenon, because we view it as marked by *uncertainty*, it runs the risk of assuming a peculiarly shadowy character, the status of an as-if. You will know perhaps that one of the most important interpreters and analysts of Kant, Hans Vaihinger, entitled his own book *The Philosophy of As-If*.[9] Orthodox Kantians have had a good laugh at this relativist misinterpretation of the *Critique of Pure Reason* that nevertheless insists on clinging to 'absolute values'. But having regard to the peculiarly shadowy character which the immanent world acquires through consciousness, I would like to say that it is not actually the true world. The metaphysical experience that I am attempting to present to you as objective – not in Kant's consciousness, but as the *objectively* inspiriting force behind Kant – seems to me to have been not inaccurately captured in Vaihinger's phrase, redolent of nineteenth-century flat-footedness though it may be. The world does in fact become a way of concealing something unknown, a kind of *Doppelgänger*, a mere spectre or illusion.

We can say – and perhaps we may be permitted to say it because there are profound links between history and the consciousness of the mentally ill – that the layer of meaning objectively expressed in Kantian philosophy here bears a certain resemblance to the consciousness of schizophrenics or of people who find themselves in a state of extreme emotional tension. In extreme psychological situations it is easy to imagine suddenly that everything that exists, all existing things, are really just signs, or allegories, as Baudelaire put it.[10] This means that they all mean something other than what they are, without our being able to say what they are. Nowadays much is said about the theory of the Absurd in Existentialist philosophy. You are all aware that critics have associated Kafka with this theory of the Absurd and you know, too, that in the philosophy of Albert Camus – one of the best-known of the French Existentialists – this concept of the Absurd has been transformed into the very medium of metaphysical truth. However, when a concept like the Absurd arises naturally – or is helped to articulate itself – in a philosophy which is not concerned to portray philosophical 'moods', but which sticks quite soberly to the analysis of the mechanisms of knowledge, this seems far more laudable to me than when a philosopher isolates a particular concept, such as the Absurd, and elevates it into an abstract principle that is supposed to explain everything and ends up explaining nothing. In general, I believe that there is perhaps a more significant existential, that is, experiential content in philosophies that do not make such a song and dance about their experiential content and boast that they are the product of experience, but which rely more on reflection and the power of reflection than can be claimed by philosophies that make experience their subject. Such philosophies are more likely to find it impossible to shake off the marks of the contingent, of what happens to have been experienced here and now, than is the case with Kant, whose philosophy is free of such marks.

In contrast to the state of experience expressed objectively in the *Critique of Pure Reason*, we are surely justified in repeating now – at the high-water mark of our study – what we claimed at the outset, to wit, that the *Critique of Pure Reason* really is an act of *salvaging*. It is an act of salvaging in the sense that through this act of immersion in inwardness, that is, in the subject, something can be discovered of that light that shines like a beacon through this metaphysical night. You all know Kant's statement (in the *Critique of Practical Reason*), one that has long since degenerated into cliché, that there are two things that fill the mind with reverence: the starry heavens above me and the moral law within me.[11] Now, given the conclusions of the *Critique of Pure Reason*, we need not attach too much importance to this reverence. For according to Kant we cannot accept the teleological proof of the existence of God – in other words, the idea that the purposive nature of the world shows that it must have a creator – as something that has been demonstrated, as a firm piece of knowledge.[12] And as in all other matters Hegel continues the trend initiated by the Kantian critique here and cuts short the 'quantitative sublime', dismissing it as a 'spurious infinity'. To the extent that reverence towards the great is not something within us he regards it as something very feeble from the outset.[13]

Kant, too, may well not have taken the talk about the starry heavens above us as seriously as the moral law within us. I have in mind here what I consider to be the most important passage of the third great Critique, the *Critique of Judgement*, at the point in the system where we might say that the starry heavens are above us, to wit, in the Aesthetics of the Sublime, which refers exclusively to the sublime in nature. He remarked there that in reality the feeling of the sublime springs not so much from the blind, quantitative might and grandeur of nature as we chance to encounter it, as from our own faculties; that is to say, it arises from our ability to assert ourselves by virtue of the moral law, the inner light, as I have termed it somewhat theologically.[14] This element is doubtless the predominant one. Thus if we wish to speak of a salvage operation in Kant, as I have done, this must refer to the feeling of confidence that a human being, objectively forsaken and metaphysically homeless as he has become, can make himself at home provided he cuts his suit according to his cloth – to speak in a very Kantian idiom. That is to say, he must confine his activity to what he knows and what lies within his competence; he must seek the guarantee of an Absolute, the warranty of authentic truth, not as an objectivity external and alien to himself, but within himself.

This appears to me to be the meaning of this theory of duplication. If it is said that the theory of duplication is a logical nonsense – and there are weighty grounds for this – we might reply, yes, indeed, it is nonsense; but this nonsense describes what is often referred to nowadays as the *condition humaine*. This means that this nonsense is the expression of the fact that while we are indeed rational and reasonable creatures, the more rational and reasonable we become, the more convinced we become of the objective irrationality and alienation of the world.

Now, however, I would like to return to our observations on the theory of cognition. The alien nature of the world that I have tried to show you to be the core of this theory of duplication in Kant cannot be detached from the specific nature of Kant's theory of cognition itself. It is possible to analyse the mechanism of alienation and to identify it in Kant's own theory of cognition. More specifically, the increasing alienation that is implicit in the knowledge that something exists out there that we do not know, and even more in our ignorance of what it is, this alienation is only one aspect – I shall not say a consequence, since we have to be very careful with concepts like cause and effect in these highly speculative contexts – but, however we describe it, we have to say it is inseparable from reification itself. I would go on to say – and I know I am demanding a lot of you here, but it is my hope that I am revealing to you something of the mystery of the *Critique of Pure Reason* – it might be thought at first that the process of subjectivization as implemented by Kantian philosophy implies a lesser degree of reification as compared to naive realism, that is, the naive belief in the reality of objects which I confront as a receptive and thinking being. Idealist philosophies of the kind advocated by Kant and Fichte see the world much more as a process, and much less as something fixed and thing-like. The interpretation of Kant that Fichte adopted should be regarded in this light. He believed that the non-idealist view – the view that refuses to conceive of the world as something 'posited' (to use the Fichtean term) by the subject – that such a view is rigid and thing-like, and that the truly living, or, if you prefer, the truly metaphysical conception and the only one worthy of human beings is the idealist one. I believe, however, that Fichte is mistaken on this point, rigorous and persuasive as his arguments undoubtedly are.

I told you earlier about the distinction between the definition of a thing as a unified point through which something like a unified consciousness becomes a real possibility, and the definition of consciousness which makes things possible thanks to its own unity. I also tried to provide you with a few examples in which Kant seems to endorse such a distinction. I would now claim that we can interpret this in a radical way as meaning not merely that there is there no incompatibility between the subjectivization of philosophy and reification, but that reification is a function of subjectivization. In other words, the more subjectivization you have, the more reification there is. There is a reifying quality in the very attempt to relate all phenomena, everything we encounter, to a unified reference point and to subsume it under a self-identical, rigid unity, thus removing it from its dynamic context. The same reifying element may be found more generally in the tendency to ground permanent existence in the idea that the rules of thought, that is, the actual constituents of subjectivity, are themselves immutable. But I would go further. With the growth of subjectivity there is a corresponding growth of reification because thanks to this process of subjectivization the poles of knowledge are drawn further and further apart. To put it another way, the more that is inserted into the subject, the more the subject comes to constitute knowledge as such, then the more that determining factors are withdrawn from the object, and the more the two realms diverge. Instead of looking for this in Kant, you can see it much more easily in its authentic form in the philosophy of Descartes, the prototype of modern rationalist idealism. In Descartes the two substances – thought and extension – are completely separate and have only been reunited retrospectively, as it seems to us today, through a rather childish coup de main, the doctrine of the *influxus physicus*.[15]

For his part Kant certainly made efforts – as indeed did all Descartes's successors who wrestled with the problem – to overcome this crude form of reification to be found at the very origins of idealism. But I should like to say that even the towering edifice of Kant's theory of cognition has not succeeded in banishing the spectre of reification. The reason for this is that in Kantian philosophy the world, reality as a whole, is turned into a product, in fact, the product of *labour*, of effort. Thinking as a spontaneous activity – that is what we do; but it is actually nothing other than labour. The distinction between thinking and receptivity, sense impressions, is precisely that we do something, we activate ourselves. Because analysis shifts the entire weight of the dynamic, the dynamic character of reality, onto the side of the subject, our world becomes increasingly the product of labour; we might say, it becomes congealed labour. And the livelier the subject becomes, the deader the world becomes. We might talk here of the 'commodity character' of the world whose rigidity and inflexibility keeps increasing thanks to this process. Thus we have these two concepts, namely, subjectivization, the dissolving of the world into the activity of the subject, on the one hand, and the reification, objectification of the world as something contrasted with the subject, on the other. It appears to me – and this is intimately bound up with the phenomenon of reification – that these two concepts have grown in magnitude and have become quite unstoppable. Moreover, what this growth of subjectivism and reification expresses is the essential antinomy of bourgeois society in general. According to this antinomy the rationality of the world has continued to advance; human beings have increasingly made the world in their own image, and the world has become progressively theirs. At the same time, however, the world has increasingly become a world that dominates them. It is a world in which they are heteronomous beings and

with which they find it ever harder to cope. It has reached the point
where ultimately they feel as impotent as we thinking people are in
the face of a world which dominates not just us, but even all the
thoughts that we are capable of mustering by way of opposition.[16]

I have now finished what I wanted to tell you about Kant's *theory
of things*. Before going on to the other, objective basic experiences
that are at work in Kantian philosophy I would like to use the coming lecture to discuss an aspect of this process of 'salvaging' that I
have talked about today. This is so that you should not run away
with the idea that this salvaging is purely a matter of apologia or
even a reactionary tendency.

LECTURE ELEVEN

25 June 1959

'Deduction of the Categories'

I told you last time that I would say a little bit more about what I have described as Kant's salvage operation as a whole. The suspicion always arises that wherever you have salvage operations you are dealing with the vestiges of theology or dogma. This holds good whether it is a matter of salvaging ontology in general or some specific thing that is alleged to have a causal effect from beyond the realm of appearances. This can easily be seen as a theological or dogmatic residue, that is, as a reactionary impulse in the face of the overall progressive movement of consciousness. Radical critics in the tradition of the Enlightenment, with Nietzsche at their head, did in fact raise this objection to Kant. But notwithstanding this I would like to warn you about the danger of a simplistic either/or thinking that claims that apologias are reactionary and to be critical and enlightened is the mark of the progressive philosopher. It is important not to fall into the trap of thinking in ready-made slogans. I think that this is not a bad moment to say something more fundamental about the intellectual climate in general.

In the nineteenth century it was widely held that everything that sailed under the flag of idealism was positive and praiseworthy. This is an important part of the German tradition, and God knows, it was not the best or most noble German tradition. There used to be a book with the title *Upwards to Idealism*; I won't swear that the author was called Dietrich Mahnke, but I think it very likely.[1] In contrast to the idealist sheep, there were the goats, that is to say, all the tendencies that were labelled materialist, sceptical, positivist, empiricist, and so forth. It really did call to mind the joke about the ancient Teutonic tribes during the Third Reich: 'What can you tell me about the ancient Teutons? Nothing but good, sir!' As far as idealism was concerned, everything was glorious and splendid, while critical thinking was denigrated from the outset and dismissed as subversive. The legend I have already spoken to you about, namely that Kant may be said to have completed the work of the Enlightenment and simultaneously have superseded it, and other nonsense of the same kind should be seen in this context. I believe, moreover, that it was *Fichte* who originally gave the signal for this very damaging tradition in German philosophy when he wrote that the kind of philosophy a man has depends on what he is like as a human being. He went on to suggest that the idealists were the good and noble people, while the non-idealists – that is to say, those who believed in the existence of the world independently of consciousness – were wicked and depraved.[2]

Your laughter tells me that this tradition has now gone for good, although I have to say that if certain questions are asked in examinations, or if you read certain examination projects you would discover that philosophers are judged with a severity that I would never dare to apply to an examination paper. On reading such papers it is hard to avoid the suspicion that this idealist tradition has not been liquidated as thoroughly as might be supposed. But what I wanted to warn you against (and what I have in mind is a general German phenomenon) is the unmediated switch into the opposite belief. I mean the belief that everything that can be construed as positivist in the widest possible sense, everything that sticks to the facts and does away with the illusions of idealism – that all this represents the kingdom of truth, that it alone is progressive, and everything else is simply reactionary. Such attitudes have deep roots in the history of the German mind. This is not a matter I can pursue today, but I can say that it is bound up with the greatest virtues of the German tradition, and in particular with its dialectical virtues. It thus tends to move from one extreme to the other. I would almost go so far as to say that nowadays statistics is about to enter into the inheritance of the trend that once went by the name of *Upwards to Idealism*. This trend seems to me to be no less dubious than the previous one – I should now like to apply what I have been saying to Kant.

The intention to salvage or preserve that I have been endeavouring to show to you in Kant is not just a matter of an apologia for what ultimately turn out to be traditional theological beliefs. It is rather a defence of reason itself – and the more closely you look at Kant, the truer this is. We are talking about something that has deep roots in the destiny of bourgeois society; I was on the point of saying that there is a pre-established harmony between the development of society and the autonomous development of mind. By this I mean that the more reason and its dominance grows, the more that dominance is undermined; the more reason is installed as the sole authority, the more we find reason being treated with contempt. In an earlier lecture I showed you in some detail how this worked in Kant.[3] Moreover, even the features of Kant to which I have drawn your attention possess this element hostile to reason. I am referring here to the absolute unknowability of the thing-in-itself and everything related to it.

Now this anti-rational element can be linked with a tendency in society in which the principle of reason comes to prevail more and more as a principle of the formal equality of the subject, while, at the same time, reason has failed to triumph in the real world and irrational relations between human beings are still widespread. I mean this as something more than an analogy, though to explore it at length would take us too far away from our theme. The critique of reason, the general movement to which we have given the name the dialectic of Enlightenment, has not remained unaffected by this tendency. To put it another way, even seemingly progressive, critical, anti-authoritarian, subversive movements are caught up in the destiny, the historical development, of mankind in general. This means that their function in that history changes and modulates over time. In the sixteenth century Montaigne argued in favour of a particular mode of scepticism that amounted to a defence of tolerance, humanity and the elimination of cruelty.[4] A scepticism of this kind is fundamentally different from what we find on the threshold of our own age in a thinker like Pareto. Pareto simply disputed the possibility of objective truth as such. He declared that every idea was the pure expression of particular interests, and in so doing he opened the door to the blind, irrational hegemony of particular interests and thus the blind interplay of conflicting forces.[5] For this reason even the concept of scepticism, the concept of the dissolution of truth or of rationalism in the old, traditional sense, cannot simply be regarded as progressive in any straightforward way. There is something diabolical at work here that Nietzsche himself initiated, but that he also described in a very open and perceptive way. This was the idea that in the search for truth not even the categories of reason (or whatever you want to call it) could be exempted and hence they, too, should be subject to scrutiny. This meant that the concepts employed in that scrutiny, including the concept, the *objective* concept of truth and the *objective* concept of reason, were themselves increasingly undermined.

Now we should not just imagine that because Kant undertook this salvage operation, his intention was simply to produce an apologia.

His motives included the desire to resist the defeatist view of reason. In other words, even if reason is subject to change and is seen to be influenced by historical conditions, it is important to retain it as a concept that represents the sole, true authority from which all critique emanates. If you wish, you can observe this duality very clearly in Kant in the division of reason into the reason which criticizes and the reason that is criticized. On the one hand, reason is subjected to criticism entirely in the spirit of the Enlightenment and Kant marshals a whole host, indeed the entire panoply, of sceptical arguments against the dogmatic transformation of reason into an absolute. At the same time, however, because reason is criticizing itself, he retains the *idea* of reason and, with it, the idea of objective truth. You see then in Kant a hesitation, an inconsistency, if you like, a disinclination simply to follow the smooth path of progress. I detect in this a particular deliberateness and conscientiousness (the situation is comparable to his contradictory position on the definition of the thing) and I feel this to be the sign of an extraordinary seriousness. That is to say, the movement of the Enlightenment can only achieve fulfilment if its own meaning, that is, the idea of truth, is retained; and if, in the midst of the dialectical movement to which these concepts are subjected, the concepts still survive. This glorious insight is present in Kant.

I believe that for once you should refrain from scrutinizing the texts from close up, and consider them more from a certain distance. You will only understand Kant properly if you really perceive these two interlocking elements at one and the same time. By this I mean, on the one hand, the apologetic or dogmatic element which is actually an aspect of Enlightened theology, as it has been called, this element of secularized Protestantism; and on the other, the element in which Enlightenment reflects on itself and criticizes itself, through which alone it can do justice to its own concept. Thus when people just repeat the old cliché that Kant overcame the Enlightenment they are quite in error if what is meant is that he places limits on reason in order to make room for faith. However, it does contain at least one element of truth. This is that thanks to this self-reflexivity he has furnished the Enlightenment with a kind of self-consciousness. This enables it to retain a hold on its own concept, that of reason and truth, instead of abandoning the field to the hegemony of what Hegel later called the 'fury of destruction'.[6] This is the situation in which every conception of truth is dissolved so that finally nothing remains but the blind domination of merely existing being. For you should not forget the difficulty here. It is perfectly legitimate to resist ideology, to distrust it and to see in it, in ideological slogans, in idealist illusions, no more than a front created by dominant forces for them to hide behind. But as opposed to this, there is an equally grave threat to humanity lurking in the naked, supposedly ideology-free hegemony of mere facts which human beings are expected to accept supinely without being able to confront them with powerful concepts, or the truth. Kant stands precisely on the threshold, the historical threshold, at which the potential, the destructive potential of heteronomy, that is, the passive acceptance of what is merely the case, has appeared menacingly on the horizon, just as on the other side of the horizon the shadows of the old dogmatism are about to be dissipated and to disappear. I believe that the dialectical image, the historical juncture, which enables us to understand Kant is precisely the moment in which these two conflicting historical tendencies arrive at a kind of stalemate, a point at which each balances the other and enters into a highly complex configuration within his philosophy.[7] I mean this not simply as a historical reflection, but, without wishing to deny that his philosophy is historically determined, it should be seen as a comment on the truth that is in the process of crystallizing in it.

Let me go on to say more about the experiences that are articulated in the *Critique of Pure Reason*. I would like to remind you – *after* the salvage operation we have discussed – of the crucial experience that there is no truth, no being, no validity, simply nothing at all in the world that has not been filtered through subjectivity, that is, not mediated, as Hegel would say. This turn to the subject has such momentous force in Kant because he does not conceive of it as in any way detracting from the authoritative nature of truth, but instead thinks of the substantial nature of truth and of things in the world as having been imported into the subject. You may wish to raise the objection that I am exceeding my brief in going beyond Kant here. Perhaps I shall be accused of arbitrarily projecting onto Kant an element characteristic of his successors. This element is that of universal mediation by the subject – that is, the idea that consciousness cannot accept anything as true, as truly being, unless it is experienced as belonging to its 'native realm of truth', as Hegel phrases it.[8] However, I cannot accept this criticism, and I should just like briefly to remind you that I cannot accept it and *why*. In the process I should like to emphasize the realm in which everything alien to the subject makes its presence felt most strongly in the *Critique of Pure Reason*.

What I have in mind is the sphere that Kant calls the sphere of sensibility or receptivity. Perhaps I may seize the opportunity to give you a brief explanation of these two concepts so that you have a clear and unambiguous idea of what is meant. These two concepts are receptivity or sensibility and spontaneity or understanding. Imagine yourselves lying down and trying to sleep. You live on a none too quiet street and the noise from the street comes right inside your room. In that event this noise is something you cannot ward off. Thus a piece of the outside world impinges on you; you are overwhelmed by definite impressions – not just without your having to make any effort, but very much against your will. In the process your stance is purely receptive. The situation is similar with emotional impressions, and to a certain degree, with optical impressions too – although here, and I may add, in the case of intensive musical listening, it is not always so easy to draw the line as I am suggesting. It is possible to gaze at something attentively, that is, with a particular kind of intensity; and it is also possible to work intensively with your ears, that is, you can think with your ears. Kierkegaard speaks of the 'speculative ear'.[9] But if you just take the normal case,[10] you can easily imagine what is meant by sensibility as a form of receptivity. It means that the data, the given impressions that come to me through my senses, present themselves to me, initially at least, as things that come to me while I receive them relatively passively. On the other hand, you will also understand readily enough that where specific mental functions are involved, such as thought, you have to 'do' something. If you have to perform some task or other, or even if you just want to remember something, you have to concentrate; you have to work at something; you 'do' something. The moment that specific mental functions are involved we have to become active on quite a different scale. If I seem to be speaking quite uncritically here in order to clarify the point for your benefit, if I talk about us as empirical, physical human beings with ears and an individual understanding, rather than just of the transcendental subject, I can only say in my own defence that Kant does exactly the same thing. Kant, too, says *we* are influenced, *we* see, *we* hear, and so on. So if I am guilty of any error in this higher sense, then I can only say that Kant is guilty of the same offence, and I shall show you next time that this error is not simply an error because there are compelling reasons to explain why such naturalistic modes of speech cannot be avoided in the theory of cognition.

The Kantian theory, then, is that our sensibility is influenced from outside; that our sensibility has forms, to wit, space and time – I shall explain this theory to you in detail[11] – and that the impressions, the data that we receive through these forms are then processed in a specific manner by our thought. This theory also seems to assume something like an objective reality, albeit on the periphery. I am not speaking here of the assumption of a transcendent thing-in-itself, but of something far less problematical: namely, of the fact that some data or other are presented directly to our consciousness. You should recollect here the assertion I wished to explain to you to the effect that in Kant even the unmediated is mediated, even though in the form I have given it to you this assertion really comes from Hegel. For, from the point of view of a systematic logic, it will be readily comprehensible that the critical juncture for this thesis is the point where the self is least in evidence, that is to say, where philosophy simply seems to be dealing with mere givens.

You then make a very remarkable discovery. Bear in mind – and you have to think ahead here, although I am sure that this theory will be more or less familiar to you, in its broad outlines, at least – that the given realities, the immediate data of our consciousness, our 'affections', as Kant terms them, are filtered according to his theory through the intuited forms of space and time. If you now wish to speak of something unmediated, that is, to speak of pure immediacy, in other words, if you wish to speak of something in which subjectivity is not already implied, you must apply a process of subtraction – I intentionally say subtraction, not abstraction. That is, you must subtract all subjective additions from these givens, including space and time and the other determining factors provided by our categories. Once that is done, what remains would be a kind of objective or trans-subjective minimum, or what Rickert subsequently termed a 'heterogeneous continuum'.[12] This would be pure immediacy.

But if – and this in my view is the proof that there is really no pure immediacy in Kant – but if you make the attempt to cleanse something given of all of its subjective elements you will be left with something entirely amorphous. To start with: for Kant a thing can only exist in time and space because we are unable to perceive anything at all other than in the forms of time and space, the forms of our 'mind' [*Gemüt*]. It might be supposed, and we occasionally hear echoes of this in Kant, that there must be some *quality* – it is terribly difficult to find an appropriate word here – that is, there must be something that falls outside this generalizing mechanism with its all-inclusive abstractions. There must be something to represent what is given in nature, something that has not been shaped in advance, and which could then be described as a pure given. I have no wish to make this any simpler than it is; I do not want to use any shortcuts in order to make the matter seem simpler and more conclusive than it is in Kant. But something of this idea that something qualitative is a given can also be detected in the *Critique of Pure Reason*. Be that as it may, putting aside time and space, if you then set out in search of properties that can be ascribed to this given, something that can be found in our consciousness quite without any input from us, you will regularly discover that all such properties have already been defined by Kant as *categories*. For example, the concept of quality that I have just referred to is itself a category. 'Quality' appears in the 'system of principles'[13] and the idea that everything that exists has qualities is one of the principles of pure reason; it is a synthetic *a priori* judgement. It is, in other words, something that is generated by the mechanism of subjectivity, quite in the spirit of Kant. So what we are left with finally, if I may sum it up like this, is the concrete pole of Kantian philosophy, the point at which the processing mechanism, the conceptual machinery, the process of abstraction of the subject, has the least impact of all. This means that whatever is to be found on what we might term the outer skin of the subject and should therefore be closest to the absolute thing-in-itself, this *ens concretissimum*, turns out to be completely abstract, as abstract in its way as the most abstract, most general concept of all, the pure 'I think'.

Just as you cannot really say of the pure 'I think', the pure function without any content, that it has any characteristic, apart from that of being pure connection, so too you will be no less hard put to it to name any characteristic of this thing 'to which everything refers'.[14] This other pole, this thing 'to which everything refers', is in its way just as indeterminate, just as lacking in qualities, just as abstract as the opposing concept. This suggests that when Hegel describes it as absolutely nothing, as pure nothing,[15] we could almost say that his assertion is nothing more than a linguistic variation of something already implied in Kant's philosophy at this point. But if that is the case, it means that there is nothing unmediated about which we can talk in a meaningful way, nothing unmediated about which we can meaningfully raise the question of truth. This means that whenever we claim to be speaking the truth the subject must be already implied. The attempted subtraction that I mentioned to you, that is to say, the attempt to isolate something not mediated, a pure immediacy, through the analysis of consciousness is doomed to failure. Moreover, this failure is entirely in the spirit of the *Critique of Pure Reason*. For even though the idea of pure immediacy somehow haunts the book, it is simultaneously cancelled out and eliminated by the critical analysis Kant has conducted.

This brings me, I believe, to a problem that is of the very first importance in a study of Kantian philosophy. I am speaking of the question of *nominalism* and *realism* – in other words, the question of whether concepts are merely the [arbitrary] additions of thought or whether something in the concepts corresponds to something in the things, whether concepts have a basis in the thing itself. I believe that you would be well advised to convince yourselves that Kant's starting-point is that of nominalism and that in this respect he finds himself in line with the rejection of a conceptual realism that has prevailed since the end of medieval philosophy. (In what follows I shall be using the term 'realism' to describe this conceptual realism and not in the sense in which realism is opposed to idealism.) Thus for Kant concepts are the products of thought – that is what you must hold onto. The concept of synthesis, that is, the gathering together of dispersed ideas into a unity, the bundling together of scattered ideas to form a unity – this is a fundamental concept of the *Critique of Pure Reason*. This concept of synthesis is nothing but the theory of nominalism brought to the highest pitch of abstraction because it declares not merely concepts, but everything that can be meaningfully discussed, to be the consequence of mental activity. Moreover, in the criticism Kant directs at metaphysics and at the absolute validity of the supreme concepts of metaphysics, we can still hear the echo of the old nominalist criticism of universals. That criticism dismissed universals as a mere 'breath of air' and this is reiterated by Kant in the sense that he maintains that we can speak meaningfully of nothing but the elements of our experience that we then combine in a synthesis.

In this sense, then, we can say that the foundation of Kantian philosophy is still nominalist. But Kant stands on the threshold of a development in which the considerations that led to a radical nominalism begin to turn against themselves. To put it another way, let me say that the importance of Kant's attitude towards universals is that he is the first to have conceived of the relation of universals to the particulars subsumed under them as *dialectical*. I would say that he saw this relation objectively as a dialectical one, that is, the content of his theory amounts to such a dialectic. However, he himself does not perceive it in that light; a dialectical way of seeing is quite foreign to him. We may say that a dialectical approach establishes itself in the *Critique of Pure Reason* against Kant's will or behind his back. On the one hand, Kant regards the objectivity of the world, the conceptual objectivity of the world, the constitution of experience, as a question of synthesis and therefore as a subjective achievement. On the other hand, however, this subjective synthesis can only come about by virtue of a particular kind of concept that, as he puts it at one point, is 'natural' to us. The ideas – and by this he means the transcendent ideas, that is, the subject of the old ontology – are just as natural to us as the categories. And elsewhere he provides this statement with the very simple and convincing gloss – and this is what provides the systematic unity – that the ideas, namely, the idea of the world, the soul and immortality – are nothing but categories

that have become transcendent. In other words, the ideas are nothing
but categories applied beyond the realm of experience – and they force
us into this because our consciousness cannot dispense with them.

Thus you have here – and I believe that I am approaching the
innermost core of the *Critique of Pure Reason* – this very characteristic duality that I would like to describe as the mountain pass linking
nominalism and realism in Kantian philosophy. This means, on the
one hand, that in the concept of synthesis you do indeed have the
total reduction of all concepts that exist in themselves to the thinking
that produces, that generates, them. This has the consequence that
these concepts are not ideas that simply exist in themselves in the
Platonic sense; they are ideas that have been made by us. On the
other hand, our thinking is organized so that it could not exist but for
a particular arrangement of concepts that may be said to be inherent
in it. In this sense we can see that our subjectivity possesses an ontological component. This means that subjectivity, transcendental unity,
exists in connection with, in a constellation with, concepts that exist
in themselves – and that can be said to exist in themselves because
without them our thinking, our activity, could not even be imagined.[16]

From here on in you will readily understand, or so I believe, the
central theme of the *Critique of Pure Reason*. In the framework of
this very broadly conceived interpretation the central theme of the
Critique of Pure Reason is this: how are we to understand the question of nominalism and realism, that is, the relation between thought
as subjectivity and the role of the categories or concepts as something
objectively valid or absolutely necessary? The clarification of this
relation, the clarification of the objectivity disguised as subjectivity,
secreted in the innermost kernel, the nuclear core of subjectivity, is
what Kant has undertaken to resolve in the chapter of which he says
so beautifully that it is 'somewhat deeply grounded',[17] and that really
does contain the profoundest thoughts ever to have been written on
this subject.

The chapter I have in mind is the one dealing with the Deduction of the Pure Concepts of Understanding. This chapter contains a
double movement in which he shows, on the one hand, that the unity
of consciousness, that is, the pure 'I think', really does entail all the
factors that are contained in the principles in the form of categories
and that finally become the ideas that constitute the reserve realm,
the zone in which ontology survives. Conversely – and this must not
be overlooked – he shows that thinking cannot be thought without
the mediation of the concepts which help to articulate it. This means
that subjectivity necessarily presupposes these concepts, namely, the
necessity of these interconnections, as its own precondition, and that

without this kind of conceptuality there can be no such thing as subjectivity at all. Kant's attempt to ground objectivity in subjectivity culminates in the attempt to equate these two aspects, that is, subjectivity as the creative, productive element, on the one hand, and the root concepts of reason as the ultimate data of reality, lying outside the scope of any criticism, on the other.

Moreover, and I would remind you here once again of the basic objectivist thrust of the *Critique of Pure Reason*, this does not mean that objectivity is simply reduced to subjectivity (as you will generally be told in philosophy lectures). The opposite is true: the innermost core of subjectivity, its secret, is revealed as something objective, as the power of objectivity itself. I have already said that Kant puts forward the idea that nothing exists that has not been mediated, that has not been filtered through subjectivity, and that he insists on this with enormous passion. But if that is the case, the particular feature of this passion is that the point at which this objectivity reaches its zenith, where it is at its most emphatic, is the point where it appears as something subjective. This is closely bound up with what I said to you at the beginning of this lecture about Kant's salvaging intentions.

For if Kant places enormous emphasis upon the concept of objective truth and objective reason, he really does so only by virtue of that realism that we have shown to be the innermost core of his nominalism. That is to say, objectivity is the secret of subjectivity – almost in a higher sense than the opposite claim that subjectivity is the secret of objectivity. I told you that the distinction between Kant and Hume is really that of a subtle shade of meaning. But at this point, it becomes quite radical. For what separates him decisively from Hume, and from Hume's scepticism, is precisely this attempt to show that what we call objectivity is generated by subjective mechanisms that can be variously valued, as indeed they are by him and by Hume. But even more important is his assertion that a quite specific mode of objectivity is the precondition of subjectivity. The model of this objectivity, moreover, is *logical* objectivity; in other words, what is involved here is the double view of logic as something concerned both with the laws of truth and with the laws of thought to which we are subject. So much, then, by way of confirming or analysing what I told you about the mediation of everything objective through subjectivity, and simultaneously as an explanation of his method in the Deduction of the Pure Concepts of Understanding.

LECTURE TWELVE

30 June 1959

Schematism

The meaning of our deliberations last time was to show you just how far Kant has taken the idea of the subjective mediation of all knowledge; and how radically the idea of the subjectivity of the objective has progressed. The essence of our conclusions was this: the distinction between form and matter, and thus between subjective and objective elements, constitutes the dualism that is so unambiguously inscribed in the topography of Kantian philosophy; but this dualism is largely qualified and eliminated in the dynamics of his thought – if I may use this notion to contrast with that of topography or geography. We might say that, contrary to his own intention or his own argument, the concept of the given is cancelled out to all intents and purposes. It is undeniable that this creates a number of grave problems for the *Critique of Pure Reason*. I have already mentioned one such problem. This is that, as the argument of the *Critique of Pure Reason* develops, it turns out that what remains of everything independent of the subject or that comes to the subject from outside is at bottom completely null and void. This means that the distinction made in the *Critique of Pure Reason* between appearances and things-in-themselves is not to be taken all that seriously because the things-in-themselves remain no more than 'a noble feature', as Brecht phrases it in *The Threepenny Opera*.[1] In other words, they survive as a reminder that subjective knowledge is not the whole story, but they are without further consequence themselves.

This difficulty is compounded by a further one, one that I drew your attention to at the start of these lectures, if my memory serves me right.[2] This is that the concept of knowledge itself becomes problematic. This occurs because not just the forms, but with the radicalization of the concept of form, the quintessence of what is known is incorporated into the subject. We might well enquire what it means to know something if that something is completely indeterminate and if knowledge is no more than the quintessence of subjectivity, taking this expression in a fairly strong sense. This contradiction survives the translation of objectivity into subjectivity and is not explicitly addressed by Kant. Perhaps the good old things-in-themselves provided him with a sufficient consolation. It may have fulfilled the function of the *other* that knowledge ultimately refers to. The only trouble is that this consolation is of the kind we generally feel at funerals. That is to say, we assert that all our knowledge ultimately refers to the thing-in-itself, since the appearances that I constitute, that I organize, are ultimately caused by the thing-in-itself. But since the process of cognition and its content are radically separated from this absolutely unknowable things-in-themselves by a χωρισμός, a rupture, in the Platonic sense, the idea of a thing-in-itself adds nothing to my actual knowledge. This means that what I recognize as an object is just that, an object in the sense that we have discussed at length; it is *not* a thing-in-itself, and always remains something constituted by a subject. Thus the problem of knowledge as a single tautology survives intact: to oversimplify grossly, it is the problem that at bottom the subject can only know itself.[3]

I told you that this difficulty in the *Critique of Pure Reason* is not explicitly addressed, and that the failure to do this is undoubtedly connected with the duplication of the concept of the thing which we have already discussed. But it would be a vast underestimation of the power of Kant's thought – as it so often is when you think you have caught Kant out in some inconsistency or other – to imagine that the difficulty of which I have just told you had not surfaced in concrete form in the course of Kant's arguments. I told you, earlier on,[4] that for a first rough orientation the structure of the *Critique of Pure Reason* should be thought of in terms of various materials falling into a machine where they are then processed; and that what then emerges as the result of this processing is my knowledge. In reality this result amounts to an arrangement of these materials (in the broadest sense), a kind of conceptual organization, in actual fact no more than a grid, in part also an abbreviated version of the given world, and something that is external to, and has nothing in common with, what there is to be known. It was not for nothing that I advised you then that you should hold fast to this idea in order to obtain a rough and ready view of the architecture of the *Critique of Pure Reason*.

And you would do well even now to keep in your mind this rather crude distinction that amounts to the distinction between form and content. Nevertheless, to be fair to Kant you need to see that this is not the end of the story. The fact is that the *Critique of Pure Reason* also contains a completely different line of thought. This is the idea that, if knowledge is to be truly authoritative, it must adapt itself to its own material. The kind of externality characteristic of a purely classificatory type of thinking – I am speaking here of externality without any derogatory connotations – is much like the externality of the natural sciences, which have become accustomed to liberate themselves from the so-called internal nature of things that dominated the natural sciences in Bacon's day and have concentrated instead on describing the phenomena they observe with the aid of external concepts... So please do not misunderstand me here. When I speak of externality I am not appealing to the facile arrogance of the German tradition of inwardness. In Kant it is an element that has on its side the entire emotional force of the history of the modern natural sciences, with all its triumphs. All this is by the way. However, as an epistemologist, Kant did not rest content with this externality. He faced up to the problem of how, in this interplay of matter and form – that is, in the immanent presence of the knowing consciousness – matter and form could possibly have anything to do with one another. In other words, he had to confront the question of how knowledge might be able to adapt itself to what it knows. And in this problem what survives within the sphere of the immanent consciousness that Kant has marked out is, after all, the idea of synthesis, the non-tautological, that is, the idea that knowledge must know more than itself; it must do more than simply reflect the form of knowledge in general.

This curious problem makes its appearance in one of the most difficult chapters of the *Critique of Pure Reason*. I shall not give you an account of its contents now; I hope to have time to do this later on.[5] Instead, I want to put you in a position where you can understand the *function* of this especially difficult and obscure chapter, where you can understand what the point of it is – something that does not generally become clear in the usual commentaries. For if matters were really so simple – if it were simply the case that the material turned up and were then enveloped as if in a cocoon – then Kant would have had no need to reflect on the way in which these different elements were mediated. But in fact he did reflect on them. The expression of these thoughts, that is, the expression of the question of how form and matter actually come together, forms the subject matter of the chapter on the *schematism* of pure reason.[6] At this point

you must think of the schematism problem as the question of
is possible for knowledge to be not just something alien to its object
but also the truth because it adapts itself to the nature of what it is
classifying, the nature of what is immediately given.

In other words, we are talking about the connection between the
two main branches of knowledge I have told you about, to wit,
receptivity and spontaneity. How can I ascertain that these two things
are linked? The question is not: When I think about something I have
perceived, when I conceptualize it, do I organize it and subsume it
under concepts in a manner external to my percept? The question is
rather: How is it possible for the concepts I use to fit the thing they
are describing? This question is of course as old as philosophy itself,
and was first formulated as early as Plato's doctrine of the proper
division of concepts. What he called for was an arrangement in which
concepts were not just ordered in a logical system (as we would say
today), were not just part of a system of classification, but were
arranged in such a way that they corresponded to the nature of the
thing being classified. As Plato put it, they should naturally fit the
nature of the things described.[7] The question we are concerned with
here and that forced itself on Kant's attention in the Schematism
chapter is the question of a discrepancy between a category and its
object. He tried to resolve it by arguing that there was a kind of
intermediate stage between intuition and concept, a kind of model or
image. These models were models of what we are perceiving and
enable us to recognize what we perceive. Now, I do not wish at
present to go into the question of what these images are, these sche-
mata that he traces back to 'an art concealed in the depths of the
human soul';[8] it amounts to an aporetic concept that signals the
presence of a perplexity, a difficulty.[9] Instead I would like at least to
convey to you some of Kant's thoughts on the subject and explain
how they lead him to this problem, that is, to the problem of how
within the space defined entirely by the subject, the *non*-subjective,
the given, somehow contrives to make itself felt.

For example, Kant says:

> In all subsumptions of an object under a concept the representation
> of the object must be *homogeneous* with the concept; in other words,
> the concept must contain something which is represented in the object
> that is to be subsumed under it.[10]

Please take note of this: the concept must contain something that is
represented in the object; this means that the concept must in some
way be influenced by the material to be perceived. The concept may

not shape it; it may not deal with it arbitrarily, but it must be so
constituted that it somehow corresponds to it. Or, in the language
used in classical philosophy to discuss these matters: the concept
must *resemble* its object in a certain sense.[11] This requirement that
there should be homogeneity, that is, a resemblance between object
and concept, implies that Kant is aware that the separation between
these two sources of receptivity and spontaneity is somehow arbitrary.
You can explain this quite simply to yourselves when you realize that
for Kant an immediate given, that is, what you appear simply to
receive from outside, contains not just the forms of intuition, but also
thought in a certain sense – namely, synthesis: the union of disparate
elements into a definite intuition. Conversely, if a concept is to be
true and not just something arbitrary it must necessarily be influenced by the nature of the object to which it refers. Thanks to the
total separation of spontaneity and receptivity in the architecture of
the work this element of a relation between these two 'pillars of
knowledge', as Kant calls them, is utterly lost sight of – whereupon
Kant then tries to retrieve it.

> Thus the empirical concept of a *plate* is homogeneous with the pure
> geometrical concept of a *circle*. The roundness which is thought in the
> latter can be intuited in the former.[12]

This sentence is not without its difficulties, since it is not entirely
clear what is meant by *thinking* 'roundness', if roundness is not
simultaneously *intuited*. To think 'roundness' means that you can
give the equation for a circle in terms of analytical geometry, that is,
as the geometrical location of all points that are equidistant from a
given fixed point, namely, the midpoint. But in such an equation the
concept or the representation of roundness is simply not present.
Kant leaves the question open for empirical concepts, but insists on it
all the more emphatically for the categories, that is, for the highest
and most universal concepts. For these concepts, you will recollect,
are supposed to have been purified of everything intuitive. It is thanks
to this purity, to this freedom from elements that can be intuited,
that they can be said to be constitutive, that is, they are made possible by virtue of synthetic *a priori* judgements and can deliver knowledge that is absolutely necessary. In consequence it is now absolutely
impossible – as Kant is quick to point out – to backtrack on this and
suddenly to ascribe sensory qualities to them. In other words, they
bear absolutely *no resemblance* to whatever is subsumed under them.
But if that is the case – and Kant is quite frank about this even
though it goes against his own interest, or the interest of his system

– if the concepts of the understanding are really free of intuited qualities, and if the intuitions are quite free of concepts (and this freedom from concepts of even the purest intuitions is something he demonstrated with great ingenuity in the Transcendental Aesthetic),[13] then we have every right to enquire how the two can ever come together. That is to say, how are we to conceive of a situation in which there is knowledge that conforms to its object, that conforms via the concept to what is given – doing justice to the given instead of simply dictating to it brutally? This is actually the lowest point of the argument since here, despite all the subjective mediation, in fact through all the subjective mediation, whatever is not proper to the subject contrives after all to make its presence felt in the *Critique of Pure Reason*. It is in this spirit that you should understand the entire thrust of the Schematism chapter – which incidentally regards *time* as the test case of the unification of intuition and concept.

Before discussing that, however, I would like to read you the passage in Kant that comes closest to showing Kant's own awareness of this problem:

> But pure concepts of understanding being quite heterogeneous from empirical intuitions . . . can never be met with in any intuition. For no one will say that a category, such as that of causality, can be intuited through sense and is itself contained in appearance. How, then, is the *subsumption* of intuitions under pure concepts, the *application* of a category to appearances, possible? A transcendental doctrine of judgement is necessary just because of this natural and important question. We must be able to show how *pure concepts* can be applicable to appearances.[14]

Please note: they would be readily applicable if it were only a matter of creating an order. But we might then object that this application is arbitrary because there would be no *fundamentum in re*, if I may use a not entirely suitable expression from earlier philosophy; that is to say, the concepts would contain nothing that corresponds to something in the matter in hand. Kant's reply to this (aside from those models or images) is that time is the factor that organizes or schematizes the givens in our experience, that schematizes our understanding with respect to appearances and their form. The reason for this is that time is the factor that is common to both thought and intuition. This means, on the one hand, that time is a form of intuition in the sense that our own experiences are given to us in the form of a one-dimensional continuum of past, present and future, independently of all our thinking. On the other hand, our thinking, as a synthesizing process, is only conceivable as something that is enacted ιe and related to time. Time is inherent in thought and constitutive of its nature, namely of the course that it runs. In Kant's eyes the fact that time is the common element is the key to our ability to subsume appearances under the concepts of the understanding without, we should add, committing a μετάβασις εἰς ἄλλο γένος, that is to say, without mixing our categories, without adding oranges and typewriters, something we would otherwise be unable to avoid.

This, then, is the point I wished to bring to your attention, the point at which Kant attempted to solve the problem of intuition and category, and with it the problem of how the non-identical, that is, the non-subjective element within subjectivity, can make itself felt. And if we are justified in talking of Kant's *profundity*, we may say that the really profound passages in Kant are those where he keeps on probing, where he refuses to be satisfied with generalities, where he is not the Kant about whom you are asked in examinations. His profundity is to be found – and this is true of every great thinker, not just of Kant – in the way he follows where the argument leads, without regard to any preconceived goal. He may be said to externalize himself, to surrender to the demands of the matter in hand and to think against his own inclinations. The greatness or importance of a philosophy may in fact be measured by its ability to do this; and the immeasurable quality of Kant's philosophy seems to me to be situated at this very point. The fact that we can learn from the nodal points in his thought where this happens appears to me to justify the claim that in Kant we have a thinker who is far from being a mere historical monument.

However, I should not like to deviate here from the task I have set myself. This was to enquire into the motivating experience that underlies this universal subjective mediation in Kant. I would point to two factors here. Firstly, it represents the reflection in philosophy of the experience of the natural sciences. The emergence of the natural sciences made possible an unprecedented expansion of knowledge through experimentation, classification and subjective intervention. This knowledge has as its only criterion the fact that it works – and that it does so because it renounces any attempt to make any statement about the nature of things, and about what things really are. It is no great exaggeration if I say that the natural sciences combine a peculiarly defeatist attitude towards the declared goal of their enquiry with a triumphalist attitude towards what they are able to discover once they have abandoned the attempt to discover anything.

This situation in the sciences – one which has not changed to this day – is one you will find reflected in Kantian philosophy. For its claim to objectivity reflects the triumphalism of science about its

success in having taken its domination of nature to the point where
an infinite world of givens has been subjugated by the human subject,
that is, it has been shown to be of the same nature as the subject.
However, this is only possible if you renounce a persistent prejudice,
namely, the insight into the essential nature of the given world. In a
sense it could almost be said that the subjectivization of the concept
of knowledge in Kant is the corollary of the real history of the natural sciences. For the sciences can be said to have achieved a real
dominance over the world only when they renounced the attempt to
gain knowledge of anything apart from what is accessible to human
organization and human shaping. This is what enabled them to find
their way around the world of human beings and to subject an ever
greater proportion of given things and events to control by human
beings. You may say then that the twofold process of resignation and
the growth in productive energy are what constitutes the nature of
the modern natural sciences in general and that this process comes to
a knowledge of itself in Kantian philosophy. This is as much as to say
that the world of experiment is actually the positive world of the
Critique of Pure Reason and that the Aristotelian world of forms
that the sciences have shaken off is the world that has received the
coup de grâce at the hands of philosophical reflection after having
long since been dismissed by the natural sciences. Henceforth that
world of forms was to be excluded from the world of science proper.

However, in my judgement this does not exhaust the potential
of Kantian subjectivism. To understand this you need to reflect
further on Kant's practical philosophy. In addition to the factor
we have just been talking about, the reflection in philosophy of the
historical advance of the natural sciences, there is also the idea of
freedom or the idea of *maturity*. As we have seen, the Kantian theory
of cognition proclaims that the world in its objectivity is actually the
product of my subjectivity. This means that the world is not just
something that has to be accepted passively, and obeyed, but that it
is something that can be mastered by me. In other words, human
beings are the subjects of their world and not just the objects. Kant's
critique of reason would not be conceivable in the absence of this
idea of the social and political emancipation of the human subject
that has ceased to act out a submissive role towards the world and
instead has discovered in the freedom and autonomy of the subject
the principle which alone enables the world to be known. That is to
say, with the discovery of its own autonomy the subject identifies the
principle of the world as such.

For many years it has been customary to ridicule idealism and
treat it as a dead duck. This trend had its roots in the writings which

marked Scheler's conversion to a materialist phenomenology. Since
then there has been no end to the condemnations of idealism as an
anachronism. I am certain that no protestations will be needed to
persuade you that I am mindful of this critique of idealism. Indeed,
I believe I have even made some pretty authoritative contributions
towards it. But I also think that we should not take it too much for
granted since, now that the untruth of idealism has been recognized
and demonstrated over and over again, we ought also to reconsider
the untruth of idealism in the spirit of dialectics and thus to perceive
it as a particular truth. This means that while we must bluntly state
that this Kantian subjectivism cannot be sustained in its pure form,
we should nevertheless acknowledge that it proclaims crucial experiences. One of these is that of the dual relation of the natural sciences
to their object which they simultaneously dominate and retreat from.
Or again, there is the idea of freedom whose potential it proclaims.
I would almost be willing to say that idealism may be false when
understood as an abstract system, as a scheme of knowledge that
asserts itself once and for all. But I would insist that it is undoubtedly
true as the index of a specific state of the self-consciousness of spirit
and at the same time as a mediated stage in the history of thought,
that is to say, one that does not naively oppose itself to reality, a type
of thought that had no precedent.

I should certainly like to underline the fact that no philosophy
which does not possess these mediations can claim to have moved
beyond Kantianism and idealism. This remains true regardless of
whether philosophies that imagine they have been cured of idealism call themselves an 'ontology' or 'dialectical materialism'. Rather,
all such philosophies regress to a more primitive stage. To echo
Feuerbach's saying, the challenge is not to be *against* idealism, but
to rise *above* it.[15] This means that the themes of idealism should
be integrated into theory, but without their being given the status
of absolutes. On the other hand, when we consider these experiences we realize that the claims of idealism cannot be sustained
and that they lead to conceptual difficulties at every turn. We must
therefore ask ourselves how that can be possible. How can a consciousness that, as I have tried to show, has so much about it that is
right nevertheless end up being wrong? My answer would be that
there is a sense in which the Kantian theory of cognition anticipates a
specific goal and does so in a mistaken fashion. Kant explicitly defined the ideas of freedom and autonomy as postulates, as regulative
ideas, and did not include them among the constituents of knowledge. On the other hand, it is obvious – and is implied in the structure
of the *Critique of Pure Reason* – that they impinge on the Kantian

system at every turn. Thus they cannot be disentangled from these issues.

What this means is that there is a sense in which Kantian philo- sophy strives to define the world as it ought to be – much as was once said in a classical τόπος that Sophocles depicted people as they ought to be while Euripides showed them as they really are.[16] We might well say that the element of ideology in Kant's philosophy can be pinpointed in the idea that as an object of knowledge the world appears as a human world, as *our* world, on a plane where that is not actually true. Precisely because it is not true (we might say), because we are still heteronomous, because we live in unfreedom, the *Critique of Pure Reason* presents us with a highly dubious mirror image, a kind of complementary ideology. By that I mean that the world upon which we may be said to depend appears to us – by virtue of a mechanism I cannot discuss in detail now – as if we were its masters. If in truth we are captives in this world, blindly dependent upon it and largely incapable of doing anything about it, this is reflected in theoretical philosophy as if we were the captives of our own selves.

From this vantage-point you can understand the comments I made at the outset about the element of tautology in Kantian philosophy. For this tautology is nothing other than the expression of captivity: as knowing subjects we know only ourselves. In this sense we are never able to get outside ourselves; we are imprisoned within ourselves. This, too, has its profound truth in Kantian philosophy because it means that the world in which we are captive is in fact a self-made world: it is the world of exchange, the world of commodities, the world of reified human relations that confront us, presenting us with a façade of objectivity, a second nature. This likewise is conveyed by that curiously tautological conception of the *Critique of Pure Reason*, but it is not given its proper name. For it to be given its true name this philosophy would have to cease being what it essentially is – an idealist philosophy. The world is all the more alien to us – we might say – the more it crowds in on us: this relationship that we register daily in our own bodies is similarly registered in the dualism and idealism of Kant's philosophy. It is my belief that it is only when you perceive this idealism in all its implications and ramifications that you will be able to avoid the idiotic choice of either embracing a philosophy that is unacceptable in this form or else of seizing the opportunity to gloat over its defects. What you must do instead is appreciate its truth content as one that contains its own untruth.

LECTURE THIRTEEN

2 July 1959

Constituens and *Constitutum* (I)

In the last few lectures we have been preoccupied with the problem of subject and object, and specifically with the problem of the subject-ive mediation of objectivity in Kantian philosophy. The situation we have now arrived at is one in which the concept of a knowable object has been eliminated, while on the other hand Kant wishes to escape from the idea that our knowledge is no more than a mere duplication of the subject. You will now wish to know what criteria he uses in the definition of objectivity. I believe I have already told you some-thing of these criteria (at the very beginning, when I was discussing the concept of synthetic *a priori* judgements) – or at least, I gave them to you in the form in which they are to be found in Kant.[1] However, I think we have now reached the point where we need to consider these criteria a little more closely, particularly since, if I understand the situation rightly, this leads us to the heart of one of the central problems of the *Critique of Pure Reason*, one that we have not really discussed as thoroughly as it deserves. I am talking about the problem of *constituens* and *constitutum*. To give you the keywords: the criteria Kant gives for synthetic *a priori* judgements and thus for genuine, valid knowledge with a substantive content, are the concepts of necessity and universality, universality and neces-sity. Now if you look these terms up in the *Critique of Pure Reason* to see how they are defined you will be sure to be disappointed. The fact is that you will not find all that much said about these concepts; Kant does not discuss at length what is meant by universality and necessity. To anticipate my general thesis about these terms, let me begin by saying that they illustrate in exemplary fashion what I have already said about the 'externality' of Kant's concept of knowledge, although I would ask you not to misunderstand me on this point. What I mean is that by knowledge he thinks of the ordering and classifying of something, subsuming it under laws and rules, without its ever being made explicit what this something is.

As far as the concept of *necessity* is concerned, the first criterion of absolutely valid knowledge in Kant, I would ask you to look in the chapter on the Systematic Representation of all the Synthetic Principles of Pure Understanding, that is to say, the point where the synthetic judgements are inferred from the Deduction of the Pure Concepts of Understanding, and following on from the Postulates of Empirical Thought. We learn there that this concept of necessity is thought of exclusively as coming within the parameters of the law of causality. Every other concept – for example, that of a necessity of thought or necessity as an internal motive, or as a necessity that follows from the nature of a thing – every other concept is actually excluded by Kant from his idea of necessity as something that acts as a guarantee of knowledge. Here is the relevant passage:

> Necessity concerns only the relations of appearances in conformity with the dynamical law of causality and the possibility grounded upon it of inferring *a priori* from a given existence (a cause) to another existence (the effect).[2]

In other words, then, that externality of which I have told you holds good even for the concept that is most powerfully opposed to it in the philosophical tradition in general, namely, the concept of necessity. For if we regard something as necessary we doubtless *also* have causality in mind, but when we reflect on it we really always think of something *more*. Thus when we say that crises are a necessary part of the capitalist system, we do not really mean to say that a specific causal sequence at particular points necessarily leads to the symptoms of crisis. What we mean is that the system as such, with its mutually conditioned growth of wealth and poverty, necessarily contains the idea of recurrent crises *in its actual concept*. That this externality is really involved here emerges with even greater clarity from a passage in the first version of the Deduction of the Pure Concepts of Understanding:

> Thus the concept of a cause is nothing but a synthesis (of that which follows in the time-series, with other appearances) *according to concepts*; and without such unity, which has its *a priori* rule, and which

subjects the appearances to itself, no thoroughgoing, universal, and therefore necessary, unity of consciousness would be met with in the manifold of perceptions.[3]

I have already told you about the peculiar ambiguity of the unity of consciousness[4] and I would draw your attention to the fact that here, once again, it is to be taken in its objective sense; that is to say, Kant speaks of the unity of consciousness in appearances, in the 'manifold of perceptions'. In other words, the unity of consciousness is not just something in me, but is always and at the same time present in the experiences concerned, because the experiences, the appearances, are in truth always only *mine*, that is, they are mediated through me. But that is by the by and I mention it because the passage very strikingly documents once again the ambiguity of the central concept of unity in the manifold and because I attach the very greatest importance to this point where subjectivity and objectivity meet in Kant. But what we should be focusing on here is something else. This is that because of the nature of our thought we can do no other than subject success-ive events to such a rule. But our thoughts are incapable of telling us anything about what might be called the internal interconnections linking these events that succeed one another in time, aside from the form of our act of subsumption. You see here with great clarity the sense in which the subjectively constituted objectivity Kant intends is really no more than an epiphenomenon, something imposed and external to the things themselves (as I have already explained in gen-eral terms).

The classical definitions of causality can be understood entirely in the spirit of these remarks. These definitions have played a major role in all the discussions about the nature of science and I only repeat them here to make sure that you really understand this Kantian con-cept of causality.

> Let us take, for instance, the concept of cause, which signifies a special kind of synthesis, whereby upon something, A, there is posited some-thing quite different, B, according to a rule. It is not manifest *a priori* why appearances should contain anything of this kind.

In other words, he is not looking into the different elements that are connected by causality – it is in this strict sense that we must speak of the *externality* of causality. For 'experiences cannot be cited in its proof, for what has to be established is the objective validity of this *a priori* concept'. Thus once again he makes a virtue of a necessity; on top of that the fact that no internal motivation can be discovered in appearances is then credited to the objectivity of the concept of causality – as is generally his practice. This is because he says, well, if this necessity arose simply from the appearances, from the given in its constantly changing nature, then it all might be different. But because it is located in the *a priori* conditions of our knowledge it simply cannot be any different; it is absolutely necessary. That is to say, the very externality, the very factor in which this classical idealist concept of causality is deficient with regard to its object, is what enables Kant to make its particular claim to objectivity. This provides backing for my thesis that in Kant the concept of objectivity is chained to the predominant power of subjectivity. For this reason it is not evident *a priori* 'why appearances should contain anything of this kind . . ., and it is therefore *a priori* doubtful whether such a concept be not perhaps altogether empty, and have no object anywhere among appearances'.[5] The criticism he makes here is the same criticism as *Hume* makes of the traditional concept of causality[6] and it is one that he appropriates here to an astounding degree.

There are few passages in the *Critique of Pure Reason* that sound as Humean as this one. But he goes on to pull himself out of the quagmire by his own hair, by inferring the objective validity of thought from the very fact that it is structured the way it is and that it is subject to this rule. In a further passage about the concept of causality – and this is the proper definition of causality in Kant – he asserts: 'For this concept [of causality] makes strict demand that something, A, should be such that something else, B, follows from it *necessarily and in accordance with an absolutely universal rule.*'[7] If you examine this statement closely you will notice a certain circularity. For you will recollect the other argument that I read out to you according to which the concept of necessity was said to be meaningful only in so far as it related to causality – and now we find causality defined in terms of necessity! I do not want to make a meal of this; all the less as the two statements arise from different versions of the *Critique* and we may probably assume that Kant regarded the second one as definitive.[8] However that may be, we are no doubt entitled to conclude that having once defined necessity in terms of causality and nothing else, and having defined causality as a regularity, namely a lawful progression in the nature of consciousness that brings together successive phenomena, that is to say, a form of synthesis – causality in Kant must be understood in terms of this synthesis and not in terms of something inherent in objects themselves.[9]

We might almost say that these two concepts – necessity and universality (which I shall discuss in a moment) – share this peculiar character of a subsumption along two axes. Causality can be placed along the vertical axis, that is, in the dimension conceptualizing the progression of events in time. For its part the concept of universality does not express a temporal progression, but defines an object universally in terms of simultaneity. If you wish to know what Kant means by *universality* in the *Critique of Pure Reason*, you will discover even less. All you will find is the mention of it in the discussion of *a priori* judgements, where it is listed as the second criterion of absolutely valid knowledge. That is to say, for a universal proposition to be *absolutely* universal it must not arise from experience because there might always be a further experience that would contradict the previous assertion. Basically it is a matter of the traditional critique of induction, of inductive statements, on the grounds that any universal proposition based on experience only applies to the phenomena or observations that have been experienced because we can never be certain that such a proposition will not be refuted by a subsequent observation. But since, on the other hand, Kant does not wish to jettison the concept of universality, he inserts it into the nature of knowledge as such without elucidating it any further. Such an elucidation would not be difficult to supply, however. The model that the Kantian concept of universality evidently follows is that of the formation of concepts in general. Thus what Kant means by universality is simply that taken as conceptual units all the individual elements that contain the characteristics defined in the concept are to be included in that concept.

I believe that a cursory glance at this question of the formation of concepts, a matter that is generally ascribed to formal logic, will suffice to enable us to understand the external nature of a process of conceptualization that is orientated towards universality. For this concept is constituted in terms of what we call extensional logic, that is to say, it defines the scope of the elements contained in it [while excluding meanings]. Thus a concept only arises through a process of arbitrary classification in which we isolate *one* feature of all the available ones and base the definition on that feature which is then supposed to fix the concept. But it is this arbitrary element, the arbitrary selection of a particular feature, instead of focusing on the thing itself, that pinpoints the element of externality that basically fails to achieve what we mean when we say that we have the 'concept of a thing'. This idea is something that Kant no longer understands; what we generally find in him in the theory of cognition is the subsumption of things under rules, on the one hand, or under the concepts of extensional logic, on the other, instead of a comprehension of the thing itself. If you wish to gain an understanding of the conjuncture at which his successors parted company with him, then you have the reason for it at precisely this point. To put it quite simply, it is that the philosophical concept as it appears in Kant is not seriously intended to be the concept of a thing, but merely something more or less imposed on the thing from outside by the subject. I believe that what I set out to tell you about the element of externality in the Kantian concept of knowledge – together with the reference, by way of correcting that, to problems of which the problem of schematism was an example – has now been satisfied by my showing you how it actually works out in the *Critique of Pure Reason* in the definition of its true object, namely the synthetic *a priori* judgements. And the conclusion is that the criteria of truth – namely, necessity and universality – are in reality no criteria at all of the truth about comprehending a thing, but only criteria of their *correctness*, that is to say, of whether we have acted correctly in the way that we have dealt with these objects, the way we have handled them.

The universality of which I have told you can be described as the universality of *subjective reason*, a universality generated simply by the constitution of the human subject that comprehends things in this way and no other. It stands in stark contrast to the objective concept of reason such as can be found with exemplary force in traditional philosophy in the thought of Plato. For Plato ascribes a rationality to things themselves; he ascribes a λόγος to things themselves, the putative objects of cognition. He then regards the task of knowledge as that of comprehending the λόγος in the things themselves. He does not see it as his task to subsume the thing or things under the rules or concepts of knowledge. However, if you now enquire more closely into the nature of this universality, you come across an interesting ambiguity, one that is not made explicit in the *Critique of Pure Reason*, but which is implied in the concept of universality itself. On the one hand, universal judgements must be universal in the sense that they are absolutely valid for all future experience. Kant justifies this by claiming that the mind is structured so that it is incapable of thinking in the absence of such universality – a claim, incidentally, that can be conceded, since without concepts, without abstraction, that is, without the mechanisms that he ascribes to universality, thinking is in fact not possible; in this respect he has seen quite correctly that synthesis is not possible; we really would be faced with 'blind intuition', as he calls it,[10] that is to say, with non-conceptualized givens, from which concepts were absent and on which no light could be thrown. But aside from this meaning – which you will certainly not underestimate after what I have told you – the concept of universality contains a further element. This is something that comes very close to the concept of consensus, the agreement of all human beings.

If Kant heard me speaking like that he would make the sign of the cross, and it goes without saying that in the form in which I have stated it there is nothing remotely like this anywhere in the *Critique of Pure Reason*. If we were in a seminar now I would be minded to ask you why Kant should be so horrified by the idea. After all that we have said here I believe that you could all give me the answer. This is that, if this universality were made to depend on the consensus of all human subjects, this universality would be an empirical fact. It would depend therefore on the nature of these empirical individuals who would have to agree on it. And something merely empirical and dependent on chance cannot constitute valid, objective knowledge as Kant requires of universality. You can see here that the point I am leading up to is closely related to the question of *constituens* and *constitutum*. Notwithstanding all that, this concept of objectivity only makes sense if in fact it includes a consensus. The entire question of this universality and necessity, too, for that matter, would lack substance unless all subjects endowed with reason, *all human beings* – as Kant would insist at this point – must think in this way, and unless there is a connection between the empirical nature of their minds and the mechanism of universality that is supposed to be grounded in reason. Only if all human beings must think in this way will a proposition be truly universal. What we might call this anthropological element is therefore implicit here.

The huge difficulties we face here are evident and I would like to turn to them now. Suppose for a moment that the idea that universality should be a universality for all mankind is part of its very concept. This would then imply something to the effect – and I would ask you not to misunderstand me here – that the subject that underlies this is a *social* subject and not just an empirical one. This means that the forms we are considering here are not the forms we perceive in the analysis of every given consciousness; it is rather the case that the forms have their universality in the fact that they are the forms of all conscious persons (if I may put it like this) and that compared to them the individual consciousness is of secondary importance. Thus in this philosophy the individual consciousness stands opposed to the social consciousness in the same ratio as the relatively accidental and particular stands opposed to necessity and its laws, to the universal which operates in accordance with rules. In the *Critique of Pure Reason* Kant made the sustained attempt to make a very clear distinction between the subject that he made the focus of his analysis and the empirical subject. He arrived at this abstract subject, as is the case with every concept, by abstracting from a multiplicity of individual subjects. We might then say that I cannot meaningfully talk about the transcendental subject or what he calls in the *Prolegomena* 'consciousness as such', if I insist on discussing just one single consciousness. For the single consciousness will never yield more than what is in it, and there is no direct evidence to support the idea that what we say about it possesses universality. Instead I have to proceed from the assumption of a multiplicity of egos, a multiplicity of 'consciousnesses'. I would then have to compare them and leave out everything about them that is merely contingent, that is, everything that attaches to them from outside, psychologically or through some chance. In short, I would have to strip them down until I arrived at the skeleton that is universal.

It will at once be objected – Kant too would have joined in the protest – that this is a misunderstanding because the transcendental subject is what makes possible the multiplicity of individual, empirical human subjects. It is precisely at this point that we encounter the difficulty and that we see that this is one of the problems in which the dialectic is grounded in Kant's philosophy. For how can I feel justified in talking about such a universality if my starting-point is simply the individual subject? I have already said as much to you. But on the other hand, if my starting-point is a multiplicity rather than the connections between what is immediately given in each specific, individual consciousness – then do I not just presuppose the very thing I had set out to prove, namely, something like a subjective world? Do I not simply presuppose for the entire argument the thing that has to be constituted – society and with it an empirical reality? Kant has shown great wisdom in leaving this question unresolved. In the later version, the second version, of the *Critique of Pure Reason* there are two passages where the question is raised explicitly, namely in the Transcendental Deduction and the chapter on the paralogisms, the psychological paralogisms, that is to say, the fallacies that lead to the assumption of the substantiality of the soul. In both cases Kant took the side of transcendental logic in contrast to that curious transcendental conception that is supposed to represent a third way between the alternatives of logic and psychology, a third way that in reality is the true speculative sphere.[11]

No doubt we may justifiably claim that a concept like 'we', society, is a 'naturalistic' concept when measured against the criteria of the *Critique of Pure Reason*.[12] People who wish to criticize our dialectical attempts to operate with the concept of society as a constitutive concept of epistemology[13] really never have more than the one argument. This is that our efforts are illegitimate because philosophy has absolute priority over all social considerations and that, on the contrary, such social questions have first to be grounded in the theory

of knowledge. In consequence, so the argument goes, philosophy
would relapse into pre-philosophical scepticism if it were to start
talking about society. I believe that this is a vital issue, not only for
the *Critique of Pure Reason* but for philosophy as such, so much so
that I owe it to you to discuss it at somewhat greater length. The idea
of subjectivity in general, that is to say, of a theory of the forms of
consciousness, cannot be conceived of without consciousness itself.
As we have seen, Kant says repeatedly that concepts without intuitions
are empty; and he criticizes the ontological proof of the existence of
God by saying that the pure concept of a thing, regardless of what
properties are ascribed to it, does not permit us to infer anything
about its existence.[14] When he makes these criticisms, we ought really
to apply his arguments to the idea of the transcendental subject, that
is, to the forms of thought as such. This amounts to saying that the
idea of subjectivity cannot be comprehended in the absence of the
consciousness from which it has been separated by the process of
abstraction. It is a fundamental tenet, one that is constantly reiterated
in idealism, in particular by Fichte, who makes the claim explicitly
and with great feeling, that whatever has been abstracted from a
thing – we are talking here of the concept of pure thought or an
absolute subject, as it was called by the later idealists – has absolutely
nothing in common with the thing from which it has been abstracted.
Now it seems to me that this inference, too, is just as much of a
fallacy, a μετάβασις. To follow Kant's terminology we would have to
say that it is just as much an amphiboly of the concepts of reflection
as any of the amphibolies that Kant had criticized. That is to say,
what is at stake here is the idea that a concept of reflection – that is,
a concept that is abstracted from something given by a process of
thought, but which retains a link to that given – is subsequently
treated as if it had absolutely nothing to do with the thing to which it
referred.
    It is important here to make a distinction between the logical
validity of abstractions – which are by their nature free of the individual elements on which the abstractions are based – and what I
might call the transcendental validity of abstractions. That is to say,
whether such supreme abstract concepts are valid in themselves without the necessity for the assumptions on which they are based to be
imported into them once again; in other words, whether at this point
where Kant's philosophy is at pains to eliminate the *constituens*
through criticism, at this innermost point of the *constituens*, it comes
across the very thing that it calls the *constitutum*. What Kant has in
mind here – and we have to say that Kant is not terribly clear on this
issue – is the pure 'I think' and this cannot be distinguished clearly

from the 'I' as actual fact. This becomes evident when we perceive the failure of all attempts to define this 'I think' in its purity, and to steer clear of subjective expressions. You will find it impossible to imagine this 'I think', this ultimately constitutive problem in Kant, without some sort of 'I', however constituted. But the moment you start to talk of an 'I' that 'thinks' you may indeed imagine it as something that is not fully corporeal or existing in time and space. Nevertheless, in order to obtain any grasp of it at all you have to include something of what comes to mind when you think it; without that it would make no sense at all. That is to say: it depends on factual existence; the ontological stands in need of the ontic just as much as, conversely – if we go along with the arguments of Kant and indeed of idealism in general – the ontic stands in need of the ontological. If you completely detach this 'I think', that is, the pure transcendental subject, from the 'I' as actual fact, then not only does all talk of an 'I' lose all its meaning but it also becomes impossible to imagine what Kant means by 'context of consciousness' or 'synthesis' or 'memory' or 'reproduction'. All these categories that we encounter in Kant would lose their entire meaning. If you separate the *constituens* – that is, the pure consciousness through which the actual world comes into being – from the *constitutum* – that is, the world in its broadest sense – then the former, the *constituens*, cannot even be imagined without the *constitutum* being imagined simultaneously.[15] This point, too, was taken up in criticism of Kant by the later idealists. Only they solved the problem by means of a *coup de main*, by inventing a sort of super-ego – this trend starts with Fichte – a monstrous, gigantic, absolute subject which encompasses both these concepts – *constituens* and *constitutum*.

According to Kant himself, it is a mistake to hypostatize what results from the process of abstraction; yet he is guilty of this very thing in the case of the 'I think'. On the other hand, however, the empirical self is constituted in its own right. The soul, too, may be thought of as a 'thing', for example, in the sense that it is subject to causality. That is to say, with the aid of psychology we can establish to which laws of cause and effect our so-called psychic lives are subject, what causal dependencies may be said to govern our drives and suchlike matters. Modern psychology has made great strides in the direction of the causal analysis of the empirical subject. This contradiction that I have alerted you to amounts to saying that, on the one hand, every *constitutum* calls for a *constituens* because, as we have seen in the last few lectures, mediation is involved in everything. Conversely, however, the *constituens* stands in need of a *constitutum* because without one to refer to even the most abstract

and elementary forms cannot be imagined. This contradiction is one
that cannot be resolved by philosophy; it must instead be comprehended in its truth. If there is a point at which the transition to a
dialectical conception of philosophy is compelling, this would seem
to me to be the place to start. There is no empirical self without the
concept, without those elements not reducible to mere existence and
objectivity. On the other hand, there is no concept, that is, no such
pure 'I' that could not somehow be reduced to an empirical self. Both
of these are present in Hegel.

The decisive idea that you must grasp and that I would like to
convey to you today is this: I do not wish to leave you with the idea
that the true *constituens* is not spirit, transcendental subject, but is
instead something empirical – namely, society. Such an assumption
would be just as misguided as the assumptions made by idealism. I
believe that the misunderstandings to which we are exposed again
and again in teaching philosophy lie precisely at this point. What you
should learn here, and what I hope to have gone some way towards
persuading you of, is nothing other than that this question of an
absolute first principle is itself mistaken. There is in short neither a
constituens nor a *constitutum*, but instead these two elements mutually produce one another in a way that can be determined but not so
that the one can be reduced to the other. Moreover, the ψεῦδος, the
untruth, of the philosophical tradition – that is to say, the aspects of
that tradition that philosophy needs to rethink radically – is located
in this search for the ideal of an absolute first principle. And we
should take note that to give society absolute primacy and hypostatize
that is just as much an act of naturalistic hypostatization as to give
absolute priority to the spirit.

Next time we shall have to discuss the structure assigned to the
concept 'we' in Kantian philosophy. I would only add now that we
have been discussing this entire problem more or less without too
much reference to Kant, but that it makes itself felt in his constant
use of the word 'we' of which, strictly speaking, he ought not to avail
himself.

LECTURE FOURTEEN

7 July 1959

Constituens and *Constitutum* (II)

It seems to me that last time I was a little bit hasty and casual in my treatment of an idea that is in fact of central importance for the *Critique of Pure Reason*.[1] Moreover, I did not display enough of the gift of sympathetic exposition which, admittedly, Kant confessed that he did not possess either.[2] However, Kant's confession is but a poor consolation and for that reason I believe that I owe it to you to provide a further description of at least the fundamental ideas in the hope that you will be able to understand them – simply because I believe that they provide the key to our efforts here in general. However, since it is not my habit to repeat a lecture, I would like to structure the arguments rather differently from last time, and this may have the advantage that those of you who did after all derive some benefit from my none-too-well organized account will not be too bored on this occasion. Thus my starting-point now is a fact to which philosophers have often taken exception and which has been a focus of criticism in discussions of the *Critique of Pure Reason*. This is Kant's use of the word 'we', which constantly recurs whenever he talks about the faculty of cognition. I believe that you will have no difficulty in understanding the problem, for, as you know, the task the *Critique of Pure Reason* has set itself is to ground, or as Kant writes, to 'constitute', experience, and with it the construction of an objective world.

However, if I now speak of 'we', this obviously refers to something that is already constituted; that is to say, the faculty of cognition we are discussing here is tacitly ascribed to already-existing,

actual, real, human subjects, individual persons. It may be said, therefore, that Kant has already anticipated, has already presupposed, the
very thing that ought to emerge from the *Critique of Pure Reason*.
We might wish to pass over this by assuring ourselves that this use of
'we' is no more than a linguistic slip, but this would be a vain consolation. For at such a crucial point, one which is of pivotal importance
for the structure, the innermost core, of the *Critique*, one to which,
as we have already remarked, the entire work is attached,[3] it would
be reasonable to expect Kant to have chosen his words with extreme
care. Such an expectation would not be excessive. Moreover, the
moment you attempt to replace this 'we' with something more precise, you will discover that this is no easy task; I would even go so far
as to say that it is impossible. For the moment you start to use such
expressions as 'the transcendental subject' or 'the subject as such' or
whatever, you will see that you have uncovered a mare's nest by way
of explanations and reservations that are otherwise absent from the
Critique of Pure Reason. Such a confusion would create scope for
a host of conflicting interpretations. But the greatest difficulty of all –
to come right to the point – lies in the fact that we cannot eliminate
this 'we' – or, on occasion, this 'I' – because all the concepts that
actually make comprehensible the transcendental, that is, the sphere
of the *constituens*, the sphere through which experience is made
possible – because all these concepts designed to explain the transcendental sphere refer back to something like an 'I', to personal
consciousness.

I believe, therefore, that it is better not to allow ourselves to be
fobbed off with the paltry consolation that Kant, like Homer, occasionally nods off and that his use of the word 'we' should not be
taken too seriously. Instead, we should try to clarify for ourselves
what is implied by this Kantian 'we'. What strikes us first about that
is what formed the subject of the last lecture, namely the concept
of universality. That is to say, he commonly says 'we', generally in
preference to 'I'. He uses 'I' mainly when giving specific examples,
such as the famous analogy of the thalers, but not in the course
of discussions of principle. Now, when he talks of 'we' he means
something universal, not the empirical individual but something prior
to empirical individuals. The fact that he does this is something on
which a certain evidence, a certain insight can be based. This concept
of the 'we' is simply the thing that underpins thought: it is what
thinks. At bottom, it is nothing but the self-reflecting, critically
reflected *res cogitans*, Descartes's thinking substance. If you reflect for
a moment upon what takes place in the process you would call thinking, you will find – at least in the models that underlie the *Critique*

of Pure Reason, that is, in the propositions of pure mathematics in the first instance – that you are not essentially involved in it as an empirical person. Whereas the thing that thinks is underpinned by each and every one of us and presupposes as a possibility the existence of individuals – we are unable to conceive of any other kind of thinking – in its objective content it is not tied in any obvious way to you and me, or to any individual. Initially, at least, we do not appear to participate in any comparatively universal totality, that is to say, we do not enquire into the judgements or mental processes or conclusions (or whatever) of other people. The 'I' that thinks, thinks – if it thinks in the strong sense of the word – not as a private individual but as the executor of a thought content. I should like to remind you of the idea that I have already referred to a number of times and which really is of central importance for the question of philosophical systems, for the proper grounding of the theory of knowledge. This is that when we utter a judgement, a synthesizing judgement, this synthesis is not simply something imposed on us arbitrarily by things external to us. Rather, 2 + 2 must actually *be* 4 in order for us to be able to express the judgement 2 + 2 = 4. For without that synthesis the proposition 2 + 2 = 4 could not even *be thought*. This element of reconstruction, of adapting ourselves to something that is the case, but which is only the case (I should almost want to say) because we adapt ourselves to it, is what defines the specific nature of the act of thinking. This experience is what is meant when people speak of the universality that is ascribed to Kant's synthetic *a priori* judgements and that are expressed in this 'we'.

At the same time, however, if we take it seriously enough to credit it with programmatic importance, the expression 'we' refers to a plurality of persons. That is to say, this plural is meaningless if by this 'we' we do *not* mean a plurality of individuals, if it does *not* refer to such a plurality of individuals. Logically, there can only be a plural, the linguistic expression for plurality, if there is also an expression for singularity. Plurality is in general only meaningful as a synthesis of singularities. Unless I can conceive of an individual, an 'I', however constituted, all the talk of 'we' makes no sense. Now, if you quickly confront this idea with what we spoke of previously, you will realize that faced with the mere individual, the singular, individual consciousness to which this 'we' implicitly refers, Kant only speaks in the plural as if to redeem the individuated consciousness from its arbitrary nature; to relate it to the element of universality of which we have been speaking. But only where a distinction is made between a plurality and a singularity, a plurality of subjects and an individual subject, can such a thing as a plural be said to exist. This has far-reaching implications not just for the argument we are concerned with here, but for the *Critique of Pure Reason* as a whole. For it means that if the factors or conditions relating to the transcendental, to the possibility of synthetic *a priori* judgements, are to be meaningfully possible, there has to be such a personal singularity, that is, a coherent, monadological consciousness in the sense of the Kantian critique.

In short, without an 'I', an 'I' moreover that is thoroughly individuated, there can be no such thing as the 'I think' that accompanies all my representations. This corresponds to the development of the argument of the *Critique of Pure Reason*, in particular the chapter on the Deduction of the Pure Concepts of Understanding. We are saying, then, that the unity on the side of subjectivity is the possibility of combining all my ideas. This unity, which Kant claims is the only guarantee of objectivity, is the unity of personal consciousness. What Kant understands by this combinatory process, this mechanism of synthesis, that is, the mechanism involved in combining both simultaneous and successive ideas, is possible only in the context of an individuated or, as we would say, a personal consciousness. Thus an individual consciousness is constitutive of the concept of the transcendental and hence for the concept of the constitutive factor itself. In the *Critique of Pure Reason* the constitutive factor is itself constituted by such a unified, individuated, individual consciousness.

The question we are discussing here has obviously always been one that the philosophical tradition has been highly conscious of and has repeatedly debated. In the idealist tradition that followed Kant, which may also be called the tradition of conceptual realism, what I have just been saying has generally encountered the objection that we are just talking here about the form of personality. In other words, the universal element that I have described to you as being characteristic of thought, this 'it' that thinks, occurs only in the form of a single, individuated consciousness. However, in its substance, its actual content, it is still independent and hence not tied to the individual, the particular. There is something in this, and it is quite certain that Kant himself intended something of the sort. We are saying that just as we cannot dismiss the idea that synthesis points to personal consciousness, so too we cannot dismiss the idea that in the *Critique of Pure Reason* this personality is conceived as a form that points to plurality, universality. The synthesizing process can only thrive in the form of individuality; but the validity of this synthesis is independent of this individuation. The judgements that he calls synthetic *a priori* judgements are never intended as merely individual judgements. But

I believe that in making this concession we should take care not to make things too easy for ourselves. We may not take the easy route of saying, well, we live in an individualistic society and the universal that resides in thought, in the λόγος, only actualizes itself in single individuals, but intrinsically it has nothing to do with these individuals and with individuation. To say this would be to gloss over the problem. I believe that some of Kant's successors, Fichte in particular, were really too superficial at this very point where they thought they were being especially deep in their attempts to evade factuality, the specific nature of individuality. This came about because they underestimated the profundity of the interconnections between the *principium individuationis* that furnishes the possibility of synthesis, on the one hand, and the objectivity of truth, on the other, and they failed to reflect sufficiently on that relationship.

What I want to say is that it is true that in the *Critique of Pure Reason* Kant reflects only on the *form* of an individual consciousness; that is to say, on the most general facts concerning such an individual consciousness. For example, he reflects on the fact that all the experiences that form part of an individual consciousness have some characteristic in common, namely that they are the experiences, the contents of the consciousness, of this specific individual (and cannot be replaced by those of any other individual, since that would instantly invalidate the process of synthesis). Or again, he has in mind facts which are universal, but tied to the individual, facts such as memory, the reproduction of the imagination which (as I have already mentioned) represent the core of Kant's argument about the transcendental. But even if we must concede that we are not dealing here with the specific experiences of specific, individual persons, but with universal constituents of the individual, we must nevertheless add that these universal forms would have no meaning apart from actual individuals, apart from the personal consciousness of actually existing individuals in whom this synthesizing process takes place. Thus they are only valid in so far as such a thing as an empirical consciousness actually exists. Or, to put it slightly differently, the universal forms we are dealing with here are abstractions that are intended to construct the unity of consciousness. But philosophy was in error when it supposed that it could simply cut the umbilical cord, thus separating the abstractions from the things from which they were being abstracted. It is true that an abstraction is only meaningful if it does not contain the totality of the thing of which it is an abstraction. If it were not, there would be no concepts, and abstraction would be nothing more than a dull-witted repetition of each τόδε τι, each individual, existing thing. On the other hand, however, the validity – and hence the substantiality – of every such abstract concept must always be related to the thing from which it has been abstracted. This applies with particular force here. It means that only where an actual empirical consciousness exists can we speak of a transcendental consciousness.

Kant developed these ideas very incisively and with great force in the Amphiboly chapter of the *Critique of Pure Reason*, in particular in the great note on the concept of amphiboly [pp. 281–96]. It is very remarkable that it did not occur to him that his critique of amphibolies, that is, his critique of the confusion between the abstractions and the things themselves, also applied to his own doctrine of the transcendental. I cannot deny myself the pleasure of reading out to you a few sentences from his argument. He talks here of the concepts of reflection and by these he means the supreme intellectual concepts, that is, the concepts that are known only through the intellect, as opposed to intuition and experience, concepts to which Leibniz and Wolff ascribed 'being in itself'. 'The absolutely inward [nature] of matter, as it would have to be conceived by pure understanding, is nothing but a phantom' – and here you have the justification, Kant's apologia, for what I described to you in one of the recent lectures as the element of externality in the *Critique of Pure Reason*, without, incidentally, any desire to belittle it.[4] 'For matter is not among the objects of pure understanding, and the transcendental object which may be the ground of this appearance' – that is to say, the celebrated thing-in-itself – 'that we call matter is a mere something of which we should not understand what it is, even if someone were in a position to tell us. For we can understand only that which brings with it, in intuition, something corresponding to our words.'[5]

But if this is true it must hold good for the categories and above all for the hierarchy of categories that Kant developed. That is to say, we can only speak meaningfully of an 'I' if it refers to an actual empirical consciousness. At this point in the Amphiboly chapter Kant advances beyond the critique of reason, in what we might call the critical spirit, particularly in the passage where he talks of the concept of the 'I':

> The relation of sensibility to an object and what the transcendental ground of this [objective] unity may be, are matters undoubtedly so deeply concealed that we, who after all know even ourselves only through inner sense and therefore as appearance, can never be justified in treating sensibility as being a suitable instrument of investigation for discovering anything save always still other appearances – eager as we yet are to explore their non-sensible cause.[6]

I believe that here we have to be more Catholic than the Pope, that is to say, more Kantian than Kant, if we are to arrive at the immanent necessity of a dialectical conception of philosophy. The fact is that Kant is inconsistent here – and I would say that this is not one of the famous contradictions that the schoolmasters take note of, but rather a kind of pause in the argument which, however, we cannot accept. Thus with regard to external meaning he scorns to say anything definite about things-in-themselves; but at the point I have just read out to you he assumes such an extremely radical agnosticism about the things-in-themselves that, if we were to take him at his word, he would not even be able to employ the concept of things-in-themselves. But when it comes to the 'I think', in contrast, to the inner meaning, that is, to what we can know about things in the shape of appearance and not as things-in-themselves, he speaks as if he were talking about the thing on which appearance is grounded.

I believe that this is the cardinal point and I should like to repeat it so that you all understand it. According to Kant, the transcendental sphere is supposed to provide the foundation of the connections between the phenomena, relations in general, by means of which we have such things as a world and experience. This sphere is the legitimizing reason for the very existence of such a thing as appearance. But likewise according to Kant – in particular the very thesis from the Amphiboly chapter I have just read out to you – we have knowledge of such matters only in the shape of phenomena, of appearance. The pure 'I think', the absolute 'I', the secret basis for the establishment of these connections or of this process of synthesis, is just as deeply concealed as the transcendent, that is, as the transcendent thing-in-itself. When it comes down to it, Kant had no right to speak undialectically of such things existing in themselves, of such fixed forms given to us in reality once and for all. Instead, when he states that the world only comes into existence by virtue of the connections that are contained in these transcendental factors, these hierarchies of consciousness, he should really add that these hierarchies only exist and we only know of them because we have appearances, because we have phenomena. In other words, what Kant calls the constitutive sphere, the *constituens*, should not be made into an absolute, any more than should the *constitutum*. In the case of the latter Kant had shown that so-called naive realism would in fact lead to inconsistencies and meaningless statements. To fail to make a comparable argument in the case of the *constituens* is to succumb once more to the very pitfall he had unearthed in Leibniz and exposed so incisively. It is to succumb to the amphiboly of the concepts of reflection, in other words, the confusion between abstract concepts and what they represent, what they refer back to, just as truly as these referents point back to those concepts.

In other words, then, the concept of the transcendental, that is, all the elements through which something like experience may be said to arise, the so-called constituents of our consciousness, are none of them directly known to us, as you might have inferred from the analysis in the Deduction of the Pure Concepts of Understanding. They are rather mediations, the abstractions of a specific element of cognition – and this element is then hypostatized in the *Critique of Pure Reason*. Kant does exactly the same thing with the 'I think' that he so rightly criticizes in the Amphiboly chapter in the case of the ontological employment of the concept of Being, the concept of matter and all those other naturalistic concepts. The fact is that when I use the expression 'I think', I cannot dispense with the 'I' and this is reflected in Kant's linguistic usage, which was our starting-point. It proves that if our somewhat long-winded discussions are persuasive, the 'I' is not the pure, valid and thus already constituted logical form. With this I touch on a point at which I cannot avoid a disagreement with my otherwise greatly esteemed colleague Wilhelm Sturmfels.[7] You will constantly hear him polemicizing against psychologistic interpretations of Kant with the argument that the transcendental is actually nothing more than the purely logical. In my view this is a primitive reduction of Kant and just as much a simplification as the psychologistic view that was so prevalent in the nineteenth century. It is my belief that you will only understand the deeper problems at the heart of the *Critique of Pure Reason* if you can free yourselves from this interpretation.

If it were actually true that the sphere of the transcendental involved no more than logical unity, an idea of conformity to the laws of thought that, incidentally, presupposes thought and refers to it, if it were really nothing more than that, then Kant would surely have not taken the trouble to insist, in the introduction to the Transcendental Logic, on the distinction between a merely formal logic and a transcendental logic, that is, a logic that relates to objects and is for that reason bound up with objects at a far deeper level. I should like to draw your attention here to Section II of the introduction to the Transcendental Logic where he distinguishes transcendental logic from logic in general or formal logic. He says there that if matters stood as the above interpretation implies and if it were therefore possible to dismiss the problem of a logic relating to objects simply by formalizing it, then – so Kant maintains – formal logic 'would also treat of the origin of the modes in which we know objects'; 'whereas general logic has nothing to do with the origin of knowledge'.[8]

The *Critique of Pure Reason* is an investigation that is concerned essentially with the *origin* of knowledge – and not with the laws that govern the modes of knowledge that have already been crystallized and have become established. As a genetic question, as a question concerned with origins, it does not move within the parameters of a purely formal logic, but rather in a realm which is designed to ground the phenomenal, the world of objects, even though at the same time, in order for it to exist at all, it must relate to that world of objects. I believe that you can grasp this most easily – I want to insist on this point because I believe that it really does form the innermost core of the *Critique of Pure Reason* – if you reflect for a moment upon the concept of spontaneity. By spontaneity I mean the activity, more particularly the involuntary activity, as which Kant conceives of thought, as opposed to mere intuition. For this spontaneity is something that we really cannot predicate on a purely logical entity. It is quite impossible for us to imagine how a purely logical entity that has no content, no thing that can function, nothing that is over and above a pure abstraction, might generate an activity of any sort, no matter how intellectualized the concept of 'activity' might be – unless, that is, we wished to ascribe to Kant the kind of metaphysical view that he would have called spiritualism and repudiated in no uncertain terms. It is impossible, then, to imagine anything active in a pure concept – and the concept of an entity is a pure concept. It is possible to subsume something under such an entity, but an entity *qua* entity creates nothing, has no function and brings nothing about. But this element of bringing something about, of activity, is contained phenomenologically in the ' "I think" that accompanies all my representations'. And if I did not possess the consciousness of such an 'I do', then there would be no such thing as an ' "I think" that accompanies all my representations'. It is in this circumstance that we see why the transcendental form depends on an element of content – however sublimated, however abstract – as the precondition of its possibility and vice versa. Kant would no doubt concede that it [i.e. the transcendental form] can only generate valid judgements where it relates to intuitions – that is in fact the content of the *Critique of Pure Reason*. But what we are doing here, the argument we are pursuing here, goes beyond this in important respects. It asserts nothing less than that quotidian existence, factuality, is just as much a precondition of the possibility of thinking about mere forms as is its claim that without these forms the contents of experience could not come about at all.

This brings us to what I described last time, I believe, as the *quid pro quo* in the concept of the transcendental:[9] the *quid pro quo*

between *constituens* and *constitutum*. The reason why I am making
such strenuous efforts, if I may say so, is that what is at stake here
are the foundations of the philosophical position I myself uphold and
that I believe I can expound in connection with these reflections on
Kant. And what I would like to persuade you of is that neither of
these two elements of *constituens* and *constitutum* is reducible to
the other. Thus it is not my aim.to demonstrate that the so-called
constitutum has an ontological priority over the *constituens* – after
everything I have said that would not be possible. I would just like to
bring you to the point where you can see that these two elements are
related to each other. Remember – and I say this so that you should
grasp this idea in as pointed a fashion as I can manage – that in the
lectures up to now we have discussed in detail how Kant maintained
that the subject is the universal, and thus is contained in every particular. I even went so far as to show you that in this sense even
intuition can be thought of as conceptually mediated, not as mere
immediacy. I pointed out that at this point in Kant's philosophy
Hegel's later idea of universal mediation is objectively implied, even
if he did not express it in this way. But I did demonstrate this to you
with reference to a number of significant passages in Kant. In other
words, then – and this is what we might term the official thesis, this
is the Kant you will find in Baedeker: there is no *constitutum* without
a *constituens*; there is no world without a transcendental subject,
without an ' "I think" that accompanies all my representations'. When
I say that there is no world, you must understand that in principle,
as Kant has already admitted, the actual, empirical subject is part of
the world and belongs in this world. This means that as empirical
persons we are *constituta* and not automatically *constituentes*.

Conversely, however, the conclusion of our analysis today is that
the *constituens* stands in need of an individual subject as the precondition of its existence, and thus of a *constitutum*. Thus the very
thing that is secondary according to the Kantian critique turns out to
be the precondition of what is primary, just as much as the primary is
its precondition. If I may for once adopt the most facile philosophical
way of talking, our discussions today have provided a critique of the
general thesis of idealism in tune with the Kantian system just as,
conversely, they criticize the general thesis of a so-called naive, that
is, undialectical realism. If we take this really seriously, that is to say,
if we regard the insolubility of this contradiction as proven, the only
possible inference in my view is that we must renounce any attempt
to reduce one pole of cognition to the other. In other words, we must
abandon the principle of an absolute *first* principle to which all knowledge can be reduced. This in turn implies the impossibility of an

ontology, an ontology of Being, both in its idealist version of the sort that thrives here in West Germany, and also the crudely materialist ontology to which dialectics have regressed in East Berlin. The question of determining the relation of these two poles to each other simply cannot be resolved by reference to so-called origins.

In this way our criticism of Kant's philosophy as a philosophy of origins turns into a criticism of a philosophy of origins as such. This means that we have to abandon the search for an absolute first principle which would be the authentic, ancient truth. In other words, what I have demonstrated to you today amounts to a variation of the famous Kantian project of 'the *critical* path that alone is open'.[10] We shall indeed adopt this Kantian project of the critical path. What I have been doing was very consciously carried out in the spirit of an immanent critique of the *Critique of Pure Reason*. My arguments have been moving within the conceptual apparatus and the lines of thought developed by Kant. At the same time, their aim was to break out of the prison of the so-called problem of what constitutes what. They terminate in the proposition that the *dialectical* path alone is open.[11]

LECTURE FIFTEEN

9 July 1959

Constituens and *Constitutum* (III)

I should like to begin with a very witty remark of Dr Schweppenhäuser's following the last lecture.[1] He said that what that lecture
proved was that the *constituens* of the *constituens* is the *constitutum*.
I believe that, given the discussions we have had up to now, we can
feel secure from the misunderstanding that by taking transcendental
idealism at its word, my aim is to replace it with a transcendental
realism, or rather, with a pre-critical, naturalistic realism or a subsequent development of such a realism. I shall have something to say
about that today. However, what I attempted last time was to show
you that the relationship at work here is one of reciprocity. The
inference I drew from that and which I greatly prize is that what may
be called the first principle in philosophy is not what usually goes by
that name; and even more importantly, you must make the speculative leap – one that is hard to achieve, given the power of tradition
– of renouncing the need for any such concept as a first principle
in philosophy. Incidentally, I would like to add at this point that
all philosophy of first principles, all 'first philosophy', all *prima
philosophia* – as we are accustomed to using the term, following
Aristotle's πρώτη φιλοσοφία – is *idealism*, whether it likes it or not.
For in the light of our discussions of the way in which knowledge is
universally mediated, the assumption that we can discover such an
ultimate, conclusive principle on which everything else can be based
necessarily implies the claim that whatever exists, whatever forms the
object of philosophical investigation, will be reducible to a single
principle. Only if we proceed from the assumption that our thinking

is adequate to the task of discovering such an absolute foundation will we be able to discover one and assert that it is the Absolute. In this sense even so-called metaphysical materialism can be said to be an idealism in terms of its form. This idealism in terms of its form is no mere formality; a whole series of the features of idealism, and even idealist ψεῦδοι, fallacies, keep cropping up in such philosophies. We might mention such ideas as wholly self-consistent systems, complete deducibility, all-inclusive coherence and so on.

Now, after the arguments I sought to present you with during the last two lectures you might wish to raise the following objection, an objection concerned, one might say, with the economy of thought. You might say that these are the worries of philosophers. They tear one another apart for the sake of slight nuances that can barely be understood. For when it comes down to it, why does Adorno insist on the reciprocity of *constituens* and *constitutum* in this way? Why does he deny the existence of an absolute first principle? After all, that's more or less what the priest, namely Kant, says too.[2] That is to say, we are told countless times in the *Critique of Pure Reason* that the transcendental conditions of knowledge yield knowledge only if they are applied to the contents of experience. Is there really such a terribly great difference from what Mr Adorno is telling us in such a complicated and difficult manner? As when he tells us, for example, that the *constituens* is a precondition of the *constitutum* and vice versa? Well, I would wish to reply to this by saying – and this is a remarkable feature of philosophy that has never been properly investigated and that has never really been reflected upon as it deserves – that the great distinctions, the distinctions that really matter, are always concealed in the most minute details. The two philosophical systems of Kant and Hume are generally considered to be starkly opposed to each other. It is my belief, however, that if you were to expound them to an unprejudiced observer he would say that there is no very great distinction between the claim that objectivity is constituted by the interaction of subjective conditions and the claim that these are mere conventions. But that is not really the issue at stake. After all, when Kant says that, since our knowledge is subjectively conditioned, it can tell us nothing about things-in-themselves, this is not actually too terribly far away from Hume. Nevertheless, in terms of their mood, their intellectual horizons, these two philosophies are radically different from each other, as we are right to infer from the concepts of scepticism, sceptical empiricism, on the one hand, and transcendental idealism on the other. The two philosophies breathe an entirely different atmosphere.

I may perhaps be allowed to interpose a comment here that is quite indispensable for an understanding of philosophy. This is that it is not a matter of the literal appropriation of the tenets of particular systems; we do not have to take them absolutely literally just as they appear on the page of the text. In certain circumstances the same concepts, the same tenets, may express quite different experiences – if I may be allowed to borrow this emphatic concept of experience from our discussions. Even where the form of words is identical in different philosophies, it may have quite different meanings. An example is when Spinoza seems simply to adopt the identical concept of God that Descartes had used, but then interprets it differently, namely as infinite substance. And what we then have is not just a different definition of the Cartesian conception of God, but a completely different – mechanistic and materialist – philosophical climate. However, in order to specify these differences – and this is the problem I wish to bring to your attention – you need an insight into minute distinctions. An instance is the distinction I have drawn between my elaborate deduction of the necessity of dialectical interpretation and Kant's own transcendental logic. It is only if you really scrutinize the subtlest nuances of the ideas involved that you can truly obtain a grasp of the whole, and this is where Aby Warburg's claim that God is in the detail really comes into its own.[3] You must realize that in the spirit of what I said the day before yesterday the proposition that the forms do not exist without the *constitutum*, that strictly speaking without the *constitutum* you can no more speak of them than you can of the *constitutum* without the forms – that this means a fundamental change in the problem of constitution. The nuance of meaning we are examining here is not that the forms stand in need of the *constitutum* in order to be satisfied and hence to produce truth, but that the *conditions of the possibility* of transcendental forms are the very elements that are said to be constituted by those forms. This, this seemingly difficult nuance of meaning, which I can only hope that you have understood as completely as I hope I have presented it to you – this nuance means a fundamental change in the problem of constitution. That is to say, the concept of a first or fundamental principle, a fundamental philosophy – and this applies to Kant as much as to Aristotle or Descartes or any other traditional philosopher – this concept has been dissolved.

The entire procedure may be thought of as residual. Philosophers believed – and this started as far back as Plato – that by eliminating the ephemeral, the accidental and more or less external you would then arrive at the pure concepts which would be a residue that is left behind and you would thus become conscious of the Absolute, the truth and the 'authentic'. However, should it turn out that on examining these residual concepts you then discern within them, as if through a kind of nuclear fission, the very things that they are supposed to determine – then it will become evident that this entire method of abstracting or subtracting in the hope of being left with what is permanent and eternal – that this entire philosophical method has to be discarded. This *residual theory of truth* is one which includes Descartes as much as Kant, who may be regarded as a self-reflecting Cartesian. It emerges that Kant has paid his tribute to this kind of dogmatism despite his having made heroic efforts to turn it upside down. I should like now to mention something that I shall be unable to explore fully in this course, but of which I must remind you if I am to avoid confusing you. This is that this reduction of a reduction that we have undertaken, this double process of reflection, does not mean the disappearance of the distinction between *subject and object*. What results is not that famous night of indifference in which all cats are grey.[4] What ceases is merely the mutual opposition of these elements, frozen in an eternal stasis, with the subject as form, on the one side, and an external content approaching me from outside, on the other. For such an inflexible and static separation is impossible; these elements can indeed be distinguished in every single piece of knowledge but it is not possible for one element to be reduced to another once and for all. It follows that the distinction between subject and object is dynamic; it has the character of a process, but should not be made into an absolute, a fundamental structure of being any more than in the spirit of the *Critique of Pure Reason* the concept of Being may be posited as such a basic structure. Subject and object – this distinction is not given for all time; it enters into *history* and is therefore capable of being historically determined in its various phases.

I believe that, if you have followed me thus far, I shall have furnished you with the crucial tools for the transition from the *Critique of Pure Reason* to Hegel's *Phenomenology of Spirit*, which contains the idea that the subject–object problem should be treated so as to ensure that these two elements do not oppose each other in a static, inflexible manner. Instead, the element of reciprocal mediation between them that I have tried to isolate immanently in Kant is now interpreted historically. That is to say, the relation between subject and object is equated by Hegel with history itself. Conversely, history is interpreted by him as the determination of subject and object, but in a way that distances them fundamentally from their general definition as constant, unchanging entities. Hegel, of course, remained an extreme idealist. In consequence this movement, this historical movement between subject and object, was only possible for him because both elements flowed into a third one, namely into the Absolute, the idea, so that finally they are first elevated and then reconciled in

identity. This need not concern us here, nor need we be concerned at
present with the criticism these ideas have attracted. At any rate, this
transition from the antithesis between subject and object that prevailed in philosophy from Descartes to Kant to a dynamic relationship between subject and object is the decisive step taken by philosophy
in that period. In this connection I cannot resist drawing your attention to what I regard as a peculiar regression in philosophy today.
We need only see how people today restrict the scope of philosophy
and consider the emotional reaction that a philosophy attracts if it
refuses to be confined in this way. On the one hand, you have a
conception of philosophy that limits it to the realm of the abstract in
precisely the sense we have been defining with respect to Kant. On
the other hand, it is easy to see how such a view of philosophy is
resisted by a work like the *Phenomenology of Spirit*. In that work
there is a constant interaction between the categories of consciousness,
the positioning of the subject and the objective events of history –
such as the feudal system, master–servant relations and above all the
French Revolution. Thus these very real historical processes are in
continuous engagement with the problems of constitution.

Now it is hard to avoid the thought that according to the view
that prevails today this Hegelian philosophy would not be thought
of as philosophy at all. We might say that philosophy today has
relapsed to the pre-Hegelian, Kantian standpoint. More specifically,
Kant's allergic reaction towards the empirical, and indeed towards
everything that stands in opposition to pure essence, a reaction that
was banished and exorcized in the great systems that came *after*
Kant, that allergy has reappeared in full force again today, as a com-
plement to the advances in the positive sciences. The more there is of
mere factuality, mere science, on the one side, the more philosophy is
reduced simply to a doctrine of abstract essences on the other – and
even the concept of history is diluted to that of 'historicality'.[5] The
decisive point here, the point I want most to emphasize in these
lectures, is that the element of mediation between these two areas of
interest – what Fichte meant when he said magnificently that the *a
priori* and the *a posteriori* are the same thing[6] – has vanished entirely
from the purview of philosophy today. While philosophy imagines
that it is streets ahead of so-called idealism, it has in fact fallen behind the subsequent advances and without noticing it has lapsed into
a full-blooded and extremely crude idealism. This may enable you
to understand why in my remarks on the implications of Kant's
philosophy I am adopting such a critical view of his ontological
interpreters[7] – and of the concept of ontology itself. I should emphasize, however, that in doing so I remain on Kantian terrain since the

impossibility of ontology is among the explicit tenets of the *Critique of Pure Reason*. In other words, even though the distinction between subject and object emerges in the *Critique of Pure Reason* with a somewhat unsettling bluntness, it is not possible to look behind it in search of a primordial unity that would bring the two together.

Having explained to you the problem of this rigid opposition of subject and object, form and content, form and matter – or however it may be termed in Kant – the temptation to regress to some prior stage becomes very pressing. The need to dissolve this rigid opposition lies in the fact that it involves an unsatisfactory and rigid separation of elements while at the same time we are constantly being compelled to recognize that one cannot exist without the other; that is to say that each is so defined as to be constantly referring to the other. The decisive factor here – and one that is always being overlooked in the case of Hegel and the dialectic – is that by seeking to transcend this Kantian dualism, and by failing to do so, you regress to an earlier stage and relapse into sheer immediacy. The only escape route from this impasse is the one we have been trying out here in a modest way, and that is to transcend it by advancing *through* this dualism, that is to say, by demonstrating that what is divided is *itself* mediated. In other words, then, the answer is to search for a so-called unity prior to this disintegrating duality. Kant himself repeatedly called for such a unity, whether secret or concealed, whether it was to be found in the 'depths of the soul' or in the transcendent thing-in-itself. Instead, what has to be done is to hold fast to this differentiation – and that is what I meant earlier on by the determinate nature of subject and object. What has to be done is to hold fast to this ineluctable duality, a duality that cannot be ignored and that recurs in concrete form at every stage of history, but at the same time, within this state of differentiation, to define the element of unity as its other. This is what philosophies fail to do when they imagine that they can eliminate the antinomies, the unsatisfactory nature of mere antitheses, by the arbitrary assumption of an underlying unity. This has the further consequence of enabling philosophy resolutely and finally to emancipate itself from the very thing that is demanded of it today, to wit, a concern with the highest abstractions. Thanks to the combination of present-day ontological trends with so-called philosophical anthropology it is often claimed today that categories such as 'states of mind' that commonly emerge from such schools of thought are not abstract but concrete in the highest degree. But such claims are quite specious. It can be shown that wherever such concrete specificities are claimed they involve a sleight of hand in reality – Kant would say a psychological sleight of hand – and that

they have been illicitly given the status of the highest abstractions
with which this philosophy can alone be concerned.

Once we have reached the point of admitting that in a very important sense philosophy is related to the concrete events of history, this
must lead us back to the problems of society, which is where we
started when we launched into the whole analysis we are concerned
with at present – that is to say, when we began our discussion of the
Kantian use of 'we',[8] a term we took so seriously because it was
irreplaceable. The argument we are considering here and which is
advanced to counter the objections we have made – an argument
which Kant would probably have endorsed in preference to the points
we have made – this argument claims that what philosophy wants
above all is to prepare the ground for Being; and that if we wish
to place it in an *essential* relation to society, that is, a constitutive
relation rather than one based on analogy, we will be turning it into
just such a piece of factual reality which it is the task of philosophy
to *ground*, to illuminate. In consequence we end up putting the cart
before the horse. In reply I would begin by reminding you that this
line of argument itself depends on that very philosophy of origins,
that quest for an absolute first principle, that we have been criticizing. We had come to the conclusion that this quest could not be
sustained.

In the pre-fascist era in which he experienced his philosophical
prime Martin Heidegger once described sociology as a 'cat burglar'
in contrast to philosophy. It clambers around on the outside of the
building of philosophy, stealing whatever the honest philosophical
craftsmen are building and growing (or it may have been farmers or
whatever he may have had in his mind).[9] Of course, for Heidegger to
speak in this way implies a certain defensiveness. The substance
of that defensiveness is precisely that rigid antithesis between the
validity of the truth and its *genesis*, its origins. For our part we have
come to the opposite conclusion – and I would remind you here of
our discussion of the concept of function and of doing, or spontaneous action.[10] Our conclusion there was that this separation of genesis
and validity was no Absolute either, but that genesis dwells in the
heart of validity. In other words, we decided that origins, the historical
moment as I have called it today, are immanent in truth and, as I like
to express it, the truth is not present in history, but history in the
truth.[11] Heidegger's defensiveness is easy to understand; it is no
accident. No more is the note of denunciation it contains a mere
accident. Consider the arbitrary nature of such existential categories
as 'anticipating death' – why exactly should anticipating death be a
category constitutive of existence? – 'thrownness' or 'resoluteness',[12]

all of them categories taken from psychology and transposed into the transcendental. We find all such categories beguiling; we are tempted to cling to them dogmatically whenever anyone starts to scrutinize their arbitrary nature. They are based on assumptions that are merely asserted rather than something that emerges from the nature of the thing itself. This is best done by denigrating the intention underlying such scrutiny, as if the critic really desired to dissolve the concept of truth itself. Whereas in reality the opposite is the case: the aim is to overcome that age-old delusion according to which truth is identified with the permanent, immutable, identical – while the genetic, the emerging, whatever has not always existed, are classified as the untruth from the outset. The idea of genesis is intolerable in these philosophies because the things they defend have cause to fear reflection on their origins.

However, we have demonstrated – and I attach the very greatest importance to this – that this genetic factor cannot be isolated from the question of validity. This means that we have shown that what are alleged to be the most highly abstract and universal factors governing knowledge, the factors that must be present for knowledge to be conceived of in the first place, presuppose the element of factuality, of actual existence, that they are supposed to explain. Thus reflection on the fact that subject and object or transcendental factors and human reality are mutually interdependent is at the same time a necessary pointer to the fact that I must not make absolutes of these transcendental factors, I may not hypostatize them. This means that I may not separate them from their genesis, their origins in factual reality, any more than I can detach factual reality or judgements about the world of things from their subjective mediation and hence from their historical roots. In this sense, therefore, the studies we have undertaken, the ideas we have brought to the surface in Kant through our interpretations, are directly suited to nullify the kind of separation of genesis and validity that was first introduced into philosophy by Franz Brentano in his book *The Origin of our Knowledge of Right and Wrong*,[13] which was based on certain Scholastic traditions, and was subsequently developed formally by Husserl.[14] This trend culminated in the emergence of fundamental ontology.

In other words, the transition from the so-called problem of constitution in Kant to history was already implicit in Kant himself. The process of constitution was actually implemented for him by *time* – I would remind you here of the role of memory in Kant – and if that is so, you have a strong pointer to history. For it is not possible to speak of time in the absence of some inner intuition, something inwardly present that experiences time in itself – and in this recourse to something that *possesses* time the historical is necessarily implied. It is an arbitrary act to stop short at the experiential time of individual human beings who happen to form the point of departure for philosophy, but then to refuse to take this recourse to time seriously. To take it seriously would mean fully appreciating the historical origin of our categories. On the other hand, however – and I should like to stress this as one of the most important findings of our Kant analyses – we are no less critical of a really misguided sociologism than we are of these ontologizing interpretations of Kant and their resultant ontologies. We are saying, then, that just as it is impossible to see the categories other than in relation to their origin and to history, it is equally impossible simply to *derive* concepts like space, time and the categories from history and to reduce them to social phenomena. I use the term 'sociologism' with some hesitation because in their polemics against sociologism you often hear Pharisaical overtones creeping in on the part of critics who imagine that they have a permanent monopoly on 'sacred goods' and are convinced that they have to defend them against relativism. But on the other hand – and I believe that I can say this without fear of being thought old-fashioned and stuffy – it goes without saying that there is, of course, a kind of sociologism that has dissipated its own enlightened impulses in the sense that it has ceased to acknowledge any concept of truth at all and thus finds itself in conflict with its own intentions.

In particular I have in mind here comments that are relevant in the context of our discussion of the historical dimension of philosophical explanation. That is to say, I am thinking of the sociology of knowledge, which in the German tradition is generally regarded as the domain of Scheler and Mannheim, although in reality our greatest debt in the field of the sociology of knowledge is owed to Emile Durkheim. Durkheim made a serious attempt to give a sociological explanation of space, time and a series of categories and above all, the forms of logical classification. For example, he derived temporal relations from the sequence of the generations and thus described them as something entirely social in origin.[15] Durkheim's account is just as antinomic as Kant's, whose antinomies I have described to you during the past few lectures with reference to the concept of universality as something detached from the particular human subject. I cannot go into these questions here, but I owe it to you at least to indicate the crucial points so as to secure what I have just said against the misunderstanding that I am myself guilty of sociologism. Durkheim's mistake can be easily summarized: his account of historical origins, for example, of time and space, constantly employs concepts that already presuppose the forms of intuition – to use a Kantian terminology – of time and space. For example, it is not possible to talk of a sequence of generations if you have no conception of events succeeding one another in time. And if you assert that people have arrived at the idea of space from the way fields are separated off from one another, from individual properties bordering upon one another, then you evidently presuppose the concept of space, since this idea of properties bordering one another can only have a spatial meaning. But if sociologism is really doomed to failure at this its most radical point, the point where it has really tried its hardest, then the entire enterprise must be extremely problematic. My view would be that the objectivity of time – which appears in Kant as a transcendental condition, a pure form of intuition – should be separated from reflections on time or the creation of a concept of time. The creation of a concept of time – and by analogy, of course, the same thing holds good for the concept of space – is something that takes place within history and depends, therefore, on social conditions. It is precisely at this point that we can see that the research of the later Durkheim School has been so extraordinarily productive. I am thinking here of the work of Henri Hubert and Marcel Mauss. But, naturally, there can be no question of dissolving space and time into their social roots or suggesting that they are simply things posited by society and not, if I may use the medieval expression, concepts that also have their *fundamentum in re*. On the other hand, however, we must repeat that *without* subjectivity, and that means: without real subjects interacting with one another, all talk of an objective concept of time as a concept that has priority over the consciousness of time, would be meaningless. Instead, the truth is that these two concepts are mutually interdependent.

LECTURE SIXTEEN

14 July 1959

Society • 'Block'

Last time I attempted to show you that our reflections on the relations between *constituens* and *constitutum* and the connections we established between them and that Kantian 'we', which we saw as a subject with a social dimension, did not amount to a sociologism. By way of demonstration I offered a brief critique of a view opposed to that of Kant, namely, that of Durkheim, who incidentally was well versed in Kant's philosophy and had made the attempt to provide a social explanation for the Kantian forms of intuition and some other important logical and epistemological categories.[1] We perceived that such explanations necessarily presupposed the forms or categories they set out to explain, and conversely that these forms or categories refer to existing things, realities. My aim was not only to demonstrate to you the impossibility of an epistemological sociologism, but also to show you that the question of which comes first – actual existence or formal category – is misguided. That is to say, these different elements simply cannot be separated from one another; and that this is the case points ultimately to the fact that their apparent existence as separate entities is itself the product of the reflecting mind rather than something that can be ascribed to being or existing things as such. On the other hand, you must not forget that this Kantian 'we' contains a reference to the social – that is, not just the individual – nature of the transcendental subject. His inability to dispense with such an expression as 'we' does not simply reflect an old-fashioned linguistic usage, a kind of politeness – in which an 'I' is replaced by a 'we', whereby it remains unclear whether it does not also express something of the royal 'we'.

It contains in addition a very important epistemological insight. You can picture this to yourselves by saying that if epistemology expects from each of us sitting in this room (as it traditionally does) that each person can regard himself as the fount of all knowledge, then this claim is made arbitrary in the extreme by the fact that each person, who of course looks after his own interests, can be replaced by every other subject. Furthermore, the point of departure is not final, if only because an expression 'I' that can be replaced by every *other* 'I' must be occasionalist in nature: it proves that the 'I' that is being appealed to is not being taken seriously *as* an 'I'. On the other hand, this kind of epistemology, by which I mean this entire strand of subjectivist philosophy, cannot avoid the issue since experience can be generated only through the reference to a personal subject. If immediacy is elevated into the ultimate criterion of knowledge, then of course every consciousness is 'immediate' only to itself. That is to say, the facts of consciousness are given immediately only to each individual concerned. The facts of consciousness of others are only ever given indirectly, through communication, by making inferences from analogous situations, through empathy – or however we wish to describe it. You can see here a very remarkable antinomy in this general explanatory framework of epistemology as a whole, which must be deemed to include Kant's *Critique of Pure Reason*. This is that, on the one hand, the talk of an 'I' necessarily implies a 'we', so that as an 'I' it cannot be taken seriously. On the other hand, if no appeal is made to this 'I', the idea of an immediate point of departure, the experience which stands at the beginning of all knowledge cannot be maintained. Traditional epistemology has never succeeded in overcoming this contradiction. This is one more reason, I would say, for abandoning the entire approach. As the foundation of epistemology, the 'we' is not immediately given, but highly mediated. In exchange it is saved from arbitrariness. In contrast the 'I' is immediate in every instance, but as a starting-point it is always arbitrary in comparison to the 'we'. Thus, taken in isolation, as inflexible models, both these points of departure are relatively arbitrary and problematic. I do not wish to say more about them at present. Those of you who would like to pursue the question further should look up what I have to say about it in chapter 4 of *Against Epistemology*.[2]

At any rate, you cannot escape the fact that social factors lie concealed in the crucial attributes that Kant assigns to the subject. Hegel's *Phenomenology of Spirit* may in a manner of speaking be regarded as the attempt to explicate the latent social motifs that are objectively present in the so-called problem of constitution. If you reflect for one moment that the basic defining feature, the attribute that underpins everything else in Kant's concept of subjectivity, is the dichotomy between spontaneity and receptivity, or activity and passivity, then this points unequivocally to the social process in which two elements are always present. I am referring to *work* and *nature* on which work operates. There has long been an idea that knowledge really just repeats what has always existed in the actual process of human labour; that we are dealing with a kind of raw material, on the one hand, that is then given shape by consciousness, on the other – something of this idea reverberates through the whole of the *Critique of Pure Reason*. We can doubtless say – and this has been explored a number of times in detail, for example, by the late Franz Borkenau in his book on seventeenth-century theories in the age of manufacture[3] – we can doubtless say that in their objective form theories of cognition are a kind of reflex of the labour process. Not in the sense that they have been brought forth causally by the labour process, but in the sense that, when consciousness reflects upon itself, it necessarily arrives at a concept of rationality that corresponds to the rationality of the labour process. I have in mind here the qualities of the division of labour and the planned processing of materials given in nature. On the other hand, it would be quite misguided to say – and I must confess to you that I have on occasion been very tempted by this idea – that the transcendental subject actually *is* society. It undoubtedly has one feature in common with society. This is that only the global social subject – not the contingent individual subject – possesses that character of universality, of all-encompassing totality, that Kant ascribes to his transcendental subject. We may add that behind the idea of constitution stands that of labour as social labour – and not just isolated, individual labour. On the other hand, however, in contrast with that global social subject which may be regarded as the summation of all the concrete factors of society, the Kantian transcendental subject, that is, the famous ' "I think" that accompanies all my representations', is a complete abstraction that has nothing in common with it.

Needless to say, this social interpretation of the transcendental subject should not be thought of as arbitrary. We can say that in its relation to society thought *qua* the Kantian 'I think' is *both things*. On the one hand, it is the truth of society, its 'universality'. It points beyond the merely contingent nature of individual existence and, ultimately, even beyond the conditional and ephemeral form that a society possesses at certain stages of its history. It is truly the λόγος of society, the overall social rationality in which the utopia of a rationally organized society is already implicit. On the other hand, this transcendental subject also contains, if I may risk a rather bold statement, the untruth of society. That means, the abstraction characteristic of this transcendental subject is nothing but the internalized and hypostatized form of man's domination of nature. This always comes into being through the elimination of qualities, through the reduction of qualitative distinctions to quantitative forms. It is therefore objectively always abstract in character. We may say, then, that the deepest reason for our refusal to identify the concept of truth with society is not to be found in the fact that there is a pure kingdom of truth entirely separate from society, a κόσμος νοητικός – of the kind that Plato was still able to imagine.[4]

It is rather the case that the concept of truth of which social factors form constituent parts points beyond the shape of society as it happens to exist. Furthermore, in the form ratified by epistemology it bears the stigmata of the historical process in the shape in which it has come down to us. That is all I have to say for the present about the relation of Kantian philosophy to society. I may perhaps add only that the ideas I have presented to you here with their rather complex implications are not so alien to Kantian philosophy as they may appear to be to the actual text of the *Critique of Pure Reason*. In the *Critique of Practical Reason* the elimination of empirical elements is taken much further than in the *Critique of Pure Reason*. In the later text the fear of contact with the empirical, with actual reality, is taken to such lengths that the object of practical reason, namely, action, is declared to be simply independent of empirical reality and to be something that has arisen purely from the subjective imagination, in contrast to the objects of theoretical reason. Thus the *Critique of Practical Reason* goes well beyond the formalism of even the *Critique of Pure Reason*, but ends up after a very complicated trajectory with ideas of a just society, a conception of mankind that is actually inconceivable on the basis of the Kantian programme if we were to preserve that pure distance from the facts. It would be an interesting project, one that really ought to be tackled seriously at some point, to show how the apparently extreme formalism of Kantian philosophy actually contains elements of transmutation into a kind of materialism.

I should like now to say a few words about the Kantian *block* which I have mentioned several times in a more or less desultory way.[5] I would like to discuss it in connection with the ideas that we have been considering and with which we are still concerned, and in particular with the kinds of experience that are articulated by Kant's philosophy. I believe I observed at one point that this Kantian block can be understood as a form of unmediated Cartesian dualism that is reflexive, that reflects upon itself. It is a dualism in which a great chasm yawns between inner and outer, a chasm that can never be bridged.[6] This chasm is the chasm of the alienation of human beings from one another, and the alienation of human beings from the world of things. This alienation is in fact socially caused; it is created by the universal exchange relation. Through the idea that our knowledge is blocked Kantian philosophy expresses as an experience the state of philosophy at the time. In particular, it expresses the idea that in this universally mediated society, determined as it is by exchange, in this society marked by radical alienation, we are denied access to existing reality as if by a blank wall. This is an experience, incidentally, that was suggested to Kant by his reading of Rousseau, which as we know today played a major role in the formation of the entire Kantian system. I believe that it is important in this context for you to realize that this idea of a block, of unbridgeable chasms between different realms, is in fact ubiquitous in the *Critique of Pure Reason*; it does not refer simply to the single point where it first makes its appearance, namely the question of the unknowability of the so-called things-in-themselves. For when Kant says that the ideas are not valid objects of knowledge, but merely 'regulative' ideas, this is effectively to assert the χωρισμός, the disjunction, between truth in the ontological sense and our ability to comprehend. In the light of this emphatic assertion of a qualitative leap between the ontological world of ideas and the possibility of our obtaining valid knowledge, the salvaging efforts I told you about earlier,[7] all have something of the flavour of an insurance policy. In fact the position with Kant – and this too is something rightly criticized by his successors – is that the two spheres of the understanding – that is, the really valid knowledge relating to experience – and reason – that is, the knowledge of ideas – point in opposite directions and are incapable of being reconciled. This remains true even though the organ of knowledge, namely the λόγος of man himself, in other words thought, is identical in both cases. This is an unmediated piece of thinking that is at bottom difficult to reconcile with Kant's ambition – and he did have such an ambition – to create a self-consistent system. Thus we really are talking here about what Nietzsche meant when he said that 'I am banished from all truth.'[8] What he had in mind was the disenchanted world which has been emptied of meaning, a topic I have tried to explain to you at some length.[9] This motif of radical enlightenment has become fused with the theological idea that always accompanies it, to wit, that as finite, conditioned beings we can only have finite and conditional, not unconditional, knowledge.

But I should like to add to what I have already said and mention something that has not been said up to now and goes beyond it in important respects. I believe that it is worthwhile reflecting here a little more deeply on Kant's relation to the *natural sciences*. If I am not mistaken, Kant is the last of the major philosophers who thought of himself as being in agreement with the natural sciences, while at the same time holding fast to the traditional themes of philosophy, that is, of metaphysics. After him – and here Hegel's case is exemplary – the two branches of knowledge diverged completely. That is to say, philosophers who understood something of science generally came to conclusions that were bluntly hostile to philosophy and they basically regarded logic and the methodology of science as the only possible and valid form of philosophy. Conversely, those philosophers who were unwilling to abandon their metaphysical impulses strove to maintain them as a pure realm on their own, isolated from the mathematical sciences, as far as was possible. The first symptom of this development was in fact the Hegelian system. This system did try to synthesize these strands of thought in an external manner but it manifestly failed in the attempt as far as science was concerned, that is to say, in Part Two, The Philosophy of Nature, of the *Encyclopedia*. I mean by this that what he says there is in flagrant contradiction to the facts of science.

Kant is initially rather more successful here. But if I understand this doctrine of a Kantian block more or less correctly, in particular in its implications for the unknowability of the thing-in-itself, then you begin to see – perhaps for the very first time – how Kant can be said to represent a historical watershed leading to subsequent developments in philosophy, much as could be said of the bourgeoisie of his age. You begin to see, in a kind of premonition that is not clearly articulated, the idea that science does not necessarily represent the last word about nature. Kant was enough of a scientist and was sufficiently self-confident to refrain from calling for a kind of knowledge that would reveal the 'true' essence of nature. In this respect he differed from the great Romantic philosophers. I am thinking here of Ritter and Schelling, and even, in a sense, of Schopenhauer. Kant, however, did not do this; he would certainly have rejected all such aspirations as obscurantist. But he knows, or rather, I should not really say 'he knows'. I should say instead that it is a metaphysical experience implicit in the doctrine of the block in the *Critique of Pure Reason* that the object of nature that we define with

our categories is not actually nature itself. For our knowledge of
nature is really so preformed by the demand that we *dominate* nature
(something exemplified by the chief method of finding out about
nature, namely the scientific experiment) that we end up understanding only those aspects of nature that we can control. In addition
there is also the underlying feeling that while we are putting out our
nets and catching more and more things in them, there is a sense in
which nature itself seems to keep receding from us; and the more
we take possession of nature, the more its real essence becomes alien
to us.

I said to you at one point in an earlier lecture[10] that the categories
of subjectivism and reification are not incompatible opposites, but
corollaries. That is to say, the more subjectivism there is, the more
reification, and vice versa. This means that the more we appropriate,
the more we find ourselves alienated from what we are really looking
for, and what we do actually appropriate is only a kind of lifeless
residue. This feeling (if I may for once make use of a highly dubious
psychological expression), this experience, is hard to express in rational
terms, because the sphere of rationality is the sphere that contradicts
experience. Nevertheless, this feeling is deeply embedded in Kant's
philosophy. Thus we may say that what Kant shares with positivism
is the insistence on the finite nature of knowledge and the rejection
of metaphysics as a 'wild extravagance'. But we must add that the
atmosphere which informs his entire way of thinking is extremely
unlike that of positivism (if indeed we can speak at all of 'atmosphere' in connection with positivism). That is to say, we have a situation in which knowledge is illusory because the closer it comes to its
object, the more it shapes it in its own image and thus drives it
further and further away, much as civilization has driven the wildest
and most exotic animals into the most inaccessible jungles. This is
what is reflected in the doctrine of the block; it is a kind of metaphysical mourning, a kind of memory of what is best, of something
that we must not forget, but that we are nevertheless compelled to
forget. This memory is quite alien to positivism, just as positivism
has no room for any theory that propounds the idea of a block on
knowledge. Instead, positivism would say that this is all nonsense,
these are all obsolete fantasies; stick to the 'positive' facts, to the
given realities – nothing further lies behind them.

However, Kant's historical consciousness (or whatever you want
to call it) stretches to the point of refusing to be fobbed off with this.
The memory of the questions philosophy formerly asked is still so
powerful in him that even against the grain of his own positivistic
rationality, he retains at least a notion of what lies beyond reason.

You can see, then, that his relation to science is contradictory. Science is still the model, as in older philosophy, but now that it is under the aegis of the block, of the fact that knowledge gives us only phenomena and not noumena, it is already as problematic as it was to become in post-Kantian thought. You can see from this – and if you wish you can turn this into a criticism of Kant – that he is inconsistent here, that he does not follow his arguments through to their logical conclusions. On the one hand, he cannot bring himself to venture at least some statements about this authentic world that is slipping from our grasp and about its nature, but leaves it so empty of content that to all intents and purposes it really does amount to nothing at all. On the other hand, he lacks the logical consistency of the positivists who hold fast to what is given, its interconnections and its forms, while dismissing everything over and above that as mere phantoms. Faced by these alternatives Kant can be described as a vacillating thinker, unable to make up his mind.

But I should like to remind you here that his reluctance to follow his ideas to their logical conclusion is the expression of what might be called the metaphysics of the block. To follow through his ideas to their logical conclusion would mean ignoring this block and the experience underlying it. It would mean creating an unambiguous identity governed by the dominance of the understanding, whereas the decisive feature of Kant is that the ἀνάμνησις, the power of memory, thrives because that identity is *not* possible. Kant prefers to accept that illogicality; he would rather acquiesce in the inconsistencies to which we have repeatedly drawn attention than create a seamless intellectual harmony which nevertheless would prevent him from delivering on his specific philosophical ambitions. To take matters to their logical conclusion means denying the existence of the block and laying claim to absolute identity. The dialectical or antinomic structure of Kantian philosophy means that it aspires to create a system, to provide a central point, which is that of the idea that can construct reality – but at the same time, it refuses to regard the world as identical with that idea. This implies a vast effort to square a circle and it is very easy to criticize him for the errors that spring from it. I believe that this is the deepest thing to be found in Kant. On the one hand, he holds fast to the intention of philosophy to understand reality as a whole, to decode the totality. At the same time, he declares that philosophy is *incapable* of this, and that the only form in which the totality can be grasped is the expression of the fact that it cannot be comprehended.

I have formulated this in a very pointed, perhaps overstated way, and many of you will perhaps be shocked by it. Nevertheless, I believe that I have been completely faithful to the Kantian idea here which I perceive to be deeply paradoxical. It is the attempt to give an account of the totality, while simultaneously conceding that this totality is no such thing, that subject and object do not seamlessly fit together – and that ultimately the absence of this seamless fit, which is what the block amounts to, is itself what a Romantic artist once named the innermost life of the world.[11] I should like to emphasize that, with hindsight, this seems to me to provide the justification for the procedure I have adopted in this course of lectures. This procedure is one that places far greater emphasis on the ruptures, the immanent antinomies in his thinking, than upon its harmonious, synthetic form. This is because these ruptures can almost be said to *constitute* the Kantian philosophy, for the reason that they reveal the innermost core of his thinking. This core is encapsulated in the idea that the totality that the mind is just able to encompass is no more than the fact that as *mind* it is *unable* to comprehend the totality; but that it somehow contrives after all to comprehend what it does not comprehend and the fact that it cannot comprehend it.

With this observation we have reached a critical point in our discussion of Kantian philosophy. Like all intellectual phenomena, a philosophy does not stand outside time; it exists within time – not merely in the sense that it can be forgotten, or subject to different interpretations, but rather in the sense that its own meaning unfolds in time, forming a variety of configurations that release meanings and generate meanings that were not remotely considered at its inception. This is particularly true of the question of the block about which I have attempted to say something today by way of conclusion. If I am not mistaken, we are looking here at the deepest aspect of Kant, at his attempt to say what cannot be said – and his entire philosophy is actually nothing more than a form of stammering, infinitely expanded and elevated. Like the act of stammering, it is a form of Dada, the attempt to say what actually cannot be said.[12] And just as this motif of the block is the deepest aspect of Kant, it is highly paradoxical that it is this aspect that Kant has bequeathed to the stock of bourgeois wisdom and has thus become the feature that will have made Kant look so old-fashioned to you. When I tell you about the Kantian χωρισμός, the Kantian block, I am reminded of a commonplace hit-song or student song that I learnt from my parents and that must have been current at about the turn of the century. It contained the lines – 'The soul soars high into the air / The body rests upon the chair'. This unspeakably pathetic piece of bourgeois wisdom represents in a sense the ultimate degradation, the ultimate fate of Kantian philosophy in the dire form to which it had sunk in the normal consciousness of the bourgeoisie. It is my view that this is a side of the Kantian philosophy that we have to think through so as to become fully aware that this degenerate form is not simply something that the wicked bourgeois have done to Kant, but rather something that is teleologically implicit in his philosophy from the outset. The structure of the block that I have attempted, perhaps over-emphatically, to convey to you is one that faces both ways; it faces not just towards metaphysical experience, but also towards the *world*. And the side it turns towards the world is all too similar to the world to which it turns. From this vantage-point of the χωρισμός or the dualism of Kantian philosophy what is involved is a sort of arrangement between naturalism, the empirical world, on the one hand, and non-binding ideals on the other.

Before going into this question I should like to draw your attention to a very characteristic feature of Kant's philosophy. This is that the huge effort that he has made to ground experience has actually done that experience no harm. We might also say that it is a philosophy in which the distinction between *appearance* and *essence* does not occur to a significant degree. More precisely, it is to be found in the distinction between phenomenon and noumenon, but, characteristically, nothing is said about essences, only about appearances. In other words, the world of appearances, the ordinary world of things, the ordinary world of cause and effect, and of the empirical self – all of this survives unscathed in this philosophy just as it does in everyday consciousness. In this sense Kantian philosophy is a philosophy of reconstruction; it merely reconstructs in scientific form what ordinary consciousness contains anyway. It may be said, therefore, to be far less radical and far less profound than, say, Hume's philosophy. Hume provided a penetrating critique of significant naturalistic concepts such as the self, causality and the thing. In so doing, he really did change the world to the point where it could be said that the self was lost beyond all redemption, as Mach expressed it.[13] In the same way, it could be said that for Hume there is no causality, there are no things.[14] Kant avoids such radical conclusions. Instead, in its entire vast profundity and effort, his philosophy amounts to recreating anew the world as it presents itself to consciousness, to producing with the enormous power of the productive imagination the world as it already exists. This feature of Kant contains as its implicit goal a possibility I have already mentioned. This is that in contrast to the rethinking of all deeper matters, in contrast to utopian thinking or to the realities of alienation, this grandiose metaphysical system was able to become the world view of alienation and of the blunted consciousness of the bourgeoisie.

LECTURE SEVENTEEN

16 July 1959

Ideology • The Concept of Depth

I tried last time to show you some of the features of Kant's philosophy that have contributed to its particular status as the standard philosophy of the so-called educated middle classes along the lines caricatured by Thomas Mann in the figure of Wulicke, the headmaster in *Buddenbrooks*, who never failed to allude to 'the categorical imperative of our great fellow citizen from Königsberg' when delivering himself of his thunderous speeches in honour of the Kaiser's birthday. It is nevertheless remarkable that such a vulnerable and eccentric philosophy as Kant's should have had this effect even though outward success was really the last thing on his mind. It is my opinion, however, that, as I have already pointed out, this philosophy must not be looked at abstractly on its own, but it must also be viewed as a social phenomenon and that these are matters that must be given more weight than is usually the case. I have also said that perhaps the deepest reason for this lies in a quality of Kant's philosophy that we have only touched upon. This is that in the upshot, despite its much acclaimed critical and anti-dogmatic elements, the world, or what English philosophers (in particular Sir William Hamilton) dubbed 'the world of common sense',[1] managed to survive Kant's onslaught more or less unscathed. In other words, despite his transcendental idealism the normal world of straightforward realism remains intact. I would add that this confirmation of the accustomed picture of the world, the accustomed concept of experience as characteristic of a world picture we can all live with, nevertheless contains an element that seemed more or less predestined for ideology because it implicitly negated the contrast between façade, between appearance, and essence. It tells us that even if the world we know is not the true and absolutely real world, it is one we *can*, and indeed *must*, come to terms with because all we really know of the other world, the world of essence, is that it is different from *what* we know, and that is really all we can say about it. This gave a boost to the uncritical consciousness, the normal consciousness of the ordinary philistine who simply wants to acquiesce in a more or less conventional view of the world without having to trouble himself further. You therefore find yourselves confronting the paradox that a philosophy like the Kantian that never ceases to insist on its claims to be critical ends up fostering uncritical thought. In this respect it stands at the opposite pole to Hegel, who had proclaimed that the existing world was rational, but who had made up for this with the concept of *dialectics*, the absolutely mediated nature of every existing thing. By doubting whether every existing thing is in reality what it immediately appears to be, Hegel ends up with a much more radical element of critique than there was in Kant.

Apart from this factor, however, it seems to me that there is a particular reason why Kant should have become complicit in, or have contributed to, that strange homespun philosophy, admittedly at the cost of sacrificing the critical and enlightened impulses to which I have drawn your attention now so often. This reason is connected with the element of χωρισμός, with the block or blocks, thanks to which a whole series of realms are compartmentalized and kept in isolation from one another. People may find it convenient to have one philosophy for weekdays and another for Sundays; or to have an empirical world in which you do just as you like, and then another, quite separate world of ideals into which you can retreat for more or less edifying purposes, without any real implications in practice. Lastly, you may discern in this χωρισμός a reflex of the universal division of labour that ends up encroaching upon the inner economy, the personal world of the subject. Thus the subject divides itself up into a subject that knows and a subject that believes, a subject that acts and a subject that hopes and that neatly separates the true, the beautiful and the good from one another. This has the effect that you cannot ask of the beautiful whether it is true in its innermost reality, for that would be to intrude on the comfort of the beautiful. By the same token, you cannot ask of the true whether it is also good since this would mean disturbing the general direction of the world in which we live by making the attempt to take our ideals seriously.

Take a look at the sententious poetry of Schiller, who was a Kantian and had good reason to think himself a Kantian. He wrote a number of very important theoretical essays which are without doubt the most productive contributions to the further development of Kantian aesthetics. If you look at his poetry from this point of view you can witness this process in which these neatly separated spheres are clearly transformed into more or less independent pictures for decorative domestic purposes. For example, when he writes in a poem on women that women 'weave heavenly roses into earthly life',[2] this already amounts to the idea that beauty or utopia, which he quite rightly associates with the erotic, has no binding authority. In other words, nothing is really left of this utopia that is embodied in those aspects of life that have not been entirely domesticated but a kind of ornament, a kind of illusion that helps to make the prosaic and banal life of the workaday world a little more bearable, but must on no account attempt to change it. All that remains are the 'heavenly roses' that are woven into it, almost as if utopia or the idea of the beautiful were a sort of transcendental funeral parlour. This element is already implicit in Kantian philosophy itself.

I believe it is quite useful to point these things out since this is usually not done in the normal course of education. On the one hand, you will have been told at school about classical literature and classical philosophy. They will have been represented to you as something exemplary, authoritative and even miraculous. On the other hand, as independent, thinking people you will have noticed that there is something fishy somewhere. But it is just as misguided to be blindly in awe of traditional cultural achievements as it is to condemn them all out of hand on the grounds that they are obsolete or out of tune with the spirit of our age. If such achievements are condemned today, it is because they incorporate this element of untruth that I have been attempting to show you by examining their central core, their genuine philosophical substance.

As I have indicated, the essential component of this corrupting tendency that is implicit in the meaning of Kantian philosophy from the outset appears to me to arise from the circumstance that the disaggregated elements constitute separate realms, like countries on a map, lying contiguously, but independently of one another – an image that Kant constantly uses by way of illustration. These separate realms have no authority over one another. The ideal only has power over life in the shape of *duty*, that is, in the shape of a completely formal principle that, because it is formal, can be interpreted at will – although that was undoubtedly the last thing in Kant's mind. It can be transformed at will into the famous or notorious 'dictates of the moment', that is to say, the demand that everyone should do his duty, as far as is possible, at the point where he happens to be and in the situation in life he has been assigned to. In other words, people have to satisfy all the heteronomous demands that are made upon them. I should like to say in more general terms, even though strictly speaking it does not belong in this lecture course, that the problem of the relation between duty and freedom – terms that are basically conflated by Kant in the practical philosophy – is left completely unresolved in the *Critique of Practical Reason*. The position is much the same in the *Critique of Pure Reason* with the epistemological model of this problem, namely the relation of universal and particular, of *a priori* and the contingent, the empirical.

By the same token, however, experience is not binding upon the ideals. That is to say, they are immune to criticism, they are suspended, as has been said, inalienably from the heavens[3] – although at the same time I can never quite rid myself of the idea that these ideals are like the famous herrings hanging from the ceiling that people are only allowed to snatch at,[4] and that these ideals are never subjected to productive criticism, an interactive exchange at the hands of living experience. This does not emerge clearly in the *Critique of Pure Reason*, but if you were to examine the principles of Kant's teachings on jurisprudence, in all their unprecedented rigour, teachings that have been derived from this idealism, you would very quickly perceive how lacking in experience such an ethics really is, and how open it is to exploitation for repressive purposes. This lack of authority can also be related to the fictional quality that I have been at pains to emphasize. This refers to the fact that we have knowledge neither of the true *reality*, nor of the *true* reality. And corresponding to this fictional quality we find the same process of the neutralization of culture in Kant. This neutralization is structural and can be seen in the pure lack of purposiveness of the beautiful that cuts off beauty from the sphere of knowledge, on the one hand, and from pure objectivity on the other. That is to say, it is cut off from total determination by the laws of causality which operate in the realm of true knowledge, while for its part the latter is made completely independent of the interventions of freedom, of the realm of practice. At this point there really is a pre-established harmony between the neutralization that has been characteristic of culture in the history of the 150 years following Kant and a tendency that is actually expressed in his philosophy – even though, in contrast to this, the idea of culture in Kant himself is still conceived of as the realization of reason.

In this respect, too, Kant finds himself, as I have remarked on more than one occasion, at a watershed of bourgeois consciousness. In a sense he provides the model for a habit of thought that has been widespread in normal bourgeois consciousness down to our own day. This is that curious synthesis of scepticism and dogmatism that each and every one of you will probably have experienced during your youth and from your family circumstances; it is, incidentally, a combination that does not fit badly with Kant himself since his philosophy represents a forced alliance of Humean scepticism and the dogmatism of classical rationalism. By scepticism I mean basically the bourgeois gesture that expresses the idea, well, what is truth? and which presumably likes nothing in the New Testament better than the passage when Pilate asks that very question: What is truth?[5] We should note that the only purpose of this question is to exclude every theoretical authority, every authoritative intervention of thought from the realm of experience. This was an attitude that made its contribution to the readiness of the bourgeoisie to swallow fascism and other forms of totalitarianism. On the other hand, however, certain ideas are supposed to remain inviolate and to be immune to all criticism. Such ideas remain dogmatic; they must not be touched. These two elements: the doubt that anything can be true and the unquestioned authority of norms that are regarded simply as givens within existing reality – this situation corresponds fairly precisely to the division that is rooted in Kant's philosophy.

I have tried at least to point out these things to you. It is my belief that they have not been fully spelt out in this way in the literature on Kant because Kant criticism, in so far as it has a social dimension, has focused on the concept of duty and the disguised theology it contains, but not on these aspects of Kant that I actually think much more important. I have only emphasized this to prepare the way for a discussion of a question to which I said at the very start of this course I would try and provide you with some sort of answer.[6] In the light of these tendencies, tendencies, you should note, that are not inherent in Kant's own consciousness, but what we might call ideas that have thrived in his shadow, the question we must ask is this: What is it that explains the authority of Kant, an authority that has established itself in the tradition in a completely different way? For to assert that Kant possessed all these features and that in all these respects he had succumbed to ideas characteristic of the history of the bourgeoisie after him, does not of course even begin to explain the unprecedented authority of his philosophy. That authority consists in an element through which Kant is transcended – if you will permit me the expression – that is to say, an element thanks to which Kant elevated himself above the prevailing consciousness of his age and that enabled him to tap a level of experience that had not really been accessible to consciousness before him. This is the phenomenon or aspect of Kantian philosophy usually referred to in the idiom of 'Sunday phraseology' as Kantian 'depth' – though of course we must note how this concept of *depth* has come down in the world. To cite one example, Marcus, the Old Kantian and late orthodox thinker, entitled one of his rather absurd books *From the Depths of Knowledge*[7] – a title that condemns itself. By depth he meant simply that what Kant reveals is not knowledge but instead the preconditions for the possibility of knowledge, that is to say, the transcendental mechanism. If that were the case, then any *theory* of knowledge would appear deep when juxtaposed to any *actual* knowledge. But might we not then be justified in asking whether in reality every piece of knowledge that throws light on something, every piece of knowledge that genuinely illuminates something, is not deeper than such an analysis of the machinery that is supposed to explain how such knowledge comes about?

If we are to take the claims of Kantian philosophy at all seriously, we cannot possibly be satisfied with such a concept of depth. It is clear, furthermore – and I should like to take the opportunity of saying something not just about the meaning of depth in Kant, but also about the concept of depth *per se* – that as it is generally used in Germany there can be no doubt that the concept of depth has had a catastrophic effect. This is because it is irrationalist and hostile to Enlightenment. According to such a concept thinking can only be deep if it refers to forces that lie beyond reason. To put it mildly, then, it stands in flagrant contradiction to the explicit intentions of Kant's philosophy. Kant would have retorted that the deepest foundation of his philosophy is in fact reason, that reason is the element unifying it in all its aspects and that anything that has claims to greater depth than reason cannot be contemplated. In fact he was quite consistent here and in his practical philosophy he was adamant in his rejection of that catastrophic concept of depth as something that could be combined with the irrational. In fact he designated reason as the sole legitimate source of right action. An action is only good if it is performed in accordance with the law of morality, and the law of morality is basically nothing but reason itself, as far as it determines our actions. Kant did not admit the existence of any concept of lawfulness other than what is to be found in reason and its immanent laws.

In contrast to this, the so-called irrational forces that have been glorified in the name of depth, especially in Germany, with such catastrophic consequences, are only to be found in Kant under the appellation of *affects* – and here he is following the rationalist tradition, particularly as it is expressed in the philosophy of Spinoza. These affects are things that have power over me; in so far as they have power, I am not free. They are supposed to be external to me, something merely empirical. For that reason his philosophy resists them with a determination that verges on the callous. Incidentally, I would not wish to hide the fact that his aversion to this entire sphere

of experience has its reactionary side, something of the yew hedges
of the eighteenth century. It is responsible for certain formalistic
elements of his aesthetics that unfortunately I cannot go into today.
At all events, what is usually referred to as 'deep' in the German
tradition is something he would have described as heteronomous.
Horkheimer once said that when people say that something is deep,
what is generally meant is that human beings should not prosper too
much in life. It is better that they should suffer and this justification
of suffering, the preference for the negativity of existence, the duplication of this negativity of existence, is what characterizes the concept
of depth that is so fashionable among us. This concept of depth, which
we have good reason to call masochistic, is in fact contradicted by
Kantian philosophy as a whole. This is confirmed by the positive use
of the concept of externality in the chapter on the Amphiboly of the
Concepts of Reflection and its apparent repudiation of the concept of
interiority that is generally associated with that of depth.

It has often been pointed out – and with some justice – that Kant's
philosophy is deeply imbued with *Protestantism* and particularly with
this concept of interiority. But we might object that in his hands
interiority is intensified to the point where precious little is left of
its core meaning, namely, the individual soul. In consequence what
survives of interiority is merely the abstract unity of reason, which,
admittedly, is purified of all externality. At the same time, Kant
relegates everything we generally associate with interiority to the realm
of the external. It is demoted to the level of mere psychology and
hence heteronomy, so that we end up with interiority itself becoming
the object of criticism. It is turned into something external, namely,
mere logical determinacy which lacks the wealth of interiority, but
which precisely because of this radicality of the concept actually transcends interiority or at least finds itself strenuously opposed to it.
Even though it is perfectly true that the turn towards inwardness
stems from the Protestant tradition, as do other features such as the
rigorous antithesis between belief and knowledge, it simply will not
do to reduce Kant, or indeed any other important philosopher, to his
so-called origins. If you can learn anything from what I have to tell
you perhaps it really should be to emancipate yourselves from this
question of origins. By this I mean you have to free yourselves from
the illusion that you have understood a problem better once you
know that it comes from this or that source. It is undisputed that the
tradition of Protestant interiority is the source of the rigour with
which Kant separated belief from knowledge, and also of his concept of duty. What is overlooked in the process is that the concept of
the individual as the soul in need of salvation, which is the idea

underlying this traditional Protestant concept of interiority, is dissolved by the development of the concept, that is to say, by the Kantian critique of reason – so that what we are left with is the very antithesis of what had been originally intended.

Of course, we must add – and I have no wish to conceal from you the complexity of Kant's argument – that the radical separation of idea and phenomenon, of phenomena and noumena, is objectively not entirely alien to the concept of *tragedy* that is generally associated with that of depth. This means that the finite is defined simply as the finite, as indeed is death. The meaninglessness of merely empirical existence and the fact that the empirical as such is finite, is separated, χωρίς, from its own meaning – has been made into a structural feature of this finitude and in a sense may be said to have been ratified by it. In this respect Schiller, whose concept of tragedy descends directly from Kant's philosophy, and who put this conception to work in his own plays, was an authentic Kantian. This concept of the tragic in its Kantian form asserts the complete incompatibility of the world of appearances in which we live as finite beings with the world of the idea that overtaxes us in principle and ensures that we come to grief. This concept of tragedy has a long German tradition in which tragedy is directly equated with depth. With the passage of time, however, this notion of the tragic has been exposed as superficial. That is to say, it amounts to the declaration that its meaninglessness is its true meaning and to the belief that we are in the presence of metaphysics, that the meaninglessness is a necessity, something that must be so and not otherwise. The sense of satisfaction that derives from the way in which 'the soul soars into the air' while the body is left behind like a corpse that 'rests upon the chair', simply blinds us to the truth that depth remains what it really is, namely what Hegel called 'the consciousness of distress',[8] that is to say, the reflexive form of suffering. It is my view that it is high time for a critique of the category of tragedy, not as a sublime and permanently valid expression of the human spirit, but as an heirloom from the stock of possessions of the middle classes.

So that is what I wanted to say to you about the concept of depth in Kant. In other words, that it should be distinguished from traditional ideas about depth of feeling, depth of interiority and all such matters. This remains the case even though in this thesis of the irreconcilability [of appearances and the idea], in what we have described as Kant's anti-utopian streak, this depth does meet up again with the conventional idea.

Furthermore, what I am giving you is not just an interpretation of Kant, but what might be termed a plan for a phenomenology of the concept of depth in philosophy; in other words an exposition of what might be covered by the idea of depth. You must be clear in your own minds that in Kant what we mean by depth has nothing to do with psychological depth because the mere term psychoanalysis is one that people in general still find shocking. It is well known that some people are so shocked by it that they instinctively feel the need to produce a psychosynthesis to oppose to psychoanalysis. This is why the attempt has been made to replace the concept of psycho-analysis with depth psychology. It sounds more reputable and it may be thought to contain something of that crypto-philosophy of depth[9] to the understanding of which I hope to have made some contribution. Whatever the situation may be with regard to nomenclature, the depth that Kant aspires to is not that of psychology, or the depths of the unconscious. If we were to misconstrue Kant by arguing that he had penetrated to the depths of the soul – as a great psychologist may well succeed in doing – this would be as alien to Kant as the common-or-garden metaphysics of depth which I have been discussing with you. For all *psychology* in Kant – and this brings me to the specific view of psychology contained in the *Critique of Pure Reason* – is no more than a science of psychology and if I may speak, as it were, topologically, in terms of a concept of depth, it would not even be present, be localized, in the field in which something like depth could be said to be situated. So-called depth psychology, too, would be nothing more than an empirical science in his eyes.

Incidentally, we should note the curious hostility to psychology that pervades German thought. It argues that psychology is an empirical science, while the soul because of its interiority is removed from the realm of the empirical. It follows that psychology must be a reprehensible and evil science. This hostility to psychology goes down to Husserl and even beyond Husserl to Heidegger and has all sorts of ramifications, right down to modern educational theory and God knows what else. It is very likely that this hostility is related to Kant's own fear of contact with the sphere of factual reality in the realm of the soul. Furthermore, if I may anticipate, you should be clear in your minds that Kantian philosophy shares this phobia. However, Kant's philosophy really does stand on a dividing line in this respect too. As philosophy, that is to say, as a discipline concerned with absolute validity or truth, it excludes psychology as a legitimate source of insight, albeit not completely. On the other hand, it is Kant's great merit – and this is his achievement when compared to the English philosophers – that he was the first to realize that the realm of the soul which in the tradition of German psychology was thought to be situated *outside* psychology, in fact belongs within it. He realized that there are facts of the soul, and that such facts of the soul are facts, much like other facts, and not *vérités éternelles*. Nowadays, there is a certain abuse of the ambiguity of the 'I' of the kind we have variously observed in Kant. By ambiguity I mean the fact that Kant cannot escape from the psychological dimension of the 'I', while at the same time he hypostatizes its logical form. By abuse I mean that the categories or forms of thought that are supposed to refer only to the intelligible 'I' are used to refer to our knowledge of the actual, empirical 'I'. Here, too, Kant is not wholly without blame since he taught – in a bold and very convoluted argument that can scarcely be reconstructed nowadays – that the empirical 'I', that is, the character that each individual human being happens to possess, is a repository of freedom, that is to say, it is a self that it has essentially given to itself. But in the first instance the relation of the *Critique of Pure Reason* to psychology is this: on the one hand, the analysis of the 'I', the analysis of the subject is sharply distinguished from the study of psychology. We are told that what psychology can teach us – namely, the idea of the soul and whatever it contains – is identical neither with the pure forms to which the critique of reason can be applied, nor with their concrete content. Instead, the soul is said to be a purely empirical matter. He goes on to say, however, or at least to imply, that the essential determinants of the life of the soul as it exists are to be kept within the confines of empirical science. We must add, however, that at this point his argument breaks off prematurely.

Next time I should like to bring together all the observations that follow from this and relate them to the concept of depth. I shall then attempt to give you some at least of the important arguments to be found in the Kantian critique of rational psychology, that is to say, of the psychology that attempted to make absolute, to hypostatize, various psychological categories by inferring them from pure reason. We shall see then that Kant's position is very much that of modern psychology, rather than of the obscurantists. This means that he treats the categories of psychology as empirical categories, even though, for that very reason, he excludes them from those of philosophy. The effect of this is that the arguments concerning his own depth, transcendental depth, must not be confused with arguments concerning psychological depth. I shall trace out the implications of this line of thought because I wish to confront you with its limitations, in particular with the question: What is the meaning of depth if it belongs neither to metaphysics nor to logic nor even to psychology? I believe that this will give us a crucial insight into the nature of Kant's philosophy.

LECTURE EIGHTEEN

21 July 1959

Psychology

I should like to remind you that in our discussions of the concept of depth and the meaning of talk about 'depth' in the *Critique of Pure Reason* we made the discovery that this depth was not psychological in nature, even though it involves immersion in the sphere of subjectivity. This may well strike you as very illuminating at first blush, and you will all have heard something or other about the non-psychological nature of the general thrust of Kant's thought and his preoccupation with *a priori* knowledge. But when you immerse yourselves in the text it turns out to be anything but obvious. For example, when you read that schematism is a hidden mechanism of the soul,[1] it is very difficult to conceive of this in other than psychological terms. The position is similar in the *Critique of Practical Reason* when Kant describes the coercion and sense of obligation that emanate from conscience.[2] Here modern depth psychology has even confirmed his insights, since today we know that what we may regard as the psychological counterpart of that Kantian concept, namely the super-ego, in fact exerts a kind of coercive psychological force that corresponds entirely to the effect that Kant ascribes to the moral law. Thus when you resolve to face up to the full implications of the question of Kant's *relation to psychology* you will be led back to what I have already said on a number of occasions, but you will see it in a new light. This is that as soon as you try to visualize what is meant by depth in Kant you will find yourselves in the realms of facticity, of factual realities or, in this instance, facts of the soul, concrete psychological elements – but with the distinction (as we shall see in due course) that the entire Kantian line of argument attempts to pull itself up by its own bootstraps. What I mean is that it owes its existence in great measure to these psychological or other material factors, but, at the same time, it is forced to interpret them in such a way that their factual nature is ignored. At all events, it is undoubtedly true that Kant's intentions are hostile to psychology.

It is likewise true that the difference between him and Hume is that you have the same turn towards the subject in both thinkers, but that in Kant it cannot be thought of in psychological terms. You can imagine this for yourselves; it has its own underlying motivation – that is to say, it is not a kind of arbitrary metaphysicizing act on Kant's part. Rather it reflects the fact that the real psychological mechanisms that Hume refers to – above all, those of association, that is, of the resemblance of experiences to one another or their contiguity[3] – are based on an assumption that is not made explicit in Hume's *Treatise*. This is the case even though they have been derived from what might be called experimental psychological observations. The assumption I am referring to concerns the unified consciousness which binds these associations together. In other words, when Hume criticizes the concept of the self which we are also concerned with in Kant, and dismisses it as a dogmatic prejudice, he is guilty of a certain naivety, since without a concept of the self it is not possible to conceive of the factors that it describes as psychological and that are supposed to replace the concept of the self. To put it another way, however our consciousness is conceived, if there *are* no unifying factors, if there is nothing to unify our experiences in the way that Hume describes when he talks about associations, then the concept loses its meaning. The distinction between the anti-psychological Kant and the psychological Hume at this point is not one of ideology. It derives from Kant's greater insistence on the data under scrutiny: that you cannot reduce the self to matters of fact that depend for their existence upon a concept of the self.[4]

Kant's repudiation of psychology is documented in countless passages as early as the *Critique of Pure Reason*, but with incomparably greater bluntness and explicitness in the *Critique of Practical Reason*. It became significantly more marked in the course of Kant's development, as can be seen from the fact that the changes introduced in the Second Edition of the *Critique of Pure Reason* are largely concerned with psychology. This rejection of psychology has two consequences that may be thought of as dialectically interrelated. I should like to discuss them with you now. The first is that a kind of demotion of psychology, and with it of all inner realities, is implicit in the fact that Kant develops the idea of *a priori* thinking in such a way as to assert that it is subjective in nature, but that it is independent of all psychologizing. This curious demotion of psychology begins in the *Critique of Pure Reason* and has survived as one of the most influential features of Kant's philosophy, one that has left its mark on German philosophy as a whole. This even holds good for the ontological and phenomenological trends in German thought that have explicitly set themselves up in opposition to Kantianism. I once described this situation by saying that in Germany the soul is too refined to have anything to do with psychology. Psychology has for its part insisted on its scientific status and separateness from philosophy, much as philosophy liked to think of itself as a *Weltanschauung* distinct from psychology. It responded to my rebuke by asserting that it wanted to have nothing to do with the soul. It is not difficult – and Nietzsche developed this idea on several occasions – to discern a theological legacy in this aspect of Kant's philosophy and the German tradition as a whole. That is to say, the soul must be sacrosanct; the soul must not be allowed to be involved in experience or to be contaminated by the contingent nature of experience. This is to protect the attributes of indivisibility, identity and immortality that were first formulated by Plato in the *Phaedo* and subsequently passed via Augustine into the entire Christian tradition. Thus this German philosophical tradition makes a sharp distinction between itself and psychology, and finds offensive everything that smells of psychology. Nevertheless, to be fair, it must be pointed out that for all this strange fear of contamination characteristic of German philosophy, it has long since become far too sophisticated to make use of the concept of the 'soul', which in a sense it regards as too empirical.

You will be aware that the latest attempt to gain freedom from psychology, and at the same time to preserve for philosophy categories that actually owe their existence to psychology, is the philosophy of Heidegger. In Heidegger's philosophy the term 'state-of-mind' [*Befindlichkeit*] refers to a whole series of attributes that form part of the actual, concrete, psychic life of human beings. Despite this they are treated as if they were characteristics of pure Being [*Sein*] as Being, which latter only possesses the peculiarity of revealing itself in a specific form, namely that of 'being there' [*Dasein*].[5] This has the effect that where psychological matters are referred to, they are transformed at a stroke into something that purports to testify to a meta-psychological realm. This entire phenomenon is responsible for tendencies in German philosophy and the German intellectual tradition that are inimical to every shade of Enlightenment. At the beginning of this course of lectures I told you that the Enlightenment was a failure in Germany.[6] This shows itself nowhere as vividly as in the attitude towards psychology, a subject which has largely been left to the mercies of the obscurantists. The attempt to isolate subjectivity from the empirical categories of psychology from which it draws its substance and to define it as a superior mode of being leads to a denial of the instinctual elements that are part of the subject and that constitute the genetic precondition of all knowledge.

For we know today that the ego principle – that is to say, the rationality that scrutinizes reality – is actually a form of energy that has been diverted from the reservoir of drives in our possession in the interests of self-preservation. This instinctual element, which under-lies every act of cognition in one way or another, as everyone can observe in himself as a knowing subject, is denied and resisted. This denial involves an act of repression, such as is found in the glorifica-tion of self-control [*Haltung*], a particular kind of demeanour that allegedly arises from the direct passage of metaphysical experiences into one's everyday mode of experience – while the psychological study of how this process is supposed to work is dispensed with. For example, I am aware of the situation in psychiatry, in German psychiatry, where schizophrenia is sometimes described with the Heideggerian term 'loss of being'; or even as a lack of self-control, as if a military bearing had priority over psychology and might even protect people from psychotic disturbances.

But at the same time I should like to emphasize that Kant's own theory of the soul and his critique of Wolff's rational theory of the soul call a halt to all these tendencies even though they may derive their authority from the anti-psychological tradition that goes back to his own philosophy. In this respect, too, as in many others, Kant represents a sort of watershed. That is to say, he does indeed try to establish a sphere – one which I can only describe as a *transcendental sphere* – that is supposed to be distinct from logic or metaphysics or psychology. On the other hand, however, thanks to the construc-tion of this sphere – which is indeed the most important task still remaining to us in this introductory course of lectures – the sphere of psychology may be said to have been liberated. Precisely because the actual psychic life of mankind is deemed not to be the legitimate source of the truth to which reflections upon the transcendental sub-ject are dedicated, this has the effect in Kant of making that life of the soul the object of empirical science. It thus becomes the very opposite of what has been made of it by the irrationalist tradition in Germany. We may add without exaggerating that the parts of Kant that can be seen to be the most advanced expression of the Enlightenment are those in which – despite his radical separation of the transcendental sphere from that of psychology – he turns psychology into an empirical

science and in which he largely concedes that the realm of psychology
is governed by the laws of cause and effect. It is this that I should like
to turn to now.

What I have in mind is to take a look at the chapter on the
Paralogisms. These passages were neglected for a long time, but they
have perhaps achieved a new topicality today because of their enlightened character.[7] What they are concerned with is a critique of
so-called rational psychology, that is to say, the attempt to derive the
soul as an entity, as a unified, self-identical, indestructible being from
pure thought by the processes of logic. This was the kind of project
that could be found in Leibniz's philosophy and its systematic formulation by Wolff and this is the object of Kant's critique. Kant's fundamental idea here is formulated programmatically, as it were, in the
introduction to chapter 1 of Book II of the Transcendental Dialectic,
and I should like to read you a few sentences from there and at the
same time make use of them to catch up on a few things concerning
the internal structure of Kant's philosophy that I may not have
explained to you as clearly as it was my duty to do. 'The following
general remark may, at the outset, aid us in our scrutiny of this kind
of argument' – that is to say, of the paralogism. A paralogism is a
fallacy that believes that it is possible to infer substantive knowledge
of one kind or another simply from pure concepts.[8]

> I do not know an object merely in that I think, but only in so far as I
> determine a given intuition with respect to the unity of consciousness
> in which all thought consists. Consequently, I do not know myself
> through being conscious of myself as thinking, but only when I am
> conscious of the intuition of myself as determined with respect to the
> function of thought.[9]

In a sense we are concerned here with two concepts of the self that
must be kept apart, because of their different referents, if we are to
understand what Kant intends in this passage. In the first place,
we have the self of which I am conscious when I think. It is really
nothing other than our good old synthetic unity of apperception, the
' "I think" that accompanies all my representations'. As you will
recollect, we said of this self that it really just means that all my
representations come together in the unity of my personal consciousness. This process of becoming conscious of myself as someone thinking, however, has nothing of psychology about it. It means nothing
but the simple objective fact that some sort of a connection between
experiences can arise only if they flow into an identical stream of
experiences, as Husserl would phrase it. However, this pure flow of

experiences, purified of all empirical characteristics, this purely abstract identity, tells me nothing about me in the second sense. This
sense is the idea that the self is a specific thing, a soul with this or
that substance and some characteristics and qualities or other. The
fallacy that Kant now wishes to demolish once and for all is the idea
that it is possible to take this formal account of the subject as a unity
that brings together that subject's experiences and deduce from it the
actual existence of a substantive self – whereas the truth is that the
concept of substance stands in need of intuitions if it is to be fulfilled.
That is to say, it would have to contain specific real contents, specific
experiences. We should note that Kant realized perfectly clearly and
without panicking that the concept of intuition or the empirical would
have to be applied to so-called inner experience, to what I know of
myself, just as much as to external reality. This means that what I
apprehend in myself under the heading of the *principium individuationis*, to wit, as a temporal, actual experience, is just as much a
factual reality, an empirical intuition, as any external intuition that I
happen to have of objects in space. My immediate self-consciousness
of some concrete conditions or other in which I happen to find myself
is an experience *of something*; it has a subject matter and substance
of its own, and is therefore in no wise to be distinguished from my
experiences of the external world.

I should also like to discuss this passage for a different reason, one
that is not quite appropriate at this point, but which at least gives me
the opportunity to emphasize something more strongly than I have
done up to now. It says here, 'I do not know an object merely in that
I think, but only in so far as I determine a given intuition with respect
to the unity of consciousness in which all thought consists'. In other
words, then, one factor that determines my experiences is that they
are subsumed into the unity of my consciousness, and that they are
my experiences and not those of another person. They enter into
relations with all the other experiences of *this* particular individual
subject, thanks to which they acquire their meaning. Now it seems to
me that I have used this *concept of unity* with a certain naivety, as a
matter of course, without really thinking about it and without saying
what ought necessarily to be said. I should have said that this concept of unity is one of Kant's constitutive concepts, we might almost
say, one of the most fundamental experiences that exist. You know
that the concept of synthesis plays a great role in Kant and that, as an
activity, synthesis consists simply in creating a synthesis out of a
diversity. Concepts like synthesis have a very different complexion in
different philosophies, and it may be of use to you to be able to
identify the specific complexion of the Kantian notion. Synthesis in

Kant does not mean what may be suggested to us unconsciously by the subsequent philosophy of Hegel. That is to say, it is not a mediation between opposites whose identity is defined from within. Synthesis in Kant means merely that a manifold, an assemblage of diverse things, is brought together in a unity. It is actually the decisive factor by means of which Kant may be said to have signed up to the tradition of a *philosophy concerned to dominate nature*.

The foe of this thinking – if I may be permitted to exaggerate somewhat – is the diverse, the many, that which is opposed to the autonomy of a self-controlling rationality. This includes the diffuse that always captivates us precisely because it is not uniform, because it is ambiguous. We are familiar with the diffuse from the countless myths in which elemental beings of a hybrid nature hover between man and beast, nature and man, shimmering and enticing us to follow them. In contrast, unity is the category of something like consciousness of self. It could almost be said that in Kant everything of metaphysical substance that is opposed to diversity has been gathered together in this idea of unity, of whatever is identical with itself. This is confirmed by the way in which this concept of unity plays a decisive role in the *Critique of Pure Reason* and the categories themselves all emanate from unity, to wit, the unity of consciousness, while the concept of unity is never discussed or deduced from anything else. Instead, it represents the canon by which everything else can be judged. That knowledge is *one* and the fact that this one has primacy over the many may be said to be the metaphysical premise of Kantian philosophy. It is also the point at which Kant concurs with the Enlightenment in the broadest possible sense, as indeed with early Greek thought and with Christian thought in its entirety. This emphasis on unity at the expense of diversity is a feature of the tradition that Kant adopts without reflection. I would say that the operations that lead to an escape from this kind of thought and of which I have attempted to give you at least an inkling are all connected with the possibility of thinking critically about the concept of unity – which is inseparably connected to the concept of the first principle. At the same time – and this characterizes it as something I have described as a fundamental experience of the *Critique of Pure Reason* – this concept of unity cannot be said to be a mere abstraction that has been applied retrospectively.

Kantian unity – and this may be seen as an aspect of the profundity of Kant's philosophy – is not a mere homogenization that results from depriving a mass of diverse, varied things of their differentiating features, while retaining the one thing they have in common. This unity is understood by Kant to be modelled on the unity of consciousness itself; it is in a sense prior to all knowledge in the shape of the identity of the subject that is then correlated to the unity of any object that manifests itself. To that extent it is not so much the product of knowledge as its essence. If you like, we might say that in this sense the *Critique of Pure Reason* culminates in the thesis that unity is not something produced by consciousness, but it is the essence of knowledge that arises from a consciousness, which itself is nothing other than unity. The ' "I think" that accompanies all my representations' means nothing but the unity that combines to make all my representations *mine*, and not those of another human subject. Thus unity is truly the metaphysical centre to which everything else is 'attached'. Put another way, thinking and unity are actually the same thing in Kant. I believe that he would have accepted a statement along these lines, even though it instantly throws up the question of how such a unity manages to do anything – and the even more difficult problem of how such a unity is in fact mediated by the many to which it relates. Now, the organ, the mediating category by means of which this absolute unity is related to the plurality of things is the unity of personal consciousness, without which no representations are possible. This is because it consists in the plurality, that is, in the many, in the experiences that combine to make me into a subject and to form such a unity simply because they are *my* experiences. Its function as the mediating factor, the only possible mediating factor between the hypostatized unity and the plurality that is the deepest reason for the privileged position ascribed by Kant to the subject – namely, to personal consciousness, the unity of consciousness – about which we have learnt in the passage we have just been examining.

As for the individual arguments against the paralogisms, the fallacies, even though I believe that I have sufficiently explained the principle to you, I should like to illustrate it with a few characteristic models. For example, we can look at the concept of *substance*. You must bear in mind that in Kant substance is a category, that is to say, substance is not an existent being as such, but that whenever we speak of substance we are in the presence of a necessity of thought that is grounded in the transcendental mechanism of thought as such. However, this mechanism of thought only yields valid knowledge if it refers to something we can intuit, if it has a content, but it degenerates into vacuity, baselessness and empty assertion if it has nothing to get its teeth into.

> In all judgements I am the *determining* subject of that relation which constitutes the judgement. That the 'I', the 'I' that thinks, can be regarded always as *subject*, and as something which does not belong to

thought as a mere predicate, must be granted. It is an apodeictic and indeed *identical* proposition; but it does not mean that I, as object, am for myself a *self-subsistent* being or *substance*. The latter statement goes very far beyond the former, and demands for its proof data which are not to be met with in thought, and perhaps (in so far as I have regard to the thinking self merely as such) are more than I shall ever find in it.[10]

This final sentence may be said to be a lethal blow to the concept of the substantiality of the soul because it amounts to the following statement: In a sense I can know myself as an Absolute since as a thinking subject – as the thinking that accompanies all my representations – I am the necessary and indispensable precondition of every external and internal perception. But this does not mean that anything at all is said about me as an object, and thus as an empirical 'I', let alone as anything absolutely enduring. The fact that without the form of this 'I' no contents can be thought does not imply that it can become an object, can be reified; it does not mean that we may think of it as we might think of it once it has been filled with data. Since the data are determined by time, since they change and are modified by time, it could be said – and this is implicit in Kant's argument – that these data do not empower us to grant the soul the status of absolute being, presiding over the changes in its concrete contents, its concrete manifestations which I perceive within myself in the shape of internal intuition. This assertion represents a damaging blow to the idea of the substantiality of the soul. An even more damaging one is perhaps contained in the following passage that I should like to read you because it marks the point – and after all we have said about Kant I regard this as a piece of fair play that I owe him – because it comes closest to the point we have reached in our deliberations concerning the relation of the one to the many and in general concerning that of the transcendental self to the individual self.

> That the 'I' of apperception, and therefore the 'I' in every act of thought, is *one*, and cannot be resolved into a plurality of subjects, and consequently signifies a logically simple subject, is something already contained in the very concept of thought, and is therefore an analytic proposition.[11]

Here Kant quite unambiguously asserts what I have told you about and what you will have difficulty finding so clearly stated elsewhere in the *Critique of Pure Reason*. This is that the sentence 'I think' only has a meaning if it refers to the singularity of a specific self whose experiences are connected and are functionally interrelated by the fact that they are *his* experiences and not those of anyone else. We may note in passing that this admission contains the implication that the attempt that we find in so many interpretations of Kant to draw a sharp line between subjectivity and psychology of every kind is simply not tenable. For by making such a singularity the foundation – instead of a universality or a plurality – Kant already points to a factual existence and even to an already constituted individual existence. 'But this does not mean that the thinking "I" is a simple *substance.* That proposition would be synthetic.' This means it would be a proposition that only comes into being by synthesizing a series of different elements, that is to say, by combining intuited elements into a unity, while the substantial cannot be conceived of in a formal unity without regard to its possible content.

> The concept of substance always relates to intuitions which cannot in me be other than sensible, and which therefore lie entirely outside the field of the understanding and its thought. But it is of this thought that we are speaking when we say that the 'I' in thought is simple.[12]

This statement contains nothing less than the admission that the identity of the subject, personal identity, is so formal that it almost reduces itself to the tautology that the experiences of a singular subject are his experiences and not those of anyone else. But it insists that beyond that the expression of identity does not imply something like a substantial identity of human beings with themselves.

And this conclusion, we may say, really only differs by a hair's breadth from Hume's criticism of the concept of the self. In any discussion of empirical psychology, psychology as science, you would really need a magnifying glass to see the difference between empiricism and the *Critique of Pure Reason.* It has to be said that it has taken a long time to digest this last proposition. It has taken a very long time really to liberate ourselves from the mythology of the identity of the soul and to realize that this bond of identity is so tenuous that quantity reverses into quality. I mean by this that when we think of ourselves as having a permanent identity, we mean something so formal that, actually, we do not mean anything at all. Proust's entire cycle of novels could be said to be a single magnificent attempt to portray the non-identity of the psychological subject within its identity. And if you are interested in the original experience underlying the thought and the ideas of Gottfried Benn, you will encounter there a similar phenomenon.[13] All of these very advanced things can already be found in the *Critique of Pure Reason.* I would not like

to let the opportunity slip to point out that one element of the greatness of the *Critique of Pure Reason* is that a whole series of its
speculative propositions, propositions that were well in advance of
its age, have now either been absorbed into the individual sciences or
else have been reflected in major works of art.

LECTURE NINETEEN

23 July 1959

The Concept of the Transcendental (III)

I should like to begin by taking up the thread of our examination of Kant's views on the so-called rational psychology which we have been looking at as a preliminary to making secure our understanding of the concept of depth in transcendental philosophy. I should like briefly to discuss a few more passages from the chapter on the paralogisms so as to give you the core of the argument. Here, as elsewhere, I am of course acting in accordance with the principle of paradigmatic learning. This means that by interpreting particularly crucial passages – passages of key significance – I believe that I can not only focus on the essential features of Kant's thinking but also enable you to extrapolate from these passages to others elsewhere in the argument. What I want you to understand is that you should make the effort to apply what you have learnt from the interpretations I have given to other passages that you have studied for yourselves.

So what I am concerned with here is the proposition about my identity with myself. Kant states:

> The proposition, that in all the manifold of which I am conscious I am identical with myself, is likewise implied in the concepts themselves, and is therefore an analytical proposition.

The unity of personal consciousness is indeed identity in the most abstract possible sense. It means that all the contents of consciousness, all the facts of consciousness are to be referred to this self, this individuality, that is identical and present in them.

But this identity of the subject, of which I can be conscious in all my representations, does not concern any intuition of the subject, whereby it is given as an object, and cannot therefore signify the identity of the person, if by that is understood the consciousness of the identity of one's own substance, as a thinking being, whatever changes it may undergo. No mere analysis of the proposition 'I think' will suffice to prove such a proposition; for that we should require various synthetic judgements, based upon given intuition.[1]

You see here as in a test tube the prototype of the arguments that constantly recur in the so-called negative part, the critical part in the narrower sense, of the *Critique of Pure Reason*. We might describe the position simply by saying that the fallacies of reason or the reasons for the mistakes of reason are always to be found in the one circumstance. This is that something that is merely subjective, a merely reflexive concept, a form, mistakes itself for something objective, something independent of all the specific facts of experience – and it does so because all the elements of the knowledge of substantive contents require these subjective, formal components.

The entire proof of the antinomies, of the paralogisms as well as the amphibolies, all the things that Kant has criticized, that he has 'smashed', all say the one thing, again and again. This is that something subjective, namely, the form – which possesses validity only in relation to a matching content, and fulfils any sort of objectivizing function only in relation to this content – that this subjective element claims to be objective. We might say that this is the pattern of the amphibolies, the pattern of the confusion on which all the fallacies of reason are based. And what you can take home with you is what I have already told you. This is that there is a sense in which the *Critique of Pure Reason* fits into the general movement of the Enlightenment. For as in André Gide's play about Oedipus, the Enlightenment states – and here it goes against all mythological ideas, all metaphysical underpinnings – that what you think of as an existing, objective thing is in reality none other than yourself. What it comes down to is simply man and nothing besides.[2] Thus, as I believe I already pointed out to you last time, the argument is that this formal identity of consciousness is just what it says. The fact is that all my experiences are defined as *mine* and not those of anyone else. They tell us nothing about the objective, substantive identity of the individual. It is not the case that this identity is permanently present in me in concrete terms. So what we have here is a confusion between the *pure conceptual form* of identity and a material identity, something actually existing.

And finally, here is one last passage, probably the most crucial of all, from the chapter on the paralogisms:

> That I distinguish my own existence as that of a thinking being, from other things outside me – among them my body – is likewise an analytic proposition; for *other* things are such as I think to be *distinct* from myself. But I do not thereby learn whether this consciousness of myself would be even possible apart from things outside me through which representations are given to me, and whether, therefore, I could exist merely as a thinking being (i.e. without existing in human form).[3]

I read this passage out to you with a certain muted exclamation of triumph because it is the passage in the *Critique of Pure Reason* where Kant directly expresses the idea that I have rather laboriously been trying to convey to you. This is the idea that all the talk of an 'I' and all the other features that are claimed to be transcendental elements in Kant actually presuppose something like an empirical individuality.

When Kant says that I could probably not exist 'merely as thinking being', without *being* a human being, in other words, without my being an object of anthropological study, or without my being an empirically determinate, factual reality – then this means that the critique of the claim to absolute apriority, to the absolute primacy of the ' "I think" that accompanies all my representations' may be adjudged a success. The only difficulty – and we shall have to concern ourselves with this in what follows – is that Kant refuses here and in many other places to accept the full implications of his own assertion. Instead he leaves the matter standing with the logical priority of the 'I think' over mere factual reality, without drawing any conclusions from the question of whether we may speak meaningfully of an 'I think' in the absence of an actually existing 'I'. At this juncture, then, he has indeed arrived at the insight we have been labouring over, but at the same time it fails to have any consequences for his construction of apriority. You can see here Kant's refusal of consistency, the gesture which Brecht once expressed as taking the form of 'whoever says A, need not say B'. You can see that this gesture is of enormous importance for its insistence that the world is fissile, that there is no reconciled unity of subject and object. However, his refusal also has its negative aspect because the theory remains inconsistent in its own terms, and so crucial parts of it become untenable. What is being said here is nothing less than that this naive self which forms the starting-point of so much epistemological speculation – as we find, for example, in the English psychological philosophers, Locke and

Hume – has absolutely no priority over any other notion of the self. Furthermore, this self has a content and even its physical personality cannot be simply ignored, in other words, we cannot just overlook the fact that we are dealing with a particular psycho-physical being called 'man'. It is perfectly clear that this delivers a severe blow to our ability to use as our starting-point the absolute self-certainty of the self that directly apprehends some data or other, as well as all the implications of this that we have discussed in such detail. I do not wish to emphasize those things here. Instead what I wish to stress is that the ontological primacy of the empirical person as a soul can in fact no longer be sustained as it was by rationalist psychology. That primacy turns out to be no more than what latter-day neo-Kantians would have called a merely methodological primacy, that is to say, a primacy of presentation, not a primacy that emanates from the nature of the matter in hand.

I should like to make two further points to round off what we have said about the chapter on paralogisms. On the one hand, I believe that Kant's critique has made matters too easy for itself; it is *too* radical in one sense. This is because he offered a number of definitions relating to the world of the outer senses, the world of things, without paying heed to the fact that they could be applied just as easily to the world of the inner senses, to the psyche. You constantly come across turns of phrase that indicate that where this psychological factor is empirical, it is intangible, ephemeral, a relation between aspects, rather than something with substance. You must remember here that according to Kant substance is a category, in other words, a form of thought that is indispensable if we are to bring order into our intuitions. If you consider, further, that the character of the phenomenal that he ascribes to the content of everything concerning the psyche applies in equal measure to external realities, then you will surely realize that Kant has failed to see that the phenomenon of *reification* must apply to the phenomena of the psyche too. By this I mean the phenomenon that such a relation permits specific expectations for the future and specific memories of the past, just as he had shown this to operate in the case of external objects. Cast your minds back to my detailed interpretation of a passage in the chapter on amphibolies,[4] which says how startling it is that a thing really consists of relations, namely, the relations between its different phenomenal aspects – the scientists would talk in terms of functional equations. Exactly the same thing might be said of inner phenomena and indeed a pupil of Max Scheler – I believe he was called Haas – wrote a book in the 1920s in which he developed the implications of this idea,[5] admittedly from different philosophical assumptions. These assumptions were those of a material phenom-enology, leading to talk of a psychological world of things. In other words, then, it is possible for enduring, substantial structures to develop within the economy of the psyche, the realm of the intuitions given to us in the course of experience. These structures are subject to the laws of causality and in their turn they set up rational expecta-tions in exactly the same way as in the case of events in the external world. Kant failed to see this possibility of objective realities in the psyche and thus overlooked the element of truth that is after all to be found in the rationalist doctrine of the soul that he was combating. This element of truth is that there really is such a thing as personal identity, an empirical identity of the individual which takes the form of a thing-like relation between psychological phenomena, between individual modes of reaction.

All this may seem to you to be mere pedantry, but what depends on it is nothing less than the category of *character* in psychology. Only via this route that I have sketched for you can psychology be in a position to provide a science of character. And to me at least, the development of such a science is the most important goal that psy-chology can aspire to. A school of psychology that postpones the establishment of a science of character to the Greek calends – and many schools of psychology do just that – is really just fooling around in its own forecourt, instead of pressing forward to the heart of the matter, while this corrosive critique of rational psychology leaves absolutely no room for the concept of character at all. This has major implications for the Kantian system because in Kant's ethics – which is closely connected at this point to his theory of knowledge – the concept of character is defined as intelligible character: that is to say, as the cause of a person's individual actions which can, therefore, be said to be subject to the causality exercised by his character. In this sense Kant is in complete agreement with the idea of a psychology of character. For we know that people who have a definite character, a neurosis, for example, constantly repeat specific actions of a specific type, and these actions have causes that are independent of their conscious will. For example, they repeatedly behave in such a way as to bring about their own failure in their profession because they unconsciously undermine their own activities. We call these modes of behaviour character neuroses and this describes a particular type of character. Kant sees this when he says in the *Critique of Practical Reason* that my individual actions are mediated with my character by causality.[6] Only he adds – and this may be taken as his reply to his 'oversight' on this point in the *Critique of Pure Reason* – that I originally give myself this character through an act of freedom.[7] This declaration, on which the doctrine of freedom of the *Critique of Practical Reason* is actually based in so far as it possesses a positive content, this declaration is completely incompatible with the idea of psychology as a science. I mean by this that anyone with the faintest notion of the psychology of character will be aware that character is formed in early childhood on the basis of specific conflicts with the surrounding world and the resolution of these conflicts. It follows that it is utterly absurd for Kant to ascribe this achievement – as he explicitly does – to the autonomous reason of the child, who has no knowledge of himself. Likewise, if you take the concept of *conscience* you will discover a similar ambiguous attitude towards the insights of psychology which is very relevant in this context. At the phenomenological level Kant gives a very satisfying account of the compulsive, inexorable and coercive features of conscience.[8] However, he goes on to claim conscience as an absolute, whereas, as Hegel would say, it is really something that is itself asserted; that is to say, it emerges from the dynamics of the psyche. And its coercive elements in particular, which are hypostatized by Kant, are in reality nothing less than the stigmata of oppression and failure.[9]

These are the essential points that I wanted to convey to you in connection with Kant's critique of the psychological paralogisms. This is the point where his criticism of them goes too far and condemns itself to sterility. On the other hand, we must also say that in one respect he does not go far enough. For when Kant claims that concepts like identity, substantiality and singularity – concepts that he criticizes – can only be said to have an application if they refer to phenomena, to specific intuitions, he ought really to make the same claim with regard to the idea of the synthetic unity of apperception. For this is the foundation that underpins the transcendental philosophy, namely the simple 'I think'. Now, he does in fact do this up to a point. He says that this transcendental subject must not be understood to be an empirical reality but that it is meaningful only if it is filled with intuition. However, he is not entirely consistent here, but leans towards the establishment of a realm of pure forms without realizing that these pure forms are mediated, as his successors would say, by their content, just as their content is mediated by their form. This process is described in one of the greatest chapters of Hegel's *Logic*,[10] with a simplicity of which, remarkably enough, the *Critique of Pure Reason* did not show itself to be capable, despite its much more elementary nature. In actual fact a further consequence of the chapter on the paralogisms ought to be that the concept of the subject it contains, and that might be said to be nothing other than the legacy of this rational psychology, should not be allowed to stand as a pure *a priori* concept. Its *a priori* nature and the intuitions which are required to give that *a priori* nature substance – these two realms ought really to stand in a relation of mutual reciprocity. However that may be, I believe that I have said enough to persuade you that Kant's so-called profundity cannot be taken to mean profundity in a psychological sense. One reason for this is that the entire sphere of psychology is demoted to the level of mere appearance and is not even assigned to the *a priori* world. Another is that within psychology itself he completely fails to take cognizance of its own depth, to wit, the unconscious mechanisms by means of which such things as identity and non-identity, harmony and disharmony arise in the realm of the psyche.

I shall continue with the question of depth in Kant. If I am not mistaken, the concept of depth closest to us, if we were to make use of it nowadays, would be the *concept of essence* as contrasted with the façade, the superficial appearance. I shall not enquire who or what is responsible for this curious turn of phrase. It is not clear whether we should blame Hegel's *Phenomenology* and its descendants for dredging medieval realism and the medieval concept of essence from the past – the *essentia* – or whether this notion of essence and essentiality is an unconscious legacy of Hegelian philosophy itself, in which 'essence' occupies a central position. I do not wish to adjudicate on this matter. At all events, the distinction between essence and appearance does not really appear in Kant. The point at which it might have appeared is the chapter entitled The Ground of the Distinction of all Objects in General into Phenomena and Noumena.[11] This, incidentally, is a chapter I would like to recommend that you read because there is a sense in which it has been constructed in accordance with the principle of 'Once your work is done, it is good to rest'. That is to say, once the extraordinary efforts required by the transcendental analysis have been completed, this chapter takes a backward look and collects up, with something of a magisterial gesture, the essential insights that have been established. From this vantage-point much light is shed retrospectively on what are in part the very difficult and impenetrable analyses of the earlier chapters.

To repeat: by phenomena, by appearances, Kant understands not just the actually given appearances that I perceive at any moment, but the entire world of appearances, that is to say, the world of things in so far as they are known to us, that is, in so far as there are interconnections between appearances. This includes the entire realm of inner experience, the experience of psychological phenomena. The world of noumena, in contrast, would be the world as it is in itself

or, to put it another way, the world as it is revealed to us as a result
of pure thought, independently of any given intuitions. In fact the
chapter on phenomena and noumena is the only chapter in which the
word 'essence' [*Wesen*] occurs in Kant. He speaks there of 'sensible
essences' and elsewhere of 'intelligible essences' – although it is not
absolutely clear what he means by them. We are left with the feeling
that it is something of a makeshift term for 'objects'. The passage
reads:

> At the same time, if we entitle certain objects, as appearances, sensible
> entities [*Sinnenwesen*] (phenomena), then since we thus distinguish the
> mode in which we intuit them from the nature that belongs to them in
> themselves, it is implied in this distinction that we place the latter,
> considered in their own nature, although we do not so intuit them, or
> that we place other possible things, which are not objects of our senses
> but are thought as objects merely through the understanding, in op-
> position to the former, and that in so doing we entitle them intelligible
> entities [*Verstandeswesen*] (noumena).[12]

Here, then, in this distinction between sensible entities or essences
and intelligible entities or essences we plainly have the concept of
'essence' – quite without elucidation and if I am not mistaken this is
the only passage in the *Critique of Pure Reason* where it occurs.

However, it is highly symptomatic that the *Critique of Pure Reason*
does not contain a doctrine of essence. It is in general not a bad idea
when attempting to appropriate the specific nature of a philosophy
not to confine oneself to an examination of the concepts it contains;
particularly since the concepts that occur in one philosophy are for
the most part also to be met with in others. Thus it is very difficult to
grasp the distinctions between two philosophies by focusing on the
differences in their basic vocabularies. But it is much easier to isolate
the particular features of a philosophy by examining the concepts
that it does *not* contain. I once confided to Walter Benjamin my plan
to give an account of a philosophy purely in terms of the concepts
that were taboo in it, not those that it employed.[13] He was very
enthusiastic about the idea. I carried out this plan, at least in part, in
both the texts that I published on Benjamin.[14] I believe it would be
worth the effort to produce such an *index verborum prohibitorum*,
an index of forbidden concepts, in the case of Kantian philosophy.
The concept of 'essence' would merit a place of honour in such a list.
I may remind you here of the passages I read out to you from the
chapter on the amphibolies,[15] in which Kant says explicitly and with
some feeling that the defining features that the understanding can

regard as imparting valid knowledge are all external; they are the defining features of a synthesis that brings together all the appearances as a unity, but that does not venture to unlock the phenomena from within in the way that all the idealists insisted on, even including Schopenhauer on the most crucial point.

The reason for Kant's rejection of the concept of essence and the resultant deviation of Kantian depth from what is generally understood by that term will be obvious to those of you who have followed my argument up to now. It is that the insight into the essentials of being, insight into the noumenal world that would constitute such a world of essential being, is simply denied to us; we can have absolutely no knowledge of whatever lies *behind* the façade, *behind* the appearances. If then *after* Kant, above all in Hegel, the concept of essence was able to spring back to life, that was a function of the restructuring process that the entire system underwent in post-Kantian idealism. To make the point another way: I have told you that post-Kantian philosophy ignored the Kantian block; that it said that the things-in-themselves which we find in Kant are nothing but an empty phrase, and that, moreover, the things-in-themselves are *after all* cognizable by us – simply because things-in-themselves are nothing but reason conscious of itself. Since reason is empowered to have knowledge of the Absolute, it is likewise empowered to have knowledge of essences – without, of course, remaining fixated on them. Instead Hegel had the brilliant insight that the two spheres which point in two different directions in Kant – the world of phenomena and the world of noumena, which are separated by one of those trenches so familiar in Kant – stand in a necessarily reciprocal relation to each other. This means that there is no essence without appearance and no appearance without essence. You can picture this quite easily to yourselves by reflecting that it makes absolutely no sense to say that a thing has an 'essence' unless you realize that the same thing must also have a surface, an appearance. Conversely, it is meaningless to speak of the façade or the surface of a thing unless you simultaneously postulate the existence of its essence. Because of the Kantian χωρισμός, because knowledge is not in control of its own true object, this element vanishes from the scene in his philosophy. Formally, as I have said, space has been reserved for the noumena and therewith for the essential. But Kant says quite explicitly that the consciousness we have of them is quite empty and we can make absolutely no use of it.[16]

I should now like to move on and try to confront in all seriousness the question of what can be said to survive; what actually is the substance of this Kantian philosophy – and I hope that none of you will take this to refer to the category of 'substance' about which I have told you more than enough. What I mean to ask is what is the *substantial meaning* that we are left with in Kant? The answer lies in a revision of the concept of the transcendental that we have to undertake and that will simultaneously introduce us to the way the concept is employed by Kant's successors – by Fichte, Schelling and to a certain extent as early as Reinhold.[17] You should begin by adopting the negative approach I have outlined today. Consider all the things that do *not* come within the compass of the transcendental. In the first place, the sphere of the transcendental, that is, the realm of the constitutive, of the *a priori*, of the conditions upon which all experience, all content, is based, is not psychological. For psychology is part of the science of the world; it belongs to the everyday, just like zoology or geography or astronomy – and it therefore presupposes intuition. According to Kant, transcendental philosophy may not be based on that. I am repeating all this so that you should have Kant's ·concept of the transcendental clearly before you, namely the relatively straightforward and generally comprehensible definition of the transcendental which we took as our starting-point. This is the idea that Kant calls all investigations transcendental that are based on the possibility of synthetic *a priori* judgements. Thus they cannot be psychological even though there is a remarkable similarity between psychological analysis and transcendental analysis. If you take the trouble to examine the mechanisms by means of which Locke – who, curiously enough has the greatest similarity to Kant of all the great philosophers, even though Kant would turn in his grave at the mere thought – if you take the trouble to look at the stages by means of which the concepts of reflection, in other words the only valid form of knowledge, come into being, as contrasted with the ephemeral impressions of the senses, you will discover that this psychological account of the mechanisms of knowledge in Locke is startlingly similar to that of Kant.[18] And it has turned out again and again that so-called transcendental analyses – that is to say, analyses of the mechanisms by means of which our knowledge comes into existence – orientate themselves towards the canon of psychology, in other words towards the canon of the interconnections between the elements of consciousness in the empirical consciousness and the elements abstracted from it. Looking in one direction, transcendental analysis is always the abstraction from something psychological – accompanied by declarations to the effect that it has nothing at all in common with psychology. It is nevertheless a remarkable state of affairs that, overtly or tacitly, all philosophers from Kant to Husserl have assumed a kind of parallelism between psychological and transcendental analysis. At the same time, they allow it to escape them again from fear of dirtying their hands with empirical reality and hence of losing touch with the truth in all its purity.

However, it is also true that the sphere of the transcendental in Kant must not be a sphere of pure logic. I can show you what this means in a rather pedantic fashion by drawing your attention to one point. This is that if the formal principle of identity were identical with the proposition of the ' "I think" that accompanies all my representations', this would spare Kant the inconvenience of making any distinction between formal logic and transcendental logic as a logic that establishes the possibility of experience. For in that event the principle of identity that you find in formal logic would be identical with the basic tenet of transcendental philosophy. Moreover, attempts to prove this very point have repeatedly been made. That is to say, attempts have been made to interpret the proposition A = A, the pure principle of identity, the supreme law of formal logic, as if it were identical with the proposition of the ' "I think" that accompanies all my representations'. Please do not misunderstand me here. It is not possible to wish this piece of extreme formal logic away from its position at the very heart of the *Critique of Pure Reason*. Without this element of the identity of propositions, without the demand that all the judgements in a consciousness should be mutually compatible, the idea of a transcendental consciousness, of the ' "I think" that accompanies all my representations' would not be possible. For the idea that this 'I think' provides for the unity of all the individual representations contains the logical implication that the 'I think' brings all those representations into a logical relation to one another. It follows that any representations that are incompatible with others in this unity must logically be excluded from it. On the other hand, however, in the *Critique of Pure Reason* – and this is the crucial factor – this formal identity is a necessary, but not a sufficient factor to establish the nature of consciousness. Further elements are called for. Above all, according to the first version of the *Critique of Pure Reason*, in Section 2 of the Deduction of the Pure Concepts of Understanding, he calls for the [synthesis of] reproduction in the imagination,[19] that is to say, the presence of an absent thing. Needless to say, I can only speak of reproduction in the imagination[20] if I include a temporal element as a necessary factor. However, formal logic has nothing to say directly about time – although Kant does indeed say at one point that the mathematical (i.e. arithmetical) operations that we are accustomed to today should be regarded as the operations of a logical calculus and hence of formal logic; as such they would necessarily pass through a temporal sequence.[21] Thus in this sense the *Critique of Pure Reason* or the sphere of the transcendental cannot be called logical either, if we have to think of it as the summation of everything to which the possibility of synthetic *a priori* judgements can refer. Nor – a final point, which I can propose here only in a sentence – can the sphere of the transcendental be metaphysical. This means that it may not surpass the bounds of possible experience; it must not be hypostatized; the concepts of reflection may not be treated in the sphere of the transcendental as if they were things-in-themselves. I shall have more to say on this point next time.

LECTURE TWENTY

28 July 1959

The Concept of the Transcendental (IV)

Our discussions had reached the point where we were considering
the meaning of the concept of the transcendental in Kant, but in a
somewhat broader sense, at a distance from the literal meaning of the
text. If the transcendental, or rather the transcendental subject, that
is to say, the most general point of reference that is supposed to
guarantee the possibility of universally valid and necessary knowledge, is really no more than a merely logical unity, we could not
imagine how spontaneity or activity could be ascribed to it. How
something that is not in any sense individuated in time and space,
that is essentially no more than a factor that unifies different things
– and is thus no more than a logical abstraction – is able to generate
representations, remains completely obscure. The problem we are
facing here is something you must take very seriously indeed because
you must not forget that the concept that actually characterizes the
entire transcendental logic in Kant is the concept of spontaneity.
Moreover, even where he describes these transcendental connections
as relations, functions, so that we need not think of them as having
been produced by anyone or anything, they are nevertheless referred
to, in one famous passage of the Transcendental Deduction, as activities.[1] But by the same token, if Kant's transcendental subject were a
psychological subject – in however etiolated a sense – it would still be
something individuated in time and space and in accordance with the
categories. In terms of the distinctions made in the *Critique of Pure
Reason* this means that it would be an appearance. It would, therefore, be constituted by transcendental conditions rather than being a

constituens, as the transcendental subject really should be according to the system of the *Critique of Pure Reason*. You are aware that we have returned again and again to the point that the concepts of *constituens* and *constitutum* are reciprocal, and that one *cannot* be reduced to the other. Moreover, this is an idea that holds no terrors for us. However, lest you precipitately read it into Kant, I ought to tell you that nothing could be further from his thoughts. For as soon as you actually take what amounts in his theory to the *constitutum* and interpret it as the precondition of the *constituens*, you will destroy the entire system. Literally. Because this would be to make the transcendental dependent upon the temporal and it would become subject to change and modification. It could, therefore, no longer be thought of as something that always remained constant and that organized all appearances in a necessary and unchanging way. In such a situation there is always a way out, a third alternative (if we can speak of a third alternative); at any rate, we can speak of a third possibility which we may call the metaphysical possibility. This is the idea that the transcendental realm is neither psychological nor logical, but something beyond these two realms; it is a unifying point that gives rise to these two realms and from which they follow.

The attitude of the *Critique of Pure Reason* to this third possibility is not wholly unambiguous. Nor do I wish to represent matters in this difficult text as being simpler than they are. I set much greater store by using the so-called contradictions in the text to point to the objective difficulties of the matters under discussion and show you how they are reflected in the complexities of the theory. This is surely preferable to looking for the cheap satisfaction of making everything fit together by suppressing whatever does not belong and thus ending up with a simple, satisfying Kant for home consumption. You will not discover a Kant of this kind in these lectures. On the one hand, you will find numerous turns of phrase in the *Critique of Pure Reason* that seem to concede the possibility of an ultimate unifying factor that is designed to mediate between the two spheres of intuition and thought. The best-known of these passages is the one in the Schematism chapter which speaks of the art 'hidden in the depths of the human soul' that relates intuition and thought to each other.[2] This is the passage that Heidegger arbitrarily makes the pivotal point of his entire interpretation of Kant.[3] But there are other passages of the same kind. One is to be found in the Deduction of the Pure Concepts of Understanding, where Kant discusses why we have these categories and not others and why therefore the '"I think" that accompanies all my representations' is the ultimate condition. He suggests that it is a mystery not capable of further elucidation.[4] Lastly

– and most simply of all – you could point to the concept of the transcendent thing-in-itself which, as I have repeatedly told you, has not been resolved by Kant, any more than it had been resolved by Locke. Incidentally, there is an extraordinarily profound similarity between Kant's epistemology and Locke's. It is to be seen in the fact that both have an analysis of consciousness while retaining the idea of an underlying thing-in-itself that is not completely coextensive with consciousness. This similarity is one that to the best of my knowledge has never been as thoroughly explored as it deserves. But all these features that might be said to prepare the way for a metaphysical interpretation of the transcendental face the obstacle of Kant's resolute repudiations of it in the form of statements that such a realm as existence in itself or the Absolute – or however you wish to describe it – does exist, but that the concept of that realm is quite empty and no use can be made of it. One instance of this is the passage from the chapter about noumena and phenomena that I referred to last time.[5]

> Thus the concept of pure and merely intelligible objects is completely lacking in all principles that might make possible its application. For we cannot think of any way in which such intelligible objects might be given. The problematic thought which leaves open a place for them serves only, like an empty space, for the limitation of empirical principles, without itself containing or revealing any other object of knowledge beyond the sphere of those principles.[6]

Thus it is clear that if the concept of 'pure intelligible objects' can be applied to anything at all then it must be applicable in an emphatic sense to the objects of the *Critique of Pure Reason*. It must be applicable to the transcendental conditions of all knowledge. These must be independent of experience because they constitute experience and they are what Kant sets out to deduce from an ultimate unifying factor, namely, their merely logical function, the function of thought.

But he says here not only that this concept of 'pure intelligible objects' is 'completely lacking in all principles that might make possible its application' – and it has to be said that there is a certain contradiction here to what we find in the Transcendental Deduction – but also that 'we cannot think of any way in which such intelligible objects might be given', even though, when it comes down to it, the Deduction of the Pure Concepts of Understanding does precisely that. For that chapter contains the attempt to make comprehensible a way in which these pure concepts of understanding can be given. That is to say, it attempts to show how a unity of consciousness can be

produced only from the discrete components of that unity. The categories are then nothing other than these components of the unified
consciousness within which the 'I think' necessarily unfolds, only
they have been functionally joined together and reduced to a formula.
I should like to add as a footnote that strictly speaking – that is,
logically speaking – the Deduction of the Pure Concepts of Understanding is not a deduction at all because Kant does not draw inferences from a major premise. What really happens here is that he
demonstrates that there is a structural equivalence between the unity
of the 'I think' – that is, a purely logical unity – and the components
of consciousness, namely, of apprehension and reproduction. In other
words, if there were no such thing as a unity of consciousness and
unity of the object, in short, absolute identity, there could be no such
things as the discrete components of the synthesis. On the other hand,
in the absence of these components of the synthesis, the assertion
of such a unity of consciousness would be quite vacuous. It is only
because there is such a thing as a living unity of personal consciousness that actualizes itself in these different stages that we can say
anything at all about this purely formal 'I think'. I believe that you
will only understand the point of this central passage of the *Critique
of Pure Reason* rightly if you appreciate the importance of this reciprocity between the 'I think' and the individual components of the
deduction and finally the categories. Kant is quite consistent when he
remarks, in the passage just quoted,[7] that neither the categories, in
other words, neither the individual components of which this unity
is composed, nor the unity itself can be further explained, but must
simply be accepted. After what I have said to you it will be evident
that a metaphysical interpretation of the transcendental – that is to
say, of the sphere in which the deduction of the pure concepts of
understanding is situated – must be excluded from the *Critique of
Pure Reason*, just as much as logical or psychological interpretations.
This means that Kant would have to apply the critique that I have
just read you from the chapter on phenomena and noumena,[8] a critique that can be found in countless passages in the *Critique of Pure
Reason* – my choice of that particular passage was quite arbitrary.
He would have to say that we cannot really say anything about this
transcendental sphere because it is an intelligible object; the entire
sphere comes within the province of the *Critique of Pure Reason*; it is
itself subject to that critique.

I believe that the observations we have made have led us to an
aporia. I have tried to spell out for you all the relevant defining
features, or rather, all of the relevant negative defining features, the
delimitations – and in the light of the passages I have just read out to

you I specifically want them understood as negative defining f‹
Now if you take all these defining features together, and if you take
them quite literally, they really preclude all propositions about the
transcendental. I believe that with this we have reached a decisive
point. I believe this will enable you to understand why there had to
be a transition from the *Critique of Pure Reason* to German idealism,
as I have indicated to you on a number of occasions. We have thus
reached the point where this necessity becomes explicable. This aporia
really contains an objective confession of failure; the failure of Kant's
intentions in the *Critique of Pure Reason*. It is not possible to reconcile the different postulates which are advanced simultaneously: on
the one hand, the postulate of fulfilment through intuition so that
I can utter meaningful propositions; on the other hand, the postulate of pure apriority, so that I do not lapse into the realm of mere
experience.

Now, what Kant does – and I believe this is perhaps the final point
to be made about the method of the *Critique of Pure Reason*, about
its inner logic – is to override his own prohibition. Recollect what I
said about his explicit warning in the Transcendental Dialectic not to
'stray into intelligible worlds'; his explicit warning not to attempt to
derive binding propositions from pure thought unless they are filled
with the content of experience. What you find in the *Critique of Pure
Reason* can perhaps be most easily and most profoundly described
– particularly at the crucial defining moments – by saying that Kant
does *the very thing that he forbids reason to do*. He constructs something from pure thought, he stipulates something (I use this word in
preference to the misleading 'postulates'), that cannot be delivered by
experience, by the phenomenal world. For there are no phenomena
that might vindicate the use of the categories or the unity of consciousness or (as we shall see) the so-called pure intuitions of space
and time as he requires of every cognitive act that aspires to be more
than formal. You cannot discover intuitions corresponding to the
categories *qua* categories or the unity of consciousness *qua* unity of
consciousness that would legitimate propositions about them in the
way that authoritative knowledge should be legitimated according to
the doctrine of the antinomies and the entire transcendental dialectic.
The path chosen by Kant instead is in actual fact a path constructed
of pure concepts: he seeks through pure thought what absolutely
must be thought if experience is to be at all possible. But such a process of logical deduction from pure thought is something he himself
prohibits.

Perhaps you will recollect what I have said to you already about
the concept of aporia. I call concepts aporetic if they arise at a point

where no content or intuition can be discovered to correspond to a thought, and where for that reason the thought must advance beyond its own possible content in order to achieve a coherent, internally consistent meaning. The situation is like that of the mathematicians who have invented certain numbers, negative numbers and then the imaginary numbers that have no correlatives in the series of natural numbers, but have been introduced because of a logical necessity, even though they do not really exist in terms of the theory of number the mathematicians started out with. This movement from the necessity of thought to a realm which in a sense does not exist could be regarded as directly analogous to what is meant by speculation, the speculative movement of the concept, in the philosophy that succeeded Kant. In other words, the difficulties Kant encounters in defining the innermost ground of his own methodology drive him objectively to exactly the speculation that he censures in his rationalistic predecessors, Leibniz and Wolff. In this sense post-Kantian idealism was quite consistent, since what it did was no more than to bring to consciousness what Kant had done before it when it nullified the distinction between transcendental logic and transcendental dialectic, between mere reflection and speculation, and when it elevated into an organ of cognition the transcendental dialectic which Kant had inexorably been drawn into. I am spending so much time on this point because I believe – and this fits with some of the ideas I have told you about earlier in the course – that every theory of knowledge necessarily finds itself caught up in aporetic concepts and a dialectical movement of this kind. For every theory of knowledge must, if it is to be a theory, that is, a coherent body of ideas, resolve the problems of identity and non-identity, subject and object, in such a way as to shift the entire emphasis – I almost said the entire substance – into the subject and draw knowledge purely from the analysis of the subject (because such an analysis of the object simply cannot be undertaken *a priori*, that is, independently of changing historical contents).[9]

However, if I may speak ontologically for once, the belief that the object can be made to coincide entirely with the subject, that the object really *is* the subject, is itself false; it is simply not the case. You will recollect that I have demonstrated this shortcoming to you by showing that the pure subject presupposes objectivity, just as, conversely, objectivity presupposes subjectivity. A price has to be paid for this shortcoming by a subjectively orientated analysis such as epistemology. The price is that ultimately all the concepts it creates prove to be inadequate. Each concept may be said to be an IOU that can be redeemed only by a further concept. Expressed more vulgarly, epistemology resembles the man who can only block up one hole by digging another. The entire history, the internal history of epistemology, is actually the history of this debt relationship; that is to say, the history of the repeated postponement of this debt, this deferral of the non-redeemable share in knowledge of an object to a further piece of knowledge that recedes further and further from the object of redemption, from the moment of fulfilment through the act of knowing. It is this process that ends up by making such makeshifts as the transcendental an unavoidable necessity. This explains also what is truly profound in Kant. On the one hand, from the point of view of positivism in the broadest sense of the term, equivalents, objective correlatives, cannot be discovered for what he calls the transcendental. On the other hand, however, his construction of this entire edifice is governed by a coercive force that thinking cannot resist. Thus in the 'mistakes' that Kant makes we see the protest of the entire epistemological method. And I do indeed hold the view that the profundity of a philosophy can only be measured by the profundity of its errors – rather than by the smooth success of its harmonious conclusions.

You may well ask me now: How should we think about the relations of the categories or these aporetic concepts to one another? How should we think about the entire configuration; and how should we think about the profundity of a philosophy that collides with all the given data but which is entirely coherent in its own terms? I believe that I can best explain this with the aid of that metaphor of debt. Incidentally, this metaphor of the debtor and of debt relationships is one that recurs frequently in Kant and plays an important role in it, and that includes the practical philosophy. The same may be said of the aphorism of Anaximander[10] which stands at the very inception of Western philosophy. I merely point to this fact without being able to pursue it further here.[11] The way it works is that these aporetic concepts, that is, concepts that cannot achieve in their isolation what they are supposed to achieve, that these concepts borrow from one another; they borrow from the concept adjacent to themselves.

We may say that the sphere of the transcendental is a no man's land,[12] or more precisely it is *not* a land at all if by that we mean something with fixed features. It is rather a gigantic credit system in which the final IOU cannot be redeemed. To put it in more concrete terms: from the realm of logic the idea of unity and coherence has been borrowed, that is to say, the idea of non-contradiction. For synthesis means that things have to be brought together in such a way that they do not contradict one another or – to put it in the language of the old philosophy of Leibniz and Wolff – they must satisfy the requirement of 'compossibility', of mutual compatibility. This idea is borrowed from logic – or perhaps it was not even borrowed, but was the foundation of the entire edifice. A further borrowing came from psychology, from what had already been constructed. This was the element of activity, of temporality – all the elements that relate to a possible realization. This loan was a very shamefaced loan, since in ordinary life people who borrow things do not tend to shout about it from the rooftops. But in this case it is only through this loan that it becomes possible to establish relations between the sphere of logic and the sphere of intuition to which it must be related according to Kant's own postulate. If there were no affinity between the transcendental subject and the sphere of perception or experience; if Kant had not assumed such an affinity – earlier, in antiquity, philosophers would have spoken of a 'resemblance'[13] – it would have been quite simply impossible to conceive how intuitions could be subsumed under concepts in the first place. For how could that be done unless the concepts themselves contained what transcendental logic actually prohibits, to wit, elements that arise from intuition, from experience? The final borrowing comes from metaphysics. This is the claim to absolute validity, which amounts *after all* to the claim of an intelligible realm.[14] This is supposed to legitimate itself albeit in a manner that never becomes fully transparent in Kant because it is always conceived of in a specific relation, namely a constitutive and self-fulfilling relation to experience. What we have here then is a highly tortuous process in which these three fundamental concepts or fundamental spheres borrow from one another in order to survive and to ensure that the two antagonistic realms can be brought together. This is the way in which we have to imagine how this curious imaginary realm of the transcendental actually comes into existence.

If we reflect for one last moment on the entire situation, and consider it from a metaphysical point of view, we will have to conclude that we are looking at an attempt at secularizing the realm of *transcendence*. Of course, transcendence was originally a theological concept, but now it is to be given a dispensation from every assertion, that is, from every claim to a factual existence. At the same time, this aporetical edifice is designed to ensure that its status of absolute otherness, its absolute separateness from immanence, is secure. This is done in such a way that if you dig deeply enough within immanence, into its innermost core, there you will discover transcendence as the condition of its existence. By focusing on the idea of transcendence here my aim is to confront you with a final, decisive point. We are agreed – and Kant would have admitted as much – that the logical categories or the forms of intuition have no factual existence, even a second-order factual existence. They are merely what he calls concepts of reflection, that is to say, they follow necessarily from the reflections we are compelled to make concerning the transcendental. However, we can discover no form of existence which – as Husserl would subsequently think of the matter – would correspond to these categories or forms of intuition.

If you put this together with the idea of discovering transcendence at the innermost core, it follows that pure spirit [*Geist*], the 'I think' which is the end point of the *Critique of Pure Reason*, has to become an entity, an existent thing-in-itself, and ultimately an Absolute, if it is truly to be able to act as the precondition of everything that exists. In this sense it was Kant's successors, Fichte and Hegel, who actually hypostatized the concept of spirit. By insisting that it should not derive from experience, that it should not be an individual human consciousness and that it should be the absolute preconditioning element, they transformed it into a genuine transcendence. This is undoubtedly true of Fichte and a similar claim can be defended with regard to Hegel, although I am fully conscious of the enormous difficulties that we encounter in Hegel on this point. At all events, we are left with this idea that spirit, which is where a subjectively based analysis culminates if it is not to regress to mere factuality, has to be a metaphysical entity: it must be the Absolute. And this idea is objectively implicit in Kant in the structure of the aporetic concept. This means that only if the sphere of the transcendental is really thought of as something transcendent will it be able to do what Kant wants it to do. In this sense we can say that the hypostasis of spirit, the elevation of spirit into God that was implemented by the later idealist philosophers, is the ultimate aporetic concept. To put it another way: we are thus left with the proposition that the 'I think' is the true essence of things; it creates and generates everything else, while at the same time this 'I think' is emancipated from everything connecting it to a merely empirical 'I' that is supposed to be contained in it. The moment we take this step it is hardly possible to arrive at any other conclusion than of elevating this spirit to the status of absolute spirit. In this respect the concept of the transcendental in Kant actually arrives at the insight that is subsequently made thematic by Hegel with his idea of the identity of logic and metaphysics. By this he meant that logical unity is all-inclusive – and if the transcendental dialectic ceases to be separated from knowledge and becomes instead its organon, it really is all-inclusive. And if that is the case, then we really have arrived at metaphysics.

In other words, then, let us come back to our three key features, the three aporetic concepts that are under discussion here: logic, psychology and metaphysics. If we consider them once more we can say that the peculiar conflation of logic and psychology which, however, remains something less than psychology leads to a situation in which logic leads an existence of its own and thus transcends metaphysics. It means also that the *Critique of Pure Reason* is turned into a metaphysics, namely a metaphysics that, by turning towards the subject, seeks to salvage transcendence by concealing its existence at the heart of subjectivity. This is what ultimately explains the profound impact of this book and what provoked the preoccupation with profundity in the first place, a profundity which I have undertaken to decode for you, at least in outline.

I believe that from here on you will be able to understand what I have *failed* to discuss systematically in this course of lectures – no doubt to the horror of no small numbers of you. And what I have failed to discuss is what is normally the very first topic you come to when looking at the *Critique of Pure Reason*, namely the Transcendental Aesthetic. What I have said puts you in a position to understand why Kant shows such an indescribable interest in the *a priori* nature of time and space, which is the thesis of the Transcendental Aesthetic. On the one hand, the *Critique of Pure Reason* is dependent on the relation to intuition, since without that relation there can be no valid knowledge; and if there were no intuition, knowledge would be empty of content. On the other hand, however, what I intuit is an immediate given to the senses in the here and now; it thus falls victim to the criticism of being merely empirical, a criticism that constitutes the fundamental motif of the *Critique of Pure Reason*, as powerful a criticism as that other one of straying into intelligible worlds. In consequence Kant is compelled to construct a sphere which consists of intuition but which is also *a priori*. What this sphere takes from intuition is the idea that it is the source of certain universal contents of knowledge, while on the other side it is supposed to receive dispensation from the curse that this knowledge will be *merely a priori*. This is the underlying foundation of the Transcendental Aesthetic. In this connection I would ask you to take very seriously the idea of aporetic concepts – the idea that the difficulties of a philosophical question impel us to further acts of conceptualization. If you take this idea as seriously as I would like you to, and approach the matter from the coercion formed by the consideration of such difficulties, you will understand the edifice of the Transcendental Aesthetic far more easily than by simply confronting the text, weighing up the arguments and dissecting them. In other words, to put the matter rather crassly, the Transcendental Aesthetic – that is to say, the theory of intuition, of pure intuition – depends on logic. It is a mere illusion of the *Critique of Pure Reason* that logic is erected on the foundation of the Transcendental Aesthetic. That is really the schoolmasterly notion that priority belongs to the pure forms into which contents, the affects, then flow – and these are followed in turn by the understanding which processes and shapes it all. This is indeed how I presented it to you at the outset because that is what the primer tells us to do, but of course this approach does no justice at all to the actual structure of the *Critique of Pure Reason*. I believe that now you have reached the point where you understand that the structure of this Transcendental Aesthetic is a function of logic and that what I am attempting to do is to resolve the aporia between intuition and logic, you will be in a much better position to grasp the particular shape of the Transcendental Aesthetic.

I should like to devote the whole of the final lecture to an interpretation of the Transcendental Aesthetic. This means that I shall bring these lectures to a close at the very point where trivial accounts of the contents of the *Critique of Pure Reason* normally begin.

LECTURE TWENTY-ONE

30 July 1959

'The Transcendental Aesthetic'

You will remember that last time I explained that we should post-pone our necessarily abbreviated discussion of the Transcendental Aesthetic to this last lecture. The reason for this is that it is clear from what I have argued that the Transcendental Aesthetic is a function of the Transcendental Logic and not vice versa. I could now take the route of showing you in detail how this works, much as I did in the case of the Schematism chapter, which was revealed as the chapter that mediated between the Aesthetic and the Logic. (Although, of course, that chapter is not situated where it really belongs, which in fact would be between the Aesthetic and the Logic. This is because it makes clear that there is a sort of neutral zone between Aesthetic and Logic, namely the element of *time* which is actually the scheme in accordance with which the objects of intuition are simultaneously defined as potential objects of the intellect.) So today I should like to refer you again to the Schematism chapter, the interpretation of which we shall have to forgo for reasons of time.[1] Instead I should like to turn now to the Transcendental Aesthetic and give you a brief ac-count of some of the salient points in it, and after that I shall attempt to draw a number of conclusions for our examination of the *Critique of Pure Reason* as a whole.

The teaching of the Transcendental Aesthetic, its principal thesis, is probably familiar to you all. It is the assertion of the *a priori* nature of time and space. This *a priori* nature of time and space is not a matter of concepts, that is to say, of the forms of thought. It is a matter of the forms of sensibility, the pure forms of intuition by means of which we necessarily apprehend all immediate givens without the involvement of the element of activity, of spontaneity, in other words, the element of thought. These are forms in the true sense of the word; they do not call for any activity on the part of the subject, but really are just empty forms into which the affects simply fall. By affects we mean the emotions, which in Kant are caused by things-in-themselves. More specifically, these forms of intuition are said to be subjective in nature. This means that they are not attributes of things-in-themselves, but forms of our cognition; they are not an inherent part of the individual intuitions, but the constitutive conditions that ensure that there is such a thing as intuition in the first place. This theory of Kant's is known to everyone familiar with the basic elements of the *Critique of Pure Reason* and is not one I wish to dwell on at length. What is important is that this basic thesis breaks down into four assertions or four key arguments, and it is these key arguments or theses that I would like to discuss in greater detail now.

The first point Kant makes is that space and time are not empirical concepts derived from experiences of the external world.[2] You must think back here to what I have been saying in the last few lectures. In particular I have in mind the obligation, a sort of compulsion in Kant, to keep the constitutive conditions that he wishes to isolate in the transcendental analysis free from all merely empirical matter, since otherwise they will presuppose the very thing for which they are supposed to supply the basic premises.

Now this assertion that space and time are not empirical concepts, that is to say, they are not concepts derived from any given concrete intuitions, is a claim that contains a very serious problem. To start with, there can be no doubt that our ideas of time and space are shaped by empirical experience. I should add here that Kant conceives of space as the form of our outer sense and time the form of our inner sense. However, these definitions are not conceptual, but intuitive; for only if you already know what 'spatial' means can you conceive of something being 'outer', namely distributed in space, and 'inner', namely not located in space. In this sense these definitions simply fail because we are evidently not dealing with essences or elements of knowledge that are incapable of being reduced to more basic ones and thus cannot be expressed in terms of something other than what they are. (I say all this lest I be held to have failed to inform you of the essential distinctions that Kant makes at this point.[3])

As I say, then, it cannot be denied that our ideas of time and space are shaped by our empirical experiences; they are not simply given, as Kant seems to imply in the Transcendental Aesthetic. Looked at from the point of view of individual development, ontogenetically, a child does not start out with the idea of time or space; a child sets out with no more than a 'this thing here', a perceptual field and also a temporal perceptual field. He or she only gradually arrives at something like ideas of time or space after a process of abstraction and through a definite process of transcending these immediate givens. I believe I have already pointed out[4] that the important factors as far as ontogenesis is concerned are familiar to everyone who has observed children; all such observers have realized that these ontogenetic factors are also valid in phylogenetic terms. This was perfectly clear to members of the Durkheim school, who were able to show that our conceptions of time and space emerge simultaneously with particular property relations. They showed that the primordial designations for spatial relations are always based on the limits set by juridical title of one sort or another to the real ownership of land. And similarly, our representations of time are based on the underlying model of the relations between the different generations.

We must add, however, that whatever their particular origins may happen to be, all the expressions in use objectively presuppose the existence of time and space. If I refer to this space or that field lying adjacent to my field, this assumes that I am positioned in a continuum to which these concepts can be applied. And if I do the same with regard to adjacent chunks of time or segments of time – since there are no such things as 'pure' segments of time in the continuum of experience – we find ourselves in a similar situation. In other words, you can see here the essence of the problem of origins and validity in a nutshell; you can see the problem of the relation of origins to validity – these terms by no means always coincide and cannot be reduced to a common formula.[5] This situation is that for the subjective consciousness, for the process of reflection and designation, such things as time and space are secondary phenomena; they arise from elsewhere and are *not* simply givens. At the same time, however, if you ignore this fact and simply concentrate on the objective contents of any proposition concerning time and space, every such proposition presupposes the existence of something like space or (in this instance) plane surfaces or the like that enable us to distinguish between two fields. This remains true even if you are speaking only of what seem to be particular objects, so that you say something like this space lies next to mine, or this field is adjacent to mine. In other words, reflection on our ideas of time and space, that is, on their objective forms, is something that at first seems to be totally different from the fact that they are objectively presupposed in every act of knowledge, since only if we know what time and space are, are we capable of understanding particular temporal or spatial expressions. I do not know what space is without the experience of a determinate, that is, finite space; nor do I know what time is without the experience of determinate, finite instances of time. On the other hand, however, I can know nothing of determinate instances of space and time unless I can relate them by way of comparison to that more general principle of the supreme sensible forms that Kant has elaborated. What follows from this is the element that I have repeatedly identified as the crucial feature of the theory of knowledge in the course of these lectures, namely the reciprocal relationship between the categories or forms of cognition. In other words, then, Kant undoubtedly made the great discovery (and it is one I have no wish to belittle) that the meaning of particular spaces and particular instances of time objectively implies some such thing as the idea of an infinite space and an infinite time. But he neglected the other side of this reciprocal relationship, namely its dependence upon the determinate and the particular without which it cannot exist. To put it another way, he has once again attempted to solve the riddle in one direction only, by reducing it to the pole of subjectivity – whereas it is precisely this one-sided resolution that is so dubious. This is because a sufficient theory of time and space can only be arrived at through the concrete relation between temporal and spatial phenomena, on the one hand, and the forms of time and space, on the other.

The next argument is closely related to the first but merely gives a different twist to the same Kantian assertion that space and time are not empirical concepts, or not concepts derived from the empirical realm. On this occasion it is the positive formulation that space and time are necessary *a priori* representations.[6] Of course, the first point to be made is that this claim is open to the same objection that I have raised with respect to the first one, but it calls for an important corollary in addition. Thus we speak of representations and we claim that space and time exist in our consciousness, however this is to be understood; at the same time we assert that we cannot make the same claim about their existence outside our consciousness. The corollary of which I am speaking is that we are then under an obligation to pursue this question and to enquire whether there actually is what Kant calls a 'pure intuition' of time and space. However, as far as I can tell, there is no such intuition. If you have nothing better to do, or if you find yourselves unable to sleep in the first night of the vacation because of the strenuous mental efforts you have been making, you could spend some time experimenting with the attempt to imagine pure time or pure space without any specific empirical contents. You will then make the remarkable discovery that you cannot

really conceive of such an absolute space without thinking of some empirical substratum or without imagining some feature that identifies a space as a space. The same holds good for time: unless you imagine alongside time something that *has* time or that occurs in time, that unfolds in time or takes place in time – that is to say, without something with which to measure time, you will find yourselves unable to imagine it at all. Instead you will discover that these extremely general ideas of space and time contain a relation to what is known in modern logic as a referent, that is, the relation to whatever it is that they refer to. If you cannot conceive of any substratum from which time can be read off, or any such substratum from which you can derive space (if only as a limiting concept) – then what you are left with is not simply an abstract, empty space or an abstract, empty time, but absolutely nothing at all. In the absence of a reference to some such thing you will be unable to imagine anything at all. And to confuse this nothing with empty space or empty time seems to me to have one disastrous consequence; it seems to me to be a serious intellectual error. For instance, if you reject the notion of a substratum from which space or time can be derived, you would no longer be able to distinguish time and space from each other; the two would amount to the same thing. But there would no longer be any specific difference, any defining feature, that would enable you to grasp what time and space actually are. In that event the proposition about the necessary, *a priori* nature of time and space as infinite things would cease to have any meaning. The fact is that they are not only the precondition of all intuitions; strictly speaking, they are also conditioned by intuition, since they can be imagined only if they contain actual intuitions. Thus the relation of form to content is not that of an empty form into which a content flows, as generally appears to be the case in Kant, but here, too, the situation is one of reciprocity. That is to say, this form only exists if it has a content, because it is form only as the form of a content, just as, on the other hand – as Kant correctly perceived – a content can only exist if these forms can actually be said to exist.

The third of Kant's arguments is that the distinction between space and time is not a matter of concepts.[7] I believe that this is one of the most inspired insights of the entire *Critique of Pure Reason*; and when Schopenhauer asserted that the Transcendental Aesthetic was the most important section of the *Critique of Pure Reason* I think that he can only have had this part of the argument in mind.[8] For it seems reasonable to say, well then, if time and space have no determinate content, but are to be thought of in terms of an extreme formal universality, they must be concepts like any other. If Kant is justified in distinguishing between sensibility and understanding, receptivity and spontaneity, his justification for doing so must lie in the really stringent proof that time and space are not conceptual in nature. The situation here is as follows. Every concept is confronted by the individual things or individual elements or individual some-things of which it is composed. In English they would be called 'items'; German does not possess such an apposite expression as English. The relation between them is one of the general to the particular, of abstract to concrete. If you form the concept of a 'book' you set aside the features relating to particular books; you ignore the fact that one book has a green binding and another one red. You show no interest in the fact that one book contains the *Critique of Pure Reason* while another has a novel by Ganghofer.[9] Such matters have no relevance in this context. Instead, to establish a defining concept you take an object that consists of a large number of printed pages that are bound together; you assume further that these printed sides generally pos-sess a meaning, although that is not absolutely essential. In this way you arrive at the concept of a book as something that comprehends all these qualities. Kant perceived – and I believe he was really the first to do so – that the position with space and time is quite different from this. Space does not relate to individual spaces like an abstract concept to the individual items of which it is composed. You do not take so-and-so-many spaces – nowadays in Germany, thanks to the war and the military culture, we speak of the 'space', for example, the area of Hesse [*Raum Hessen*] (in which people look for their future wives in the partners-wanted advertisements) or of the 'space' of North-Rhine Westphalia, or whatever. Now, the concept of space is not formed by saying that the space of Hesse and the space of North-Rhine Westphalia and the space of Schleswig-Holstein all have something in common, which is that they are a 'space'; and that the most general quality they have in common forms the concept of 'space'. Instead – and this explains why space is a representation, a pure intuition, and not a concept – you form the general representa-tion of space by adding together all these existing spaces so that they fit together. There is nothing further to be said about it; it really is a matter of this additive process. So if you wish to imagine the Federal Republic of Germany as a space, you do not subtract the abstract concept of space which is what is left over from the different regions of the Federal Republic as their presiding concept; instead you have to look at the map and fit the different regions together – Hesse, North-Rhine Westphalia, Rhineland-Palatinate, Bavaria, etc. – and what you have at the end is the space of the Federal Republic. And taking this method further you eventually finish up with the general

European space. You can even take the whole process a stage further and you then end up with cosmic space; this is not as hard as might be supposed since nowadays the idea of cosmic space has lost its terrors for us. You can see that the way you arrive at the relationship between space in general and the individual spaces is completely different from the relation of a concept to the individual things, elements or whatever they are called that it comprises. Obviously, the same holds good for time, which as a continuum is the sum of all particular instances of time, and not the conceptual unity of all the different times. I believe that no objection can be raised to Kant's argument and that he really gives a very rigorous explanation of the non-conceptual nature of time and space, the two forms of intuition. Kant, we should add, customarily employs the term 'forms of intu-ition' rather than just 'intuitions' and he varies this occasionally with the expression 'pure intuition'. They are not meant to be intuitions in the true sense, in the particular sense of a replete, concrete, sensible intuition, since in that event they would be givens that were subject to change; they would be empirical. Instead they are supposed to be the form of such intuitions. The term 'form' alternates with the term 'pure intuition', and that is no coincidence. After all, as I have just pointed out, Kant has shown that space and time are no concepts; and this means that a particular space and a particular time do not relate to space and time as a particular to the general. Space and time are not more general than spaces and times, nor are they more abstract, but the latter are simply the components of the former. It is in this sense that we are not dealing with concepts. Now reflect for a moment on the curious implications of this situation. We have reached the point where we perceive that space and time are neither concepts, that is to say, they are not mental constructs that have been derived from concrete particulars; nor, however, are they straightforwardly empirical. This again raises the question we asked in the course of our discussion of the aporetic concepts. If they are neither concepts nor intuitions, what are they? For a 'pure' intuition – if by that we mean an intuition which is not a given, which is not therefore em-pirical and thus subject to the critique of the empirical – has in fact nothing that corresponds to it. A pure intuition that is neither conceptual (since that has been precluded by our argument) nor an intuition in the concrete sense (and it cannot be that since it is sup-posed to be a pure intuition separated from everything empirical) – can only be yet another *speculative construct* without any proper correlatives, even though we are supposed to be dealing with some-thing non-conceptual. It is therefore lacking in everything that would enable it to be properly identified or defined.

This whole question can perhaps be clarified with reference to the fourth thesis of the Transcendental Aesthetic, which I shall say a few words about now. This is the thesis that space and time are infinite, given magnitudes.[10] It is extremely curious that having characterized the concept of the infinitude of a given magnitude as an impossibility in the Transcendental Dialectic,[11] Kant should now postulate this same infinite, given magnitude for the forms of intuition, without noticing that the critique of the antinomies must hold good in this instance too. If Kant had wished to evade the consequences of his demonstration that the antinomies arise only because ideas, conceptual assertions, stray beyond the possible limits of experience, he would probably reply, if he were here amongst us, that non-conceptual things like time and space are not concerned with such matters, but with pure intuitions. However, that is not rigorous since for one thing the idea of filling time and space with intuition – in other words, the very thing that would make of them a positive given – is the very thing that was precluded at this point. If, however, you make the attempt to picture to yourselves an infinite space in a pure act of the imagination, in a pure variation of the imagination, as Husserl would have called it, you will find yourselves in difficulties that are just as great as those that arise from trying to imagine space as a finite magnitude. This means that both concepts lead to difficulties at the level of representation, let alone that of thought. If you think back to the concept of compossibility that I used last time to refer to a Leibnizian legacy in Kantian philosophy – these concepts lead to nonsense and to inconsistencies. You cannot imagine anything infinite because all imaginings necessarily contain the element of limits – at any rate, as long as they contain a sensory element, and are therefore not purely intellectual. Just make a serious attempt to imagine an absolutely infinite space, and you will find that you can never imagine anything bigger than a very, very, very big sphere or something of the sort. But actually to picture it to yourselves in its infinitude will be beyond you. At best you will have the image of something diffuse, that is, something whose boundaries you cannot make out. But to *picture to yourselves* this diffuse thing as a positive infinitude (as opposed to *thinking* about it) is a trick that I believe you will be no more able to master than I was, even though I have made sincere efforts to do so. On the other hand, however, you will of course be able to imagine space as a finite space and time as a finite time. But this will not bring you much joy either. For it is evident that, *however* large the space and time that you picture to yourselves, you will always be able to imagine a *further* space and a *further* time outside them. You will always be able to go beyond the greatest possible picture that you can imagine – so that the idea of space or time in their totality as a finite idea leads to damaging inconsistencies just as the idea of an infinitude is one that we cannot picture to ourselves at all. We cannot imagine an infinitude, and all imaginings are limited. Finite imaginings always allow the imagination to go beyond them. And this means that Kant's thesis that time and space are infinite givens is in fact untenable. It is a kind of speculative construct. By the way, one of the most important points here concerns the way in which Kantian philosophy has been affected by the positive sciences. The Kantian doctrine of the infinite nature of space has evidently been superseded by relativity theory and is no longer tenable. As against this, our imaginations, that is, the sheer disposition of our minds on which Kant continually reflects, refuse to accept the notion that space is finite. It follows that the antinomy I have just shown you still persists. In general – as I trust I may say today, in this final lecture – it looks as though the discoveries made by science over the last sixty years or so have enabled us to discover a small window of opportunity which permits us to look out from the prison imposed upon us by our anthropological intellectual constitution. The discoveries I have in mind are those of relativity theory and quantum mechanics, and to some extent also atomic theory. Thanks to these developments Kant's belief that what we know is determined exclusively by our own intellectual disposition can now be dismissed; it has effectively been refuted.[12] But here I just wish to point you in this direction because the problem of the Transcendental Aesthetic has played an extraordinarily important part in the philosophical debates of recent decades. I need only remind you here of the controversy between Max Born and Ernst Cassirer.[13]

We can summarize what I have told you today by saying that Kant is surely right to say that it is meaningless to speak of the temporal and the spatial in the absence of time and space. But this proposition has to be supplemented by the further statement that it is no less meaningless to speak of space and time in the absence of the spatial and the temporal. In other words, here, too, there is a reciprocity between the form of knowledge and its material. To put it another way, if the pure forms of intuition are juxtaposed to their possible contents directly and without any mediation, this will inevitably result in contradiction.[14]

I should like to close now by making a point that may appear very subtle, or perhaps even over-subtle to you. It concerns what I regard as a problem in the arrangement of the chapters in the *Critique of Pure Reason* – a problem that then recurs in Hegel's *Logic* in the section where he deals with the dialectic of form and matter.[15] I

pointed out earlier that for Kant the Transcendental Aesthetic is made
to precede the Transcendental Logic as a kind of fundamental stratum
of knowledge. I argued there that this rigid disjunction appears
untenable and that the Transcendental Aesthetic should be seen as a
function of the Transcendental Logic; and I hope that in the course of
this lecture I have been able to show you by our examination of the
text that this is truly the case. Nevertheless, in his original claim Kant
was guided by something that we should not be too ready to dismiss.
This brings me back for the last time to the second principal motif
that I have sought to pursue in these lectures. This is the idea that
Kantian dualism, the Kantian χωρισμός, that is, the antithesis of form
and content, stands in need of mediation, but that it cannot simply
be abolished or liquidated. Rather, it is fitting that a dialectical mode
of thinking whose elements I have tried to elucidate for you through
a discussion of Kant should try to keep a hold on this distinction
even while subjecting it to criticism. Now, if we speak of universal
mediation; if, as in the present case, we have to say that the pure
forms of space and time are mediated by their content, just as everything spatial and temporal is mediated by the forms of space and
time into which they enter – none of this entitles us to do away with
the idea of *immediacy*. I believe that the very most that dialectics
can require of us is this: even if you do not regard the concepts of
immediacy and mediacy as absolutes, as something conclusive, but as
things that are mutually mediated, you must hold fast to the realization that a universal mediation still insists that there is such a thing
as immediacy. Unless you retain this notion, you run the risk of misunderstanding the idea of universal mediation and will end up in a
superficial functionalist theory. You can only conceive of mediatedness
in relation to something that is mediated. This is comparable to my
telling you that the idea of an infinite space and an infinite time
devoid of all empirical baggage can only be imagined if mediated by
something that is actually spatial and temporal. Thus, notwithstanding this universal mediation, there is something of this sort within it
– I should like to call it a difference of weighting. It is one thing to
say that the forms are mediated by the contents to which they relate;
it is quite another to say that the contents are mediated by the forms
to which they relate. The forms are in fact *essentially* mediated by
contents and cannot be conceived at all in their absence. The contents, however, always contain a reference to something that is not
fully coextensive with form and cannot be fully reduced to it. Now
when Kant rather idiosyncratically opposes the stratum of the Transcendental Aesthetic to the intelligible sphere, when he defines it as
something that we absolutely have to respect and to accept, in contrast

to the realm in which our freedom and our activity is rooted, he has given voice to what might be termed a *materialist motif*. In other words, the mediation of the unmediated is different in a sense from the mediation of forms by the immediate; it is different from the mediation of the mediated.[16] This element is ultimately identical with the element of the threshold, the Kantian block, of which I have so frequently spoken. It means that there is a priority over the form that amounts to the statement that our knowledge does not exhaust itself in pure mediation, in its purely formal aspect, but that it remains attached to something to which it refers. And – a final point – the *Critique of Pure Reason* is actually the first attempt on a grand scale to bring together this element of something that cannot be further reduced, this element, then, of an existing something that cannot be completely dissolved into form – to bring this together with the idea of universal mediation by form. With this the *Critique of Pure Reason* represents the first great attempt in modern times – or perhaps we should say the first and also the last great attempt, and one doomed to failure – to master through mere concepts all that cannot be mastered by concepts. And what the concepts express is that by establishing identity they are simultaneously compelled to acknowledge the fact of *non-identity*.[17]

BIBLIOGRAPHICAL
REFERENCES

Translator's Note

References to existing English translations have been provided wherever possible. The most commonly used are given here, along with the German editions used where no suitable English translations are available. With the exception of the lecture titles, material added by the translator is enclosed within square brackets, both in the body of the text and in the notes. Except where indicated all notes are those of the editor.

Theodor Adorno

Against Epistemology: A Metacritique, trans. Willis Domingo, Basil Blackwell, Oxford, 1982.
[with Max Horkheimer] *Dialectic of Enlightenment*, trans. John Cumming, Allen Lane, London, 1973.
Hegel: Three Studies, trans. Shierry Weber Nicholsen, MIT Press, Cambridge, Mass., and London, 1993.
The Jargon of Authenticity, trans. Knut Tarnowski and Frederic Will, Routlege and Kegan Paul, 1973.
Minima Moralia, trans. E. F. N. Jephcott, New Left Books, London, 1974.
Notes to Literature, ed. Rolf Tiedemann, trans. Shierry Weber Nicholsen, Columbia University Press, New York, 1992.

GS Gesammelte Schriften, ed. Rolf Tiedemann, with the assistance of Gretel Adorno, Susan Buck-Morss and Klaus Schultz, Suhrkamp, Frankfurt am Main, 1973.

NaS Nachgelassene Schriften, the posthumously published writings, which have appeared in six sections. They include 16 vols of previously, unpublished lecture courses.
Vo Unpublished single lectures.

Georg Wilhelm Friedrich Hegel

Aesthetics: Lectures on Fine Art, trans. T. M. Knox, Clarendon Press, Oxford, 1988.
Hegel's Science of Logic, trans. A. V. Miller, London, George Allen and Unwin; New York, Humanities Press, 1969.
Phenomenology of Spirit, trans. A. V. Miller, Oxford University Press, Oxford, 1977. [*The Phenomenology of Mind*, trans. J. B. Baillie, London, George Allen and Unwin, 1964.]

Martin Heidegger

Being and Time, trans. John Macquarrie and Edward Robinson, Oxford University Press, Oxford, and Cambridge, Mass., 1995.

Max Horkheimer

Gesammelte Schriften, ed. Alfred Schmidt and Gunzelin Schmid Noerr, Frankfurt am Main, 1987.

David Hume

A Treatise on Human Nature, ed. L. A. Selby-Bigge, Clarendon Press, Oxford, 1896.

Immanuel Kant

Critique of Judgement, trans. James Creed Meredith, Clarendon Press, Oxford, 1973.
Critique of Practical Reason, trans. and ed. Mary Gregor, Cambridge University Press, Cambridge, 1997.
Critique of Pure Reason, trans. Norman Kemp Smith, Macmillan, London, 1928 (subsequent editions retain the original pagination). In accordance with common practice, references to the first and second German editions are given as A and B. I have also consulted the translation by Paul Guyer and Alan W. Wood in the Cambridge Edition of the Works of Immanuel Kant, Cambridge University Press, 1997.
Kant: Political Writings, ed. Hans Reiss, trans. H. B. Nisbet, Cambridge University Press, Cambridge, 1970.
The Metaphysics of Morals, trans. Mary Gregor, Cambridge University Press, Cambridge, 1991.

Prolegomena to Any Future Metaphysics, the Paul Carus translation, extensively revised by James W. Ellington, Hackett Publishing Company, Indianapolis, 1977.

Where no translations were available, reference is to Immanuel Kant, *Werke in sechs Bänden*, ed. Wilhelm Weischedel, Wissenschaftliche Buchgesellschaft, Darmstadt, 1964, repr. 1983.

Friedrich Nietzsche

Thus Spake Zarathustra, trans. R. J. Hollingdale, Penguin Books, Harmondsworth, 1969.
Twilight of the Idols / The Anti-Christ, trans. R. J. Hollingdale, Penguin Books, Harmondsworth, 1968.

Arthur Schopenhauer

The World as Will and Idea, trans. R. B. Haldane and J. Kemp, Kegan Paul, Trench, Trübner and Co., London, 1909.
Parerga and Paralipomena, trans. E. F. J. Payne, Clarendon Press, Oxford, 1974.
On the Basis of Morality, trans. E. E. J. Payne, Berghahn Books, Providence, RI, and Oxford, 1995.

EDITOR'S NOTES

Lecture One

1   Comparisons between Copernicus's heliocentric reform and all sorts of changes in the intellectual superstructure have always been very common, both before Kant and since. Kant himself regarded his 'intellectual revolution' as an 'analogy' to the Copernican revolution: 'We must ... make trial whether we may not have more success in the tasks of metaphysics, if we suppose that objects must conform to our knowledge ... We should then be proceeding precisely along the lines of Copernicus's primary hypothesis. Failing of satisfactory progress in explaining the movements of the heavenly bodies on the supposition that they all revolved around the spectator, he tried whether he might not have better success if he made the spectator to revolve and the stars to remain at rest.' For Kant's 'new method of thought' this means 'that we can know *a priori* of things only what we ourselves put into them.' (Kant, *Critique of Pure Reason*, pp. 22–3, B xvi, xviii). Walter Benjamin, with whose ideas Adorno closely identified himself, wrote of 'a Copernican turn in historiography' analogous to Kant's epistemological grounding of objectivity in the depths of the subject. According to this, true insight into past events was reserved for a process of remembering anchored in present actualities (see Walter Benjamin, *Gesammelte Schriften*, vol. 5, ed. Rolf Tiedemann and Hermann Schweppenhäuser, Suhrkamp, Frankfurt am Main, 1982, pp. 490–1 and 1006). Adorno spoke of *Beethoven's Copernican revolution* by means of which Beethoven derived the traditional forms of music once again from the subject (*Beethoven. Philosophie der Musik. Fragmente und Texte*, ed.

Rolf Tiedemann, *NaS*, section I, vol. 1, p. 99). On Kant's Copernican revolution see also Lecture Three, p. 32, and also n. 13.

2 *Critique of Pure Reason*, p. 12, A xvi–xvii.
3 Ibid.
4 The concept of *salvaging, rescuing* [*Rettung*] is crucial to Adorno's interpretation of Kant. Kant only used the word casually, for example, in connection with the idea of freedom (cf. Kant, *Critique of Practical Reason*, p. 80. Adorno quotes the passage in *Negative Dialectics*, *GS*, vol. 6, p. 250). For Adorno the nominalism that both accompanies and conditions the history of the increasing domination of nature terminates in the abolition of metaphysical entities and reaches a culminating point at which the entire process goes into reverse: the *Kantian urge to rescue* the intelligible sphere, to cite a formulation from *Negative Dialectics* (*GS*, vol. 6, p. 378), corresponded to the final limitation of knowledge to the world of 'appearances'. In the same way the young Horkheimer talked in a lecture of 1927 of the way in which Kant 'was compelled to discover new ways to salvage metaphysics and a faith capable of rational explanation'. Max Horkheimer, *Gesammelte Schriften*, vol. 9: *Nachgelassene Schriften* [Posthumous Writings] *1914–1931*, p. 471. On the concept of salvaging in Kant, see also Lecture Three, p. 31.
5 [This phrase was famously used by Karl Marx to describe the oblivion into which Hegel had fallen in the middle of the nineteenth century, and has been regularly used in the Marxian tradition since then. (See *Capital*, vol. 1, Lawrence and Wishart, London, 1967, 'Afterword to the second German edition', p. 19.) *Trans.*]
6 [The Great Elector, i.e. Friedrich Wilhelm von Brandenburg (1620–88), is remembered for his role in building up the power of Brandenburg Prussia, both by foreign conquest and by administrative modernization. As a result, Prussia became a kingdom a few years after his death. *Trans.*]
7 This was the lecture *Erfahrungsgehalte der Hegelschen Philosophie* [Experiential Contents of Hegelian Philosophy] that Adorno gave to the Conference of the German Hegel Society on 25 October 1958 in Frankfurt. See the expanded version in *GS*, vol. 5, pp. 295ff.
8 Reichenbach's book appeared in Berkeley/Los Angeles in 1951.
9 'Immanuel Kant has acted the inexorable philosopher; he has stormed the heavens; he has put the entire garrison to the sword; the overlord of the world is wallowing – unproven – in his own blood; there is now no universal mercy; no paternal kindness; no reward in the next world for self-denial in this one; the immortality of the soul is in its final death-throes – how it gasps and groans – and old Lampe is standing by with his umbrella under his arm, a distressed onlooker, cold sweat and tears pouring down his face.' Heinrich Heine, *Sämtliche Werke*, ed. Hans Kaufmann, Kindler, Munich, 1964, vol. 9, p. 250. [Lampe was Kant's servant. *Trans.*]

10   See especially Bernhard Groethuysen, *Die Entstehung der bürgerlichen Welt- und Lebensanschauung in Frankreich* [The Origins of the Bourgeois View of Life and the World in France], 2 vols, Halle, 1927–30; cf. Adorno's discussion of this book in *GS*, vol. 20.1, pp. 205ff.

✳ 11   'If you wish to enter the realm of the infinite, just explore the finite in every direction.' J. W. von Goethe, 'Gott, Gemüt und Welt' in *Gedenkausgabe der Werke, Briefe und Gespräche*, vol. 1: *Sämtliche Gedichte*, part 1, 2nd edn, Artemis Verlag, Zürich/Stuttgart 1961, p. 410.

12   'The critique of this pure understanding . . . does not permit us to create a new field of objects beyond those which may be presented to it as appearances, and so to stray into intelligible worlds; nay, it does not allow of our entertaining even the concept of them.' *Critique of Pure Reason*, p. 294, A 289/B 345.

13   Cf. the Preface to the First Edition, p. 8, A ixf.

14   [*Critique of Pure Reason*, Introduction, p. 55, B 19. *Trans.*]

15   Adorno has addressed this question in the Introduction to *Against Epistemology*: 'Kant reckons to be sure about the reconstruction of truth out of the immanence of consciousness. And the "How is it possible?" forms the determining figure of all his questions, since for him possibility itself poses no problems. Thus, like Hegel after him, he assumes the burden of carrying through that reconstruction on all fronts.' *Against Epistemology*, p. 34.

16   Note the correction at the beginning of Lecture Two.

Lecture Two

1   Kant himself adduces these examples in the Introduction to the *Critique of Pure Reason*: 'If I say, for instance, "All bodies are extended", this is an analytic judgement. For I do not require to go beyond the concept which I connect with "body" in order to find extension as bound up with it. To meet with this predicate, I have merely to analyse the concept, that is, to become conscious to myself of the manifold which I always think in that concept. The judgement is therefore analytic. But when I say, "All bodies are heavy", the predicate is something quite different from anything that I think in the mere concept of body in general; and the addition of such a predicate therefore yields a synthetic judgement.' *Critique of Pure Reason*, Introduction, pp. 48f, A 7/B 11.

2   On this point Adorno largely follows the arguments of Hans Cornelius (1863–1947), who had taught him philosophy and who had passed his doctoral thesis in 1924, although he had in fact rejected his first dissertation for the second doctorate, the *Habilitation*. 'The distinction between analytic and synthetic judgements that is of such crucial importance for the entire work [i.e. the *Critique of Pure Reason*] suffers . . . from a lack of clarity. The proposition "All bodies are heavy" is only synthetic if the concept of the "body" is taken in the sense of a *geometric* body. If, in contrast, "body" is used in the way it normally

occurs in a chemistry laboratory, then it would contain the meaning of "weight" in it and so the above-mentioned proposition becomes analytic. This example shows that the distinction between analytic and synthetic *varies* unless it is made clear which attributes are contained in it and which are not.' Hans Cornelius, *Kommentar zu Kants Kritik der reinen Vernunft*, Erlangen, 1926, p. 31.

3 'That *logic* has already, from the earliest times, proceeded upon this sure path is evidenced by the fact that since *Aristotle* it has not required to retrace a single step, unless, indeed, we care to count as improvements the removal of certain needless subtleties or the clearer exposition of its recognized teaching, features which concern the elegance rather than the certainty of the science.' *Critique of Pure Reason*, Preface to the Second Edition, p. 17, B viii.

4 Probably in conversation. At any rate, this term has not been discovered in Adorno's published writings.

5 Here Adorno sums up in two sentences an idea that stands in the centre of his own thinking from the book on Kierkegaard down to *Negative Dialectics*. This is the critique of idealism as a critique of the philosophy of origins. This critique was most fully developed, not long before the present lectures on Kant, in the Introduction to *Against Epistemology*, a book whose spirit pervades almost the entire course of lectures. 'Idealism, which through reduction to the absolute unity of the "I think" was the very first to be amenable to a systematics developing on all fronts, has, by the measure of its own radicalism, revealed how questionable is the residue it had crystallized. *Prima philosophia* came to awareness of this in the doctrine of the antinomies in the *Critique of Pure Reason*. The search for the utterly first, the absolute cause, results in infinite regress. Infinity cannot be posited as given with a conclusion, even though this positing seems unavoidable to total spirit. The concept of the given, the last refuge of the irreducible in idealism, collides with the concept of spirit as something to which everything can be reduced, viz. with idealism itself. This antinomy explodes the system, whose only idea is the attained identity, which as anticipated identity, as finitude of the infinite, is not at one with itself.' *Against Epistemology*, pp. 29f. And, on the 'problem of history': 'The problem of the first itself is retrospective. Thinking which, like Plato's, has its absolute in memory has no real expectations of anything further. The praise of the unchanging suggests that nothing should be otherwise than it has always been. A taboo is issued about the future' (ibid., p. 32). Then, in the *Negative Dialectics*, Adorno defined his own philosophy as an 'attitude' that 'refuses to act as the custodian of the primordial and the certain and yet, if only through the trenchant nature of its own narrative, is so far from making concessions to relativism, the brother of absolutism, that it comes close to doctrine ... But by setting thought free from the primal and the fixed it does not validate itself as something free-floating. That very act of setting free ties it to something other than itself and destroys the illusion of autarchy.' (*GS*, vol. 6, p. 44). The central themes

of the lectures on the *Critique of Pure Reason* take up ideas from the Introduction to *Against Epistemology* that had been written two years previously. And in the same way, without simply repeating himself, Adorno continued to develop most of the ideas contained in the lectures in his subsequent writings, above all in *Negative Dialectics*.

6   Adorno has in mind here the Note to §16 of the Transcendental Deduction in which Kant states: 'The synthetic unity of apperception is therefore that highest point to which we must *ascribe* [*heften* = attach. *Trans.*] all employment of the understanding, even the whole of logic, and conformably therewith, transcendental philosophy.' *Critique of Pure Reason*, p. 154, B 134 [Editor's emphasis].

7   'I know no enquiries which are more important for exploring the faculty which we entitle understanding, and for determining the rules and limits of its employment, than those which I have instituted . . . under the title *Deduction of the Pure Concepts of Understanding.*' *Critique of Pure Reason*, p. 11, A xvi.

8   *Critique of Pure Reason*, p. 161, B 145.

9   Ibid., B 145f.

10 Kant himself speaks of 'intelligible contingency' in the Observation on the Fourth Antinomy of Pure Reason, where he writes that 'we cannot argue from an empirical contingency to an intelligible one.' (*Critique of Pure Reason*, p. 420, A 459/B 587). In his commentary on this passage Cohen then speaks literally of 'intelligible contingency'. See Hermann Cohen, *Kommentar zu Immanuel Kants Kritik der reinen Vernunft*, 2nd edn, Leipzig, 1917, p. 150.

11 Adorno writes about Kant's respect for the 'irreducibility' of existent beings to their concepts in 'Aspects of Hegel's Philosophy', the first of his *Hegel Studies*, written in 1956–7: 'Just as, on the one hand, the categorial forms of the "I think" need a supplementary content that does not arise out of them themselves in order to make truth, that is, knowledge of nature, possible, so on the other hand the "I think" itself and the categorial forms are respected by Kant as a species of givens; to this extent at least the *Critique of Pure Reason* is more a phenomenology of subjectivity than a speculative system. In the "us" that Kant, in his introspective naivety, continues to use unreflectively, he acknowledges the relationship – and not only in their application, but in their origin – of the categorial forms to something existing, namely human beings, that arises in turn from the interplay of the forms with sensory material. Kant's reflections break off at this point and thus testify to the impossibility of reducing the factual to the spirit and this points instead to the intertwining of these opposing elements.' *Hegel: Three Studies*, pp. 14f.

12 Cf. Franz Kafka, 'Reflections on Sin, Suffering, Hope and the True Way', in *Dearest Father: Stories and Other Writings*, trans. Ernst Kaiser and Eithne Wilkins, Schocken Books, New York, 1954, pp. 38f. 'The more horses you harness to the job, the faster the thing goes – that

is to say, not tearing the block out of its base, which is impossible, but tearing the straps to shreds, and as a result the weightless merry journey.'

13 'For it [i.e. metaphysics] is nothing but the *inventory* of all our possessions through *pure* reason, systematically arranged. In this field nothing can escape us. What reason produces entirely out of itself cannot be concealed . . .' *Critique of Pure Reason*, Preface to the First Edition, p. 14, A xx. In the Introduction, in the version found in the Second Edition, he says: 'Transcendental philosophy is only the idea of a science, for which the critique of pure reason has to lay down the complete architectonic plan. That is to say, it has to guarantee, as following from principles, the completeness and certainty of the structure in all its parts. It is the system of all principles of pure reason.' Introduction, p. 60, B 27.

14 In Adorno's view the reaction of philosophical consciousness to the Kantian 'block' is of crucial importance for the question of truth and falsehood. In the second of his *Hegel Studies* he had written in the previous year: 'The debate between Kant and Hegel in which Hegel's devastating argument had the last word is not yet over; perhaps because what was decisive, the superior power of logical stringency, is untrue in the face of the Kantian discontinuities. Through his critique of Kant, Hegel achieved a magnificent extension of the practice of critical philosophy beyond the formal sphere; at the same time, in doing so he evaded the supreme critical moment, the critique of totality, of something infinite and conclusively given. Then he highhandedly did away with the barrier after all, with the experience of something that cannot be dissolved in consciousness, which was the innermost experience of Kant's transcendental philosophy, and he stipulated a unanimity of knowledge that becomes seamless through its discontinuities and that has something of a mythical illusory quality to it.' *Hegel: Three Studies*, p. 86. Adorno did not come to a fuller discussion of the 'Kantian block, the theory of the limits of possible positive knowledge' until 1966, in *Negative Dialectics* (*GS*, vol. 6, pp. 378ff).

15 *Critique of Pure Reason*, p. 59, B 25.

16 Writing of the Table of Categories, Kant remarks: 'This division is developed systematically from a common principle, namely, the faculty of judgement (which is the same as the faculty of thought). It has not arisen rhapsodically, as the result of a haphazard search after pure concepts . . . It was an enterprise worthy of an acute thinker like *Aristotle* to make a search for these fundamental concepts. But as he did so on no principle, he merely picked them up as they came his way' (*Critique of Pure Reason*, p. 114, A 80f/B 106f).

17 *Critique of Pure Reason*, p. 41, B 1.

18 On the idea of the theory of knowledge as a *no man's land* between the established branches of knowledge, see Lectures Three and Twenty, p. 32 and p. 219 above.

Lecture Three

1 In *Against Epistemology* Adorno pointed to Plato's *Meno* as an instance
of the 'mathematicization' of philosophy: 'Just in order to enforce continuity and completeness, it must eliminate everything which does not
fit from whatever it judges. The poverty of philosophical systematics
which in the end reduces philosophical systems to a bogey, is not at first
a sign of their decay, but is rather teleologically posited by the procedure itself, which in Plato already demanded without opposition that
virtue must be demonstrable through reduction to its schema, like a
geometrical figure.' *Against Epistemology*, p. 10.

2 In his Introduction to *Against Epistemology* Adorno understands the
residual theory of truth to refer to the self-abasement of philosophers
that is the corollary of the 'privileging of the subject', the consistent
theme of philosophies of origins: 'Just to avoid error – since that is how
they promote themselves – they abase themselves and would like best of
all to eliminate themselves entirely. They use their subjectivity to subtract the subject from truth and the residue they call objectivity. All
prima philosophia up to Heidegger's claims about "destruction" was
essentially a theory of residue. Truth is supposed to be the leftover, the
dregs, the most insipid thing of all.' *Against Epistemology*, p. 15 [trans-
lation slightly amended]. In the first of the *Hegel Studies*, written at
almost the same time, Adorno equated 'the residual theory of truth
according to which the objective is left after the so-called subjective
factors have been eliminated' with 'the static analysis of knowledge into
subject and object that the currently accepted logic of science takes for
granted.' (*Hegel: Three Studies*, p. 7).

3 *Critique of Pure Reason*, p. 41, B 1. See also Lecture Two, p. 21,
above.

4 The quotation from Thucydides was evidently incomprehensible on
the tape and it is represented in the transcript by dots and a question
mark. The quotation given in the text is conjectural, based on the
version given in Karl Reinhardt, 'Thukydides und Machiavelli' in his
Vermächtnis der Antike [Legacy of Antiquity], *Gesammelte Essays zur
Philosophie und Geschichtsschreibung*, Göttingen, 1960, p. 190.

5 The following criticism of the idea that the truth endures goes beyond the
corresponding passages in the Introduction to *Against Epistemology* in
important respects (cf. ibid., pp. 17ff).

6 See *Critique of Pure Reason*, p. 505, A 599/B 627. See also p. 42 and
the wording of the whole analogy in n. 10 to Lecture Four.

7 For the connection between abstract knowledge and the universal rule of
exchange value, see *Negative Dialectics*, in particular the section entitled
'Negative Dialectics. Concept and Categories' (*GS*, vol. 6, pp. 137ff, and
esp. p. 180). Here, based mainly on Kant, Adorno gives his development
of the theory of knowledge, in so far as we may still speak of one.

8 As an example we may cite the following statement from Cornelius's
Kommentar zu Kants Kritik der reinen Vernunft, Erlangen, 1926, p. 29:

'That gold differs from water we know only from experience. But this knowledge is undoubtedly universal and bears the character of necessity.'

9   This example, too, can be found in Cornelius's commentary (ibid., p. 42). Cornelius adds in a footnote: 'This example, which I first used at the beginning of my academic career, has made its appearance since then in so many scholarly publications without giving the source that I think it only right to point out its origins here.'

10 In the Preface to the *Prolegomena to Any Future Metaphysics that will be able to Come Forward as Science* Kant writes: 'I openly confess that my remembering David Hume was the very thing which many years ago first interrupted my dogmatic slumber and gave my investigations in the field of speculative philosophy a quite new direction.' *Prolegomena to Any Future Metaphysics*, p. 5.

11 This translates the text as given in the draft. However, Adorno may have said 'the timeless, absolutely valid truth independent of experience'.

12 See p. 2 above and also Lecture One, n. 4.

13 See p. 1 above and n. 1. According to *Negative Dialectics* Adorno believed that the Kantian critiques were unable to free themselves from 'pre-critical thinking' since it too 'let itself be seduced into thinking of reason not as the instrument, the court of appeal, of reflection, but as a *constituens* . . . The hypostatization of the means, which today has become a matter of course, lay theoretically in the nature of the so-called Copernican revolution. Not for nothing does Kant use this as a metaphor whose substantial meaning is the very opposite of the revolution in astronomy.' (*GS*, vol. 6, p. 196).

Lecture Four

1   See Martin Heidegger, *Kant und das Problem der Metaphysik*, 2nd edn, Frankfurt am Main, 1951.

2   See esp. §35, 'The Originality of the Previously Laid Ground and the Problem of Metaphysics' where he sums up his position with the words: 'Kant's laying of the ground for metaphysics leads to the transcendental power of imagination. This is the root of both stems, sensibility and understanding. As such, it makes possible the original unity of ontological synthesis. This root, however, is rooted in original time. The original ground which becomes manifest in the ground-laying is time. Kant's laying of the ground for metaphysics . . . becomes the question of the possibility of ontology in general. This poses the question concerning the essence of the constitution of the Being of beings, i.e., concerning Being in general. The laying of the ground for metaphysics grows upon the ground of time. The question concerning Being, the grounding question for a laying of the ground for metaphysics, is the problem of *Being and Time*. This title contains the guiding idea of the preceding interpretation of the *Critique of Pure Reason* as a laying of the ground for metaphysics.' *Kant and the Problem of Metaphysics*,

trans. Richard Taft, Indiana University Press, Bloomington/Indianapolis, 1990, p. 138.

3   Adorno's statement is not to be taken quite literally either since the System of all Principles of Pure Understanding is the second of three chapters of Book II of the First Division of the Transcendental Analytic, which also has an Appendix. It cannot therefore be regarded as the 'conclusion' of book II.

4   [*Critique of Pure Reason*, trans. Paulauyer and Alau Wood, pp. 147f, B 20–3. *Trans.*]

5   Adorno cites the passage – the beginning of the First Preface – in the next lecture, see p. 51. See the *Critique of Pure Reason*, p. 7, A vii.

6   See Lecture One, p. 7 above, and also n. 13.

7   That is to say, in section VI of the Introduction in the 2nd edn. Cf. p. 57, B 22.

8   'Since these sciences [i.e. pure mathematics and pure science] actually exist, it is quite proper to ask *how* they are possible; for that they must be possible is proved by the fact that they exist.' *Critique of Pure Reason*, p. 56, B 20.

9   The Impossibility of an Ontological Proof of the Existence of God, *Critique of Pure Reason*, pp. 500–7, A 592–602/B 620–30.

10   Kant's words in the section on the impossibility of the ontological proof of the existence of God are: 'Otherwise stated, the real contains no more than the merely possible. A hundred real thalers do not contain the least coin more than a hundred possible thalers. For as the latter signify the concept, and the former the object and the positing of the object, should the former contain more than the latter, my concept would not, in that case, express the whole object, and would not therefore be an adequate concept of it. My financial position is, however, affected very differently by a hundred real thalers than it is by the mere concept of them (that is, of their possibility). For the object, as it actually exists, is not analytically contained in the concept, but is added to my concept (which is a determination of my state) synthetically; and yet the conceived hundred thalers are not themselves in the least increased through thus acquiring existence outside my concept.' *Critique of Pure Reason*, p. 505, A 599/B 627. See also Adorno's use of Kant's analogy of the thalers in *Negative Dialectics*, GS, vol. 6, p. 189.

11   Cf. Max Scheler, *Der Formalismus in der Ethik und die materielle Wertethik. Neuer Versuch der Grundlegung eines ethischen Personalismus*, 4th edn, Bern, 1954 (*Gesammelte Werke*, vol. 2). In *Negative Dialectics* Adorno insists that 'The formalism of the Kantian ethics is not just worthy of the condemnation with which it has been stigmatized, from Scheler on, by reactionary, academic German philosophy. *On the contrary*, it stipulates the universal norm of justice. In this sense, despite or even because of its abstract nature, a matter of substance, namely the idea of equality, survives in it.' (GS, vol. 6, pp. 234f).

12   On the relations of form and content in Kant see also pp. 87f and 97 above, but above all the Introduction to *Against Epistemology*, where

he writes that 'the analysis of consciousness brings to light that it does not contain some such absolutely first thing, independent of its material, of what "befits" consciousness. The ontologically first thing does not come first ontologically, and this undermines the whole idea. Kant's attempt to use the distinction between form and content in order to extricate himself from this awkward situation is both ingenious and artificial. The definition of contradiction and its necessity, which in effect prohibits any mediation of the kind Kant himself sought, represents the more unforgiving truth, in comparison with later idealism. But as apologist for *prima philosophia* he nevertheless continued to advocate the primacy of form. The reciprocal dependence of form and matter which he himself arrived at could not be allowed to affect the system as a whole. The forms as givens in their own right become for him the absolute first things. As the second version of the Transcendental Deduction says, no "further ground" can be given for those forms. . . . Kant certainly seeks to unravel the secret and deduce the somewhat paradoxical givenness of the forms. Thus he arrives at pure identity, pure thought itself, the subject which as "pure" and cut off from all content, is made into a simple non-existent thing, but is simultaneously hypostatized. The Transcendental Deduction flows into reason as absolute being; the Transcendental Dialectic criticizes the absoluteness of both being and reason. So in a certain way the Deduction lags behind the doctrine of the antinomies. In spite of this, the antinomies presuppose the Deduction and the proof of the subjective character of the category in order to ward off the "naive", unreflecting positing of the infinite. By the retreat to formalism, for which first Hegel and then the phenomenologists reproached him, Kant paid homage to the nonidentical. He disdained to absorb it into the identity of the subject without residue. The price he paid for this, however, was to narrow the very idea of truth which no longer expected more than to classify the heterogeneous by means of concepts of order.' (*Against Epistemology*, p. 30).

Lecture Five

1   *Critique of Pure Reason*, p. 21, B xiv.
2   The transition from Kant's critique of reason to the speculative thinking of the post-Kantian idealists is a theme that permeates Adorno's entire philosophy. Here is just one early example from the book on Kierkegaard of 1932 which illustrates it in the process of formation. He says of the forms of consciousness that they 'paid with abstraction; [that] the principles are "necessary" only in so far as they are "universal". The idealist systems undertook once again to recover the lost content of ontology through the elimination of the contingency of the "material" which is itself derived from the synthetic unity of apperception, developed as "content" out of the subjective forms from which "ontology" can be

deduced and through "development" posited as identical with subject-ivity.' *Kierkegaard: Construction of the Aesthetic*, p. 74.

3 Kant contrasts dialectics as a 'logic of illusion' to the 'logic of truth', which is equated with the Transcendental Analytic. See *Critique of Pure Reason*, p. 176, A 131/B 170.

4 *Critique of Pure Reason*, p. 7, A viif.

5 See p. 15 and n. 4, above.

6 Cf. *Against Epistemology*, pp. 3–40.

7 *Critique of Pure Reason*, p. 9, A xif.

8 Ibid., A xii.

Lecture Six

1 *Critique of Pure Reason*, p. 10, A xiii.

2 See *Dreams of a Spirit-Seer Elucidated by Dreams of Metaphysics*, in *Theoretical Philosophy 1755–1770*, pp. 301–59.

3 *Critique of Pure Reason*, p. 10, A xiii.

4 See pp. 76f, above.

5 Adorno has in mind the first of the four rules that Descartes took as a guiding principle in part II of the *Discourse on Method* of 1637: 'The first rule was to accept nothing as true which I did not evidently know to be such, that is to say, scrupulously to avoid precipitance and prejudice, and in the judgements I passed to include nothing additional to what had presented itself to my mind so clearly and so distinctly that I could have no occasion for doubting it.' René Descartes, *Discourse on Method*, in *Philosophical Writings*, selected and trans. by Norman Kemp Smith, Macmillan, 1952, p. 129. This was the only one of the four rules that Adorno did not discuss in 'The Essay as Form' (cf. *Notes to Literature*, vol. 1, pp. 3–23). However, in his own copy of Artur Buchenau's translation of Descartes he noted in the margin: 'in Kant: critique'.

6 See pp. 4 and 27f and *passim*, above.

7 See *Kant-Lexikon*, a reference work to *Kants Sämtliche Schriften, Briefe, und handschriftlicher Nachlaß* [Kant's Complete Writings, Letters and Posthumous Unpublished Writings], ed. Rudolf Eisler, Hildesheim, 1964 (reprint of the edition of Berlin, 1910), p. 49. The last sentence is taken from the *Critique of Pure Reason*, p. 598, A 747/B 775, while the previous sentences are Eisler's summary of Kant's position.

8 *Kant-Lexikon*, p. 49. Only the passage starting with 'Enlightenment is . . .' comes from the *Idea for a Universal History with a Cosmopolitan Purpose*, in *Kant: Political Writings*, p. 51. The first sentence comes from Eisler's commentary.

9 *An Answer to the Question: 'What is Enlightenment?'* in *Political Writings*, p. 54.

10 *What is Orientation in Thinking?*, in *Political Writings*, p. 249.

11 *Kant-Lexikon*, p. 50. The phrase in double inverted commas is a literal quotation from *An Answer to the Question: 'What is Enlightenment?'*, p. 55; the rest is a quotation from Eisler.
12 Cf. the opening of the book: 'In the most general sense of progressive thought, the Enlightenment has always aimed at liberating men from fear and establishing their sovereignty. . . . The programme of the Enlightenment was the disenchantment of the world. It aimed at the dissolution of myths and the overthrow of fancy by knowledge.' *Dialectic of Enlightenment*, p. 3 [translation amended, *Trans.*].
13 See p. 43, above.

Lecture Seven

1 Fichte himself mentions Kant's negative view of the *Wissenschaftslehre* in the 'Second Introduction to the *Wissenschaftslehre*', cf. Johann Gottlieb Fichte, *Sämmtliche Werke*, ed. I. H. Fichte, section 1, vol. 1, Leipzig, n.d. [*c.*1844], p. 469.
2 *Critique of Pure Reason*, p. 29, B xxixf.
3 The term *lumen naturale* was used from Thomas Aquinas down to Leibniz to refer to the 'light of reason'. Its meaning can be gleaned from Descartes's essay 'The search for truth by means of the natural light' and particularly from its subtitle: 'This light alone, without any help from religion or philosophy, determines what opinions a good man should hold on any matter that may occupy his thoughts, and penetrates into the secrets of the most recondite sciences'. See *The Philosophical Writings of Descartes*, vol. 2, trans. John Cottingham, Robert Stoothof and Dugald Murdoch, Cambridge University Press, Cambridge, 1984, p. 400. Kant appears not to have used the expression.
4 *Critique of Pure Reason*, p. 29, B xxx.
5 Adorno criticizes Kant's statement even more sharply from the vantage-point of Hegel's 'antithesis' in his *Encyclopedia*: 'Hegel sensed the regressive and tyrannical moment in Kant's modesty and opposed the famous saying with which Kant's Enlightenment endeared itself to obscurantism: "I have therefore found it necessary to deny knowledge, in order to make room for faith. The dogmatism of metaphysics, that is, the preconception that it is possible to make headway in metaphysics without a previous criticism of pure reason, is the source of all that unbelief, always very dogmatic, which wars against morality." Hegel's antithesis to this reads, "The sealed essence of the universe has no power that could withstand the spirit of knowledge; it is compelled to open itself to it and lay out its riches and its depths and offer them for its enjoyment." In formulations like this, the Baconian pathos of the early bourgeois period is extended to become that of a mature humankind: we may yet succeed.' *Hegel: Three Studies*, pp. 67f.
6 See the 'Last Sermon in Wittenberg': 'And what I say of passion, which is a great sin, must also be understood of reason: for the latter violates

and insults God in His spiritual gifts and has far more horrible whorish evils than a whore . . . Do you hear this, you scabby, leprous whore, you holy reason . . .' Martin Luther, *Werke*, ed. Buchwald, Kawerau, and others, third series, Berlin 1905, pp. 97 and 99; quoted from Friedrich Wilhelm Pohl and Christoph Türcke, *Heilige Hure Vernunft. Luthers nachhaltiger Zauber*. Berlin, 1981, p. 60.

7 *Critique of Pure Reason*, p. 294, A 289/B 345. [The English translation 'stray', although accurate, is less obviously erotic than '*ausschweifen*' with its connotations of 'leaving the straight and narrow', 'run riot' or 'indulge to excess'. *Trans.*]

8 The quotation has not been identified.

9 See the end of Lecture Six, p. 67f, above.

10 See Lecture Six, p. 63, above.

11 In the *Critique of Pure Reason* Kant speaks of 'merely pseudo-rational, merely dialectical concepts' (p. 533, A 644/B 672), and similarly 'the dialectical conclusions of pure reason' are said to deserve 'rather to be called *pseudo-rational* than rational' (p. 327, A 339/B 397). In *Negative Dialectics* Kant's language is said to provide evidence of a more extensive tendency towards antinomy: 'The pure logic of consistency, pandering to self-preservation without self-reflection, is itself deluded and irrational. Kant's loathsome talk of the pseudo-rational – echoes of which can still be heard in Hegel's term "reasoning" [*Raisonnieren*] – pillories reason without making any valid distinctions and arrives at an accommodation with the hypostasis of reason beyond all rational purposes, despite the flagrant contradiction. *Ratio* turns into an irrational authority.' (*GS*, vol. 6, p. 258).

12 Cf. Adorno's further discussions of depth on pp. 185ff, 207ff and 222. Furthermore, this may be compared with the introduction to *Negative Dialectics* in which Adorno makes his final statement about the ideology and truth of talk about profundity in philosophy. See *GS*, vol. 6, pp. 28f.

13 See p. 61, above.

14 Adorno probably had in mind Schopenhauer's often repeated interpretation according to which Kant destroyed theology only in order to re-establish it on the basis of morality (cf. Arthur Schopenhauer, *On the Basis of Morality*, p. 44, and *Sämtliche Werke*, vol. 5: *Parerga et Paralipomena* II, §115, Darmstadt, 1965, p. 260).

15 Cf. 'What emerges from this consideration is, therefore, *first*, that the law of identity or of contradiction which purports to express merely abstract identity in contrast to difference as a truth, is not a law of thought, but rather the opposite of it; *second*, that these laws contain *more* than is *meant* by them, to wit, this opposite, absolute difference itself.' G. W. F. Hegel, *Science of Logic*, p. 416.

16 Julius Ebbinghaus (1885–1981). For his work on Kant, see esp. section I of his *Gesammelte Aufsätze, Vorträge und Reden*, Darmstadt, 1968.

17 Cf. Klaus Reich, *Die Vollständigkeit der kantischen Urteilstafel* [The Completeness of the Kantian Table of Judgements], Berlin, 1932; 2nd edn, 1948.

Lecture Eight

1 Adorno doubtless has his own experiences in mind. A few years before in the context of the 'Group experiments' – a study undertaken by the Institute for Social Research in 1950–1 – he had carried through a qualitative analysis of the reactions of his interviewees to such themes as 'concentration camps', 'terrorism', 'the genocide of the Jews', 'wars of aggression', and produced a monograph on the subject with the title *Guilt and Defence-mechanisms* (cf. *GS*, vol. 9.2, pp. 121ff).

2 'Therefore it must be itself that thought thinks (since it is the most excellent of things), and its thinking is a thinking on thinking.' Aristotle, *Metaphysics*, 1074b, in *The Complete Works of Aristotle*, ed. Jonathan Barnes, vol. 2, Princeton University Press, 1984, p. 1698.

3 [Adorno used the English word. *Trans.*]

4 G. W. F. Hegel, *Science of Logic*, p. 442.

5 Ibid.

6 No reference has been found. [Heinrich Rickert, 1863–1936, professor of philosophy in Freiburg and Heidelberg, was the founder of the southwest German school of neo-Kantianism. *Trans.*]

7 The motif of 'expression' as applied to Kant's philosophy reaches back into Adorno's early youth and according to an essay of 1964 was something for which he was indebted to Siegfried Kracauer: 'For years Kracauer read the *Critique of Pure Reason* with me regularly on Saturday afternoons. I am not exaggerating in the slightest when I say that I owe more to this reading than to my academic teachers. Exceptionally gifted as a pedagogue, Kracauer made Kant come alive for me. Under his guidance I experienced the work from the beginning not as mere epistemology, not as an analysis of the conditions of scientifically valid judgements, but as a kind of coded text from which the historical situation of the spirit could be read, with the vague expectation that in doing so one could acquire something of truth itself. . . . As he presented it to me, Kant's critical philosophy was not simply a system of transcendental idealism. Rather, he showed me how the objective-ontological and subjective-idealist moments warred within it, how the more eloquent passages in the work are the wounds this conflict has left in the theory. . . . Without being able to account for it fully, through Kracauer I perceived for the first time the expressive moment in philosophy: putting into words the thoughts that come into one's head. The opposite moment, the moment of rigour, of compelling objectivity in thought, took second place to it. For quite a while after I first encountered it in the practice of philosophy at the university it seemed academic to me, until I found out that among the tensions that are the lifeblood of philosophy the tension between expressiveness and rigour is perhaps the most central.' 'The Curious Realist: On Siegfried Kracauer', in *Notes to Literature*, vol. 2, pp. 58f.

8 'I recently made the acquaintance of the modern, so-called Kantian philosophy – and I must tell you my thoughts about it, since I need not fear that it will move you as deeply, as painfully, as it did me. . . . If

men had green glasses instead of eyes, they would have to believe that the objects they saw through them were *green* – and they would never be able to decide whether their eyes showed them things as they were, or whether they did not add something to them that belonged not to them, but to the eye. The same is true of the mind. We cannot decide whether what we call truth is truly true, or whether it only appears so to us. If the latter, then the truth we amass here does not *exist* after our death – and all our striving to acquire possessions that will follow us to the grave is in vain.' Letter of 22 March 1801 to his fiancée, Wilhelmine von Zenge, in Heinrich von Kleist, *Sämtliche Werke und Briefe*, edited by Helmut Sembdner, vol. 2, 5th edn, Munich, 1970, p. 634. See also a similar statement in the letter of 23 March 1801 to his sister, ibid., p. 636.

9   The epithet goes back to Moses Mendelssohn, who wrote in the Preface to his *Morgenstunden oder Vorlesungen über das Dasein Gottes* [Morning Hours or Lectures on the Existence of God], which appeared in 1785, 'I know of ... the writings of the great men who have made a name for themselves in metaphysics – the works of Lambert, Teten, Platner and even the all-destroying Kant only from the inadequate reports of my friends or from learned notices that are rarely more informative.' Moses Mendelssohn, *Schriften über Religion und Aufklärung*, ed. Martina Thom, Berlin, 1989, p. 469. Schopenhauer then refers to 'Kant, the all-destroyer'. See Schopenhauer, *Parerga and Paralipomena*, vol. 1, 'Fragments for the History of Philosophy', pp. 29ff, and ibid., p. 190, 'On Philosophy at the Universities'.

10 *Critique of Pure Reason*, p. 32, B xxxvi.

11 The intertwining of critique and the salvaging of ontology was positioned at the centre of Kant's theoretical philosophy as early as Adorno's *Kierkegaard* of 1932. 'Critique of pure reason was a critique of rational ontology, specifically, of Wolff's ontology. This ontology was subjected to its most severe test: that of the contingency of the categorically undeducible material of intuition. If ontology is not to be rescued as the content of experience, then it may be conceived only as the form of experience. It shrinks to a synthetic *a priori* judgement to the extent that it is not relegated to the secure and powerless transcendence of the postulates. The gap between the inner and the contingent outer is still mastered in the system of principles: subjectively produced by means of the synthetic unity of apperception, they belong to the immanence of consciousness; as constitutive conditions of all objective knowledge, they are themselves objective. Ontology is preserved in their double meaning: it is protected from contingency through the systematic strength of the spontaneous centre and protected from the deceptions of speculative thought through experiential validity. The cost of this security is abstractness; the principles are "necessary" only in so far as they are universal.' *Kierkegaard: Construction of the Aesthetic*, trans. Robert Hullot-Kentor, University of Minnesota Press, Minneapolis, 1989, pp. 73f.

12   See I. Kant, *Werke*, vol. 3, p. 590 ('On the Prize Question: What is the true progress achieved by metaphysics in Germany since the age of Leibniz and Wolff?').

13   See Adorno's 'Critique of Logical Absolutism' in Husserl, in ch. 1 of *Against Epistemology*, pp. 41–88.

14   In the first of his *Hegel Studies*, 'Aspects of Hegel's Philosophy' Adorno writes, formulating what might be termed the birth certificate of the new dialectics: 'For Hegel's idealism, reason becomes a critical reason in a sense that criticizes Kant once again, a negative reason that both preserves static elements and sets them in motion. The poles that Kant opposed to one another – form and content, nature and spirit, theory and praxis, freedom and necessity, the thing-in-itself and the phenomenon – are all permeated through and through by reflection in such a way that none of these determinations are left standing as ultimate. In order to be thought, and to exist, each inherently requires the other that Kant opposed to it.' (*Hegel: Three Studies*, p. 8). And Adorno's negative dialectics maintains the connection with Kant's Transcendental Philosophy no less than with Hegel's *Logic* when he begins the conceptual section of *Negative Dialectics* with the anacoluthon, 'No existence without existing entities.' (*GS*, vol. 6, p. 139).

15   Adorno followed his teacher Cornelius in his interpretation of the position adopted by the Kantian critique towards Hume's philosophy with reference to the key themes of the self, causality and the thing: 'The dogmatic slumber that held Kant and with him the entire philosophy of the Continent in its spell consisted essentially in the fact that the concepts of a *thing existing in and for itself*, independently of our perception, of *cause* and of the *spiritual personality*, concepts that had been taken over from pre-critical thought, were being applied uncritically and used to lay the foundations for a unified explanation of the universe, in other words, a metaphysics.' (Cornelius, *Kommentar zu Kants Kritik der reinen Vernunft*, p. 2).

16   Namely in the Transcendental Deduction of the Pure Concepts of the Understanding [pp. 129–75]. In his lectures up to now Adorno has dealt essentially with the two Prefaces and the Introduction.

17   See, above all, the Deduction of the Pure Concepts of the Understanding in the Second Edition, and particularly §16, The Original Synthetic Unity of Apperception: 'It must be *possible* for the "*I think*" to accompany all my representations; for otherwise something would be represented in me which could not be thought at all, and that is equivalent to saying that the representation would be impossible, or at least would be nothing to me.' *Critique of Pure Reason*, p. 153, B 131f.

18   See p. 191, above, together with Lecture Eighteen, n. 3.

19   Adorno subsequently supplied a critique of the Kantian concept of causality in *Negative Dialectics*: 'The famous, highly formal Kantian definition of causality asserts that everything that takes places presupposes a prior state "which it follows inevitably according to a rule". Historically this definition is aimed at the school of Leibniz and at the

interpretation of a succession of states as proceeding from an inner necessity, an existence in itself. On the other hand, it distinguished itself from Hume: without the regularity of thought that Hume ascribes to convention, to chance, an experience about which we agree is not possible. Hume himself has of necessity to speak the language of causality in order to persuade us of what he would like to trivialize by making it a matter of convention. For Kant, in contrast, causality becomes a function of subjective reason with the consequence that whatever we imagine by it becomes increasingly attenuated. It dissolves like a piece of mythology. Thus causality comes close to the principle of reason as such, namely, thought according to rules. Judgements about causal connections tend to turn into tautologies: reason discovers in them what it itself brings about by virtue of its laws. . . . Once causality has been so utterly shorn of its magic, as if by a taboo on the inner determination of objects, it collapses in on itself. What gives Kant's salvage operation its only advantage over Hume's denial is that what Hume swept away is perceived as innate in reason, as it were, its necessary nature, if not an anthropological accident. Causality is to arise, not in the objects and their relations, but instead merely in the subjective necessity of thought. The idea that one state can have an essential, specific connection with a following state is in Kant's eyes too a piece of dogma.' (*GS*, vol. 6, p. 245). On the concept of causality see also pp. 108, 140, above, as well as Lecture Thirteen, n. 6.

Lecture Nine

1   This was the term given according to his own account by Hans Cornelius to the concepts of a *thing existing*, independently of our perception, *in and for itself*, of *cause* and of the *spiritual personality*, concepts that had been taken over from pre-critical thought: 'I have referred to these concepts as "naturalistic concepts".' (Cornelius, *Kommentar zu Kants Kritik der reinen Vernunft*, p. 2). In his *Einleitung in die Philosophie* [Introduction to Philosophy] Cornelius wrote that the naturalistic concepts constituted a 'source of dogmatic explanations' which provided 'metaphysical systems with powers of resistance that enabled them constantly to spring back into life in defiance of all criticism.' (Cornelius, *Einleitung in die Philosophie*, 2nd edn, Leipzig/Berlin, 1911, p. 48).

2   See p. 91f, above.

3   This is probably not to be taken literally. According to Horkheimer, Kant 'probably made the acquaintance of Hume's theoretical philosophy . . . only in the form of the little *Enquiry*'. Max Horkheimer, *Nachgelassene Schriften 1914–1931*, p. 470. More recent research, however, inclines to the view that at the very least Kant had read the partial translation of the final part of book I of the *Treatise* which was published anonymously in 1771 by Hamann (cf. Gerhard Steininger, *David Hume*, 2nd edn, Reinbek bei Hamburg, 1992, p. 131).

4   *Critique of Pure Reason*, pp. 344ff, A 367ff.

5   Namely in the first of the *Meditations on First Philosophy*, in *The Philosophical Writings of Descartes*, trans. John Cottingham, Robert Stoothof and Dugald Murdoch, vol. 2, Cambridge University Press, Cambridge, 1984, p. 15.

6   For Kant's polemic against Berkeley's idealism see pp. 243f, B 274f. However, the concept of 'dreamy idealism' is not to be found there. Adorno may have confused it with the 'mystical and visionary idealism' that Kant uses to describe Berkeley. (*Prolegomena to Any Future Metaphysics*, p. 37).

7   *Critique of Pure Reason*, p. 172, B 163f.

8   Later on, in *Negative Dialectics*, Adorno formulated his objections to Kant's solution to the 'central question' of the *Critique of Pure Reason*: 'That it [i.e. reason] prescribes nature's laws, or rather, law, signifies no more than the subsuming of nature under the unity of reason. Reason transfers this unity, the principle of its own identity, to the objects and then misrepresents this as knowledge of them.' (*GS*, vol. 6, p. 245). And: 'For Kant's primary principle, the synthetic unity of apperception, . . . every definition of the object is an investment of subjectivity in non-qualitative diversity. This applies without regard to the fact that the determining acts which he takes for spontaneous achievements of transcendental logic also include an element alien to themselves; and that we can synthesize only what permits and requires synthesis. Active determination is not something purely subjective and therefore the triumph of the sovereign subject that dictates laws to nature is hollow.' (*GS*, vol. 6, p. 142).

9   See p. 130f, above, and also Lecture Twelve, n. 5.

10 *Critique of Pure Reason*, p. 131, A 98ff and p. 171, B 161f.

11 An allusion to the opening of Hegel's *Science of Logic*, p. 82.

12 *Critique of Pure Reason*, p. 172, B 164.

13 Ibid., pp. 172f, B 164f.

14 Adorno also discusses at length the epistemological implications of *Gestalt* theory in the lectures on epistemology of 1957/8. Cf. for the time being the pirated version, Theodor W. Adorno, *Vorlesung zur Einleitung in die Erkenntnistheorie* [Introductory Lectures on Epistemology], Junius-Drucke, Frankfurt, n.d., pp. 104ff.

15 In a subsequent course of lectures Adorno says about 'the Kantian concept of apprehension' that according to it 'a kind of synthesis takes place directly even before the indirect functions of reproduction and recognition intervene'. Cf. Adorno *Philosophische Terminologie. Zur Einleitung* [Philosophical Terminology. An Introduction], vol. 2, ed. Rudolf zur Lippe, 5th edn, Frankfurt am Main, 1989, p. 143: 'We might almost say that there is . . . something like a passive synthesis and it would not take much to persuade us that what is incidentally the very difficult Kantian concept of apprehension in intuition actually intends something of the sort. By this I mean that this "my" . . . that is to be found in what falls into "my" consciousness . . . is a nexus of

qualities, and that a direct connection already exists prior to all indirect connections based on concepts such as recognition and memory' (ibid., p. 142).

16 The concept of adumbration [*Abschattung*] stems from Husserl. See, for example, §41 of the *Ideas Pertaining to a Pure Phenomenology and to a Phenomenological Philosophy*, 1st Book, trans. F. Kersten, Martinus Nijhoff Publishers, The Hague/Boston/London, 1982, p. 88.

17 *Critique of Pure Reason*, p. 291, A 285/B 341.

18 Ibid.

19 Ibid., pp. 291f, A 285/B 341.

Lecture Ten

1 [In English in the original. *Trans.*]

2 *Critique of Pure Reason*, p. 156, B 137.

3 See p. 89f, above.

4 *Critique of Pure Reason*, p. 441, A 494/B 522.

5 See *Thus Spake Zarathustra*, 'Of the Afterworldsmen' [or 'Otherworldsman' – *Trans.*], pp. 58–61. There is no sign of any reference to Kant in this section. Adorno probably confused Nietzsche's metaphor of the 'otherworldsman' with the following passage from *Twilight of the Idols*: 'I bear the Germans a grudge for their having blundered over *Kant* and his "back-door" philosophy, as I call it – this was *not* the pattern of intellectual integrity' (p. 88).

6 See, for example, §43 of the *Ideas*: 'The holders of this view are misled by thinking that the transcendence belonging to the spatial physical thing is the transcendence belonging to something *depicted or represented by a sign*. Frequently the picture-theory is attacked with zeal and a sign theory substituted for it. Both theories, however, are not only incorrect but countersensical. The spatial physical thing which we see is, with all its transcendence, still something perceived, given "in person" in the manner peculiar to consciousness. It is not the case that, in its stead, a picture or sign is given.' Edmund Husserl, *Ideas Pertaining to a Pure Phenomenology* (Lecture Nine, n. 16, above), p. 92.

7 Cf. Kant, *Critique of Practical Reason*, pp. 82f.

8 It is not Stauffacher but Tell himself who says in the penultimate scene of the play, 'Here I am again! Here is my hut! I am standing on my own property once more!' Friedrich von Schiller, *Wilhelm Tell*, Act V, scene 2, ll. 3134f, in *Sämtliche Werke*, ed. Gerhard Fricke and Herbert G. Göpfert, 4th edn, Munich, 1965, vol. 2, p. 1023.

9 Cf. Hans Vaihinger, *Die Philosophie des Als ob. System der theoretischen, praktischen und religiösen Fiktionen der Menschheit auf Grund eines idealistischen Positivismus. Mit einem Anhang über Kant und Nietzsche.* [The Philosophy of As-if: A System of the Theoretical, Practical and Religious Fictions of Mankind on the Basis of an Idealist Positivism. With an Appendix on Kant and Nietzsche.] 4th edn, Leipzig, 1920.

10 'Tout pour moi devient allégorie.' Charles Baudelaire, 'Le cygne' (II).
11 'Two things fill the mind with ever new and increasing admiration and
reverence, the more often and more steadily one reflects on them: *the
starry heavens above me and the moral law within me.*' *Critique of
Practical Reason*, Conclusion, p. 133.
12 Cf. 'The Impossibility of the Physico-Theological Proof', *Critique of
Pure Reason*, pp. 518–24, A 620ff/B 548ff.
13 Cf. book 1 of the *Science of Logic*: 'The *infinite quantum* as *infinitely
great* or *infinitely small* is itself implicitly the infinite progress; as great
or small it is a quantum and at the same time it is the non-being of
quantum. The infinitely great and infinitely small are therefore pictorial
conceptions which, when looked at more closely, turn out to be nebulous
shadowy nullities. . . . Quantum as degree is unitary, self-related and
determinate within itself. Through this unitary nature, the otherness and
determinateness in quantum are sublated, so that the determinateness is
external to it; it has its determinateness outside it. This self-externality
it has is in the first place the *abstract non-being* of quantum generally,
the spurious infinity.' *Science of Logic*, p. 238 [translation altered].
Hegel treats the question of the teleological proof of the existence of
God in vol. 2 of *Lectures on the Philosophy of Religion*, Werke,
Suhrkamp, Frankfurt am Main, 1971, vol. 17, pp. 501ff.
14 Adorno may have in mind the 'General Remark on the Exposition of
Aesthetic Reflective Judgements': 'The object of a pure and unconditioned intellectual delight is the moral law in the power which it exerts
in us over all *antecedent* motives of the mind. Now since it is only
through sacrifices that this power makes itself known to us aesthetically, . . . it follows that the delight, looked at from the aesthetic side
(in reference to sensibility) is negative, i.e. opposed to this interest,
but from the intellectual side, positive and bound up with an interest.
Hence it follows that the intellectual and intrinsically final (moral) good,
estimated aesthetically, instead of being represented as beautiful, must
rather be represented as sublime, with the result that it arouses more a
feeling of respect (which disdains charm) than of love or of the heart
being drawn towards it – for human nature does not of its own proper
motion accord with the good, but only by virtue of the dominion which
reason exercises over sensibility. Conversely, that, too, which we call
sublime in external nature, or even inward nature (e.g. certain affections) is only represented as a power of the mind enabling it to overcome *this or that* hindrance of sensibility by means of moral principles,
and it is from this that it derives its interest.' *Critique of Judgement*,
pp. 123f.
15 *Influxus physicus*, physical influence, in Descartes refers to 'the force
with which the souls of men or angels move their bodies.' (René Descartes, *Die Prinzipien der Philosophie*, 7th edn, Hamburg, 1955, p. 52).
In Cartesian philosophy the theory of 'influctionism' gained great
importance as a counterweight to that of 'occasionalism'. In the chapter
on the paralogisms in the first edition Kant criticized the system of

physical influence as one of the three possible 'theories in regard to the communion between soul and body', together with those of a *predetermined harmony* and *supernatural intervention* (cf. pp. 358ff, A 390ff). In the earlier lecture course of 1957/58 Adorno gave the following, somewhat simplified account of 'physical influence': 'The mediation between the two substances had already caused Descartes the very greatest difficulties, and he was only able to resolve them with the aid of a highly artificial argument, one that appeared far-fetched even in his own day. This was the theory of the so-called *influxus physicus*, namely, of physical influence; this theory described how the physical world, and hence the world of bodies, might gain influence upon the soul. In the process he made the somewhat fanciful and bold discovery that a particular gland, namely, the pineal gland, possessed the magic gift of transmitting this influence of the body on the soul; and he ascribed this faculty to this gland in what was, it must be said, a crassly dogmatic way.' (Cf. the pirated version of the *Einleitung in die Erkenntnistheorie*, pp. 84f.)

16   In *Negative Dialectics* we can find Adorno taking up and developing further his reflections on reification as a function of subjectivization and on labour as the innermost secret of thought: 'The more autocratically the self rises above existing things, the more it imperceptibly turns into an object and thus recants ironically its constitutive role. It is not just that the pure self is ontically mediated by the empirical self that unmistakably shines through as the model of the first version of the deduction of the pure concepts of the understanding; but the same thing holds good for the transcendental principle itself, which philosophy regards as its own first principle as opposed to actual existence. Alfred Sohn-Rethel was the first to point out that in this principle, in the universal and necessary activity of the spirit, social labour lies hidden. The aporetic concept of the transcendental subject, a non-existent thing that nevertheless must act, a universal that must nevertheless have particular experiences, would be a will-o'-the-wisp; it could never be gleaned from the autarchic immanent matrix of a consciousness which is necessarily individual. Nevertheless, as contrasted with consciousness, this concept is not merely more abstract, but thanks to its ability to impose its authority, it is also more real. Beyond the magic circle of identity philosophy the transcendental subject can be decoded as society unconscious of itself. . . . Ever since the *Critique of Pure Reason* the essence of the transcendental subject has been functionality, the pure activity that manifests itself in the achievements of individual subjects and simultaneously transcends them. It is a projection of free-floating labour onto the pure subject which is regarded as its origin. If Kant damped down the idea of the functional nature of the subject by declaring it to be null and void in the absence of any material coming from beyond it, he nevertheless had no qualms in insisting that social labour is a labour on something. His idealist successors were more consistent here since they did not hesitate to eliminate this. However, the universal nature of

the transcendental subject is that of the functional context of society as a whole.' (*GS*, vol. 6, pp. 178–80).

Lecture Eleven

1 Dietrich Mahnke, a former high-school teacher, wrote a book called *Das unsichtbare Königreich des deutschen Idealismus* [The Invisible Kingdom of German Idealism], Halle, 1920. Adorno may have had this in mind.

2 Cf. the 'First Introduction to the Science of Knowledge': 'The kind of philosophy you choose depends . . . on the kind of human being you are: for a philosophical system is not a piece of household furniture that you can acquire or dispose of at will, but it is animated by the soul of the man who has it. A character that is lax by nature or that has become worn out and misshapen by spiritual servitude, acquired luxury and vanity will never elevate itself to idealism.' Johann Gottlieb Fichte, *Sämmtliche Werke*, Section I, vol. 1, p. 434. Adorno's copy notes in the margin of the first sentence: 'No. Existential motif. Kierkegaard'; and next to the second sentence he wrote: 'bad'.

3 See p. 63f, above.

4 Just as the preceding sentence alludes to the *Dialectic of Enlightenment*, so here Adorno evidently refers to Horkheimer's essay of 1938, 'Montaigne and the Function of Scepticism' (cf. Horkheimer, *Gesammelte Schriften*, vol. 4: *Schriften 1936–1941*, pp. 236ff).

5 Adorno's essay 'Beitrag zur Ideologienlehre' [Contribution to the Theory of Ideologies] of 1954 contains a similar account of Pareto: 'Pareto accepts . . . the full implications of sociological relativism. He denies all truth to the world of the mind in so far as it goes beyond mechanical science; that world is dissolved into mere rationalizations of particular interests, justifications of every conceivable social group. The critique of ideology is transformed into a spiritual law of the jungle: truth is reduced to being a mere function of the prevailing power.' (*GS*, vol. 8, pp. 467f).

6 Cf. the chapter on 'Absolute Freedom and Terror' in the *Phenomenology of Spirit*. 'Universal freedom, therefore, can produce neither a positive work nor a deed; there is left for it only *negative action*; it is merely the *fury of destruction*.' Hegel's *Phenomenology of Spirit*, p. 359. [This is the usual translation of the phrase *die Furie des Verschwindens*. It literally means 'the fury of disappearance' and is used by Hegel to describe the Reign of Terror in the French Revolution. *Trans.*]

7 The concepts of the dialectical image and the configuration [*Konstellation*] are among those which were introduced into philosophy by Walter Benjamin and characteristically modified by Adorno. For Benjamin's use of these concepts, see Rolf Tiedemann, *Dialektik im Stillstand. Versuche zum Spätwerk Walter Benjamins* [Dialectics at a Standstill. Essays on the Late Works of Walter Benjamin], Suhrkamp, Frankfurt

am Main, 1983, pp. 32ff. For Adorno's use of these concepts, see R. Tiedemann, 'Begriff Bild Name. Über Adornos Utopie der Erkenntnis' [Concept, Image, Name. Adorno's Utopia of Knowledge] in *Frankfurter Adorno Blätter* II, Munich, 1993, pp. 92ff.

8 'With self-consciousness, then, we have therefore entered the native realm of truth.' (*Phenomenology of Spirit*, p. 104).

9 Some light may be thrown on what Kierkegaard meant by this by a passage in *Either/Or* which Adorno sidelined in his copy of the book: 'Language, regarded as medium, is the medium absolutely qualified by spirit, and it is therefore the authentic medium of the idea.... Language addresses itself to the ear. No other medium does this. The ear, in turn, is the most spiritually qualified sense.' See Søren Kierkegaard, *Either/Or*, vol. 1, trans. Howard V. Hong and Edna H. Hong, Princeton University Press, Princeton, 1987, pp. 67f. [Kierkegaard writes: 'Just as the speculative eye sees things together, so the speculative ear hears things together.' By way of explanation he argues that in order to understand Donna Elvira's aria, 'Ah, chi mi dice mai', in Act I of Mozart's *Don Giovanni*, we must be aware that Giovanni's 'unparalleled irony' lurks concealed inside Elvira's 'substantial passion'. In other words, to understand her love–hate we must hear Giovanni's mockery, which inflames it, as part of her passion. Ibid., p. 122n. *Trans.*]

10 The transcript has, presumably in error, 'the extreme and normal case'.

11 See the final lecture, p. 224f, above.

12 Rickert uses the term in a somewhat different sense: 'What enters into our consciousness when we think of the reflective knowledge of the reality situated in time and space consists in the fact that this reality is *different* at each point from what it is elsewhere, and therefore that we do not know how much that is new and as yet unknown will be shown to us. For this reason we may call the real a *heterogeneous continuum*, to distinguish it from the unreal, homogeneous continuum of mathematics...' Heinrich Rickert, *Die Grenzen der naturwissenschaftlichen Begriffsbildung. Eine logische Einleitung in die historischen Wissenschaften*. [The Boundaries of Scientific Concepts: A Logical Introduction to the Historical Sciences], 3rd and 4th edns, Tübingen, 1921, p. 28.

13 He means the 'Table of Categories', cf. *Critique of Pure Reason*, p. 113, A 80/B 106.

14 Adorno seems to assume that his audience is familiar with §16 of the Transcendental Deduction of the Pure Concepts of the Understanding (*Critique of Pure Reason*, pp. 152–5, B 131ff). It is also possible, however, that there is a missing passage in the tape recording or the transcription.

15 Cf. '*Being, pure being*, without any further determination.... Being, the indeterminate immediate, is in fact *nothing*, and neither more nor less than *nothing*.... Nothing is ... the same determination, or rather the absence of determination, and thus altogether the same as, pure *being*.' G. W. F. Hegel, *Science of Logic*, p. 82.

16 On the question of nominalism and realism in Kant's philosophy see
    ch. 1 of the post-doctoral dissertation of Karl Heinz Haag, *Kritik
    der neueren Ontologie* [Critique of Modern Ontology], Stuttgart, 1960,
    pp. 10ff.
17 *Critique of Pure Reason*, p. 12, A xvi.

Lecture Twelve

1 ['Denn für dieses Leben / Ist der Mensch nicht schlecht genug / Doch
   sein höh'res Streben / Ist ein schöner Zug.' 'For this life man is not
   bad enough. But his constant striving for higher things is a noble feature.' Bertolt Brecht, *Gesammelte Werke*, vol. 2, Werkausgabe ed.,
   Suhrkamp, Frankfurt am Main, 1968, p. 465. *Trans.*]
2 See p. 69f, above.
3 In *Against Epistemology* Adorno calls the 'duplication' of the subject
   the 'scandal of idealism': 'the fact that what is subjectively created is
   supposed to remain an *objectum* as well, opposed to the subject . . .
   Kant himself spoke of a paradoxicality in his own philosophy which he
   hoped "to explain" through the Transcendental Deduction of the Pure
   Concepts of Understanding. In the *Critique of Pure Reason* the ego
   constitutes things by applying categories to the sensible [*Sinnliches*].
   The traditional concept of truth, however, that of the correspondence
   [*Angemessenheit*] of knowledge to its object, remains valid. Accordingly, what the subject knows is true, if it corresponds with what the
   subject itself has constituted. The subject's knowledge of the objective leads – considering the radical indeterminacy of the "material" –
   right back to the subject and is thus in a certain sense tautological.'
   Against Epistemology, p. 174.
4 See pp. 49f and 98f, above.
5 Adorno never did provide a discussion of schematism that went beyond
   what is given in this lecture. A thorough analysis of the problems
   surrounding schematism can be found, for example, in Günter Ralfs,
   *Sinn und Sein im Gegenstand der Erkenntnis. Eine transzendental-
   ontologische Erörterung* [Meaning and Existence in the Object of Knowledge: A Transcendental, Ontological Discussion], Tübingen, 1931,
   pp. 25ff.
6 [Cf. *Critique of Pure Reason*, pp. 180–7, A 137-7/B 176–87, The
   Schematism of the Pure Concepts of Understanding. *Trans.*]
7 Plato's theory of concepts can be found above all in the late dialogues,
   the *Sophist*, the *Statesman* and *Theaetetus*. For Plato the definition of a
   concept meant 'to separate one concept from another by eliminating
   what is alien and retaining what is proper to it in a fitting manner'
   (261a). 'When one perceives first the community between the members
   of a group of many things, one should not desist until one sees in it all
   those differences that are located in classes, and conversely, with all the
   various unlikenesses among the multitude of objects, one should not be

deterred into stopping before one has enclosed all the related things within one likeness and actually included them in one real class' (285). *Statesman* in Plato, *Complete Works*, ed. John M. Cooper, Hackett Publishing Company, Indianapolis/Cambridge, 1997, pp. 300 and 328. [Translation altered. *Trans.*] Whether Adorno had this passage in mind or a different one is not a matter on which the editor can venture an opinion.

8   'This schematism of our understanding, in its application to appearances and their mere form, is an art concealed in the depths of the human soul whose real modes of activity nature is hardly likely ever to allow us to discover, and to have open to our gaze.' *Critique of Pure Reason*, p. 183, A 141/B 180.

9   However, see p. 217f, above.

10   *Critique of Pure Reason*, p. 180, A 137/B 176.

11   On the question of classical theories of resemblance as well as the theme of resemblance in Adorno's philosophy see n. 13 to Lecture Twenty, below.

12   *Critique of Pure Reason*, p. 180, A 137/B 176.

13   See also p. 228f, above.

14   *Critique of Pure Reason*, p. 181, A 137f/B 176f.

15   Adorno cites, or rather, modifies an aphorism of Feuerbach's: 'Do not be *against* religion, but *above* it. Knowledge is more than faith. Even if we know but little, this little is greater than the nebulous "more" that faith has over and above knowledge.' Ludwig Feuerbach, *Sämtliche Werke*, ed. Wilhelm Böhm and Friedrich Jodl, vol. 10, Stuttgart, 1911, p. 236. Cf. also Adorno, *NaS*, section IV, vol. 15: *Einleitung in die Soziologie* [Introduction to Sociology], p. 134, where Adorno 'varies' the same quotation.

16   According to Schadewaldt this saying is attributed to Sophocles himself: 'Or take a different saying. He himself depicts people as they ought to be, Euripides depicts them as they are. A subtle contrast: Euripides was more realistic. Sophocles was not what we would call idealistic, but he saw human beings more in terms of their own proper ideal existence which is perhaps their real existence.' Wolfgang Schadewaldt, *Die griechische Tragödie. Tübinger Vorlesungen* [Greek Tragedy. Tübingen Lectures], vol. 4, ed. Ingeborg Schudoma, 2nd edn, Frankfurt am Main, 1992, p. 191.

Lecture Thirteen

1   See p. 9f, above.

2   *Critique of Pure Reason*, p. 248, A 227f/B 280.

3   Ibid., p. 139, A 112.

4   See p. 94, above.

5   *Critique of Pure Reason*, p. 124, A 90/B 122.

6   Cf. the following summary of his analysis of causality that Hume gives in Book II of the *Treatise*: 'All those objects, of which we call the one *cause* and the other *effect*, consider'd in themselves, are as distinct and separate from each other, as any two things in nature, nor can we ever, by the most accurate survey of them, infer the existence of one from that of the other. 'Tis only from experience and the observation of their constant union, that we are able to form this inference; and even after all, the inference is nothing but the effects of custom on the imagination.' David Hume, *A Treatise of Human Nature*, ed. L. A. Selby-Bigge, Clarendon Press, Oxford, 1896, p. 405.

7   *Critique of Pure Reason*, p. 125, A 91/B 124.

8   Adorno has in mind here the passage referred to in n. 2, above (i.e. p. 248, A 227f/B 280). It should be observed, however, that both this statement and the preceding one (p. 125, A 91/B 124) stem from the first edition and were taken over into the second.

9   See also p. 91, above, and n. 19 to Lecture Eight. Adorno discusses the general crisis of causality today in detail in the chapter on freedom in *Negative Dialectics* (cf. *GS*, vol. 6, pp. 262ff).

10 'Thoughts without content are empty, intuitions without concepts are blind.' *Critique of Pure Reason*, p. 93, A 51/B 75.

11 In the second of his *Hegel Studies*, written shortly before the present lectures, Adorno had given a definition of *experiential content*, the social content of the subject in every epistemology, but without mentioning Kant by name: 'The personal consciousness of the individual, which was analysed by traditional epistemology, can be seen to be an illusion. Not only does the bearer of personal consciousness owe his existence and the reproduction of his life to society. In fact, everything through which he is specifically constituted as a cognitive subject, hence, that is, the logical universality that governs his thinking, is, as the school of Durkheim in particular has shown, always also social in nature. The individual who considers himself the legitimate basis of truth by virtue of what is supposed to be immediately given for him, obeys the web of delusion of a society that falsely but necessarily thinks of itself as individualistic. What the individual holds to be primary and irrefutably absolute is derived and secondary, down to every individual piece of sensory data.' *Hegel: Three Studies*, p. 63.

12 On the question of 'naturalistic' concepts see Lecture Nine, n. 1, above.

13 In addition to his own writings on Hegel and Husserl, to which copious reference has been made, Adorno has in mind above all the *Dialectics of Enlightenment* that he wrote together with Horkheimer, as well as the latter's *Eclipse of Reason* (Horkheimer, *Gesammelte Schriften*, vol. 6: *Zur Kritik der instrumentellen Vernunft*, pp. 19ff).

14 See p. 41f, above.

15 In *Against Epistemology* Adorno summarizes his dialectical analysis of the problem of constitution in a few sentences: 'The static contrast of *constituens* and *constitutum* is insufficient. If epistemology had worked

out that the *constitutum* needed the *constituens*, then analysis, on the other hand, must relate the facts of consciousness – which are supposed to hold as constitutive according to the content, indeed the possibility of epistemology – to what traditional epistemology claims is just constituted. Otherwise, epistemology would advance its brand of ideality with the naivety that naive realism advances reality' (*Against Epistemology*, p. 145).

Lecture Fourteen

1 The start of this sentence is a conjecture on the part of the editor. The typescript of the tape contains only the words '. . . (the opening is missing) entirely.'

2 Cf. the Preface to the Second Edition: 'Now, *as regards the second edition*, I have, as is fitting, endeavoured to profit by the opportunity, in order to remove, wherever possible, difficulties and obscurity . . . As to the mode of *exposition*, . . . much still remains to be done; and in this edition I have sought to make improvements . . .' *Critique of Pure Reason*, pp. 33f, B xxxvii–xxxviii.

3 See p. 16, above, as well as n. 6 to Lecture Two.

4 See p. 139, above, and *passim*.

5 *Critique of Pure Reason*, p. 286, A 277/B 333.

6 Ibid., p. 287, A 278/B 334.

7 Wilhelm Sturmfels (1887–1967) had his intellectual roots in the neo-Kantianism of the Marburg School. He taught as Professor of Philosophy at the Johann Wolfgang Goethe-University in Frankfurt am Main in 1932–3 and then again from 1946. For his ideas on Kant see W. Sturmfels, 'Kant und die Philosophie' in *Kant und die Wissenschaften* [Kant and the Sciences]. Lectures given on 12 February 1954 on the 150th anniversary of the death of Immanuel Kant, Frankfurt, 1955 (*Frankfurter Universitätsreden*, 12), pp. 15ff.

8 *Critique of Pure Reason*, p. 96, A 55f/B 80.

9 Not in the previous lecture, but in *Against Epistemology*, where he talked about the *quid pro quo* of *constituens* and *constitutum*. See the reference in Lecture Twenty-One, n. 14, below.

10 *Critique of Pure Reason*, p. 668, A 856/B 884.

11 In *Hegel: Three Studies* Adorno explicitly finds the source of the idea of a reciprocity between *constituens* and *constitutum* in Hegel's philosophy: 'In Kant's sense no world, no *constitutum*, is possible without the subjective conditions of reason, the *constituens*, and Hegel's self-reflection of idealism, similarly, adds that there can be no *constituens* and no generative conditions of the spirit that are not abstracted from actual subjects and thereby ultimately from something that is not merely subjective, from the "world". By virtue of this insistent response the deadly legacy of traditional metaphysics, the question of an ultimate principle

from which everything must be derivable, became meaningless for Hegel'
(*Hegel: Three Studies*, p. 9).

Lecture Fifteen

1   In 1959 Hermann Schweppenhäuser (1928–   ) was Adorno's assistant
    in the Philosophy Seminar in Frankfurt University.
2   ['I think the priest says something like that too / Just in the wording
    there's a difference' is a line from *Faust*. It is spoken by Gretchen and
    its effect is to undermine Faust's evasive reply to her question about
    whether he believes in God. See J. W. Goethe, *Faust*, part one, trans.
    David Luke, Oxford University Press, Oxford, 1987, p. 109. *Trans.*]
3   According to Ernst Gombrich, the author of the biography of Aby
    Warburg, 'there has been no final clarification' of the actual source
    of the saying 'God is in the detail', which is constantly attributed to
    Warburg. 'Warburg noted it as one of the mottoes for his first seminar
    in Hamburg University (1925–6); but he probably did not claim to
    have invented it. The French version "le bon Dieu est dans le détail"
    . . . has been attributed to Flaubert.' Ernst H. Gombrich, *Aby Warburg.
    Eine intellektuelle Biographie*, trans. from the English by Matthias
    Fienbork, Frankfurt am Main, 1981, p. 28n.
4   [Despite the change of image Adorno is alluding here to Hegel: 'Dealing
    with something from the perspective of the Absolute consists merely in
    declaring that, although one has been speaking of it just now as some-
    thing definite, yet in the Absolute, the A = A, there is nothing of the
    kind, for there all is one. To pit this single insight, that in the Absolute
    everything is the same, against the full body of articulated cognition,
    which at least seeks and demands such fulfilment, to palm off its Abso-
    lute as the night in which, as the saying goes, all cows are black – this is
    cognition naively reduced to vacuity.' *Phenomenology of Spirit*, p. 9.
    Trans.]
5   The concept of historicality is to be found in Hegel, and plays an even
    greater role in Dilthey. But what Adorno has in his sights here are the
    fashionable Existentialist overtones the term acquired after its use by
    Heidegger in *Being and Time*. In *Being and Time* Heidegger writes 'In
    analysing the historicality of Dasein we shall try to show that this entity
    is not "temporal" because it "stands in history", but that, on the con-
    trary, it exists historically and can so exist only because it is temporal in
    the very basis of its Being.' And, 'Only authentic temporality which is
    at the same time finite, makes possible something like fate – that is to
    say, authentic historicality.' *Being and Time*, pp. 428 and 437. Benjamin
    had been an early critic of Heidegger's concept: 'Heidegger vainly seeks
    to rescue history for phenomenology abstractly, through "historicality".'
    Benjamin, *Gesammelte Schriften*, vol. 5, p. 577. Adorno's critique can
    be found in *Negative Dialectics*: 'Through the transposition of history

into the existential concept of historicality the salt of history is eliminated, the claim of all *prima philosophia* to a theory of the unchanging
is extended to what does change: historicality tacitly transforms history
into the unhistorical, unconcerned about the historical conditions which
shape the internal composition and configurations of subject and object'
(*GS*, vol. 6, pp. 134f).

6 Cf. the conclusion of the 'First Introduction to the Theory of Science':
'In so far as we regard the final conclusions of idealism as the result of
reasoning, they are so *a priori*, in the human mind; and in so far as we
regard them, assuming that reasoning and experience truly coincide,
as given in experience, they are so *a posteriori*. For a fully developed
idealism the *a priori* and *a posteriori* are not two different things, but
the same; we simply look at them from two different sides and the
difference is merely the method by which we arrive at them' (Fichte,
Sämmtliche Werke, section 1, vol. 1, p. 447).

7 Adorno's attitude towards an ontological interpretation of Kant was
less unambiguous, doubtless for pedagogical reasons, than may appear
from the lectures. We can see this from a statement about Benjamin in
connection with the latter's essay 'Fate and Character': 'Although the
effort to produce an ontological interpretation of Kant continued long
after this relatively early work had been written, today it is evident that
antecedent to these efforts Kant's thoroughly functional thinking, aimed
at "activities", had already petrified into a kind of ontology under
Benjamin's medusan, fixating gaze. The concepts of the phenomenal
and noumenal, which are bound together in Kant by a selfsame reason
and which reciprocally determine each other even in their opposition,
became for Benjamin spheres of a theocratic order.' 'Introduction to
Benjamin's Writings' in *On Walter Benjamin*, ed. Gary Smith, MIT
Press, Cambridge, Mass./London, 1988, p. 11.

8 See Lecture Fourteen, p. 149f, above.

9 Adorno repeatedly cited Heidegger's saying about sociology, for
example in his Inaugural Lecture in 1931: 'One of the most effective
academic philosophers of the present day is said to have replied when
asked about the relationship between philosophy and sociology that
whereas the philosopher, like a master-builder, produces the plan of
building and then carries it out, the sociologist is a cat burglar who
clambers around on the outside of the walls, picking up whatever he
can reach' (*GS*, vol. 1, p. 340). In 1931 Adorno still thought: 'I would
be inclined to accept the simile, but to turn it to the advantage of the
function of sociology for philosophy. For the building, the large building, has long since become dilapidated, right down to the foundations,
and threatens not only to crush everyone in it, but also to destroy all
the things that have been stored in it, many of which are irreplaceable.
If the cat burglar steals these objects, individual, often half-forgotten
things, he does a good deed since at least they will be saved; he will
scarcely hang on to them for long since he will think them of small value'
(ibid.). In the 1954 essay 'Contribution to the Doctrine of Ideologies',

written after the experience of fascism, Adorno was no longer inclined to put such a harmless gloss on such defamatory views of the social sciences: 'It is well known that a highly authoritative German philosopher of the pre-fascist era compared sociology to a cat burglar. Such ideas, which have long since percolated into the popular mind and contributed to the mistrust in which sociology is held, must give us pause (GS, vol. 8, pp. 457f).

10 See p. 121f, above.

11 See, for example, Against Epistemology, 'It is not, as relativism would have it, truth in history, but rather history in truth.' At this point Adorno refers to the immediately following quotation from Benjamin's 'Arcades project': 'Now is the time for decisive renunciation of the concept of "timeless truth". Yet truth is not, as Marxism claims, a temporal function of knowing, but rather bound to a core of time which resides both in the knower and the known' (Against Epistemology, p. 135 [translation altered]. The quotation from Benjamin is to be found in Gesammelte Werke, vol. 5, p. 578). Adorno frequently discussed the relationship between genesis and validity. For example, he did so in detail, in connection with Husserl (in Against Epistemology, pp. 74ff), but also in the introduction to the Positivist Dispute in German Sociology of 1969, one of his last works: 'The epistemological metacritique denies the validity of the Kantian claim to the subjective a priori but affirms Kant's view to the extent that his epistemology, intent on establishing validity, describes the genesis of scientistic reason in a highly adequate manner. What to him, as a remarkable consequence of scientistic reification, seems to be the strength of subjective form which constitutes reality is, in truth, the summa of the historical process in which subjectivity – liberating itself from nature and thus objectivating itself – emerged as the total master of nature, forgot the relationship of domination and, thus blinded, re-interpreted this relationship as the creation of that ruled by the ruler. Genesis and validity must certainly be critically distinguished in the individual cognitive acts and disciplines. But in the realm of so-called constitutional problems they are inseparably united, no matter how repugnant this may be to discursive logic. Since scientistic truth desires to be the whole truth it is not the truth' (The Positivist Dispute in German Sociology, trans. Glyn Adey and David Frisby, Heinemann, 1976, p. 22).

12 These are categories of Heidegger's fundamental ontology; cf. Being and Time, especially §38 and §§46–60 (pp. 219ff and 279–341). Adorno also discussed the categories of 'anticipating towards death' and 'resoluteness' in the Jargon of Authenticity, pp. 158ff.

13 Franz von Brentano, The Origin of our Knowledge of Right and Wrong, ed. Oskar Kraus, trans. R. M. Chisholm and E. H. Schneewind, Routledge and Kegan Paul, London/New York, 1969.

14 In Against Epistemology Adorno has quoted what is here the crucial sentence from vol. 1 of the Logical Investigations: 'The question is not how experience, whether naive or scientific, arises, but what must be its

content if it is to have objective validity: we must ask on what ideal elements and laws such objective validity of knowledge of the real is founded – more generally, on what any knowledge is founded – and how the performance involved in knowledge should be properly understood. We are, in other words, *not* interested in the origins and changes of our world-representation, but in the objective right which the world representation of science claims against any other world-representation, which leads it to call *its* world the objectively true one' (*Against Epistemology*, p. 74). (The quotation from Husserl can be found in the *Logical Investigations*, vol. 1, trans. J. N. Findlay, Routledge and Kegan Paul, London; Humanities Press, Atlantic Highlands, NJ, 1982, p. 207.)

15   Cf. Emile Durkheim and Marcel Mauss, 'De quelques formes primitives de classification', in *L'année sociologique*, 1st ser., 6th year, 1901–2, pp. 1ff, and also Emile Durkheim, *Les formes élémentaires de la vie religieuse. Le système totémique en Australie*, 3rd edn, Paris, 1937, pp. 12ff and 627ff.

Lecture Sixteen

1   See the writings of Durkheim referred to in Lecture Fifteen, n. 15, above.

2   Cf. *Against Epistemology*, pp. 186ff.

3   See Franz Borkenau, *Der Übergang vom feudalen zum bürgerlichen Weltbild. Studien zur Geschichte der Philosophie der Manufakturperiode* [The Transition from the Feudal to the Bourgeois Picture of the World: Studies in the History of Philosophy during the Age of Manufacture], Paris, 1934.

4   κόσμος νοητικός is a conjecture by the editor; the transcript only has a question mark at this point.

5   See p. 34f, 66, above, and *passim*.

6   Adorno probably has Lecture Ten in mind. See p. 114ff, above.

7   See pp. 31, 85, 117, and *passim*.

8   Cf. Zarathustra's Song of Melancholy: 'So sank I once / From my delusion of truth, / From my daytime longings, / Weary of day, sick with light, / Sank downwards, down to evening, down to shadows: / Scorched and thirsty / With one truth: / Do you remember, do you, hot heart, / How you thirsted then? / *That I am banished from all truth, / Only a fool! / Only a poet!' Thus Spake Zarathustra*, pp. 310f.

9   See p. 110ff, above.

10   See Lecture Ten, p. 115, above.

11   The Romantic artist is perhaps Goethe or rather Faust, who desired 'a vision of Nature's forces / That bind the world, all its seeds and sources / And innermost life . . .' See *Faust*, part one, trans. David Luke, Oxford University Press, Oxford/New York, 1987, p. 15.

12   Adorno evidently intended a riposte to the last sentence of Wittgenstein's *Tractatus*, 'What we cannot speak about we must pass over in silence'

(translation by D. F. Pears and B. F. McGuinness, Routledge and Kegan Paul, 1974, p. 74). Cf. also *GS*, vol. 8, pp. 336f and *GS*, vol. 6, p. 21: 'Against both [Bergson and Husserl] we must insist on the goal they pursue in vain; against Wittgenstein, on saying what cannot be said. The simple contradictoriness of this challenge is that of philosophy itself; it qualifies philosophy as dialectics before becoming embroiled in its individual contradictions.'

13   Cf. Ernst Mach, *Die Analyse der Empfindungen and das Verhältnis des Physischen zum Psychischen* [The Analysis of the Sensations and the Relation of the Physical to the Mental], Jena, 1922, p. 22: 'The self is beyond redemption.'

14   On Hume see also p. 89ff.

Lecture Seventeen

1   [Adorno used the English expression. *Trans.*]

2   See Friedrich Schiller, 'Würde der Frauen' [The Worth of Women]: 'Ehret die Frauen: sie flechten und weben / Himmlische Rosen ins irdische Leben'. [All honour to women, they plait and weave / Heavenly roses in life on earth.]

3   The source of this allusion has not been identified.

4   [The idea, familiar in Central and Eastern Europe, is that when times are hard, the household has to share a herring which hangs from the ceiling. You are not allowed to eat it, but only to touch it with your potato on a fork so as to get some of the flavour. *Trans.*]

5   John 18: 38. Cf. also Luther's marginal note, 'Ironia est. If you wish to speak of truth / you are lost.'

6   See p. 179f, above.

7   Cf. Ernst Marcus, *Aus den Tiefen des Erkennens. Kants Lehre von der Apperzeption, der Kategorialverbindung und den Verstandesgrundsätzen in neuer verständlicher Darstellung. Ein Kommentar zur transzendentalen Logik* [From the Depths of Knowledge: A New, Comprehensible Account of Kant's Doctrine of Apperception, the System of Categories and the Principles of the Understanding. A Commentary on the Transcendental Logic], Munich, 1925.

8   Adorno's repeated citation of this quotation from Hegel is based on a misunderstanding. For example, he writes in *The Philosophy of Modern Music*: 'When the immediate self-certainty of unquestioningly accepted materials and forms has vanished from the foundations of art, then at least one region of obscurity will have healed over, will have relieved that boundless suffering [i.e. 'consciousness of distress' – *Trans.*] whereby the substance of intellectual conception is brought to consciousness.' *The Philosophy of Modern Music*, p. 15. Adorno claims to have quoted the text as given in the second edition of Hegel's *Lectures on Aesthetics* brought out by H. G. Hotho, Berlin, 1842. However, what Hegel writes is: 'Music, for example, which is concerned only with the completely

indeterminate movement of the inner spirit and with sounds as if they were feeling without thought, needs to have little or no spiritual material present in consciousness' (*Aesthetics*, vol. 1, p. 28). In other words, music has little or no need of any spiritual material; the expression 'to have need' [*hat von Nöthen*] is antiquated. Adorno's misunderstanding has not escaped the attention of the critics; cf., for example, Jürgen Trabant, 'Consciousness of Need'. Philologische Notiz zum Fortleben der Kunst in Adornos ästhetischer Theorie, in *Theodor W. Adorno*, ed. H. L. Arnold, 2nd edn, Munich 1981, pp. 130ff (Text + Kritik, Sonderband). ['Die Musik hat wenigen oder keinen geistigen Stoff im Bewußtsein von Nöthen.' The mistake (which is easily made) is as follows: Adorno attached 'consciousness' to 'distress','need'; hence he read the sentence as if it said: 'Music has little or no spiritual material in its consciousness of distress.' Syntactically, this is a possible, though unlikely, reading. Hegel's phrase is 'music has no need . . .' and the whole sentence reads: 'Music has little or no need of spiritual material in its consciousness.' *Trans.*]
9   A conjectured reading for 'crypto-philology'.

Lecture Eighteen

1   *Critique of Pure Reason*, p. 183, A 141/B 180. See also Lecture Twelve, n. 8, above.
2   Kant treats of conscience above all in the Metaphysical First Principles of the Doctrine of Virtue, the second part of the *Metaphysics of Morals*. Adorno may well have had in mind a passage such as the following: 'Consciousness of an *internal court* in man ("before which his thoughts accuse or excuse one another") is *conscience*. Every man has a conscience and finds himself observed, threatened and, in general, kept in awe (respect coupled with fear) by an internal judge; and this authority watching over the law in him is not something that he himself (voluntarily) *makes*, but something incorporated in his being. It follows him like his shadow when he plans to escape' (*Metaphysics of Morals*, p. 233). Similarly, in the only passage of the *Critique of Practical Reason* where the word 'conscience' occurs, it is credited with passing 'judicial sentences' (*Critique of Practical Reason*, p. 82). Since conscience is the voice of the moral law, Kant also entrusted his arguments about compulsion and constraint to the *Critique of Practical Reason*: 'The consciousness of a *free* submission of the will to the law, yet as combined with an unavoidable constraint put on all inclinations though only by one's own reason, is respect for the law. . . . An action that is objectively practical in accordance with this law, with the exclusion of every determining ground of inclination, is called *duty*, which, because of that exclusion, contains in its concept practical *necessitation*, that is, determinations to actions, however *reluctantly* they may be done' (ibid., p. 69). Adorno discussed the connection between Kant's concept of

conscience and the super-ego of psychoanalysis, in the chapter on freedom in *Negative Dialectics* (*GS*, vol. 6, pp. 267ff).

3 See David Hume, *A Treatise of Human Nature*, Book I 'Of the Understanding' (pp. 10ff). In Section IV, 'Of the connexion or association of
ideas', Hume writes: 'The qualities, from which this association arises,
and by which the mind is after this manner convey'd from one idea to
another, are three, *viz. resemblance, contiguity* in time or place, and
cause and *effect*' (p. 11).

4 In *Negative Dialectics* Adorno writes about the difference between Kant
and Hume 'at this point': 'Hume's critique of the self glossed over the
difficulty that facts of consciousness would not exist unless they were
registered in a particular consciousness, not in some other picked at
random. Kant corrects this, but neglects reciprocity; in his criticism of
Hume he lets personality congeal to a principle beyond individuals,
to their framework. He conceives the unity of consciousness to be independent of all experience' (*GS*, vol. 6, p. 288).

5 'In *understanding* and *state-of-mind*, we shall see the two constitutive
ways of being the "there"; and these are equiprimordial. . . . What we
indicate *ontologically* by the term "state-of-mind" is *ontically* the most
familiar and everyday sort of thing; our mood, our Being-attuned. Prior
to all psychology of moods . . . it is necessary to see this phenomenon as
a fundamental *existentiale* . . . Heidegger, *Being and Time*, §§28–9,
pp. 172f.

6 See pp. 58f and 64f, above.

7 Adorno had already discussed Kant's doctrine of the psychological paralogisms at length in *Der Begriff des Unbewußten in der transzendentalen
Seelenlehre* [The Concept of the Unconscious in the Transcendental
Doctrine of the Soul], his so-called first post-doctoral dissertation of
1927. (See *GS*, vol. 1, pp. 158ff.)

8 To be accurate it should say that the only syllogism Kant regards as a
transcendental paralogism is the one in which he 'conclude[s] from the
transcendental concept of the subject, which contains nothing manifold,
the absolute unity of this subject itself, of which, however, even in so
doing, I possess no concept whatsoever' (p. 328, A 340/B 398). Adorno's
definition applies rather to dialectical inferences in general.

9 *Critique of Pure Reason*, p. 368, B 406.

10 Ibid., p. 369, B 407.

11 Ibid.

12 Ibid., B 408.

13 [Gottfried Benn (1886–1956) was a leading poet of the Expressionist
movement before the First World War. During the Third Reich he
expressed some support for the Nazis and became notorious for his
attack on émigré writers and artists. He later detached himself from the
Nazis and was a leading representative of what was called the 'inner
emigration'. Following a period of neglect after 1945 he enjoyed a
second phase of celebrity, partly because his writings expressed a nihilism fashionable during the Cold War and partly from the need for the

West-German cultural world to produce a writer to counterbalance Brecht's growing reputation in East Berlin. At the time Adorno was giving these lectures Benn was widely regarded as the greatest living German poet. The ideas Adorno alludes to are to be found mainly in prose works like *Das moderne Ich* [The Modern Self], *Provoziertes Leben* [A Provoked Life], and the novel *Roman des Phänotyp* [Novel of the Phenotype]. *Trans.*]

Lecture Nineteen

1 *Critique of Pure Reason*, pp. 369f, B 408f.
2 A reference to words spoken by Gide's Oedipus to his sons: 'As a young man at the beginning of his career each of us encounters a monster, and it presents us with a riddle that aims to stop us in our tracks. And even if the Sphinx asks each of us a different question, you may be sure, my children, that to all its questions the same answer remains; in fact, there is only one answer to such different questions; and this one answer is: man. And this single man is for each of us, oneself.' André Gide, *Oedipus*. Drama in Three Acts, 1931, in Gide, *Theater. Gesammelte Stücke*, trans. E. R. Curtius, Stuttgart, 1968, p. 206.
3 *Critique of Pure Reason*, p. 370, B 409.
4 See p. 102f, above.
5 Wilhelm Haas, *Die psychische Dingwelt* [*The Psychic World of Things*], Bonn, 1921.
6 Adorno probably had in mind a passage from the *Critique of Practical Reason* in which Kant writes: 'This could not happen if we did not suppose that whatever arises from one's choice (as every action intentionally performed undoubtedly does) has as its basis a free causality which from early youth expresses its character in its appearances (actions).' *Critique of Practical Reason*, p. 84.
7 Cf. here *GS*, vol. 6, pp. 286f, where Adorno analyses the passage from Kant referred to in the previous note.
8 See Lecture Eighteen, p. 190, above, as well as n. 2.
9 In *Negative Dialectics* this is made even more explicit: 'The criticism that in the objectivity of the moral law subjective reason is inflated into an absolute would be unworthy. Kant expresses, fallibly and in a distorted manner, what would be quite justifiable from the point of view of society. Such objectivity cannot be translated into the subjective sphere, either of psychology or of rationality, but exists for good or ill in a separate realm until particular and universal interests are truly harmonized. Conscience is the mark of shame of an unfree society' (*GS*, vol. 6, p. 272).
10 See ch. 3 of section one of the Doctrine of Essence: 'Ground', esp. Part A 'Absolute Ground', *Science of Logic*, pp. 444ff.
11 [*Critique of Pure Reason*, pp. 257–76, B 295–315/A 236–60. *Trans.*]

12 *Critique of Pure Reason*, pp. 266f, B 306. [Adorno is evidently talking about 'essences', and so I have used that word to translate '*Wesen*', but *Wesen* can have other legitimate translations as well. I have therefore left N. Kemp Smith's translation of *Sinnenwesen* and *Verstandeswesen* as 'sensible entities' and 'intelligible entities', respectively, while using 'essences' for the surrounding text. Paul Guyer's version, incidentally, translates them as 'beings of sense' and 'beings of understanding'. *Trans.*]

13 In his essay 'The Character of Walter Benjamin's Writings' Adorno speaks of the latter's 'anti-philosophical philosophy'. 'It would not be stupid to present it in terms of the categories that do not occur in it. An idea of them would mediate his idiosyncratic dislike of such terms as "personality"' (*GS*, vol. 10.1, p. 245).

14 Alongside the 'Character of Walter Benjamin's Writings' mentioned in the preceding note there is the 'Introduction to Benjamin's *Schriften*'. (See Gary Smith, *On Walter Benjamin* (Lecture Fifteen, n. 7, above), pp. 2–17.)

15 See p. 154f, above.

16 *Critique of Pure Reason*, p. 275, A 259f/B 315. See also p. 215, above.

17 [Adorno is referring to Karl Leonhard Reinhold (1758–1823), a professor of philosophy in Jena and Kiel. A follower of Kant, he tried to build on Kant's philosophy. In particular he attempted to deduce reason and sensibility from the imagination. His principal book was his *Versuch einer neuen Theorie des menschlichen Vorstellungsvermögens* [Essay on a New Theory of the Imagination] of 1789. *Trans.*]

18 Locke's theory of knowledge is to be found chiefly in book 2 of his *Essay Concerning Human Understanding*, in which the author states that he wishes to show 'whence the understanding may get all the ideas it has, and by what ways and degrees they may come into the mind'. In this project Locke appeals to 'everyone's own observation and experience'. *Essay Concerning Human Understanding*, Book 2, ch. 1, Penguin Books, Harmondsworth, 1997, p. 109.

19 'Imagination' is a conjectured reading for 'power of the imagination'. [See *Critique of Pure Reason*, p. 132, A 100–2. *Trans.*]

20 A conjectured reading, as above.

21 In *Negative Dialectics* Adorno goes so far as to say that 'Among the greatest of the achievements of Kant's deductive theory one that stands out is that even in the pure form of cognition, the unity of the "I think", at the stage of reproduction in the imagination, he still preserves memory, the trace of historicity' (*GS*, vol. 6, pp. 63f).

Lecture Twenty

1 Adorno probably has in mind §15 of the Second Edition, where the 'combination of a manifold in general' is called 'an act of spontaneity' and 'an act of the understanding': 'of all representations *combination* is

the only one which cannot be given through objects. Being an act of the self-activity of the subject, it cannot be executed save by the subject itself.' *Critique of Pure Reason*, pp. 151f, B 130.

2   See p. 131, above, and the passage cited in Lecture Twelve, n. 8.

3   See Martin Heidegger, *Kant and the Problem of Metaphysics*, trans. Richard Taft, Indiana University Press, Bloomington/Indianapolis, 1990, esp. §22, pp. 69ff.

4   'This peculiarity of our understanding, that it can produce *a priori* unity of apperception solely by means of the categories, and only by such and so many, is as little capable of further explanation as why we have these and no other functions of judgement, or why space and time are the only forms of our possible intuition.' *Critique of Pure Reason*, p. 161, B 145f.

5   See p. 209, above, and Lecture Nineteen, n. 16.

6   *Critique of Pure Reason*, p. 275, A 259f/B 315.

7   See n. 5, above.

8   See p. 215, above.

9   In Adorno's eyes this quandary implied the 'ultimate failure' (cf. *GS*, vol. 5, p. 152) of all epistemology that constantly preoccupied him and, following his metacritique of it in connection with phenomenology, he arrived at a conclusive formulation in the *Negative Dialectics*: 'In the history of modern philosophy the word identity has had a number of meanings. In the first place it signified the unity of personal consciousness: the idea that throughout all its experiences a self remains the same. This was what was meant by that Kantian phrase the " 'I think' that accompanies all my representations." Then again, identity was supposed to be what was legally the same in all rational creatures, thought as logical universality. Beyond that it was the self-sameness of every object of thought, the simple A = A. Finally, in epistemological terms, it was the idea that subject and object, however mediated, coincide. The first two levels of meaning are not strictly separated in Kant. This is not the fault of linguistic laxity. It comes about because identity marks a meeting point between psychology and logic in idealism. Logical universality, as the universality of thought, is tied to individual identity without which it could not arise because without it no past event, and hence nothing at all could be maintained as the same. In its turn recourse to this identity presupposes logical universality, it is a recourse of thought. The Kantian "I think", the individual element of unity always entails the supra-individual universal. The single self is one single thing only by virtue of the universal nature of the principle of numerical unity; the unity of consciousness itself is the form of reflection of logical identity. That an individual consciousness is single is only valid on the assumption of the principle of excluded middle: that it cannot be something else. In that sense its singularity, to be possible at all, must be supra-individual. Neither of the two aspects has priority over the other. If there were no identical consciousness, no identity of the particular, there would be no universality; and the converse is equally

true. This is how the dialectical conception of the particular and the universal acquires epistemological legitimacy' (*GS*, vol. 6, p. 145n.).

10   Cf. Fragment 1 of Anaximander of Miletus: 'The origin of all things is the Unbounded, the ἄπειρον. And the things from which is the coming into being for the things that exist are also those into which their destruction comes about. For they give justice and reparation to one another for their offence in accordance with the ordinance of Time.' Quoted from the text given by Jonathan Barnes, *The Presocratic Philosophers*, vol. 1: *Thales to Zeno*, Routledge and Kegan Paul, London/Boston, 1979, p. 29, and also Hermann Diels, *Die Fragmente der Vorsokratiker*, Rowohlt, Hamburg, 1957, p. 14. In the introduction to *Against Epistemology* Adorno writes of traditional epistemologies, 'Every one of them stands under Anaximander's curse, whose philosophy of being was one of the earliest, but practically prophesied the future destiny of them all' (*Against Epistemology*, p. 25).

11   In *Against Epistemology* Adorno pursued this with reference to Husserl's epistemology which became 'locked into a debit structure' and 'unwittingly construe[d] epistemology analogously to a universal legal contest. The most enlightened epistemology still participates in the myth of the first in the figure of a contract which is never fulfilled and therefore is itself endless, self-repeating without respite' (*Against Epistemology*, p. 26).

12   See also pp. 22 and 32, above.

13   A footnote in *Against Epistemology* gives the pre-history of the motif of resemblance: 'Theophrastus asserts in *De Sensu* that Parmenides had already taught that what is perceived and what perceives resemble each other, while Heraclitus pleaded that only the unlike and contrasted can recognize the like. Plato followed the Eleatic tradition. Aristotle turned Plato's own μέθεξις back into a doctrine of resemblance, viz. the Pythagorean doctrine that things exist only in imitation of numbers (*Metaphysics*, α, 987 b). Among the proofs of immortality of the soul in the *Phaedo* the argument is indeed made that, corresponding to a likeness between the body and the world of appearances, is a likeness between the soul and the world of ideas (St. 79). It is not far from that to the conclusion that the resemblance between subject and object is the condition for the possibility of knowledge' (*Against Epistemology*, p. 143n. [translation altered]). Cf. also the continuation about mimesis 'without the addition of which, however sublimated, the break between subject and object would be absolute and cognition impossible' (*ibid.*). Then, in *Negative Dialectics*, an explanation of the motif is given in terms of the history of philosophy: 'For the more thoroughly the subject follows idealist custom of making nature equal to itself, the further it distances itself from all equality with nature. Affinity is the sharp point of a dialectics of enlightenment. No sooner does the dialectic cut through that affinity than it recoils into delusion, an external intervention without concept. Without that affinity, there is no truth: this is what idealism caricatured in the philosophy of identity. Consciousness knows of its

other as much as it resembles it, not by negating itself along with that resemblance' (*GS*, vol. 6, p. 266f).

14 An idea that leads further than appears at first sight. In *Negative Dialectics* Adorno will go on to expand it: 'Hegel's doctrine that logic and metaphysics are one and the same is implied, although not made explicit, in Kant. For Kant the objectivity of reason as such is the epitome of the validity of formal logic. It becomes the refuge of ontology, which has been subjected to lethal criticism in all material realms. This not only establishes the unity of the three *Critiques*: but as the unifying factor reason acquires that dual character which goes on to help provide the motor of dialectics. Reason for Kant is, on the one hand, the pure form of subjectivity, as distinct from thinking; on the other, it is the essence of objective validity, the archetype of all objectivity. Its dual character allows the turn taken by both Kantian philosophy and the German idealists: to teach the objectivity of truth and all substantive contents even though subjectivity with its promotion of nominalism has undermined it – and to teach it by virtue of the same subjectivity that has destroyed it' (*GS*, vol. 6, p. 233).

Lecture Twenty-One

1 However, Adorno had discussed the Schematism chapter [Book II, ch. 1 of the Transcendental Analytic, pp. 180-7 – *Trans.*] in Lecture Twelve, see pp. 130ff, above.

2 See *Critique of Pure Reason*, pp. 67f, A 23/B 38, and pp. 73f, A 30/B 46.

3 Cf. the beginning of §2 of the Transcendental Aesthetic: 'By means of outer sense, a property of our mind, we represent to ourselves objects as outside us, and all without exception in space. In space their shape, magnitude and relation to one another are determined or determinable. Inner sense, by means of which the mind intuits itself or its inner state, yields indeed no intuition of the soul itself as an object; but there is nevertheless a determinate form [namely time] in which alone the intuition of inner states is possible, and everything which belongs to inner determinations is therefore represented in relations of time' (pp. 67f, A 22f/B 37).

4 See p. 168f, above.

5 See p. 166f, above.

6 Cf. *Critique of Pure Reason*, p. 68, A 24/B 38f, and pp. 74f, A31/B 46.

7 Cf. *Critique of Pure Reason*, pp. 68f, A 24f/B 39, and p. 75, A 31f/B 47.

8 Adorno has in mind statements of the kind to be found in the Appendix to vol. 1 of *The World as Will and Idea*: 'The *Transcendental Aesthetic* is a work of such extraordinary merit that it alone would have been sufficient to immortalize the name of Kant. Its proofs carry such perfect conviction, that I number its propositions among uncontestable truths, and without doubt they are also among those that are richest in results,

and are, therefore, to be regarded as the rarest thing in the world, a real and great discovery in metaphysics' (*The World as Will and Idea*, vol. 2, p. 32).

9   [Ludwig Ganghofer (1855–1920) was a popular writer of novels with Bavarian settings. *Trans.*]

10 *Critique of Pure Reason*, p. 69, A 25/B 39f, and p. 75, A 32/B 47f.

11 Cf. the Antithetic of Pure Reason, more particularly the Observation on the First Antinomy in which Kant speaks of 'the defective concept of the infinitude of a given magnitude', and how this is understood 'in the usual manner of the dogmatists'. *Critique of Pure Reason*, p. 399, A 430/B 458.

12 Adorno advanced a similar argument in the text 'On Subject and Object', a postscript to *Negative Dialectics* written in the last year of his life: 'What speaks for the priority of the object is doubtless a factor that is irreconcilable with Kant's doctrine of constitution: that in the modern natural sciences rationality can peek over the wall it has itself erected; it catches hold of a corner of something that does not fit into its well-honed categories. This expansion of rationality shakes the foundations of subjectivity' (*GS*, vol. 10.2, p. 748).

13 It has not been possible to discover any reference to a 'controversy' between Max Born and Ernst Cassirer. Nevertheless, see Cassirer's essay 'Einstein's Theory of Relativity' of 1921, which contains a section on 'The Concept of Time and Space in Critical Idealism and Relativity Theory', in Ernst Cassirer, *Substance and Function* and *Einstein's Theory of Relativity*, trans. William Curtis Swabey and Marie Collins Swabey, New York, 1923, pp. 409–29.

14 Probably because of the pressure of time arising from the approaching end of the semester Adorno's interpretation and critique of the Transcendental Aesthetic turned out to be a little laconic. It is worthwhile reproducing here the discussion that Adorno devoted to this subject in *Against Epistemology*: 'Kant's Transcendental Aesthetic comes to terms with the *quid pro quo* of *constituens* and *constitutum* by de-sensifying sense-perception. His pure intuition ceases to have anything to do with intuition. The reference of the given to something already constituted descends in Kantian terminology to expressions such as the constantly recurring one that objects are given to "us". The contradiction between this and the doctrine of the object as mere appearance has been an obstacle since Maimon. For philosophers have not become aware of the implicit admission of the bounds of *a priority* on that *constitutum* whose constitution should be made real by that *a priorism*. But at the heart of Kant's attempt at reconciliation there abides a paradoxicality, which epitomizes the irresolvable contradiction. The contradiction is linguistically indicated by the nomenclature "pure intuition" for space and time. Intuition as immediate sense-certainty, as givenness in the figure of the subject, names a type of experience, which precisely as such cannot be "pure" and independent of experience. Pure intuition is a square circle, experience without experience. It would be of little help to interpret

pure intuition as a loose turn of phrase for the forms of intuition purified of all specific content. The fact, rather, that Kant vacillates in the
Transcendental Aesthetic between the expressions "form of intuition"
and "pure intuition" attests to the inconsistency of the situation. De-
spairingly he wishes to reduce immediacy and *a priority* to a common
denominator at a single blow, while the concept of form, as referred to
some content, itself already presents a mediation, something categorial
so to speak. Pure intuition as immediate and not conceptual would
indeed itself be sense-perceptual, viz. "experience". Pure sensibility,
siphoned off from any relation to content, would no longer be intuition,
but rather "thought". A form of sensibility which merits the predicate
"immediate" without, however, also being "given", is absurd. The forms
of sensibility are so emphatically contrasted by Kant with the categories
– among which Aristotle had indiscriminately included them, as Kant
reminds us – only because otherwise ostensibly present and immediate
givenness would be endangered in these forms. Kant would have had to
concede that the "material", with which categorial labour was supposed
to deal, would itself already be pre-formed. "Space" and "time" as the
Transcendental Aesthetic lays them out are, in spite of all assurances to
the contrary, concepts, or in Kant's expression, representations of a
representation. They are not intuitive, but rather the highest universals
under which the "given" may be grasped. The fact, however, that a
given independent of these concepts is not indeed possible, turns
givenness itself into something mediated. So much is true in the Kantian
critique of speculative idealism which fused the opposition of form
and content. No matter can be isolated from form. Nevertheless, form
exists only as the mediation of matter. Such a contradiction expresses
a comprehension of non-identity and the impossibility of capturing
in subjective concepts without surplus what is not of the subject. It
expresses ultimately the breakdown of epistemology itself. The entire
conception of the Schematism is objectively motivated by the fact that
Kant eventually became aware of the categorial essence of what he calls
sensibility. By letting what he held in the beginning to be the raw material of cognition be pre-formed by an "art concealed in the depths of the
human soul", he can declare the similarity between categorial form and
sensible content without which the two "breeds" of cognition would
simply not go together. The doctrine of the Schematism tacitly retracts
the Transcendental Aesthetic. For if in fact the Transcendental Aesthetic
did function as the architecture of the system prescribes, then the transition to the Transcendental Logic would be a miracle. If, however, pure
sensibility remained consistent to the programme of the Aesthetic and
were dispossessed of its material, then it would also be reduced to
something merely thought, a bit of the Transcendental Logic. We could
not understand how thought supervenes at all. Kant himself, who con-
tests the conceptual nature of space and time, still does not get over the
fact that space and time cannot be represented without spatial and
temporal things. To that extent they are not intuitive, not "sensible".

This aporia forces the contradictory assertions that space and time are, on the one hand, "intuitions" and, on the other hand, forms' (*Against Epistemology*, pp. 146f).

15 See Section A (b) on 'Form and Matter' in ch. 3 of the Doctrine of Essence. Adorno presumably saw a parallel to the Transcendental Aesthetic as *a kind of fundamental stratum of knowledge* in Hegel's initial discussion: 'Matter is . . . the differenceless identity which is essence, with the determination of being the other of form. It is consequently the real *basis* or substrate of form, because it constitutes the reflection-into-self of the form-determinations, or the self-subsistent element to which the latter are related as to their positive subsistence.' *Hegel's, Science of Logic*, p. 450.

16 Adorno reads Hegel's *Logic* in a similar way. In the section on 'Form and Matter' Hegel writes: 'Matter, the indifferently determinate, is the *passive* side over against form as the *active* side. The latter, as the self-related negative, is the internal contradiction: it is self-resolving, self-repelling and self-determining. It relates itself to matter and is *posited* as relating itself to this its subsistence as to an other. Matter, on the other hand, is posited as being related only to itself and as indifferent to other; but it is *implicitly* related to form; for it contains sublated negativity and is matter only through this determination.' *Hegel's, Science of Logic*, p. 451. In his copy of the *Logic* Adorno noted in the margin at this point: 'Very profound. In mediation the two elements are not "equal". Materialism.' On mediation and immediacy see also part II of *Negative Dialectics*, especially the section 'Mediation through objectivity'. [*GS*, vol. 6, pp. 172ff.]

17 Adorno supplied a final version of his interpretation and critique of Kant in the eighth thesis of *On Subject and Object*. This thesis is concerned with the relation of the thing-in-itself to the non-identical (cf. *GS*, vol. 10.2, pp. 752ff). 'In Kant the memory of non-identity survives, the element that resists assimilation by traditional logic with its insistence on consistency.' The fact that it does survive had already been noted in *Negative Dialectics* (*GS*, vol. 6, p. 286n.) where under the heading 'The Primacy of the Object' he had developed this idea into a theory of his own. In the 'Notes on Philosophical Thought' of 1964, an occasional work that belongs in the general context of *Negative Dialectics*, he had noted and resolved the contradiction that seemed to exist between the primacy he ascribed to the object and Kant's Copernican revolution in the direction of subjectivity: 'Objectivity, the truth of ideas, depends on its relation to the matter in hand. Looked at subjectively, philosophical thinking is constantly confronted with the requirement that it should argue consistently, and nevertheless that it should incorporate matter different from itself, matter that does not submit *a priori* to its own laws. Thinking as a subjective act is even more strongly obliged to surrender to external matter where, as Kant and the idealists taught, it constitutes or even produces that matter. Thinking remains dependent on such matter even where it finds it problematic as a concept

and hence sets out to establish it in the first place. There can scarcely be a more powerful argument in favour of the fragile primacy of the object, a primacy that can only be conceived of in the reciprocal mediation of subject and object, than the fact that thought has to adjust to the object, even when it does not possess one or imagines that it must start by producing it. Kant's matter of fact method has its expression at the level of content. Admittedly, his thought is indeed directed at the forms of the subject; but it seeks its goal in the definition of objectivity. Despite the Copernican revolution Kant unwittingly confirms the primacy of the object' (*GS*, vol. 10.2, pp. 601f). The aforementioned text *On Subject and Object*, a postscript to *Negative Dialectics*, sums up the position: 'Primacy of the object means . . . that the subject is an object, but in a qualitatively different, more radical sense than mere object, because it cannot be known otherwise than through consciousness, and is therefore also subject. What is known through consciousness, must be something; mediation implies something mediated. Subject, however, the quintessence of mediation, is the How, never – as something contrasted with object – the What that is postulated by every conceivable notion of the concept of the subject. The subject can potentially, though not actually, be eliminated from objectivity; however, the object cannot be eliminated from subjectivity in the same way. However the subject is defined, it is not possible to conjure away an existing being contained within it. If the subject is not something – and "something" here means an irreducibly objective factor – it is nothing at all; even as pure act it requires a relation to something that acts. The primacy of the object is the *intentio obliqua* of the *intentio obliqua*, not the *intentio recta* warmed up; it is the corrective to subjective reductionism, not the denial of subjective involvement' (*GS*, vol. 10.2, pp. 746f). On the question of the connection between his own theory of the primacy of the object to the *Critique of Pure Reason* Adorno had this to say in *Negative Dialectics*: 'Kant refused to let himself be talked out of the primacy of objectivity. He both controlled the subjective analysis of the faculty of cognition from an objective standpoint and he stubbornly defended the transcendent thing-in-itself. He was fully aware that there was no contradiction between being-in-itself and the concept of the object; and that its mediation by the subject was due less to the idea of the object than to the inadequacy of the subject. Although the object does not exist in its own right even in Kant, he refused to sacrifice the idea of its otherness. Without the object knowledge would deteriorate into tautology; what is known would be knowledge itself. This was a greater source of irritation to the Kantian concept of mediation than the incongruous claim that the thing-in-itself was the unknown cause of phenomena while according to the critique of reason the category of causality was ascribed to the subject. The construction of transcendental subjectivity was a magnificent attempt – both paradoxical and fallible – to gain control of the object through its opposite pole. But only by criticizing it is it possible to accomplish what a positive, idealist

dialectics had merely proclaimed. An ontological element is indispensable because ontology will critically strip the subject of its decisive
constitutive role but without substituting the object for the subject, in
a kind of second immediacy. Only through subjective reflection and,
specifically, through reflection on the subject, can the primacy of the
object be achieved' (*GS*, vol. 6, pp. 185f).

EDITOR'S AFTERWORD

In the early sixties, in conversation with younger collaborators, Horkheimer once gave an account of the division of labour that had gradually emerged over a long period of time between Adorno and himself. The task of developing a shared theory had fallen to Adorno, and he carried it out in such a way that it could 'stand as it was', while he, Horkheimer, had devoted himself to teaching students. Horkheimer had probably retired when he made this statement and when Adorno came to hear of it, as was no doubt inevitable, he reacted with some irritation. Did that mean that he was neglecting his duties as a teacher? Adorno did not indeed write his lectures down, but the time and effort he put into teaching was not really visible at the time outside the circle of his audience and has since been forgotten. In the year and a half the young lecturer was allowed to teach before 1933, and following his return from exile in autumn 1949, he gave a regular two-hour seminar in every semester up to his death in 1969, with only two interruptions of two semesters each. Apart from the last course, an *Introduction to Sociology*, his lectures were all devoted to philosophical subjects. Manuscript versions of a number of the courses he gave up to summer 1957 have been found among his unpublished papers, although for the most part these consist mainly of notes. A few of these earlier lecture courses have survived in the form of, for the most part, fragmentary transcripts of varying reliability. Not until the winter semester of 1957/8 did Adorno allow his lectures to be recorded on tape and written up. This means that of the thirty-five lecture courses that Adorno delivered in the course of his lecturing career fifteen have been preserved in this way.

Adorno did not publish any of his lecture courses; and for the most part he refused to allow anyone who had missed a lecture, even close friends or students he knew well, to look at the transcript of the tapes. Adorno's intention in having the tapes made was to make use of them subsequently when preparing writings for publication. How far he actually did so will become evident only once the lectures have been printed. In fact only relatively few of the transcripts show any sign that Adorno consulted them. There can be no doubt that Adorno would have refused to agree to the posthumous publication of the lectures. His reasons may be inferred from what he wrote giving his consent to the publication of a single improvised talk in 1962. He was

> conscious that in my own case the spoken and written word diverged from one another even further than was customary today. If I were to speak in the way that would be necessary to achieve the authority of a precise account, I would be incomprehensible to my audience; nothing that I say can do justice to what I demand from a text. . . . The fact that everywhere today there is a tendency to record extempore speech and then to disseminate it is a symptom of the methods of the administered world which pins down the ephemeral word in order to hold the speaker to it. A tape recording is a kind of fingerprint of the living spirit. (*GS*, vol. 20.1, p. 360)

The Theodor W. Adorno Archive has now begun to publish the lectures that have survived because it was felt that this was justified by their importance. Publication must be accompanied, however, by the explicit appeal to the reader not to forget for a single moment that he or she is not looking at a text by Adorno, but only at the record of a talk which the speaker intended to consign to oblivion.

Adorno had spent several years at Oxford, where he 'was forced', as he wrote to Walter Benjamin, 'to lead the life of a medieval student in cap and gown' (Theodor W. Adorno/Walter Benjamin, *Briefwechsel 1928–1940* [Correspondence 1928–1940], ed. Henri Lonitz, Suhrkamp, Frankfurt am Main, 1994, p. 76). He had seen through the form of the traditional lecture, which he regarded as archaic. In the medieval university and even down to the time of Hegel it had been possible and meaningful to transmit an authoritative teaching in an unbroken discourse and in an authoritarian manner – in the spirit of a theology or at least of a coherent system like that of German idealism. But this procedure had long since lost its legitimacy. In his lectures Adorno sought to make a virtue of a necessity by relinquishing the practice of speaking didactically and reading from an already fixed text that had been fully thought through and formulated in advance. This is to be taken quite literally. In his lectures Adorno always improvised freely, basing his talk on a few keywords that he had usually noted down shortly before the class. These keywords rarely included lines of argument, and for the most part were confined to a list of the order in which the points were to be discussed. In his lectures he carried out the programme he had formulated in a text written for Horkheimer in which he described the challenge facing university teaching in the present day. This was to immerse oneself fully 'in the element of intellectual freedom in the shape of reflection, interpretation, criticism and the productive elaboration of ideas.' (Cf. Max Horkheimer, *Gesammelte Schriften*, vol. 8, ed. Gunzelin Schmid-Noerr, Suhrkamp,

Frankfurt am Main, 1985, pp. 396f.) Adorno was not unaware that his lecturing style imposed excessive demands on the majority of his students. While he remained convinced that such excessive demands helped to preserve something of the humanity that was in the process of disintegration at every point, he also attempted to mitigate the feeling of being excluded that was bound to overcome some of his listeners when faced by the demands made by his way of speaking. In the present lectures this took the form of the fiction that they 'do not yet have any knowledge' of the subject to be discussed, and this can help to explain the introductory nature and the pedagogical manner that comes to the fore on occasion and was a common feature of his lectures, one that stands in productive tension with the exacting level of his thought. The latter always reflects the difficulty of the subject matter rather than springing from the supposed right of a professor to express himself in a difficult way, and for all their difficulty Adorno's lectures never lost sight of his students' needs. In a text that appeared in a student newspaper in 1955 with the title 'Studying Philosophy' Adorno addressed the false reactions that his lectures frequently encountered.

> Many students wait expectantly to see whose side the lecturer takes; they become excited if they detect an affirmative or polemical judgement and prefer a definite position to mere reflection. Extreme care must be taken to avoid any distortion of a philosophical nuance of meaning since the most important distinctions, the specific nature of an argument, most commonly lie hidden in such nuances. The overwhelming need of students to take notes reduces what is being said to summary theses so that what gives the ideas their vitality is discarded as mere ornament, to say nothing of the resentment that is felt towards ideas that limit or refute an argument. Dialectics as a school of philosophy are acceptable, but a form of thinking that actually enacts a dialectical process is a source of irritation and is sometimes regarded as an obstacle to success in examinations. But it is precisely this insistence on the 'thesis', on the expectation that the lecturer should lay down the law about what you should think and even what you should do that is the true enemy of philosophy and of the mind as such. (GS, vol. 20.1, pp. 325f)

These comments allow us to infer Adorno's own programme on the nature and function of lectures in general. At the same time we can deduce from them something of the spirit in which we should respond to his own lectures in particular.

However, the specific nature of Adorno's lectures is not confined to its propaedeutic character, something which it shares anyway with current teaching practices. In his lectures Adorno did not scorn what are known today as rhetorical techniques, or even 'mere' rhetorical techniques. *Negative Dialectics* includes a rediscovery of rhetoric: thanks to rhetoric 'expression has found refuge in thought' and has confirmed 'the linguistic nature' of philosophy (*GS*, vol. 6, p. 65). We may perhaps see the linguistic essence of Adorno's writings in his strict avoidance of all rhetorical ornamentation and it is through this that the subject matter acquires its expressive force. If that is so, in the spoken word of his lectures the subject matter puts its as yet unprocessed

aspect on display to the outside world: it is thought that has not yet discovered its authoritative formulation and can therefore 'stay as it is', sated to
a certain extent, even though it is just setting out on its journey, so to speak.
In his lectures his ideas have not yet crystallized into doctrine, into the fixed
form of scholastic thesis; they are still fluid, their end is not yet in sight.
There is an analogy with modern art in which for Adorno the idea of experiment is self-evident. In Adorno's lectures thinking frequently casts its bread
upon the waters; it finds itself compelled to take huge risks, including the
risk of total failure. Adorno approved of the title *Holzwege* [Blind Alleys]
and especially the fact that Heidegger was *in favour of* them. To accompany
Adorno along the roads and the byways of his thought is to find oneself in
situations in which the sense of the fully rounded and conclusive form that
always predominates in his writings is constantly broken up, and possibil-
ities emerge that Adorno was unable to resolve in his authoritative works.
For Adorno thinking was always inseparable from effort; he frequently cited
Hegel's statement in the Preface of the *Phenomenology of Mind* that the
important thing for the student of science is 'to make himself undergo the
strenuous toil of conceptual reflection' [*Phenomenology of Mind*, p. 116
– *Trans.*]. And he defined the Kantian concept of spontaneity as the 'experience of strenuous activity . . . that is inseparable from thinking.' (*GS*,
vol. 10.2, p. 600). When the present editor had just begun his studies he
could not refrain from asking Adorno, with all the naivety of a beginner,
whether he, too, found writing difficult; he received the well-deserved reply,
'Not writing, but thinking!' That Adorno's writings are the product of the
most strenuous thought is not likely to escape anyone. But it is only the
record of his lectures that allows us to see the effort of thought that went
into them and gives us a glimpse of the workshop in which the philosopher
hones his concepts like Siegfried forging his sword in Mime's cave. These
lectures allow us to see how 'the living spirit' works away at thought.
    Adorno gave these lectures on Kant's *Critique of Pure Reason* in the
summer semester of 1959. They are the second series of lectures to be published, following the *Introduction to Sociology* of 1968. They were neither
his first course dealing with Kant's main work on epistemology, nor the first
in which he grappled with the problems of epistemology. The dissertation he
wrote when he was twenty had been devoted to an epistemological topic,
the critique of Husserl's theory of the thing. The lecture list of Frankfurt
University in the winter semester of 1931/2, the term in which he first took
up lecturing, reveals that he gave a 'Seminar on epistemology: Husserl'. And
following his return from emigration and an initial course of lectures on
aesthetics which seems to have lasted for two semesters, he gave a course
on 'The problems of contemporary epistemology (Husserl)' as early as the
summer semester of 1951. His interest in the *Critique of Pure Reason* goes
back even further than his preoccupation with Husserl's phenomenology.
While he was still at school he had read it together with his older friend,
Siegfried Kracauer (see Lecture Eight, n. 7, above). In his courses, however, he
did not deal with Kant before the middle of the 1950s. In the winter semester
of 1953/4 and the following summer semester he offered a two-part course

of lectures on 'The problem of idealism'. The first part amounted essentially to a course of lectures on Plato; the second part, however, bore the sub-title: 'Introduction to Kant's *Critique of Pure Reason*'. This was followed in the summer semester of 1955 by a lecture course on 'Kant's Transcendental Logic'. It is easy to infer that in the previous year Adorno had not gone beyond the Transcendental Aesthetic and that this was the sequel to that first course. Apart from a few notes nothing has survived of the lecture courses just named. The earliest to have survived in the form of a transcript of the tape recording is the course entitled 'Epistemology' that he gave in the winter semester of 1957/8. Incidentally, after Adorno's death a pirated version of this course was given a limited circulation. While it is true that it is only in the last third of the lectures that it turns more specifically to providing an introduction to the *Critique of Pure Reason*, taken as a whole it is evidently an important preliminary stage to the present lecture course which he announced and then gave in the summer semester of 1959 under the title 'The *Critique of Pure Reason*'. In later years Adorno gave no further lectures on Kant's theoretical philosophy.

Adorno published no book on Kant to set beside those he wrote on Hegel, Kierkegaard and Husserl. There is only the chapter on freedom in *Negative Dialectics* in which he discusses Kant's practical philosophy. Since Kant's critique of reason is scarcely less important for Adorno's own thought than the Hegelian dialectic and since it is certainly of greater significance than the philosophies of either Kierkegaard or Husserl, we must attach all the more importance to his Kant lectures – the present ones and also the *Problems of Moral Philosophy* of 1963 that are being published simultaneously. In the last of the lectures on Kant's *Critique of Pure Reason* Adorno speaks of 'a dialectical mode of thinking' – he means his own – 'whose elements I have tried to elucidate for you through a discussion of Kant' (see p. 233, above). Adorno could not have been more explicit. His concern was not to provide an immanent exposition of the historical Kant, but rather to make use of Kant to explore issues of importance in his own philosophy. The theory of knowledge contained in his own philosophy is a metacritique of traditional – and that means Kantian – epistemology. In an unobtrusive passage Adorno remarks that he is only making 'such strenuous efforts' to interpret the question of *constituens* and *constitutum* because 'what is at stake here are the foundations of the philosophical position I myself uphold' (see p. 158, above), a position for which he subsequently coined the name 'negative dialectics'. Adorno only preoccupied himself so intensively with epistemology in order to leave it behind him so as to be able to turn to a more substantive form of philosophy. This, too, is a Copernican revolution. The materialist insistence on the dignity of experience as the organ of thought that informs Adorno's thinking is ultimately indebted to Kant. For Kant's concept of experience is nowhere reducible simply to subjective or empirical perception, but because he undertakes the construction of an objective world it always lays claim to necessity and universality. Moreover, in Adorno this includes the thesis of the 'priority of the object' as itself something objective. Again and again, ideas of central importance to which he is committed are gleaned from his discussions of Kant. An instance is the idea of non-identity which he always emphasized so strongly and which became a kind of distinguishing feature of his philosophy. Thus Adorno interpreted the idea of things-in-themselves that Kant refused to abandon as the repository of the non-identical by means of which the basic idealist fallacy of reducing all objects to their subjective constituents is exploded. Adorno's lifelong interest in epistemological problems, in particular those raised by Kant, can be seen in the problems of a *no man's land*, a term he uses frequently in the present lectures (see above, pp. 22, 32 and 219). What he means by this is the transcendental sphere that lay for Kant between logic, psychology and metaphysics. In the gaps that opened up between these carefully demarcated disciplines and their ostensible competencies Adorno sought the 'inextinguishably ontic', the non-identical aspects of things – that is to say, those aspects that were not identical with the concepts in which they were cast. In a discussion of children's games Adorno once revealed the meaning of *no man's land* in his vocabulary.

> The land ... that I occupied when playing on my own was a no man's land. Later on, in the war, the word surfaced to describe the devastated space between two fronts. However, it is the faithful translation of the Greek – Aristophanic – word 'utopia', one that I understood all the better for not knowing anything about it. (*GS*, vol. 10.1, p. 305)

Today, when nobody wants to know about this word any more because nobody has understood it, we may be allowed to express the hope that the messianic light that lies concealed in Adorno's idea of the no man's land will be refracted, dry and uninviting though it may appear in its abstract epistemological form, and notwithstanding all the deficiencies and the vagueness that are the concomitants of Adorno's experiment in improvised speech.

This edition of his lectures is based on the transcript of the tape recording that was prepared in the Institute of Social Research, for the most part directly following the lectures. Once the tapes had been copied, they were wiped clean and reused. Today the transcripts are housed in the Theodor W. Adorno Archive, where they are catalogued at Vo 4259–504.

The Editor has tried to deal with the text much as Adorno himself did when he prepared talks he had given for publication: 'He made no attempt to convert the style of the spoken word into that of writing and just concentrated on eliminating crude errors of speech and the most glaring repetitions.' (Quoted from Talks Given during the Further Education Courses in Political Science Organized by the Universities of the State of Hesse, Bad Homburg vor der Höhe, Berlin, 1955, p. 54.) Our concern was to reduce any interventions in the well-preserved text to an absolute minimum. The text was prepared by a secretary who was conversant with Adorno's own idiosyncrasies and was fully equal to the demands of the subject matter. This enabled her to introduce various improvements in the text as it was transmitted on tape. The Editor felt all the more justified in refusing to treat the text as a sacred book. Obvious errors arising from mistakes in transcription, as well as unambiguous breaches of grammar, have been simply corrected. In the same way, particles such as 'now', 'so' and 'of course' were eliminated where their only function was to give the speaker space to formulate his thoughts. The greatest liberties have been taken in the matter of punctuation, which of course had to be inserted *in toto* and where the Editor ignored the rules Adorno himself observed when preparing texts for publication. The aim here was to ensure that Adorno's meaning should be made as unambiguous and unequivocal as possible. Thus, contrary to Adorno's own practice brackets were unhesitatingly used whenever this seemed to improve the comprehensibility of the text.

In the notes the Editor has provided references for the quotations used in the text and passages to which Adorno refers in the lectures have been given in full. In addition parallel passages from Adorno's writings have been included both to clarify what is said in the lectures and to provide evidence of the complex interplay between the lectures and the published writings.

Adorno believed that 'it was not immodest to echo Rudolf Borchardt's claim that he was wont to distinguish between genres. The difference between the written word that simply does justice to the requirements of the subject matter and the spoken word that aims at communication seems to him to be of crucial significance' (ibid.). We shall do justice to Adorno's spoken words only if we refrain from measuring them against the yardstick of his writings; for his lectures are a genre in their own right.

January 1995

ACKNOWLEDGEMENTS

The translator and publishers wish to thank the following for permission to use copyright material:

Blackwell Publishers and The MIT Press for extracts from Theodor W. Adorno, *Against Epistemology: A Metacritique*, trans. Willis Domingo, Polity Press (1982);

The MIT Press for extracts from Hegel, *Three Studies*, trans. Shierry Weber Nicholson (1993);

Palgrave for extracts from Kant, *Critique of Pure Reason*, trans. Norman Kemp Smith, Macmillan (1928).

Every effort has been made to trace the copyright holders but if any have been inadvertently overlooked the publishers will be pleased to make the necessary arrangement at the first opportunity.

INDEX